Rhetoric of the Chinese Cultural Revolution

Studies in Rhetoric/Communication
Thomas W. Benson, Series Editor

Rhetoric of the Chinese Cultural Revolution

The Impact on Chinese Thought, Culture, and Communication

Xing Lu

呂行

University of South Carolina Press

© 2004 University of South Carolina

Published in Columbia, South Carolina,
by the University of South Carolina Press

Manufactured in the United States of America

08 07 06 05 04   5 4 3 2 1

Library of Congress Cataloging-in-Publication Data

Lu, Xing, 1956–
     Rhetoric of the Chinese Cultural Revolution : the impact on Chinese thought,
culture, and communication / Xing Lu.
          p. cm. — (Studies in rhetoric/communication)
     Includes bibliographical references and index.
     ISBN 1-57003-543-1 (cloth : alk. paper)
     1. Rhetoric criticism—China. 2. China—History—Cultural Revolution, 1966–1976.
I. Title. II. Series.
     PN4096.L78 2004
     808'.04951—dc22

                              2004002630

To my parents and survivors of the Cultural Revolution

Contents

Series Editor's Preface ix

Preface xi

Introduction 1

Chapter One
My Family Caught in the Cultural Revolution 10

Chapter Two
Language, Thought, and Culture in the
Chinese Political Context 28

Chapter Three
A Rhetorical Analysis of Political Slogans 51

Chapter Four
A Rhetorical Analysis of Wall Posters 73

Chapter Five
A Rhetorical Analysis of Revolutionary
Songs and Model Operas 97

Chapter Six
A Rhetorical Analysis of Political Rituals 125

Chapter Seven
A Rhetorical Analysis of Post–Cultural
Revolution Political Discourse 152

Chapter Eight
Conclusion and Implications 182

Notes 207

Bibliography 219

Chinese Names and Terms Index 237

General Index 241

Series Editor's Preface

Lucy Xing Lu's *Rhetoric of the Chinese Cultural Revolution* is a systematic and balanced depiction of the rhetoric of the Cultural Revolution and of Chinese rhetoric in the decades following the Cultural Revolution. The book synthesizes a large body of secondary literature and brings important primary sources to bear for the first time—the author's personal recollections, interviews, and translations of documents that have appeared only in Chinese. This work of scholarly reporting and rhetorical history is a major accomplishment, to which Professor Lu has added her own analysis and reflection as a scholar trained in rhetoric, which she extends into reflections on the ethics of the rhetoric and into her advice for planners and participants in the transformation of China.

This is a big, simple, true, and important book.

Rather than work from a single, a priori theoretical position, Professor Lu calls on a range of mainstream twentieth-century American rhetorical scholarship as it is appropriate to the issue at hand, drawing a wide variety of communication scholarship into the analysis in a way that keeps the focus on big questions rather than being distracted by "disciplinarity." The result is a book full of solid news about communicative practices and convincing, shrewd observations grounded in text, observation, and firsthand report, and informed by rhetorical scholarship.

The range of communicative practices is wide and well chosen. Professor Lu deals in special detail with the cultural context, production, themes, rhetorical strategies, and reception of political slogans, wall posters, music, political rituals, and public speaking. The book gives a richly textured account of the street-level experience of rhetoric in the Cultural Revolution.

While avoiding political tendentiousness, the book is unambiguously critical of the Cultural Revolution and of much post-Mao Chinese rhetoric and politics. The immediacy and rootedness of the author's personal recollections, the testimony of her interviewees, and her rhetorical wisdom combine to make this an important contribution to rhetorical scholarship.

THOMAS W. BENSON

Preface

The twentieth century ended with conflicts and violence among nations and among ethnic and religious groups, as well as much infighting among factions within nations. Despite some progress made toward peace and reconciliation, the first three years of the twenty-first century have thus far been overshadowed by terrorist attacks against the twin towers of the World Trade Center in New York City and the Pentagon in Washington, D.C.; the United States–led war in Afghanistan and Iraq; Palestinians' suicide bombings in Israel; and Israel's retaliatory military assault on Palestine. In addition to historical and cultural factors contributing to the current state of affairs, a polarized and incendiary rhetoric is largely responsible for inflaming feelings of hatred and violence toward so-called enemies. Polarized language leads to polarized thinking; the rhetoric of agitation leads to fanaticism and violence, as evidenced in human history. Moreover, violent actions and human atrocities are justified by moralistic rhetoric and the dehumanization of perceived enemies. This is exactly what occurred during the Chinese Proletarian Cultural Revolution (1966–76), one of the most catastrophic mass movements and political upheavals of the twentieth century.

This book examines the rhetorical landscape of the Cultural Revolution. In particular, I will identify the rhetorical features and persuasive effects of the symbols and symbolic practices of that time. I will explore how the rhetoric of the Cultural Revolution was constructed, disseminated, and propagated by the power elite, as well as how an entire group of people, identified as "class enemies," was marginalized and dehumanized. Further, I will analyze the ways in which the rhetoric of the Cultural Revolution has influenced contemporary Chinese thought, culture, and communication in both international and domestic arenas. My intention in so doing is to examine the role and function of political rhetoric cross-culturally. In particular, I will identify similarities between the rhetoric of Communist China and those of Stalin's Russia and Nazi Germany. Furthermore, I seek to show how the practice of rhetoric in Communist China is situated in a particular social/political context rooted in the rhetorical tradition of ancient China.

With a population of nearly 1.3 billion China remains the largest communist country in the world. Its role and influence on the world scene cannot be overstated. Relations with the Chinese at every level—political, professional, financial, educational, and interpersonal—have become increasingly significant for the peace and well-being of humanity. Unfortunately, U.S.-Chinese relations have been problematic in modern times largely because of ideological differences, cultural misunderstandings, and a lack of knowledge regarding contemporary Chinese communication patterns. Misunderstandings between China and the West have led to many stereotypes and prejudices among Chinese and Westerners alike. While some members of Western nations may be informed of traditional Chinese cultural values and practices, most may know little about the rhetoric of the Cultural Revolution in China or may perceive the chaos of the period as romantic and idealistic.

This book is intended for rhetorical scholars who are interested in political rhetoric in general as well as in the connection between language, thought, culture, and behavior in particular. It should also appeal to sinologists and rhetorical scholars who are interested in contemporary Chinese culture and communication studies.

I was strongly motivated to embark on this project for several reasons. First, my family, especially my parents, were persecuted and suffered great physical and psychological hardship during the Cultural Revolution. I witnessed firsthand how the use of rhetoric mobilized first the young people and then the entire country, elevating Mao to the status of a living god, dehumanizing "class enemies," and destroying traditional Chinese cultural values. As a young participant in and victim of the rhetorical experience of the Cultural Revolution (I was ten when the Cultural Revolution began and twenty when it ended), I am intimately familiar with all the rhetorical themes and strategies propagated at the time, and I am also deeply aware of their impact on my own thoughts and actions as well as on those of the people around me. Second, as a rhetorical scholar, I have been prepared by my academic training and research in past years to undertake an intellectual analysis of this rhetorical phenomenon and to examine the forces of Chinese rhetoric in connection with thought, culture, and communication. My cultural and academic backgrounds enable me to describe, interpret, and evaluate the rhetoric of the Cultural Revolution with historical, cultural, and rhetorical sensitivity. Finally, being a native speaker of the Chinese language allowed me to interpret rhetorical texts and to conduct and analyze interviews in Chinese.

Many people have contributed to the formation and publication of this book. I have received consistent support and encouragement from Professors Thomas Benson, Jacqueline Taylor, Vernon Jensen, and David Frank throughout the preparation and completion of this project. I am indebted to Judy Bowker and Minmin Wang for their offer to proofread the entire manuscript and for their valuable suggestions for its improvement; they both raised thought-provoking questions not only from the viewpoint of rhetorical scholars but also from their separate cultural/political experiences as an American and a Chinese reader respectively. I would like to thank Herbert Simons for his empathetic and encouraging comments on the first two chapters. I appreciate very much the positive feedback and constructive criticism from the anonymous reviewers on the manuscript.

Further, I am deeply thankful to the thirty-five informants who willingly shared their experiences and reflections with me. Their personal accounts and witness during the Cultural Revolution added to the breadth of descriptions and depth of analysis of the topic under consideration. I wish to thank Mr. Yan Peng, who offered to read the first three chapters of this book; his experience as a participant in the Cultural Revolution and his remarkable memory of the unfolding events were very helpful. Thanks also to Tara Mckinney for her careful editing and fine-tuning of the manuscript.

This project could not have come to fruition without institutional support from the National Endowment for the Humanities, which granted me a summer stipend; from DePaul University, which granted me a one-year academic leave; and from the University of South Carolina Press, which showed great interest in my initial book proposal. I particularly wish to thank Barry Blose, the acquisitions editor, for his never-failing moral support and faith in me to finish the project and Bill Adams for his helpful editorial guidance.

Last, but not least, I would like to thank my parents, who have been invaluable resources as well as sources of inspiration for me to embark on and finish this project as scheduled. I am also grateful to my husband, Licheng Gu, for being the first reader of every chapter, for his careful proofreading of pinyin (Chinese romanization system for the characters) in the book, and for his love and support throughout the writing of this project. Finally, I would like to express my appreciation to Wendi Lulu Gu, my eleven-year-old daughter, for her patience and understanding in waiting for her turn to use the computer every day and night.

Chinese Names

The natural order of Chinese names places surname first and given name second. This order has been reversed for most Chinese names that are referenced in this book for three reasons: to avoid misunderstanding in the order of names as Western readers habitually regard the first name in the order is the given name; to avoid confusion in matching up with the names in the bibliography; and to follow the conventional practice in other scholarly works with regard to Chinese names. However, the names for prominent Chinese leaders and well-known individuals are ordered in the Chinese way.

Because Chinese names share more of the same surnames, the full names of Chinese writers appear in romanized form as well as in Chinese characters for distinction in the bibliographical reference.

Translation

Few translations of the Cultural Revolutionary texts are available. Therefore, I did my own translations of the most primary texts and all the interviews for the rhetorical analyses. I also translated the titles of books and articles in Chinese language into English for the bibliography section. Translations of Chinese texts are my own unless otherwise indicated.

Chinese Characters

I used the traditional (complicated) version of Chinese characters throughout the book as that version can be recognized by both overseas and mainland Chinese readers.

Introduction

A ten-year calamity is not one person's nightmare. It has affected the people of the entire world.
If we do not understand why it happened and provide an explanation for it, how can we face
the people of the world?

Ba Jin, *Sui xiang lu* (A Collection of Reflections)

The passing of time alone is good enough reason for reexamining the cataclysm that shook
China in 1966–1976, whose legacy endures into the China of the 1990s. Like all momen-
tous events in human history, the Cultural Revolution demands constant restudy, reinterpreta-
tion, and reflection.

William A. Joseph, Christine P. W. Wong, and David Zweig, eds.,
New Perspectives on the Cultural Revolution

History remembers the mass violence of the French Cultural Revolution (1789–99),
the persecution of religious heretics during the Inquisition of the Middle Ages, the
terror of Stalin's "Great Purge" of political dissidents in 1930s, and the horror of the
Holocaust for the Jewish people during World War II. Such atrocities are documented and studied in order to understand the past and avoid repetition of the same
mistakes and tragedies in the future. Unfortunately, the past is not always well understood and history does repeat itself. China's Cultural Revolution (1966–76) is an
example of this.

In her *Origins of Totalitarianism* (1951) Hannah Arendt offers an astute analysis of the
indoctrination methods employed in Stalin's Russia and Hitler's Germany. While
finding many similarities between the two regimes regarding their ideological campaign strategies and outcomes, Arendt had to admit that in the case of China, "We
never know very well how this worked in everyday life . . . that is, who did the
'remolding' —and we had no inkling of the results of the 'brainwashing,' whether it
was lasting and actually produced personality changes" (viii). Indeed, due to a relative
lack of communication between China and the rest of the world prior to the early
1980s, it has been difficult to obtain data from which to develop an informed understanding of the indoctrination processes by which over a billion people were transformed from adherents of Confucianism to devotees of Mao Zedong. China may be

better known today because of its increased openness to the outside world since the 1980s. However, the Chinese Cultural Revolution is still less studied and understood than are comparable social experiments and human atrocities in other parts of the world.

I was ten years old when China's Cultural Revolution began in 1966. Thirty-seven years have passed, yet I still remember clearly the fanatical shouting of slogans denouncing my father as a "counterrevolutionary." I recall the horror of seeing my father's swollen face and blood-soaked shirt, the result of a heavy beating by the Rebels.[1] I can never forget the day when my mother came home crying and wanting to commit suicide because her best friend at work had publicly denounced her for her rich family background and attacked her with groundless accusations. I still have nightmares from witnessing my mother's temporary insanity when she was cast out of the denunciation rally where my father was being tortured. I remember the days when my siblings and I lived in constant fear and humiliation, and when students had nothing to do at school but recite Mao Zedong's pronouncements and sing revolutionary songs. Even so, what my family went through was trivial compared to the magnitude of horror and loss many other individuals and families experienced. My family's story is only one of millions of tragedies that occurred during the Cultural Revolution.

Known to the Chinese as the "ten years of chaos," millions of Chinese were persecuted and thousands died during the Cultural Revolution. At the height of the Cultural Revolution (1967–69) it was not uncommon to hear stories of children denouncing their parents, students beating their teachers, husbands and wives opposing each other, and employees betraying employers—all in the name of defending Mao's revolutionary cause. Human relationships, characterized by harmony and tolerance in ancient China, were filled with hatred and mistrust during the Cultural Revolution. China's rich tradition of artistic expression was replaced with formulaic political jargon and tedious ideological clichés as the most pervasive form of public discourse. China, one of the oldest and flourishing civilizations in the world, had become a nation of fanaticism and terror, a cultural wasteland, and a stage for social/political drama characterized by cultism and mass hysteria.

The Cultural Revolution ended in 1976 soon after Mao's death and the arrest of the "Gang of Four."[2] However, the shock waves of the ten-years' chaos continue to have a devastating effect on Chinese thought, culture, and communication behaviors. This tragic experience of China's painful past has become part of the collective Chinese memory. These memories cannot be easily erased or forgotten, despite efforts by the government to do so. History is the best teacher. This failed social experiment offers a wealth of potential insights into the relationship between rhetoric and behavior for the Chinese and the non-Chinese, for political leaders as well as for ordinary citizens throughout the world.

This book is not primarily about the tragic events of the Cultural Revolution, nor is it about the recovery of its victims or the redemption of its radical fanatics. The study of victimization can be an emotionally appealing theme, but it does not guarantee that

China and the Chinese people will learn the lessons of history, nor does it prevent the occurrence of the Cultural Revolution somewhere else. This book attempts to address the question of why such a human tragedy happened in China. What were the symbols and symbolic practices that instigated such an event? How did the symbols and symbolic practices foster such chaotic nightmare? How did the symbols and symbolic practices at the time influence Chinese culture, Chinese thought processes, and Chinese communication behaviors? What lessons have the Chinese learned from the experience? Do the various factors that contributed to the Cultural Revolution still exist in China today? The Chinese people need to engage in a reflective process that involves moving beyond a sense of themselves as passive victims. As Arendt (1963) implies with regard to the Jewish people, the Chinese people need to search their own souls, examine their own thought processes, and ultimately arrive at a much deeper understanding of the rhetorical phenomenon known as the Cultural Revolution.

The subject of how symbols influence the way people think and act has been the center of scholarly attention and social/political concern since ancient times. While rhetoric was a powerful means of persuasion for Greek sophists and church fathers in ancient and medieval periods respectively, it has served as a primary tool for social change and political control in both democratic and totalitarian societies of the modern era. From the much-debated Sapir-Whorf Hypothesis (language shapes thought and culture), to Michel Foucault's (1972) theory of discourse formation (discourse is shaped in relation to power and empowerment), to Hannah Arendt's (1963) discussion of "the banality of evil" (evil is committed by following certain linguistic rules), we are provided with a more sophisticated understanding of the relationships among language, thought, culture, and human behavior.

This project is premised on the scholarly claim that language influences thought, culture, and human action, and that political language influences political thought and behavior. A look at this phenomenon is taken from anthropological, philosophical, critical, and rhetorical perspectives, examining how symbols and symbolic practices were performed and enacted in political contexts to legitimize the ruling ideology and alienating a whole group of people. The primary types of symbols under examination are political slogans, official propaganda, the language of wall posters, the lyrics in mass songs, and model operas. Symbolic expression is interwoven with ritualistic practices related to cultism, denunciation rallies, political study sessions, and criticism and self-criticism meetings. In describing and analyzing these symbols and practices, rhetorical themes and features are identified and delineated. Their impact on Chinese thought, culture, and communication is discussed.

In my descriptions and analyses of these symbols and symbolic practices I will locate the construction and dissemination of symbols within the political context of the Cultural Revolution. During this period Mao and his followers controlled the official media and were largely responsible for the coining of slogans and political clichés as well as the vulgar and violent rhetoric produced by the Red Guards. The Red Guards' pamphlets and the mass-produced wall posters were basically plagiarized versions of official Communist Party discourse proclaiming itself the infallible and absolute truth in all matters related to the extermination of "class enemies."[3] I pay particular attention to the ways in which certain words, expressions, and rituals were legitimized through powerful individuals and groups, official channels of communication, and various types of rhetorical appeals. Such appeals included moral/ethical persuasion, deductive reasoning process, and the use of certain metaphors reminiscent of ancient China. Some rhetorical strategies, such as these related to cultism, conspiracy theories, and the process of dehumanization, are strikingly similar to those employed in the regimes of Stalin's Russia and Nazi Germany.

The modern history of China is characterized by cultural and ideological confrontation, destruction, and reconstruction. Confucianism, once the state ideology and cultural foundation of China, came under attack by Western-educated intellectuals at the beginning of the last century. Subsequently, in 1949, a sinicized Marxism was adopted and enforced as the official ideology of the People's Republic of China. Although Marxist ideology was originally formulated in response to the economic and political situation of nineteenth-century Western Europe, Mao Zedong and his comrades believed strongly in the applicability of this theory to the social transformation of a new China. Beginning in the early 1950s, therefore, the Chinese Communist Party launched a series of campaigns to promote and inculcate Marxist ideology. Party members and intellectuals, mostly having received a Confucian education in their earlier years, were systematically indoctrinated with the teachings of Marx, Lenin, and Mao Zedong. The Confucian system of social ethics gave way to a Marxist understanding of class struggle. During the so-called Cultural Revolution, Mao's "application" of the Marxist theory of class struggle reached a traumatic climax, bringing widespread economic devastation and cultural destruction to the country.

Starting from the mid-1950s Mao had become increasingly concerned about the new bourgeoisie arising within the governmental body and among party officials. For Mao, this bourgeois ideology, along with traditional Chinese cultural practices, had permeated every aspect of Chinese life, posing a threat to the socialistic economic system and communist ideology. Mao and his followers adopted the Leninist practice of replacing bourgeois ideology with class consciousness, believing that a change in the superstructure (ideology) would affect the base (economy). Thus, the Cultural Revolution was an attempt to completely destroy the existing bourgeois culture as well as the "four olds" (old ideology, old culture, old habits, and old customs) of traditional Chinese culture. As stated by the Chinese Communist Party (CCP) Central Committee, "Our objective [in launching the Cultural Revolution] is to fight against and crush those persons in authority who are taking the capitalist road, to criticize and repudiate the reactionary bourgeois academic authorities and the ideology of the bourgeoisie and all other exploiting classes and to transform education, literature and art, and all other parts of the superstructure that do not correspond to the socialist economic base, so as to facilitate the consolidation and development of the socialist system" (Schoenhals 1996, 33).

It was believed that Mao deliberately wreaked havoc on China by launching the Cultural Revolution in order to prevent China from embracing capitalism. In fact, two aims were acclaimed consistently in various speeches and official media at the time: (1) to prevent capitalism; and (2) to consolidate the socialist system for the ultimate realization of a communist society. Having been brainwashed by communist propaganda, the Chinese masses embraced the premise that a communist society was the ultimate end of social progression, guaranteeing a better material life for all. A capitalistic society, on the other hand, was believed to pull history backward and cause ever widening gaps between the rich and the poor. Thus the launch of the Cultural Revolution was ideologically legitimized and appealed to the Chinese desire for a good life and an equal society.

To achieve the goal of political control over China's future, Mao mobilized the Chinese youth and radicals and allowed them to organize themselves into militant groups known as the Red Guards and the Rebels. Through Mao's controlled media, speeches by Lin Biao,[4] and the Gang of Four, as well as through the Red Guards' publications, slogans were coined, wall posters were produced, revolutionary songs were composed and sung, and rituals related to the cult of Mao were performed throughout the country, permeating every aspect of Chinese life. These symbolic practices inflamed revolutionary ardor, encouraged hatred of "class enemies," polarized thinking processes and perceptions of reality, and destroyed traditional Chinese culture and communication values and practices. Ultimately rhetoric of the Cultural Revolution paralyzed the Chinese Communist Party apparatus, caused factionalism and infighting, disrupted the economy, and led the country into deeper isolation from the rest of the world. The Cultural Revolution was indeed the most tumultuous and dramatic period of modern Chinese history.

Between 1966 and 1976 China was politicized, its entire population engaged in massive destruction of traditional Chinese culture and ideological battles between the proletarian and so-called bourgeois classes, as defined by the Chinese Communist Party. During this time the cult of Mao reached its climax while, conversely, China's economy collapsed. Also at this time human rights were wantonly violated, human dignity was gravely undermined, and crimes against humanity went unpunished. Further, the system of formal education was curtailed, the administrative sector was paralyzed, and factories and farms were turned into battlegrounds of ideological and political struggle. Every facet of Chinese life was in complete shambles. All the while the entire country spoke one political language, sang the same revolutionary songs, and performed the same loyalty dances and rituals. Anyone who dared to deviate from such conformity was severely punished with torture or execution.

Western studies of the Chinese Cultural Revolution have applied Western theories of social movement and human psychology to the Chinese context (e.g., Dittmer 1979; Esmein 1973; Hsia 1972), focusing primarily on causes, factions, and major events of the movement. Others have amounted to a collection of documents and speeches of the period (e.g., Huberman 1967; Schoenhals 1996).[5] Western scholars have, in principle, agreed on three interpretations of Mao's motives in launching the Cultural Revolution. The first interpretation was that Mao engaged in a power struggle aimed at ousting Liu Shaoqi, second in command of the nation. Liu Shaoqi had been directly in charge of China's economy prior to the Cultural Revolution. Mao considered Liu a threat, believing that Liu had gained too much power within the party's Central Committee. Mao also was concerned that Liu's agenda for economic construction would lead the country toward capitalism (Dittmer 1998; Michael 1971; Yan and Gao 1986). The second interpretation coincides with claims made by Mao's followers that the Cultural Revolution aimed at rectifying the superstructure of the Communist Party apparatus, ferreting out bourgeois values in education, art, and literature and revolutionizing Chinese culture (Solomon 1998; Xi and Jin 1996). The third interpretation is that Mao started the Cultural Revolution for the purpose of revitalizing the communist agenda, restoring ideological purity, and pushing for a more radical transformation of Chinese society (An 1972; Barcata 1967; Barnouin and Yu 1993). In general, these scholars shared the belief that Mao's reason for launching the Cultural Revolution was to clear away any obstacles on the road to a communist society. They seemed to agree that the ten years of chaos that almost brought the country to the brink of ruin was not intended by Mao, who had not anticipated the ways in which his lofty principles would meet with ugly political realities. When the Cultural Revolution ended, the CCP simply characterized the movement as "wrongly launched by the leader, manipulated by a counterrevolutionary clique, and marred by an internal chaos that brought grave disaster to the Party, the country, and the Chinese people" (Shaoguang Wang 1996, 516).

All the foregoing observations and interpretations of the Cultural Revolution carry some elements of truth. However, such studies have tended to treat the Cultural Revolution as a social phenomenon or a historical event. Few have studied the Cultural Revolution as a rhetorical phenomenon or given any attention to the symbolic processes and construction that affected Chinese thought and action. Scholars' interpretations have typically not strayed far from claims made by Mao and his followers or from the evaluation of the movement offered by the CCP. This superficial coverage of the most dramatic and devastating event in China's modern history has overlooked the significant role that rhetoric played in legitimizing and justifying violent behavior and the violation of human rights. The existing studies amount to a description rather than a reflection on the aftermath and fallout of the movement. When six million Jews were killed during the Holocaust by the Nazis the atrocity was considered a heinous crime against humanity. The horror of the Chinese Cultural Revolution, on the other hand, is known to the world as an internal conflict maneuvered by Mao for the purpose of political control in the name of preventing China from embracing capitalism. Its character as a grievous violation of human rights and dignity has not been well exposed or studied.

Another category of studies on the Cultural Revolution consists of collections of personal memoirs of the movement produced by native Chinese and in some cases penned by Westerners (e.g., Heng and Shapiro 1983; Ross 1994; Huo Wang 1998; Yuan 1987; Zhai 1992). While these works offer Chinese and Western readers first-hand accounts of tragedies, hardship, and adversity involving Chinese individuals and families during the Cultural Revolution, they do not offer systematic examination and analysis of the symbolic activities and rhetorical construction of reality characteristic of this period of Chinese history. Further, these memoirs tend to depict the protagonists as victims rather than engaging in reflective and retrospective processes with regard to the impact of language on thought and behavior.

Unlike the aforementioned studies, this book engages in analyses of a wide range of rhetorical texts and practices during the Cultural Revolution, providing a careful examination of their impact on contemporary Chinese thought processes, cultural orientations, and communication patterns. Moreover, I argue that rhetoric of the Cultural Revolution appropriated certain themes and forms of rhetoric from the classical Chinese rhetorical tradition and bore a close resemblance to the totalitarian rhetoric of Nazi Germany and Stalin's Russia with regard to ideological transformation, political control, and dehumanization. My argument is supported by rhetorical analyses of political discourses of both the official media and the masses propagated during the Cultural Revolution in the interest of shaping and remolding Chinese thought and culture. I contend that symbolic practices employed and performed during the Cultural Revolution destroyed the traditional Chinese values of harmony and stability while constructing a new Chinese culture characterized by conflict and instability. I also argue that the negation of Confucianism, in conjunction with the propagation of Maoist thought, deprived the Chinese people of their ability to think critically.

The data used for the identification of rhetorical themes and features come from three sources. The first source is interview data. I interviewed thirty-five people who lived in China during the ten-year period of the Cultural Revolution. Most of them were in their youth or teenage years at the time and still have vivid memories of their symbolic experiences. Interviewees were mixed in sex composition and were born between 1946 and 1958. They currently live either in China or in the United States. Some fell into the role of perpetrators, others the role of victims during the Cultural Revolution. Most interviews were conducted face to face; some were by telephones and some by E-mail. All interviews were conducted in Chinese and were tape-recorded. I asked the following three interview questions:

1. What symbols and symbolic practices of the Cultural Revolution do you remember most?
2. What effect and impact do you think these symbols and symbolic practices had on you and the people around you in terms of thought patterns, cultural values, and communication behaviors?
3. Do you think the thought processes and communication behaviors of the Cultural Revolution still exist today? If so, what are the traces of such influence in individuals and official discourse?

During the interview process I offered elaborations of the questions, sought specific examples, probed, and in general tried to elicit relevant responses. I transcribed all the interviews verbatim in Chinese and translated those segments I used in this book. My interview questions and consent forms were approved by the DePaul University Institutional Review Board for the Protection of Research Participants.

The second source of data consisted of collections of prominent official publications such as the *People's Daily* and the *Red Flag* (the official mouthpieces of the CCP); Red Guard collections of slogans; and books that record symbols and symbolic practices, such as slogans, wall posters, songs, operas, and rituals. Some are original documents published or disseminated during the Cultural Revolution; some are collections published in later years. Another source of textual data was the on-line Cultural Revolution Virtual Museum run by overseas Chinese dissidents (http://www.cnd.org/HXWZ/newzk.gb.html).[6]

The third source of data was the memoirs of Red Guard members and those whose families suffered during the Cultural Revolution. They are either in English or in Chinese. Most memoirs were written by the authors; some were penned by English writers. These memoirs provided primary accounts of personal sufferings as well as personal experiences with symbols and symbolic practices during the Cultural Revolution.

When expert translations of certain texts were not available I used my own translations, always seeking to strike a balance between faithfulness to the original texts and comprehensibility to the reader. I am aware that translation is not merely a matter of word-for-word reproduction; it is a process of interpretation and negotiation of meanings between two languages and in this case two political/cultural contexts.

My analyses of the rhetorical texts and interviews were guided by a variety of modes of rhetorical criticism, including dramatistic criticism, cultural/ideological criticism, narrative criticism, and fantasy theme analysis (Borman 1972; Burke 1941, 1961, 1969; Fisher 1987; McGee 1980; Wander 1983). To avoid the tendency of imposing Western models onto non-Western texts, I have made a conscious attempt to interpret meanings on the basis of the original texts with consideration for the social/political context of China rather than confining myself to existing theoretical frameworks.

This book is divided into three sections: chapters 1 and 2 consist of an overview of the historical context of the Cultural Revolution interwoven with my personal observations of that time. Here, I identify characteristics of totalitarian rhetoric along with features of Chinese Communist propaganda prior to the Cultural Revolution. In this section I also review theoretical claims made from anthropological, philosophical, critical, and rhetorical perspectives. These perspectives provide frameworks for rhetorical analyses and discussion on the impact of the rhetorical phenomenon of the Cultural Revolution on Chinese thought, culture, and communication. Chapters 3–6 undertake rhetorical analyses of selected texts produced during the Cultural Revolution. The texts are divided into four categories: slogans, wall posters, revolutionary songs and operas, and ritualistic practices. Each category has its own chapter. In this part I identify major rhetorical themes and linguistic features, make connections between features of classical Chinese rhetoric and those of totalitarian rhetoric in Nazi Germany and Stalin's Russia, and discuss persuasive effects on ideological control and mass mobilization. I incorporate interview findings into my analyses and discuss the persuasive effects of these rhetorical practices on thought, culture, and communication. Chapters 7 and 8 trace the use of Cultural Revolution rhetoric in the post-Mao era and political context. In particular, I examine the characteristics of public discourse during the regimes of Deng Xiaoping and Jiang Zemin, rhetoric condemning Falun Gong, and rhetoric of anti-America sentiment. Chapter 8, the concluding chapter, summarizes the characteristics of the rhetoric of the Cultural Revolution, discusses reflections of the interviewees, and identifies various challenges China is facing in its political rhetoric and communication.

One

My Family Caught in the Cultural Revolution

Indifference to evil is the enemy of good, for indifference is the enemy of everything that exalts the honor of man. We fight indifference through education; we diminish it through compassion. The most efficient remedy? Memory.

Elie Wiesel, "How Can We Understand Their Hatred?" *Chicago Tribune*

"Forget, forget!" Loudly you shouted. But no one will forget these unforgettable ten years. Let our next generation give this chaotic period a closure and write it into history. Someone must do this work. Why can't we leave the next generation some tangible evidence of these times? Why can't we tell of our personal suffering? We cannot simply forget the pains of the past in the name of "looking forward to the future."

Ba Jin, *Sui xiang lu* (A Collection of Reflections)

Ba Jin 巴金 is a well-known writer in China. He has published numerous novels and essays and is well loved by many Chinese. During the ten-year Cultural Revolution, however, he was denounced, condemned, imprisoned, and tortured. His home was ransacked more than once; he was sent to labor camps, while his wife endured hardship and humiliation, and subsequently died of cancer. Unfortunately, Ba Jin's ordeal is only one of millions of personal tragedies that occurred during the Cultural Revolution. Since the end of that violent era a smattering of books have been published documenting the persecution of top-ranking officials, well-known intellectuals, and famous artists and writers. Despite the government's ban on research and publications associated with the Cultural Revolution, memoirs have been written in Chinese and/or English as attempts to glean some measure of redemption and meaning from the tragedy through telling and retelling of the traumatic events and personal experiences of ordinary people and families during that time. My family's story is one such unforgettable piece of the puzzle.

It is not my intention in this chapter to write an autobiographical account or memoir, however. Inspired by Ba Jin's call to "give an explanation," this chapter aims to accomplish two goals. First, it gives the reader a sense of the historical context of the

Cultural Revolution through a narrative account of the pain and suffering of an ordinary family caught up in the dramatic events of that time. Second, and more important, it gives the reader a sense of how symbols such as wall posters, revolutionary songs, and slogans were used during the Cultural Revolution. It provides a description of how rhetorical practices such as confessions, political study sessions, debates, infighting among factions, and denunciation rallies actually functioned in the lives of real people. In particular, through the lens of my own family story and accounts of related tragedies, this chapter illustrates the ways in which various symbols and rhetorical practices have influenced the thought processes and behaviors of my family members and other Chinese. In presenting this information I hope to show the world what happened, as well as to set the stage for understanding why it happened. This chapter also includes my personal observations and reflections regarding the connections between language, thought, and communication.

Before the Cultural Revolution

Before the Cultural Revolution my family lived a relatively peaceful life. We were not rich by any means, but we always had enough to eat and could afford to buy new clothes at New Year's time. Both my parents were middle-ranking Communist Party officials. My mother worked as an assistant to a party branch in the Harbin Number 2 Bureau of Light Industry, while my father was the head of the public security section of a factory. Both worked faithfully and conscientiously in their respective jobs. It was not unusual for them to come home late and to work on weekends.

My parents were introduced to each other by mutual friends, and their marriage was approved by the party after a year of dating. They embodied the values and priorities of a typical revolutionary marriage of their generation, which made political qualifications the standard for choosing one's mate. Father had a bright political career ahead of him. This asset was the determining factor in my mother's decision to marry him. Unfortunately, their marriage was not a happy one. My memories are filled with their fighting, verbal attacks, and physical abuse. But for the sake of their children they did not divorce.

We lived in a two-bedroom apartment that was considered moderately comfortable by Chinese standards. There were four children in all: I have one younger brother and two younger sisters. My maternal grandparents lived with us until the Cultural Revolution began. My grandmother, who was kindhearted and well liked by the neighbors, helped my mother raise the four of us. Grandma was born in 1895, in a time when a woman was not allowed to receive an education; she had been forced to bind her feet in order to conform to society's "fashions" and norms at the time.[1] Grandma was about five feet, six inches tall, but her feet were only about four inches long. Both of her big toes were bent under her insteps. I remember watching her wrap and unwrap her feet with many layers of white fabric every morning and night. She could walk very fast if necessary but was never able to run. I always felt sorry for her. Grandma was a devout Buddhist, and I witnessed her paying homage to the Buddha and praying for us every day. Since my parents were always busy, it was Grandma who told us stories and passed on Chinese cultural values and practices to us.

The Persecution of My Father

In March 1966 I was two months away from my tenth birthday. Father returned from a business trip in Beijing. I was excited because whenever Father came home from a trip he would bring candies or fruits for us. Recently he had brought some bananas from southern China. That was the first time in my life I had tasted a banana, and I thought it was the best food in the whole world.

To my disappointment, Father did not bring back any goodies this time; instead he brought bad news. Over dinner he told Mother that Luo Ruiqing 罗瑞卿, a high-ranking member of the Communist Party, had attempted suicide by jumping from a building after being charged with various political crimes. Luo did not die but had broken his legs and become paralyzed. At the time Father was the section head of public security at the Harbin Electric Meter Factory. Luo Ruiqing was the top minister in my father's sector. Father had a high regard for him and was saddened and disturbed by the news. He told Mother that he had seen many wall posters in Beijing criticizing and attacking top government officials, implying an internal struggle within the party. Mother then shared a few newspaper articles condemning certain top-level intellectuals and accusing them of attempting to subvert socialist ideology through their plays and writings.[2]

Within the next couple of months the Central Committee of the Communist Communist Party issued the "May 16th Announcement," which alerted the Chinese people to the fact that there were representatives of bourgeois and revisionist interests within the party, the army, and the government and officially announcing the inception of the Great Proletarian Cultural Revolution.[3] On 5 August 1966 Mao Zedong, chairman of the Communist Party, erected his "Bombard Headquarters: My Big-Character Poster," a wall poster that openly supported actions that directly targeted government officials who were perceived as counterrevolutionary, claiming that a bourgeois headquarters was hidden within the Communist Party and that certain top officials were suppressing the revolutionary spirit and leading the country to capitalism.[4] The rhetorical style of the poster was hostile and provocative. My parents' initial reaction, as events unfolded signaling an upcoming political storm, was to remain loyal to Mao and the Communist Party, just as they had always been in past political campaigns. They never imagined that they would soon become victims of this social turmoil.

Soon after Father's return from Beijing wall posters began to appear on his factory walls. Many were written by self-professed "Revolutionary Rebels"[5] and called on the workers to expose and denounce party officials and factory administrators. One day while Father was working in his office, several Rebels came in and "seized power" from him by confiscating his handgun, his handcuffs (only the section head had the authority to keep handcuffs and handguns), and his office keys.[6] Father came home that day deeply disturbed and depressed. I heard him say to Mother, "Be prepared. I may be in trouble." He shut himself in his room and did not have dinner with us that evening. It must have been a serious blow to him, as he had been a loyal party member for twenty years and could not understand why such a thing had happened.

We did not know it at the time, but that night marked the beginning of a long ordeal for our family. From 5 July to 23 September 1967 at Father's factory about a dozen enormous wall posters were hung and directly targeted Father, accusing him of being "a capitalist roader,"[7] "a daring vanguard of the Rightists," and "the most dangerous enemy of the socialist society." One Rebel constructed six of these damning posters, charging Father with five political crimes. They said the following: "(1) Lu Rong [my father] acted in collusion with other capitalist roaders in protecting bad people and persecuting good people; (2) Lu Rong concealed the fact that he was from a despotic, landlord family and was never truthful to the party; (3) Lu Rong viciously attacked the party, Chairman Mao, and the goal of the Proletarian Cultural Revolution; (4) Lu Rong's behind-the-scene supporters were Chiang Kai-shek and Khrushchev, and he was the designated successor of Chiang and a follower of Khrushchev; and (5) Lu Rong created conflicts and factions among revolutionary comrades."

Every one of these charges was pure fabrication without any basis in fact or supporting evidence. At the end of each wall poster the Rebel cursed Father with many variations of a dreadful death. He wrote, "Lu Rong will be drowned in his own urine. He will be choked to death by a crow defecating down his throat. He will be crushed to death by a car. He will be thrown into the river to feed the fish and into the manure pit to decompose." It was frightening to hear Father recounting these charges and curses against him to Mother. Father was humiliated and indignant. But he said to us calmly, "All these charges are false. I am innocent. I've never lied to the party and I never did anything bad to anybody." Then I heard him asking Mother, "Why do they hate me so much?" Mother tried to comfort Father and said, "This is a mass movement. Trust the party and trust Chairman Mao."

My father had always believed in the Communist Party and Maoist ideals largely because of the poverty he had experienced as a child. He was born in 1929 to a family of ten children. Both of his parents were peasants and illiterate, and they lived a very poor life. Father told me that he and his siblings usually ate only one meal a day and sometimes went hungry for several days. They lived in a small village in Heilongjiang Province thirty miles from Harbin (capital city of the province) in the northeast part of China. There were no schools in the village. Father managed to finish elementary school by staying with his relatives in Harbin for a few years and commuting for two years between his village and Harbin. After that his family could no longer support him, so he went back to his village and helped his family with farming. By then they owned about two acres of land, on which they grew crops and vegetables. Because the village was situated in a flood zone, their farm often flooded and a whole year's hard labor would be in vain; the cycle of poverty and hunger was repeated in this way.

In 1946 Father joined the People's Public Security Army stationed in Harbin. Their task was to protect the city and put down bandits. A few times in the battles against bandits Father almost got killed. Because of his bravery and "good deeds," he was accepted into the Communist Party and promoted to head of a local police station. Three years later Father was transferred to the Municipal Bureau of Public Security, where he worked as a detective in addition to supervising the public security of major factories in the city. In 1956 he was transferred to the Harbin Electric Meter Factory and given the job of heading the public security section. Father was proud that he was once selected as a bodyguard for Mao Zedong when Mao stayed in Harbin overnight on his way to the Soviet Union for a state visit.

Indeed, in his twenty years of service from 1946 to 1966 Father devoted himself wholeheartedly to the Communist Party cause. He was absolutely loyal to Mao Zedong, never questioning party authority or Maoist ideology. In fact, he was grateful to Mao, believing that without Mao he would still be working in the fields and living in abject poverty. Father was convinced that the party's cause was noble and just and in the best interest of the majority, especially the poor. Largely lacking in formal education, his language repertoire was limited to terminology and set phrases from official party channels. Throughout his life he read only party newspapers and journals or government documents. He had almost no private thoughts and never learned how to think critically and independently.

Now he found himself plunged into a situation he was not equipped to understand. After two decades of unwavering devotion and dedication to Mao and the party, suddenly he had become "a capitalist roader" and "a dangerous enemy" of the people. In an unguarded moment, in the presence of a close friend and former colleague, he expressed concern about Mao's judgment, saying, "Why would Chairman Mao launch the Cultural Revolution? It does not make any sense. Maybe he is too old and has become muddleheaded." What Father did not expect was that his friend later exposed him to the Rebels for his moment of doubt. His friend's betrayal brought Father extreme suffering and nearly cost him his life.

Father was soon detained by a group of Rebels, and the torture and humiliation began. During the day he was dragged to public rallies to be criticized, condemned, and cursed. Along with other "capitalist roaders" from the factory, Father was made to wear a cone-shaped dunce cap about four feet high.[8] He was forced to bend his body forward at the waist at a ninety-degree angle with his head pushed forward and hands pinned behind his back. This torturous configuration was known as "the jet plane" position. The Rebels placed a heavy iron placard around Father's neck on which his name was written in black ink and then crossed out with a bold red X. The rallies began and ended with people shouting slogans such as "Down with Lu Rong"; "Thoroughly expose Lu Rong's counterrevolutionary crime"; "Pledge to protect Chairman Mao's revolutionary line"; and "Long live Chairman Mao." A few of the Rebels denounced Father's "crimes" over a loudspeaker, cursing and spitting at him. In the evenings there were more torture and beatings. Oftentimes he was forced to stand on a narrow stool and bend his body to his feet, after which the Rebels would kick the stool out from under him, watch him fall, and beat him again.

During one incident Father was asked to kneel down and bend his body over a piece of glass. The Rebels then placed a piece of plywood on his back and played cards on it. If the wood shook because he could not hold his body still, the Rebels would beat him and curse him. When Father begged them to stop torturing him, one of the Rebels said to him, "Torturing you is a revolutionary act. You have no rights to make such a request. You are our class enemy and under our control." Another Rebel added, "People like you should be eliminated from the earth; you are all monsters." During another incident Father was dragged by two Rebels to the window of a building's third floor and forcibly encouraged to jump out of the building. He refused to do so, for he feared that he would be condemned as a "historical criminal" if he committed suicide. He wanted to protect his family from the stigma of such a label.[9]

I was eleven years old at the time. The Rebels allowed our family to send meals to Father, and as the oldest of his children, I was given that job. Most of the time I was not allowed to see my father. One time I saw him and was thoroughly shocked and traumatized by the experience. His white shirt was covered with blood, his nose was bleeding, his face and eyes were horribly swollen, and he was unable to utter even a word. When I was unable to stop crying, the guard yelled at me and then searched my pockets to make sure that Father had not given me any notes.

Mao wrote in 1927: "Revolution is not a dinner party, or writing an essay, or painting a picture, or doing embroidery; it cannot be so refined, so leisurely and gentle, so temperate, kind, courteous, restrained and magnanimous. A revolution is an insurrection, an act of violence by which one class overthrows another" (1975, 28). This quotation was widely cited and repeatedly used by Red Guards and Rebels to justify the humiliation, abuse, and torture of intellectuals and party officials accused of counterrevolutionary, antiparty, anti–Chairman Mao offenses, or any other alleged "crimes." Those who were persecuted were first dehumanized as, for example, "cow ghosts and snake spirits." Father was considered such a "monster." From the Rebels' perspective my father and people like him were not only undesirable but also should be made to suffer. Thus torture and other forms of abuse were justified in the proletarian war against "class enemies."

The torture of my father continued. The Rebels relocated him to the basement of a factory building, known as the "cowshed," a metaphor for prison. As soon as Father entered the basement a group of Rebels began to hit him until he lost consciousness. They then dragged him to a small cell, formerly used as a toilet, where water leaked all the time. Father was imprisoned in this place with forty other "class enemies." All were made to wear white cloths with their names and "crimes" displayed in black ink.

During the days Father and other class enemies were summoned to factory workshops for public denunciation. Typically each day they would be forced to endure four such denunciations, each two hours in duration. Usually before the start of these humiliating ordeals the Rebels would beat Father from head to toe and push him into "the jet plane" position. In the evenings the Rebels would force him into that position again for a few hours before he would finally be allowed to sleep. On one occasion they forced him to hold the position for the entire night until he passed out. Another common form of torture was to wake him up at midnight and make him run in the hallway of the basement until he was completely worn-out or fainted. Beatings could take place at any time. Whenever Father lost consciousness as a result of a heavy beating, the Rebels would pour cold water over his body and pull him up by his ears. Three of his ribs were broken and the soft bones of his ears were pulled off as results of these acts of cruelty.

My father's story is only one of millions such cases of torture and persecution. Actually, he considered himself lucky not to have been executed, as a staggering number of people throughout the country had been in the wake of false charges leveled against them. Indeed, the first three years of the Cultural Revolution was a period of astonishing barbarism. Red Guards and Rebels ransacked people's houses, destroyed traditional Chinese art, and beat and abused "problem people" (those of rich family backgrounds, rightists, capitalist roaders, and so-called spies and traitors). Rampant fighting between opposing factions escalated. Countless people were imprisoned, tortured to death, or driven to suicide. Although the government has never issued statistics on death toll, Shalom (1984) estimates that approximately one million people died during the first three years of the Cultural Revolution. Among those who died, 239,110 were executed on false charges of "counterrevolutionary crimes." The remaining deaths can be attributed to torture, beating, suicide, and mass killing.

On 27 August 1966, for example, Red Guards in the Beijing area killed 325 people from landlord and rich peasant family backgrounds in Daxing County. In December 1967 a large number of high-ranking Communist Party officials throughout the country were accused of spying for Guomin Dang, the Nationalist Party, and charged with treason. Among them 80,400 people were tortured and 20,959 were executed. In February 1968 counterrevolutionary charges were brought against a self-organized People's Party in Inner Mongolia. Subsequently 346,000 people were violently persecuted and 16,222 of that party's members were executed. In Dao County, Hunan Province, alone the persecution of innocent people was so rampant that within the first two years of the Cultural Revolution 7,696 people were executed, 1,397 committed suicide, and 2,146 were disabled from torture (Meng Zhu 2001, 319–22). In a Korean-minority autonomous zone 3,000 people were arrested on charges of sabotaging the Communist Party; 1,000 of them were executed (Feng Zhao 1999, 224).

Those tortured and brutalized ranged from top-ranking officials, such as Liu Shaoqi, the president of the People's Republic of China, to ordinary citizens. It was believed that one of Mao's motives for instigating the Cultural Revolution was to rid his headquarters of Liu Shaoqi, the second-ranking member of the Chinese Communist Party hierarchy. Mao was reportedly convinced that Liu had hindered the revolutionary cause by promoting a capitalist system and advancing his own interests within the party. Beginning in 1967 Liu was accused of being "a traitor, an enemy agent, and a scab." He was also labeled "the number one capitalist roader within the party" and "the Khrushchev of China," and he was expelled from the party. Liu was systematically denounced in public, separated from his family, and beaten and tortured. His home was ransacked, and his wife and children were persecuted and imprisoned. Finally he was secretly transferred to the city of Kaifeng in Henan Province while seriously ill, suffering from multiple injuries and infections. There he died without any family members at his side (Dittmer 1998; Liu, Liu, and Liu 1987).

Ordinary citizens were also victims of brutality. Reflecting on his experience as a Red Guard, Xiaosheng Liang (1998) recalled the torture of one woman whose crimes were "spying, spreading anti-cultural revolution speeches, and corrupting revolutionary leaders" (278). The Red Guards pushed her into a big stove in which asphalt was boiling. The woman struggled to get out, but she was bound and her mouth was stuffed with cotton. Her husband and daughter tried to save her from the boiling asphalt but in the process burned themselves badly (278). In fact, in endless political campaigns beginning in the 1950s countless people were charged with crimes they did not commit. The charges brought against them never went through a legal system. Those who were victimized in this way were never given apologies or reparations. There was no punishment for those who tormented, abused, and murdered millions of innocent people.

To return to my father's story, after a year of torture in the "cowshed," he was finally released, suffering from a cerebral concussion, a lung infection, a mild mental disorder, and a spinal infection. After two weeks' treatment and recovery he was sent to a factory and required to do manual labor. During this time Father was not allowed to participate in any meetings or political activities. Workers were advised that he was a class enemy. They were told, "Lu Rong must follow orders and cannot act on his own initiatives. He must reform himself through doing harsh labor." Father was forced to write confessional reports, self-examining and self-criticizing his "wrongful thoughts" and "crimes." Convinced that he had done nothing wrong, he refused to admit to the alleged crimes. As a result his confessional reports were never approved. Many times he sat in his chair staring at the wall and weeping for failing to pass the "standard." His health deteriorated, and he began to lose his sanity.

One evening a friend came to our home to warn Mother that a group of Rebels was going to kill Father that night. Father was receiving medical treatment at home for his lung infection and concussion at the time. Mother said to me, "Take your father to a safe place. I will stay at home and confront them." It was around midnight on a very cold winter night. Father and I wandered in the street. We first went to the home of Aunt Wang and her husband, our family's closest friends. When we explained the situation to them and begged them to let us stay the night, they became frightened and turned us away. We left them and wandered in the street again. I was cold and scared. Father was deeply hurt and began to weep. He told me that he never cried, even when he was beaten. But to be turned away by his best friends was too much to bear. We finally decided to go to Father's sister's house some distance away. After several hours walking in the cold darkness we arrived there at four in the morning and were taken in. I am still haunted by what we experienced that night.

In January 1975 Deng Xiaoping was reinstated as recalled by Mao to the vice prime minister, after having been charged with being the number-two capitalist roader in the country and being dismissed from the office since 1966. The first thing Deng did when he returned to power was to liberate all those who had been wronged and persecuted by the Red Guards and Rebels. Consequently, Father was "liberated" and the torment ended. Liberation in this context meant that all the charges against him were removed and his reputation restored. I will never forget the day his liberation was announced. We were all happy and relieved; it was as if a heavy stone had been lifted from our backs. Between 1966 and 1972 my father was stripped of his job and his dignity and was tortured almost to death. After all he had gone through, Father's faith in Mao and the Communist Party was seriously undermined, though he remained a party member. He has recovered from most of the injuries over the years and is now enjoying his retirement.

The Story of My Mother

My mother was born in 1930 to a wealthy family in a village of roughly three hundred households. Her family owned a grocery store, a grinding mill, and a cooking-oil factory. However, Mother's father became addicted to opium, and the family business began to decline. In 1946 the Communists came to the village and launched the land reform movement.[10] All personal property was confiscated. Landlords and members of affluent families were denounced in public; some were executed. My grandfather was arrested, and his family was classified as "rich peasant." This label stigmatized the family as exploitive and untrustworthy. When my mother subsequently offered to help the local Communist Party with land reform activities she was rejected because of her family background.

My grandfather had received some education and insisted on sending Mother and her sister to school, even though in those days girls were not expected to receive an education. After Mother graduated from junior high school Grandmother arranged a marriage for her. The man was five years younger than Mother and also from a "rich peasant" family in a nearby village. Mother did not want to marry the man, but his family insisted. One day they came to my grandparents' house with a load of betrothal gifts and wanted to take Mother away. Mother threw all the betrothal gifts out of the window and ran away. At around this time the Communist Party issued the Marriage Law edict. Fortunately my mother and the man did not meet the age requirement for marriage under the new law. For this reason she was always grateful to the Communist Party.

Mother went to the city of Harbin on her own in 1950. Her first job was as an inventory clerk in the Number 3 Rubber Production Factory. A few months after taking her first job she was accused of stealing two hundred yuan (about twenty dollars) from work. She was beaten and coerced into making a confession for something she had not done. Later her confession was corrected and her name was cleared by a work team dispatched by the party. Because of this experience Mother became convinced that the Communist Party would never persecute innocent people and would rectify any wrongdoings.

The following year Mother was allowed to join the Communist Party. After that she worked even more diligently for the party despite the fact that several times she was passed over for promotion due to her "rich peasant" family background. In order to prove her loyalty to the party she endured these "tests" and continued to dedicate herself wholeheartedly to the Communist cause. Through this process she was indoctrinated into a system that emphasized abstract love for Mao, the party, and the state over the love of a concrete person. She was also taught to relinquish her femininity and be the equal of any man. Mother was definitely in defiance of the traditional Chinese norm of a woman as a "good wife and kind mother." In all the years we children were growing up Mother showed little affection to us, her husband, or even her own mother.

Despite her loyalty and dedication to the party Mother was denounced on three wall posters at the outset of the Cultural Revolution. The first one charged her with aiding and abetting her "rich peasant" family by allowing her parents to live with her. The testimony was provided by Father's brother, who had always been resentful of the way Mother related to Father's side of the family. The second poster accused her of having an affair with a married man, a Communist Party commander, during the land reform period. This accusation was completely false, but the testimony was provided by her own brother, who later confessed that he had testified against her in order to establish himself as a true revolutionary through his willingness to expose his sister's "dark history." The third poster was written by Mother's best friend, a Rebel, and accused her of suppressing the revolutionary masses and wanting to help the bourgeoisie regain power. This charge was based on the so-called "evidence" that Mother, coming from a "rich peasant" family background, had access to the individual files of the workplace. The assumption was that people from such a background would naturally abuse their power and seek to support the interest of the exploitive class.[11]

On the day Mother first saw these three wall posters and the charges against her she was humiliated and devastated. She came home crying and distraught. Father had already been detained, and I was only eleven years old at that time. I feared that Mother might want to commit suicide; she started telling me who were the good and who were the bad people among our family and friends, and how much money we owed others. I tried to comfort her and convince her not to commit suicide. I remember saying to her, "If you commit suicide, it will only prove that what they said about you is true, not a false accusation, and your 'crime' will seem more severe." We talked and cried throughout the night, and Mother was finally persuaded by my words and emotional pleas.

During the Cultural Revolution many people committed suicide in order to avoid further humiliation or to maintain their dignity. For example, Lao She 老舍, a famous novelist who had written many popular novels, drowned himself in a river in Beijing. Fu Lei 傅雷, a prolific translator who introduced Western classical literature to millions of Chinese readers, hung himself. Jian Bozan 剪伯赞, the vice president of Beijing University and a well-established historian, took his own life by swallowing a large dose of sleeping pills. Nearly everyone knew, directly or indirectly, someone who was driven to suicide by unwarranted charges.

Once the accusations came out against Mother, nobody in the workplace would talk to her. When her colleagues were divided into two factions, neither group wanted her. She was transferred to a cafeteria, where she worked as a cook's helper for a year, and then to a metal factory for another year. During this time she was often called to attend *xuexi ban* 學習班 (study groups) and required to self-criticize her "bourgeois thoughts" and confess her "crimes" rooted in her "rich peasant" family background. Through participation in these groups Mother witnessed many instances of rumors and lies leveled against innocent people. Typically, once someone was accused of a "crime," he or she would then be subjected to verbal, and sometimes physical, assault. No proof was required, and no measures were put in place to protect innocent people.

Mother had always been a fervent proponent of the revolutionary cause and was loyal to Mao. I remember that she once had a fight with Father because she insisted on covering the four walls of our only room with Mao's portraits, while Father thought one portrait of Mao was enough.[12] Mother was furious and charged Father with disloyalty to Mao. She even threatened to expose him. Mother strongly believed that Mao and the party had given her a new life and were China's salvation. She continued to believe this even after her painful experience. She remained faithful to Mao and the Communist cause until much later when her health started deteriorating due to the accumulated stress of the Cultural Revolution.

Mother's mental and physical health were greatly compromised by the persecution of my father during the Cultural Revolution. One time several Rebels broke into our apartment, dragged Father out of bed, and took him to a denunciation rally. Father had just been released for medical treatment of injuries caused by a heavy beating. Mother tried to stop them but in vain. She then followed the Rebels to the auditorium where the rally was held, but she was not allowed to enter. Something snapped inside her, and she began to run aimlessly through the street crying and shouting like a madwoman. Many people were watching the scene on both sides of the street, but nobody tried to help. I ran behind Mother crying and begging her to return home with me. Finally she regained control of herself and went home.

Because Father had been labeled the "most dangerous enemy in socialist society," anything that was done to him and his family was considered justified. While Father was going through the ordeal of a series of public denunciations and brutal beatings away from home, we endured humiliation and fear inflicted by a loudspeaker, which was placed outside our apartment building and constantly repeated at high volume: "Down with Lu Rong"; "Lu Rong is a capitalist running dog"; "Down with all the cow ghosts and snake spirits." The loudspeaker also broadcast revolutionary songs and announced public denunciation rallies. The projected noise was so loud and terrifying that Mother got into the habit of going to the toilet every time she heard the loud-speaker, and to this day whenever she hears a loudspeaker she has to urinate immediately. It would seem that Mother's bladder was totally conditioned by the terror of the Cultural Revolution.

On 7 May 1968 Mao issued a new directive calling for the establishment throughout the country of "cadre schools," each of which was to be known as the May Seventh Cadre School. Conceived as places to reform and rehabilitate party officials and intellectuals, the schools were located in remote areas of the country. Mother volunteered to attend the one on the outskirts of Harbin. In order to demonstrate her revolutionary spirit she walked to the cadre school on the first day (about fifty miles from our home). By the time she got there her feet were raw and blistered but her spirits were high. At that time she seriously thought that this experience would prove her loyalty to the party once and for all and help her clean up any lingering bourgeois tendencies.

Life in the May Seventh Cadre School was harsh. Mother and other participants lived in caves instead of houses. During the days they were made to do strenuous physical labor in the fields. In the evenings they had to study Mao's teachings and confess any errant thoughts or conduct. One winter day Mother took me by bus to her cadre school, which was clearly more of a labor camp. The caves had no electricity or heating systems, six people shared a big bed, and everyone wore uniforms of the same color and design.[13] Each morning after a simple, coarse meal they lined up, sang a revolutionary song, and marched to the field to do intense labor. Mother told me that during the harvest season they had to make ten trips a day carrying heavy loads of crops from the field to the processing mill. Each trip was about half a mile in length.

It was believed that the harsher the condition, the more effective the thought reform of the participants. The tactics of forced labor and separation from one's family had been employed in China's imperial past to punish those officials who voiced disagreement or disobeyed the emperor's order. This type of punishment was known as *fapei* 发配, or exile, in ancient China. In contrast, the rhetoric used to promote the May Seventh experience was couched in terms of "continuing the revolutionary cause" and "taking the necessary steps to prevent bourgeois influence." In his 1999 memoir Feng Zhao (1999) describes how certain well-known dancers, writers, and artists were forced to do all manner of physical labor. In his words, "In the May Seventh Cadre School, physicists raised horses; mathematicians made bricks; engineers dug wells; doctors built houses; writers fed ducks; opera singers worked as cooks. They did not practice their own specialty, and thus wasted their time. Some had to change careers after they left the cadre schools" (85). Indeed, the harsh conditions and intensive labor characteristic of the May Seventh Cadre Schools throughout the country had serious detrimental effects on the bodies and minds of many of China's brightest and most talented people. It was truly a tragic loss of human resources and a desecration of human dignity.[14]

Even though life in the cadre school was harsh and monotonous with tedious, backbreaking work and endless study of Mao's utterances, some people managed to keep their revolutionary zeal. Mother was one of them. She came home about once a month during that time. Each time she would teach us revolutionary songs in an attempt to cheer us up. One of the songs went: "Eat millet and climb mountains; / Fight against revisionists and prevent revisionism; / Protect our rivers and mountains." The song copied the tune of one of Mao's pithy quotations that was familiar to everyone at the time: "Make up your mind. / Do not be afraid of sacrificing your life. / Overcome all difficulties; / And strive for victory." Mother did not have a good singing voice, and the song was not aesthetically appealing; however, its marching quality and connection to Mao's teaching stirred our spirits and drew us closer to Mother. Ironically, this was the only time I can remember Mother spending time with us. She never complained about her hardships but instead was proud of herself and always in good spirits.

The first time Mother left us for the cadre school she did not tell us where she was going. When she returned a month later it was only for two days. At the end of her short visit we begged her not to leave us again. My two younger sisters cried and wrapped themselves around her legs, trying to stop her from going. Mother was determined. She said firmly, "I have to go. I will be back soon. You have to learn to take care of yourselves." She then walked away without even a backward glance. It was not uncommon for many families to be separated in this way as one or both parents would be required to serve in the cadre school. Many children were left home alone or became homeless. Mother worked at the cadre school for a year, during which time her father, my grandfather, passed away. Fearing that she might be accused of having sympathy for the exploitive class, she kept the news to herself and wept secretly for several nights.

In her award-winning memoir, *Wild Swan: Three Daughters of China* (1991), Jung Chang gives a detailed account of her mother's life. Like my mother, Chang's mother broke a wedding engagement to someone she did not like, choosing a "revolutionary marriage" instead. She was inspired and motivated by Mao and the Communist cause and was even imprisoned by the Nationalist Party for underground, pro-Communist activities. However, since the Communist rule in 1949 her loyalty was constantly called into question; at every turn she faced difficulty winning the trust of the Communist Party simply because she had been born into a wealthy family. Moreover, she was targeted during the course of every "political campaign" and forced into endless confessions regarding her "bourgeois thought" and "family problems." As was the case with my mother, Chang's mother was sent to a cadre school and suffered heavily during the Cultural Revolution. Miraculously both women survived the disaster and are still alive to tell the story. My mother now lives in China and struggles on a daily basis over her health problems associated with old age and caused by her experiences during the Cultural Revolution.

Other Memories and Reflections

The Cultural Revolution began when I was in the third grade. Already I was a Young Pioneer with a red scarf tied around my neck. We were told that the red scarf represented a piece of the red flag symbolizing the communist cause. Only good students were given the honor of membership in the Young Pioneers. I was one of the best students in my class, and my parents were proud of me.

Things changed dramatically when the Cultural Revolution began. At school classes suddenly ceased; teachers were targeted. I witnessed the degrading spectacle of the school principal being paraded publicly and denounced by other teachers and sixth graders. Her hair was cut into a *gui tou* 鬼頭 (ghost hair) configuration that featured hair on one side of her head and a clean-shaven scalp on the other. In addition she was made to wear a pair of ragged shoes around her neck while students and some teachers cursed her, spit on her, and threw stones at her. Her alleged "crimes" were "promoting bourgeois curriculum" and "having an extramarital affair."[15]

Students were classified into "five red categories" (revolutionary cadres, revolutionary martyrs, revolutionary soldiers, workers, and poor and lower-middle peasants) and "five black categories" (landlords, rich peasants, counterrevolutionaries, criminals, and rightists), according to their family backgrounds. Children of the five red categories automatically became "Little Red Guards," while children of the five black categories were looked on as potential class enemies and referred to as *gou zaizi* 狗崽子 (sons of bitches).

At school classrooms were often filled with noise and fighting. Students showed no respect for their teachers. In fact, it was not uncommon for teachers to be brutally tortured by their students. This occurred throughout the country. For example, Zi-Ping Luo (1990) gives the following account of the torture of a teacher at her high school: "Xiao-yi Wu (a Red Guard) dragged Teacher Peng into the classroom where a few weeks earlier he had been master. The room was now only a place for students to read posters. Xiao-yi Wu found a broken chair. Discarding the wooden seat, he took the intact iron frame and shoved the makeshift stocks over Teacher Peng's head, arms, and chest. Then he forced Teacher Peng to walk on his knees all around the room. Xiao-yi Wu's peers were fascinated by the invention and proceeded to break the other chairs. . . . [Later], taking off his heavy leather belt, Xiao-yi Wu beat the helpless man about his body and face" (25–26).

Regarding another such incident, Wenjiang An (1998) describes his shock at seeing a formerly gentle female student suddenly begin to shout condemnations at Su Buqing 苏步青, a well-known math professor, and pour a bottle of red ink onto the professor's head. She then pushed him to the stage where the denunciation rally occurred and ordered him to crawl like a dog on the bubbling hot asphalt road (94). Many school principals were severely tortured, and some were even beaten to death. Through her research Youqing Wang (1996) pieced together atrocious acts done to schoolteachers and principals by students in several high schools in Beijing.

In September 1968 classes at my school were resumed. However, while the Cultural Revolution ran its course nothing was taught in a systematic manner. Every morning in class the first order of business was to bow to a portrait of Mao, wish him a long life, and sing "The East Is Red" and "Sailing the Sea Depends on the Helmsman," the two most popular songs at the time. Class periods were filled with reading and reciting the *Quotations from Chairman Mao,* Mao's "Little Red Book." We were required to memorize the following three essays by Mao: "Serve the People"; "In Memory of Norman Bethune"; and, "The Foolish Old Man Who Removed the Mountains." At other times we engaged in military training or dug bomb shelters. My cousin (a carpenter) made a wooden rifle for me for the military training sessions, and I truly believed that we would be going to war with the United States or Russia at any time. In addition to military training we frequently made walking trips to nearby farms and worked in the fields in order to be "re-educated" by the peasants.

The worst experience for me was Father's torture and persecution. Classmates began to call me names and publicly humiliate me. On my way to and from school bullies would shout "Down with Lu Rong," throwing stones and setting dogs to bite me. Some children wrote "Down with Lu Rong" on a piece of paper and threw it at me. They waited for the moment in class when I opened the paper and then taunted and ridiculed me. I always felt ashamed and inferior to the other students and still have nightmares about these horrible experiences. I did not dare to fight back for fear of causing further trouble. My brother got the same treatment at his school. Consequently he became resentful of Father and refused to see him or even talk to him. To this day they are estranged from one another.

When I entered junior high school I was old enough to join the Red Guard and the Communist Youth. I wanted to join because I wanted to be considered "revolutionary" and to fight for Mao's cause. After I applied many times and was rejected I discovered that I had been classified into one of the five black categories and was thus disqualified from membership in revolutionary organizations. I tried to explain to the head of the organization that my father's family background was that of a middle peasant. She responded, "Your file indicates that you come from a landlord family. How can you prove you do not?" I was dumbfounded. I could not understand how false charges against my father had gotten into my file. I ran home crying and feeling that my future was doomed. It was not until 1972 when my father was "liberated" and all the charges were dropped that the "black material," as it was called at the time, was removed from my file and I was accepted into the Communist Youth.

Since there was not much schoolwork to do, I often went to watch neighborhood debates between the Red Guards and the Rebels. Debates usually took place in the streets in the afternoons or evenings. Debates centered around the issues of criteria for revolutionary conduct, the importance in understanding the theory of class struggle, the purpose of the Cultural Revolution, the attributes that distinguished a good person from a bad person, and whether one's family background was relevant in determining a person's moral character. I was fascinated by these topics, though I was too young to understand the deeper meaning of what was said. I remember being impressed by the passion and eloquence with which some of the people expressed themselves. Some debaters were quite articulate and charismatic. They usually started their arguments with a quotation from Mao, Marx, or Lenin and then substantiated their claims with historical and present-day examples. The best speakers typically won applause and followers, emerging as leaders of their factions. The debates usually lasted five to six hours, sometimes until midnight, with members of the audience taking sides and grouping themselves according to shared political views. Oftentimes people left angry, calling each other names and hurling accusations.

When rhetoric fails, violence becomes the order of the day. As the Cultural Revolution unfolded, factions became more and more divided. Violence became the means to resolve ideological conflicts in place of discussion and debate. Though Mao issued a directive (5 September 1966, *People's Daily*) calling for the use of "words, not force" in dealing with opposing groups and class enemies, torture, beatings, and physical assault were prominent features of the Cultural Revolution. The Red Guards and the Rebels even managed to obtain and use weapons as violence intensified. For example, around my neighborhood I witnessed several fights between two factions of workers and students, both armed with guns. They took over buildings and fired at each other. At the same time each side used loudspeakers to demand the surrender of the other side. I saw people get chased down, wounded, and even shot to death. During one incident I watched in horror as several men carried a woman into a building. She was wounded and bleeding heavily. Later I learned that she was the head of one of the factions and had suffered a miscarriage after being shot. A family in our neighborhood lost their seventeen-year-old daughter in one such fight. The family was devastated by the news; the mother became disoriented, and I never saw the father speak again.

In June 1967 we were driven out of our two-bedroom, self-contained apartment and forced to move into a one-bedroom apartment with a kitchen and bathroom that were shared with another family. On moving day no one came to help, not even my father's brothers who lived nearby. Most of our relatives and friends would no longer visit us, let alone show concern or support.

During the first six years of the Cultural Revolution, Father's salary stopped. We lived only on my mother's salary of less than ten dollars a month in U.S. terms. We often went hungry and rarely had money for clothes or other daily necessities. My daily routine included picking up half-burned coals and edible weeds, lining up overnight for ten pounds of potatoes, and doing everything possible to bring home food. When Father was imprisoned and Mother was away at the cadre school, it fell to me to cook for my brother and sisters. My grandma had been forced to leave us and stay with her second son because there was no place for her to sleep in our one-bedroom apartment.

As my family descended into extreme poverty Grandma lost her only source of financial support. Desperate, she asked me to write a letter to her youngest son, who had joined the People's Liberation Army in 1949 and had not been seen or heard from since. In the letter Grandma asked him to send her some money. To our dismay her son, my uncle, wrote back accusing his mother of being a class enemy and refusing to send her any money. In closing he disowned his mother and told her not to contact him again. He wrote in the letter, "You have suppressed and exploited many people in the past. You are the target of our revolution. How can you expect me to send you money? I was not raised by you, but by the Communist Party. I would not admit that I had a mother like you."

My grandmother missed her son very much and was heartbroken by his response. After receiving his letter she never mentioned him again, not even when she was dying. In those days it was not at all uncommon to hear stories of children and parents becoming estranged from one another, wives and husbands divorcing each other, or employees betraying their bosses in order to demonstrate their revolutionary zeal. There were even extreme cases of children forced to torture their own parents. Luowen Yu (2000) shares his recollection of one such brutal torture: "Red Guards beat an elderly couple who were labeled 'capitalists' half to death and then forced their son to hit his father with weights. The son did it and became insane afterward" (62).

I considered myself one of the "children of Mao's era." My formative years coincided with his reign of influence. I was indoctrinated into his system of morality and attracted to the communist cause. From kindergarten on we were taught that we were the inheritors of the communist legacy, which promised an egalitarian society and the best possible life. Through songs, textbooks, and school rituals we learned how Mao and the Communist Party saved China and that many people sacrificed their lives to bring us the new China. At home I never heard my parents criticize Mao or the party; I heard only expressions of praise, gratitude, and loyalty. Therefore, I believed in Mao completely. I remember being devastated by his death for I feared that China would have no future without him.

Because of my blind faith in Mao, I regarded his revolutionary theories as absolute truth even though I did not understand them completely. I saw reality in black and white terms. People were either class enemies or revolutionary comrades. Things were either right or wrong. The indoctrination was so complete that I applied these categories to others even though I knew firsthand what it felt like to be on the receiving end of such extremism and had witnessed my parents being victimized in the same way. Luckily, I was too young in the first three years of the Cultural Revolution to join the Red Guards in denouncing party officials and intellectuals, searching their homes, and taking part in acts of violence against them. These activities were justified and rationalized in the interest of protecting Chairman Mao, preventing the spread of capitalism in China, and furthering the revolutionary cause. My preteen years were spent reciting Mao's Little Red Book instead of informing myself on a wide range of subjects and perspectives. Much of my adolescent and young adult period was occupied with the writing of *pipan gao* 批判稿 (denunciation papers) that conformed to the political discourse of the time, instead of engaging in critical thinking and questioning authority. As I reflected on the symbolic experiences I had at that time, the words and expressions were quite banal and clichéd. I had virtually no private thoughts and no individual expressions during those years. Even my diaries were filled with communist dogma and slogans.

Exposing my family's private suffering to public view has not been an end in itself but rather a means for reflecting on what caused such suffering, especially with regard to the use of symbols and patterns of thought. Since the end of the Cultural Revolution, I have desperately sought the answers to many disturbing questions: What made people think and act in such an inhumane manner? Why was Mao's theory of class struggle so powerful? Why was the practice of judging people by their family backgrounds so destructive? How did thinking in polarized terms affect people's attitudes toward other people and their actions? What made friends betray one another, husbands and wives turn against each other, and students become violent toward their teachers? How could such pandemonium have taken place in China when traditional Chinese culture was known for its emphasis on harmony, balance, and order? How did the rhetoric of the Cultural Revolution work to change some people virtually overnight from human beings to barbarians, from idealists to fanatics willing to commit monstrous acts? How did/does China as a nation cope with this collective trauma and the aftermath of the Cultural Revolution? How do those of us who survived the Cultural Revolution reflect on our experiences of that time? Are there still lingering influences of the Cultural Revolution on Chinese thought, culture, and communication?

My book aims to explore these questions through rhetorical analyses of the use of language, symbols, and ritualistic practices during the Cultural Revolution. To provide the reader with a sense of history as well as theoretical frameworks for adequately addressing the issues under consideration, relevant literature on the relationship between language, thought, perceptions of reality, and culture will be reviewed. An account of Chinese communist propaganda prior to the Cultural Revolution, emphasizing its rhetorical strategies for ideological transformation and thought reform, is included in the next chapter.

Language, Thought, and Culture in the Chinese Political Context

Language is a guide to "social reality." . . . It powerfully conditions all our thinking about social problems and processes. Human beings do not live in the objective world alone, nor alone in the world of social activity as ordinarily understood, but are very much at the mercy of the particular language which has become the medium of expression for their society.

Edward Sapir, "The Status of Linguistics as a Science,"
in *The Selected Writings of Edward Sapir in Language, Culture, and Personality*

Motivated by the general goals of Chinese Communism and guided by a new communication elite, this revolution has resulted in new images, new symbols, a new language, a new audience, new communication channels, new communication methods and behavior of the masses.

Frederick T. C. Yu, "Communication and Politics,"
in *Communist China: A System-Functional Reader*

Language, a symbolic system, profoundly influences who we are as human beings and how we experience reality. Through speaking, as Arendt (1958) asserts, humans "show who they are, reveal actively their unique personal identities and thus make their appearance in the human world" (179). Inquiries into language functions and their effects on thought and sense perceptions have been undertaken by scholars in various fields from ancient times to the present. On the basis of this research theories have been proposed by anthropologists, philosophers, sociolinguists, and rhetoricians regarding the impact of language in various communicative settings. As was previously discussed, certain symbol-using activities occurring during the Cultural Revolution had tragic effects on individuals and families. These symbol-using activities included the use of slogans, the spread of wall posters, denunciation rallies, the writing of confessions, ritualistic practices, and public debates. In this chapter theories on the interplay between language, thought, perceptions of reality, action, and culture will be reviewed from anthropological, philosophical, critical, and rhetorical perspectives. These perspectives provide analytic frameworks for a better understanding of the rhetoric of the Cultural Revolution to be discussed in subsequent chapters. I will then review what I consider to be the major characteristics of political persuasion and ideological transformation in Communist China since 1949. This review will provide the necessary background information regarding symbol-using activities and rhetorical practices in effect during the Chinese Cultural Revolution.

Theories on Language, Thought, and Reality

An Anthropological Perspective

According to Harry Hoijer (1965), "language as a guide to social reality" was first postulated by American anthropologist Franz Boas. An immigrant to the United States from Germany, Boas received his education in Germany but established himself in his new home country. In fact, he is recognized as one of the founding fathers of U.S. anthropology and highly regarded for his innovative practices of studying cultures on their own terms rather than through the lens of racial and cultural stereotyping. More important, Boas (1942) posits that language classifies experience and that different languages classify experience differently. Accordingly, by studying the language of a culture different from one's own, one can gain insights into the people and culture in question. In Boas's view (1974), "Language seems to be one of the most instructive fields of inquiry in an investigation of the formulation of the fundamental ethnic ideas" (28). Moreover, Boas believes that "we think, on the whole, in words" (29). Thus, certain elements of language both reflect and affect the thinking patterns of any given speech community. For example, the use of a particular abstract term would reflect the abstract thinking style of the speaker, while clear use of the term would result in clear thinking. Boas's postulates were thought-provoking advances for his time; unfortunately he did not develop a systematic theory on the relationship between language and thought.

For Edward Sapir (1974), a student of Franz Boas, "Language is primarily a vocal actualization of the tendency to see realities symbolically" (53). Further, language guides and controls human action in an unconscious and intuitive way. In Sapir's opinion, language is closely related to thought and communication in that thought "is hardly possible in any sustained sense without the symbolic organization brought by language" (52–53). In other words, only through language can a thought pattern be revealed and delineated. Further, Sapir notes that language has a socialization function capable of unifying members of the same group and altering the individual's views to conform to those of the group. In general, Sapir perceives the functions of language as providing the basis for thought, shaping societal views, and transforming social reality.

In comparing the difference between Boas and Sapir, John Lucy (1992) delineates, "whereas Boas saw language as primarily reflecting thought and culture, and only on occasion having a direct influence back on them, Sapir began to see in language a powerful shaping factor because of the impact of using this creative symbolic tool in the interpretation of experience" (23). This latter perspective on language is particularly relevant to an understanding of the rhetoric of the Cultural Revolution in that the use of slogans, songs, and rituals profoundly shaped the unconscious thought patterns and worldviews of the Chinese people.

Sapir's line of thinking on the causal relationship between language and thought was further developed by his student Benjamin Whorf. Through his study of certain linguistic features in the Hopi language Whorf (1974) observed that the Hopi language is drastically different from standard American English in lexicon and structure and, more important, that such differences result in significant variations in habit and thought between the two cultures. Whorf's observation and study suggest that language not only prescribes a sense of reality but also directs a certain way of thinking and acting. Thus, for Whorf, linguistic behaviors, such as the use of catchwords, slogans, and rallying cries, shape and determine the way people think. Even ordinary use of language can influence the formation of culture, the individual, and action. It is Whorf's (1952) position that "Each language is not merely a reproducing instrument for voicing ideas but rather is itself the shaper of ideas, the program and guide for the individual's mental activity" (5). As further explained by Hoijer (1974), " Language [for Whorf] plays a large and significant role in the totality of culture. Far from being simply a technique of communication, it is a way of directing the perceptions of its speakers and it provides for them habitual modes of analyzing experience into significant categories" (122). This view of the impact of language on thought and cultural behavior is known among rhetorical scholars as the "Sapir-Whorf Hypothesis" or "linguistic relativity."

The Sapir-Whorf Hypothesis has sparked lively discussion and debates on the subjects of language, thought, and culture, receiving endorsement as well as criticism and, perhaps most important, provoking further theoretical speculation and empirical testing. While some studies, such as Hoijer's (1965) on color and Henle's (1958) concerning the Wintu language, provided evidence to support the hypothesis, other studies (on bilingualism, cross-cultural comparison, and deaf children) seemed to invalidate the theory by indicating that language is not the sole factor determining thought patterns (Bloom 1981; Heider and Oliver 1972; Rodda and Grove 1987).[1] The debate concluded with Slobin's (1979) distinction between a "weak form" and a "strong form" of the hypothesis. In his view, a "weak form" accepts the notion that language *influences* thought, while a "strong form" holds the view that language *determines* thought. In this book I take both the "weak form" and the "strong form" positions, arguing that the rhetoric of the Cultural Revolution has influenced and to a great degree determined the way Chinese people thought and acted. Moreover, I believe that the language and thought of the Cultural Revolution mutually influenced one another, creating a cycle of rhetorical behavior that was hard to break.

The limitations of the Sapir-Whorf Hypothesis are also revealed in the research orientation demonstrated by Boas, Sapir, and Whorf. Their comparisons of European language and tribal language (Boas and Sapir call it "primitive language") may suggest an ethnocentric bias and a sense of superiority of Western languages. Further, the scholars' discussions are largely centered around the formal (structural and grammatical) aspects of language, and they do not systematically develop a theory with regard to language and thought, nor do they provide sufficient evidence to support their hypothesis.

Despite the limitations of the hypothesis and the controversy surrounding it, Boas, Sapir, and Whorf have offered valuable insights and provided a focus for studies on the power of language in society and in particular on individual perceptions and actions. Their postulates on the relationship between language, thought, and perception are relevant to an understanding of the thought patterns and linguistic behaviors of both the perpetrators and the victims of the Chinese Cultural Revolution. In particular, the framework developed by these scholars sheds light on the discussion of the linguistic structure and word choices used to create polarized thinking as well as to prescribe a version of political/social reality stressing class and class struggle.

A Philosophical Perspective

Philosophers and thinkers of ancient Greece and China were fully aware of the impact of language on human thought and behavior. The Greek philosopher Parmenides believed that truth and being were ultimate and permanent but that a sense of these eternal realities was shaped through words. In his view, "All things that morals have established, believing in their truth, are just a name" (Hyland 1973, 193). For Heraclitus, on the other hand, reality was in flux and words were the force of existence and coherence. It was his position that "Men [*sic*] should try to comprehend the underlying coherence of things: it is expressed in the Logos, the formula or element of arrangement common to all things" (Kirk and Raven 1957, 187). Inspired by Parmenides, Plato was adamant in his pursuit of absolute truth through a discursive path. In his *Cratylus,* Plato was keenly aware that logos signified things but that a thing could not be signified by one word alone, suggesting the inadequacy of language to capture reality. In his early years Plato was dismayed by the Sophists' rhetorical preaching as well as by their public presentations. He condemned the Sophists for their manipulation of language and distortion of reality through words (the *Gorgias*). An older Plato reconceptualized rhetoric, elevating it from a persuasive art form aiming for pleasure and conviction to a philosophical inquiry striving to uplift the soul (the *Phaedrus*).

During a similar time period in ancient China, Chinese thinkers and philosophers too were seeking to understand the role of language in shaping reality and perception. Gong-Sun Long (328–295 B.C.E.), a scholar from the school of Mingjia, held that the world was made known only through language, asserting that perceptions were shaped through names and concepts. Like Plato, he warned that one could easily form a mistaken perception of reality if one were to equate the conceptual world with the real world (Gong-Sun, *zhiwu lun,* 1986, 54). Confucius, a moral philosopher, recognized the power of language in maintaining social order and political control. His well-known concept of *zheng ming* 正名 (the rectification of names) was coined for the purpose of enforcing social values and prescribing proper modes of conduct through the "correct" designation and use of terms and concepts. In his words, "When names are not correct, speech will not be appropriate; when speech is not appropriate, tasks will not be accomplished; when tasks cannot be accomplished, rites and music will not flourish; when rites and music do not flourish, punishment will not fit the crimes; when punishment does not fit the crimes, the common people will not know where to put their hands and feet" (Confucius, Lun

Yu, *The Analects,* 13.3.132). For Confucius, words served as an impetus and catalyst for social transformation and behavior change; new words and concepts called for new ways of acting and perceiving reality as well as for organizational strategies regarding cultural and political meanings. In sum, in the ancient philosophical scheme of things language was both creative and destructive; its use and misuse could affect the moral state of the individual for better or for worse, maintain social order or create anarchy, and direct positive change or bring about disaster. As we shall see, this paradoxical function of language is exemplified in the ideological transformation of the Chinese people under the Chinese Communist Party prior to and during the Cultural Revolution.

In the West the philosophical tradition of epistemology continued on a discursive path. The epistemologists of England in the late sixteenth to eighteenth centuries undertook this task. In his *Novum Organum,* Francis Bacon (1561–1626) identified four "idols" that played a significant role in shaping and distorting perceptions of reality (Bacon 1952). These four idols help identify and explain types of political language and their rhetorical function in the Chinese political context. The first idol is that of the tribe. Loosely defined, it refers to the prejudice and pride held by "members of a tribe" that cloud perceptions of reality. For instance, during Mao's years those who came from the five red categories of families held prejudices against those who came from the five black categories of families. They were also prideful in that they considered themselves the only true revolutionaries carrying on the communist cause. Their habit of classifying people into fixed categories of good and evil hindered understanding of a complicated political reality. The second idol, that of the cave, refers to misconceptions derived from limited experience of the world. For example, Mao never traveled outside of China except to Russia, and although he believed that theory, truth, and knowledge came from the experiential world and material conditions, his lack of experience in the West almost certainly prevented him from considering alternative models for social change and economic development. On the other hand, Deng Xiaoping, who had experience in France as a foreign student and had traveled extensively, tended to be more liberal and more open-minded.[2] Third is the idol of the marketplace, which relates to confusion caused by the use of imprecise popular language. For example, in the Chinese context abstract and ambiguous terms such as "the proletarian dictatorship," "class struggle," and "Mao Zedong's Thought" were popular during the Cultural Revolution. Because they were widespread, politically correct slogans many Chinese people used them without giving much thought to their contextual meaning and rhetorical implications. In this way the Chinese masses were subdued into a skewed version of reality. The final idol, that of the theater, pertains to the formation of concepts through indoctrination into religious and secular dogma. For example, during Mao's years the Chinese people were taught that Marxist-Maoist ideology was the absolute truth and that it was the only doctrine that could revive and, ultimately, save China. Any alternative views were considered heresy and dismissed as counterrevolutionary. Ritualistic practices involving the worship of Mao Zedong reinforced such belief.

John Locke (1632–1704), hailed as the brightest thinker of his time in Europe, was interested in the relationship between language and mind/thought. Locke believed that words, especially moral words, held different meanings for different users. Like Plato, he recognized the power of words, when misused, to insinuate wrong ideas, lamenting that "the arts of fallacy are endowed and preferred" and that "men [*sic*] love to deceive and be deceived" (Locke [1894] 1959, 146). In his *Essay Concerning Human Understanding,* Locke contended that the fountains of knowledge sprang from both sensible experiences and reflections, including "perception, thinking, doubting, believing, reasoning, knowing, willing" (123). In sensing the world, Locke argued, the mind is passive in the reception of simple ideas such as rhetoric of myth, illusion, and falsehood. It is only through reflecting these sensations in one's own mind that a comparison of agreement and disagreement with societal norms can be made (145–46). Further, humans negotiate meanings between what Locke called "intuitive knowledge" or "our own way of thinking" and "demonstrative knowledge" gained through "reasoning" or accepted truth of authority (88–89). For Locke, demonstrative knowledge can be misleading and dangerous if the major premise is predicated on falsehood. Craig Smith (1998) suggests that Locke's theory on knowledge has implications on two types of discourse: internal and external. The internal discourse is more authentic as it tends to be based on direct understanding of ideas, while the external discourse can be distorted as it is the discourse of society, the state, and culture. Locke argued for a healthy skepticism with regard to received knowledge and called for an engagement of communicating with others in order to avoid the tyranny of the language of the marketplace. It is easy to see the relevance of Locke's views to the Cultural Revolution, given that many Chinese felt strongly that they had been deceived and enslaved by the language of authority prevailing during that time. Due to a fear of persecution and/or lack of critical thinking ability, many Chinese neither engaged in internal discourse nor challenged the legitimacy of external discourse.

Skepticism regarding the use of language and construction of belief systems was later popularized by David Hume (1711–76), who challenged the dominance of Christianity and undermined the power of theology with his approach. Hume argued that belief was not necessarily knowledge and, further, that belief was associated with feelings and impressions created by language. For this reason rhetoric was capable of creating a false sense of reality, possibly even a false system of belief (Berlin 1956, 208). Friedrich Nietzsche went further in claiming that language was merely a set of arbitrary designations that would never adequately express reality. For Nietzsche (1979), concepts and metaphors add to "the creation of a new world of laws, privileges, subordinations, and clearly marked boundaries" (84). Moreover, when concepts become edified, they display the characteristics of rigidity and dogma. In what Nietzsche referred to as a "crap game," people are divided into various groups, each holding its own conceptual worldview and version of truth. In this sense, according to Nietzsche, the "correct conception" is impossible and skepticism of all forms of idealism is warranted. Applying Hume and Nietzsche's frameworks to the Chinese Cultural Revolution makes it clear that a skewed political reality was created through slogans, songs, quotations, confessions, and rituals. Edified language was pervasive prior to and during the Cultural Revolution. "Correct conceptions" were inculcated and strictly enforced. The Red Guards and the Rebels were divided into different factions, all claiming themselves as true defenders of Mao's cause. Anyone expressing skepticism of any sort ran the risk of being ostracized, punished, tortured, or even put to death.

Philosophers such as Bacon, Locke, Hume, and Nietzsche formulated their theories in response to a thousand years of Judeo-Christian domination during which time the European masses were bombarded with Christian dogma and taught that the only legitimate source of truth was the Christian Church. Critical thinking was stifled, and acts of extreme cruelty were perpetrated against those identified as non-Christian "pagans." This situation is strikingly similar to the situation in Communist-dominated China after 1949, when Marxist-Leninist and Maoist dogma was considered the only legitimate truth and when anyone who refused to be converted to a Maoist would encounter persecution of some sort. However, while Western scholars have reflected on the rhetorical phenomena of the medieval period and Western culture has undergone the Renaissance and the Enlightenment in the aftermath of Christian domination, the same reflection and enlightenment have not taken place in China. In the Chinese context many important questions are in need of answers. For example, how do Chinese people come to terms with what they experienced during the Cultural Revolution? What explanations do they offer to the world? What strategies, if any, might they employ in order to prevent the same mass hysteria and blind faith from occurring again?

To return to the issue of skepticism in the use of language, it is interesting to note that a similar intellectual discussion can be found in the works of Zhuangzi 庄子, a Chinese philosopher of the fourth–third centuries B.C.E. For Zhuangzi, language was inadequate to the task of representing ideas and reality. Therefore, in his view, it was dangerous to take the meanings of words as truth. At best a word's meaning was always conditioned by one's illusions of the world. Thus, it was unnecessary to argue for a position of right or wrong. In Zhuangzi's words: "Suppose you and I have had an argument. If you have beaten me instead of me beating you, then are you necessarily right and am I necessarily wrong? If I have beaten you instead of you beating me, then am I necessarily right and are you necessarily wrong?" (Watson 1968, 48). Like Nietzsche, Zhuangzi did not believe in any correct, right/wrong judgments about reality. For Nietzsche, the way to avoid moral absolutism was to constantly work at reconstructing concepts and finding freedom from the prison of language. For Zhuangzi, the antidote to dualistic thinking was the attainment of the Dao: a mind-set that synthesizes diverse views and attends to the total situation; a state of freedom from illusions and deception; and an ability to integrate opposite visions into one while harmonizing right and wrong. This holistic and cautious view of language got lost under the Communist regime, which emphasized uniformity of thought and encouraged dualistic thinking. During the Cultural Revolution in particular the worldview of the Chinese people was locked into a language system that indoctrinated their minds and allowed only one version of the truth to filter through.

A Critical Perspective

The critical perspective on language can be traced to Karl Marx (1818–83), whose theory of political economy and social change had a major influence in the twentieth century and dramatically altered the lives of half the world's people. A major portion of Marx's social theory was comprised of the assertion of a "class struggle" between the bourgeoisie (the oppressors) and the proletariat (the oppressed). The clash between these two classes was regarded as the driving force behind historical progression (Marx and Engels [1848] 1965). According to Marx ([1859] 1972), the specific economic structures under which people create goods and services determine the types of political, religious, philosophical, and ideological systems. In other words, the material conditions that people live under decide their levels of political consciousness. This Marxist model of social change was appropriated by Mao and the Chinese Communist Party in the interest of overthrowing the oppressive bourgeois class and enforcing proletariat dictatorship. Surprisingly, even though Marxist theory was written in response to the social condition of Europe in the nineteenth century, it was actualized in twentieth-century China, in the sense that previously existing material conditions and economic relations were virtually turned upside down through revolution: economy came under state control, and the oppressed became the ruling class. At the same time, however, Mao extended Marx's theory on the causal relationship between material conditions and political consciousness. Instead of waiting for the desired political consciousness to emerge of its own accord as a result of change to the material condition or economic structure, Mao directed efforts to raise political consciousness and eliminate any residue of the old society.

The Marxist critique has been a major source of critical theory and inspiration for rhetorical studies. According to Marx, a "false consciousness" is created by the ruling class through mystification of the prevailing ideology in the form of political language (Aune 1994). In the West, as David Green (1987) points out, "words such as 'individualist,' 'paternalist,' 'conservative,' 'radical,' and so on serve as organizing concepts and provide people with their basic categories of thought" (2). These words also represent different ideology and a certain level of political consciousness, be it true or false. In the Chinese context, the communist ideology is communicated through a myriad of political language and ritualized slogans. Key phrases such as "class struggle," "destroying the old," "continued revolution," and "preventing capitalism" reveal political motives and serve political ends of the Communist Party. In fact Communist, Maoist ideology was successfully disseminated and inculcated through party-controlled communication channels and mass mobilization, completely transforming the way Chinese people thought and acted. By manipulating the language, Mao and his followers created a skewed version of political reality characterized by class consciousness and ideological thinking. As Bakhtin (1973) explains, "Every sign is subject to the criteria of ideological evaluation (i.e.[,] whether it is true, false, correct, fair, good, etc.)

(10). That is, "Each and every word is ideological and each and every application of language involves ideological change" (94). For Bakhtin, language use is inherently ideological and ideological signs construct the political reality. Moreover, a sense of political consciousness cannot be achieved by individuals alone; it is created by social organizations and molded through the process of social intercourse. In the case of China, ideological signs in the form of political slogans and jargons are communicated through mass participation and various levels of social interactions. In this process ideological signs exercise their force in shaping a consensus perception, one that is collectively shared and blindly endorsed.

Michel Foucault's (1926–84) approach to the relationship between power and language differed from that of Marx. Through his examination of language in medical practice and the structure of institutional domination, Foucault (1972) concluded that power and knowledge are established and maintained through institutional discourse and disciplinary claims. In Foucault's (1980) words, political power "traverses and produces things, it induces pleasure, forms knowledge, produces discourse" (119). For Foucault, discourse was not simply a tool used to gain power and dominance but was itself an expression of power in that it was "supported by a whole system of institutions which impose them [discourses] and renew them [discourses], and which act in a constraining and sometimes violent way" (Foucault 1981, 54). Moreover, such discourses, typically in the forms of narratives, religious texts, and literary works, were often repeated, recounted, and ritualized. In this sense, "Any system of education is a political way of maintaining or modifying the appropriation of discourse, along with the knowledge and powers which they carry" (1981, 64). Here, Foucault put forth a rather pessimistic outlook regarding the human ability to overcome institutional power and influence the formation of discourse. At the same time he offered important insights and critical tools for examining the process by which language is subjugated to social forces, as well as how individuals invent and reinvent themselves through exposure to culturally appropriate and politically indoctrinated discourse. The proletarian class in Communist China, once the oppressed, has become the oppressor. The political discourse was formulated and enforced by the Communist Party mouthpieces. It was taught at schools and disseminated among the masses. Such discourse was blindly accepted as the ultimate truth by the vast majority of Chinese people, effectively functioning as social and ideological control. If we are to learn from China's tragic history, we must understand how this process took place—namely, how political discourse was created and disseminated, how slogans and dogmatic thinking came to be accepted by millions of Chinese, and whether individuals were capable of resisting the social/political indoctrination imparted through language.

While both Marx and Foucault attempted to develop a theory that would accurately describe how individuals are summoned into collective thought and behavior through power structure and discursive practices, Hannah Arendt redefined the concept of evil for an analysis of speech, thought, and action. In her book *Eichmann in Jerusalem* (1963), Arendt examines the speech patterns of Nazi official Eichmann, arguing that certain rules of language usage dictated by the Nazis led to Eichmann's inhumane, amoral stance in relation to his Jewish victims. An observer at Eichmann's trial, Arendt asserts, "The longer one listens to him, the more obvious it became that his inability to speak was closely connected with an inability to think, namely, to think from the standpoint of somebody else" (49). From this, Arendt extrapolates that thought-deprivation, or the inability to think clearly, can result from an impoverishment of language. For Arendt, thoughtlessness is an aspect of human evil that she refers to as the "banality of evil." This is because the ability to commit evil does not require deliberate or conscious intent. Indeed, according to Arendt (1951), the purpose of totalitarian indoctrination is to ensure the absolute mind control of authoritarian leaders. Toward this end political discourse, often in the form of slogans and catchwords, helps establish ideological frameworks that allow such leaders to stifle freedom of thought, creating a climate in which evil will flourish. This book will address the issues raised by Arendt, in particular her notion of the "banality of evil" in the context of the remolding of thought in Communist China during the Cultural Revolution through politicized and ritualized language and symbolic practices.

A Rhetorical Perspective

The rhetorical perspective on language, thought, and action sheds light on how the use of symbols affects and changes human behavior. Kenneth Burke (1897–1993), the leading theorist on the art of persuasion and literary criticism in the twentieth century, defined rhetoric as "the use of words by human agents to form attitudes or to induce actions in other human agents" (1969b, 41). Burke developed a framework for interpreting and understanding human action centered around the notion of "dramatism," which argued that behind every human act is conscious intent and motive similar to how drama is played out. For Burke, humans are symbol-using animals and rhetoric is "symbolic inducement," that is, the use of symbols to move others in desired directions.

Burke asserted that reality was created and shaped through the use of language, in particular, specific terminology, or "terministic screens." In his words, "though man [*sic*] is typically the symbol-using animal, he clings to a kind of naïve verbal realism that refuses to let him realize the full extent of the role played by symbolicity in his notions of reality" (1966, 5). In other words, humans fail to achieve a complete view of reality because they cannot see through the artificiality and limitation of language. Further, human action is guided by words, and the choice of words directs our attention to one way or the other. Burke elaborates: "[T]he nature of our terms affects the nature of our observations. . . . much that we take as observations about 'reality' may be but the spinning out of possibilities implicit in our particular choice of terms" (1966, 46). Borrowing from Burke, it can be argued that the discourse of the Cultural Revolution created particular "terministic screens" for the Chinese, screens of black versus white, good versus evil, and friends versus enemies, for example.

In Burke's (1969b) view, persuasion took place through the means of identification. Identification referred to the process by which individuals found common ground in like-minded individuals and at the same time were alienated from those who were different. In this sense the act of identification created unity as well as division. According to Burke, this "ironic mixture of identification and disassociation" caused group conflict as well as scapegoating—for example, in Nazi Germany, where anti-Semitic discourse was characterized by the use of "impersonal terminology" and "devil-function" technique, which reduced Jews to "things" and "harmful organisms" being ostracized by society. Further, the Nazis used such techniques to promote German national identity and to justify acts of terrible cruelty against the Jews. A similar climate prevailed during the Cultural Revolution when people were classified and divided along class lines as either revolutionaries or counterrevolutionaries and forced to take sides.

An important means of achieving identification, according to Burke (1968), is through "form," defined as "the creation of an appetite in the mind of the auditor, and the adequate satisfying of that appetite" (31). Form invites the reader to surrender to the version of reality constructed by the rhetor. It works unconsciously in the minds of the audience, shaping its desire and appealing to familiar symbolic experiences such as poetry, narrative, and the progression and development of plots and characters in a drama. In other words, form "leads a reader to anticipate another part, to be gratified by the sequence" (1968, 124). For example, the form of syllogistic progression precedes the development of events from an agreed-on or shared universal principle and draws conclusions based on the principle. Further, the persuasive power of forms can, in Burke's view, be enhanced through repetition, that is, the restatement of an idea or sentiment in different ways and by adding new details. Finally, Burke treats form as a powerful means of self-persuasion in that it leads the audience to certain expectations and induces the audience's cooperation. Analysis of political language employed during the Cultural Revolution will exemplify these rhetorical features and their persuasive effects. In particular, we will look at how millions of Chinese engaged in self-persuasion and self-subjugation through the use of political rhetoric into which they had been indoctrinated. Rhetorical forms used during the Cultural Revolution, such as confession and self-criticism, are culturally rooted and were therefore already familiar to many Chinese. Such familiarity enhanced their potency in changing attitudes and inducing desired behavior.

Burke's rhetorical perspective has been applied to political/ideological context and critiqued in the works of other rhetoricians. In his article "The Ideograph" (1980), Michael McGee identifies limitations in the arguments put forth by materialists and symbolists. In his view materialists, who assert that material conditions determine political consciousness (a Marxist view), overlook the role of language in the construction of reality and overestimate power as a variable in describing political consciousness. Conversely, symbolists tend to neglect nonsymbolic elements and fail to explain the impact of material phenomena on the construction of social reality.

McGee (1980) maintains that what is needed is an analytical model that takes into account both material conditions and the manipulation of symbols in shaping ideology and maintaining political power, arguing that an ideology is produced and reinforced by the dynamic interplay of both cultural forces and political language. Terence Ball (1988) shared a similar view, asserting that ideological change is demonstrated through the use of newly coined terms or the assigning of new meaning to the old term. Ball contends that political discourse and its connection with ideological transformation are only properly understood in the context of historical specificity, which gives careful consideration to the intention and motive of the political agent, and any circumstances that may have given rise to the need for conceptual and ideological change. In examining the rhetoric of the Cultural Revolution, both symbolic practices and political/historical contexts will be considered. Regarding the former, Chinese political symbols and discourse were invented by Mao's followers as well as by the Chinese masses; regarding the latter, their meanings were deeply rooted in Chinese history and political culture.

McGee (1980) proposes two possible approaches to an ideographic analysis of political language: the diachronic approach, which examines how usage changes and expands throughout its history; and the synchronic approach, which examines how the meaning of political language is accommodated to specific situations. Building on McGee's work, Condit and Lucaites (1993) emphasize, in their analysis of the concept of equality in American culture, the significance of such approaches. In their words, "By charting the diachronic and synchronic structures of an ideograph [political language] as it is employed in the public discourse of a particular rhetorical culture, we can begin to gain insight into how social and political problems are constituted and negotiated through public discourse" (xiv).

Although ideology and culture are not synonymous terms, one cannot fully understand a nation's prevailing ideology without understanding its culture, and vice versa. Philip Wander (1984) argues that the two are inextricably intertwined, defining ideological criticism as dependent on "a historical perspective in relation to cultural artifacts and political issues" (199). Conversely, he sees cultural criticism as the practice of interpreting cultural products in the context of ideological struggles (1983, 1984). Furthermore, cultural criticism must examine the worldview conveyed by such products in order to identify "facts they do or do not acknowledge, and consequences and alternatives they do or do not ignore in light of moral, social, economic, and political issues" (1984, 497). Language, a major component of culture, both conveys and constructs a worldview, as well as formulating ideologies and belief systems for the people of any given culture. Ideological/cultural criticism allows the critic to investigate the manner in which cultural products function rhetorically within certain historical contexts and social structures, language is used to construct social and ideological reality, and certain ideological orientations affect the thought and culture of a particular group or nation. Rhetorical practices and the use of symbols prior to and during the Cultural Revolution were rooted in Chinese historical and political contexts; in addition they were reinvented and renewed in response to the new political agenda.

Chinese Communist Rhetoric Prior to the Cultural Revolution

Since 1949, with the establishment of the People's Republic of China under the leadership of Mao Zedong and the Communist Party, China has undergone a transformation in economic structure and value orientation. The goals of communication have been to mold a "new Communist person" and eradicate all capitalistic impulses from China. The rhetorical style employed to achieve these goals has been similar to that of the Soviets. At the same time this approach has found resonance with the rhetorical tradition of ancient China. In other words, it has not arisen in a cultural vacuum. In addition, the launch and participation of the Cultural Revolution are not isolated cases. The Chinese mind-set during the Cultural Revolution had been shaped by communist propaganda and various political campaigns dating back to the 1940s.[3] The purposes of the following section are to give the reader a sense of how the relationships among language, thought, and culture have played themselves out in the Chinese political context and to provide the reader with an understanding of the reasons for the ten-year Chinese Cultural Revolution.

The Transformation of Ideology

The Chinese imperial system ended with the 1911 revolution (known by the Chinese as the Xinghai Revolution) that deposed the last emperor and established the Republic of China, with its emphasis on democracy and nation building. Unfortunately, the Nationalists' efforts to build a modern China were thwarted by the infighting among warlords, civil war with the Communists, and the Japanese invasion. Though the Nationalists still managed to bring social change to China, they never attempted at the state level to abandon Confucianism, the archetypal ideology of Chinese society for over two thousand years. However, by 1949 when the Communists defeated the Nationalists and took over China, Confucianism was dismissed as a feudal ideology representing the interests of the exploitive classes and oppressing the proletarian class. The ideology that replaced Confucianism was Marxism-Leninism, which was successfully modified by Mao Zedong in the interest of achieving a communist revolution.[4]

After the Russian Revolution in 1917 Lenin elevated Marx's notion of class consciousness to the status of cardinal communist ideology. While Marx regarded class consciousness as the basis for political consciousness, generated by the transformation of economic relations, Lenin believed that class consciousness must be awakened and brought to the forefront of the revolution through ideological indoctrination (Yu 1972). Accordingly, a massive campaign of political propaganda was orchestrated by the Soviet Communists in order to raise the level of class consciousness in the struggle against the bourgeois class. This Leninist strategy regarding class consciousness was adopted by the Chinese Communist Party. A few years after the founding of the People's Republic of China in 1949, a state-owned economy had replaced the privately owned economy and the government had taken control of the means and distribution of production. However, Mao and his comrades did not believe that a new proletarian consciousness, characterized by a collective mind and hatred for the bourgeois class, would inevitably emerge as a result of the change in economic ownership.

For Mao, a transformation of the economic system (the base) was only a first step to a socialist revolution. Independent efforts must be made to transform the ideology, culture, customs, and habits of the people (the superstructure). As Mao ([1957a] 1977) reminded the party: "While we have won basic victory in transforming the ownership of the means of production, we are far away from complete victory on the political and ideological fronts. In the ideological field, the question of who will win out, the proletariat or the bourgeoisie, has not yet been really settled" (434). Mao considered traditional customs as oppressive and the bourgeois ideology as regressive, both posing threats to socialist revolution. He was acutely aware that traditional ideas and habits were deeply rooted in the minds of the people disregard the change in social/economic structure. They were the breeding grounds for feudalism and capitalism. To maintain the power of the new regime these old ways of thinking and behaving must be eradicated and replaced by proletarian values and beliefs. For Mao, eradicating the old and establishing the new was a life-and-death struggle between good and evil, between the advancement of history and history's retreat. Mao's radical view on Chinese culture and his fear of losing the proletarian control were the driving forces for his launch of a series of political campaigns.

While Mao borrowed ideas from Lenin on the transformation of ideology, he differed from Lenin both in his approach and in his attitude toward intellectuals. As Meisner (1999) observed, Lenin's version in the ideal outcome of revolution was to bring the fruits of the bourgeois culture to the masses. A new socialist culture therefore depended on the building of a modern economy. Consequently, Lenin assigned the task of consciousness raising to politicized and educated intellectuals and considered them the vanguard of the proletariat. For Lenin, then, socialism was not aimed at annihilating traditional, cultural legacies; instead, socialism must be built on those legacies (296–97). In contrast, Mao believed that the bourgeois culture was harmful to socialist revolution. A political culture could be built without economic prerequisites. Intellectuals could not be trusted as they always carried the trace of their bourgeois past. Therefore a new culture could not be built without the elimination of the old culture. In this sense Mao was far more radical than Lenin in his rationale and blueprint for social change and social control.

For Mao and his comrades, the bases for new ideas were Marxist-Leninist-Maoist doctrines centered around the notion of class struggle and the goal of revolution was to achieve a communist society. Engaging in a class struggle meant that the proletarian class had to constantly fight against bourgeois ideas and traditional behaviors in order to maintain the proletarian dictatorship and prevent China from reverting to its semifeudal, semicolonial past. A true communist society, as preached by communist propaganda, must abolish all classes, parties, and states. Everyone would enjoy equal rights and equal access. Materials and goods would be distributed according to need rather than privilege. This shining version of the future was inculcated everywhere in society—in schools, at work, and throughout all forms of mass media—attracting and seducing the entire nation. Communist ideology thus became the new religion of the Chinese people. Any use of language, thought, and action that validated communist ideology was "correct" and "revolutionary." All opposing views were considered "wrong" or "counterrevolutionary." Efforts to correct counterrevolutionary views were considered "thought struggle" or "ideological warfare." With Mao's status as the "savior of the people" intensified, Mao's ideas and utterances became the sole correct versions of truth. As Ahn (1976) observes, "[A]ll policy and processes had to be justified in terms of Mao's thought, Mao's words served as policy statements. At the peak of a campaign, Mao Tse-tung's [Mao Zedong's][5] Thought thus served not merely as a guide for action but as á source of quasi-religious inspiration" (266).

Thought Reform and Means of Conversion
Given the political motive and rationale underlying their actions, it is not surprising that the Chinese Communist Party placed tremendous emphasis on propaganda aimed at ideological transformation.[6] As Frederick T. C. Yu (1964) observed, the most striking characteristics of the Chinese Communist Party propaganda are coercion and persuasion. In his words, "[T]hey have always depended upon mass hypnotic indoctrination and stirring persuasion to facilitate the tasks of the Party leadership and to mobilize the minds and effort of the population" (3). It is interesting to explore what techniques the Chinese Communists have employed to achieve these goals.

It has been the Chinese Communist belief that "thought determines action"; thus correct thought (adherence to Marxist-Maoist ideology) would bring about correct action (acting in line with Mao's directives and the party's dogma). The Communist Party and, of course, Mao in particular faced the daunting task of thought reform on a massive scale that included party members, intellectuals, and people of exploitive-class backgrounds. The purpose of such thought reform, according to Hu (1972), was "to prevent deviation . . . and to insure complete and absolute belief in the new faith" (149). Thought reform has taken many forms ranging from "thought struggle sessions" to writing reports and making confessions. In the numerous campaigns launched by the Communist Party since its establishment, thought reform has been a common theme and rhetorical practice.

The idea and techniques of thought reform originated in Soviet Russia during the great Soviet purge trials of the late 1930s. Like that of the Chinese Communists, the Soviet propaganda aimed at raising class consciousness and securing ideological conversion to communist belief. Thought reform was a means through which the absolute obedience and commitment of party members were ensured and those who thought and acted in ways at variance with communist ideology were purged. According to Lifton (1972), the common techniques employed by the Bolshevik Party for conversion and thought reform were criticism, self-criticism, and confession.

The practice of thought reform in China can be traced to the late 1920s when the Communists made efforts to persuade the captured enemy soldiers and prospective supporters to form an alliance with the Red Army in fighting the Nationalists. A larger scale of thought reform known as *zhengfeng* 整風 (reform of work style) was instigated by the Communist Party in Yan'an (the Communist base in Shaanxi Province) from 1942 to 1944. The stated purpose of the reform was to abolish factionalism, subjectivism, and the party's "eight-legged writing."[7] The success of reform established the legitimacy of Mao Zedong's Thought. Methods of confession, self-criticism, and reeducation borrowed from the Soviets were employed within the party. The *zheng-feng* movement is significant because, as Chu and Hsu (1979) explain, "during this period Mao made some serious attempts to consolidate and strengthen the control of the Party both organizationally and ideologically, to fight against incompatible ideology, and to experiment with various methods of thought reform" (34). In subsequent thought reform and political campaigns the ideological issue of how best to counter the threat posed by party bureaucrats, intelligentsia, and the bourgeoisie continued to be Mao's major concern. Those methods used during the *zhengfeng* period proved most effective in the subsequent land reform movement, the anti-rightist movement, and the Cultural Revolution. Borrowing from the Soviet model and drawing from the Chinese Communists' own practices, Mao learned the importance of political education and the value of techniques designated to raise class consciousness in the interest of furthering the cause of proletarian revolution. Political participation of the masses in ideological transformation took various forms, such as parades and rallies. However, confession, self-criticism, and political study sessions were common forms by which persuasion and behavior change took place.

Confession. The technique of confession has been used in almost every political campaign. During the *zhengfeng* period it was used within the party on party members. Willingly or under pressure party members confessed their "wrongdoings" or "incorrect thoughts" that violated Marxist-Leninist principles. After 1949 this method was extended to nonparty members. Between 1950 and 1952 Mao launched a nationwide land reform movement whereby arable land was taken from landlords and redistributed to peasants. To justify the seizure of land, peasants were mobilized to denounce their landlords. The denunciation started with peasants "spitting bitter water," that is, exposing the landlords' evildoings and describing the sufferings and torments caused by landlords. Landlords were humiliated by being paraded in the streets, and many were even executed. In addition landlords were forced to confess their "crimes." The active participation of peasants in the land reform movement, according to Chu and Hsu (1979), was intended not only to bring about economic change in the ownership of land but also to destroy traditional hierarchical patterns of landlord-tenant relations in the rural areas and to establish "a new set of relations in the villages according to the ideals of Communism" (15).[8]

Confession has been an effective means of thought reform with regard to intellectuals as well. In confession sessions intellectuals were pressured to reveal instances of "wrong thinking" and trace those back to the old society or to their exploitive family backgrounds. Intellectuals would typically expose their "sins," providing specific times and places when the misconduct took place, reflecting on the aspects of self in need of reform, and expressing determination to embrace the party's ideology. These confessions were presented in oral form at meetings or in written form to party officials. Some confessions were published in newspapers. For example, during the 1957 anti-rightist campaign, when many well-known intellectuals and leaders of opposing parties were accused of being rightists, many were forced to write and publish their confessions.[9] In this way the party elicited a sense of commitment to the ideological conversion from the individuals in question. This process resembled the forced confession techniques employed by the Soviets as described by Lifton (1989): "the irresistible demand for an admission of criminal guilt, however distorted or false, and the prolonged interrogations, physical pressures, and incriminating suggestions used to obtain it" (389). The whole process of confession was a manipulation and exploitation of feelings and guilt.

The practice of confession had never been part of the traditional Chinese rhetorical framework. It was clearly borrowed by the Chinese Communists from the Soviet Communists. According to Lifton (1972), the Soviet Communists' emphasis on sin and evil was derived from the Judeo-Christian tradition in general and the Russian Orthodox Church in particular. Though the emphasis on sin and guilt had never been prominent in traditional Chinese culture, Chinese Communists certainly found the method effective in achieving their goals. In Lifton's view, the difference between the use of confession in Russia and that in China can be summarized as follows: "In Russia confessions have generally been associated with the purge—the 'ritual liquidation'; in China, confession has been the vehicle for individual re-education" (165). Stalin's purge of dissidents in the 1930s resulted in a communist dictatorship in Russia. In China, on the other hand, the reeducation of intellectuals led to the emergence of the new Communist person and paved the way for the Cultural Revolution.

Self-criticism. Confession was often followed by self-criticism in which one condemned his or her incorrect thoughts or wrongdoings. Those who engaged in self-criticism were typically overwhelmed by guilt and strong feelings of shame for their bourgeois thoughts or poor work performance. Self-criticism allowed them to redeem themselves and express their commitment to self-correcting their thoughts and behaviors in accordance with the party line. Self-criticism was also a common strategy for demonstrating loyalty to Mao and the party as engaging in it indicated one's sincerity and trust for the party. Indeed, not all persuasive efforts were coercive. In fact, the most persuasive strategies and methods of conversion proved to be those that instilled in people a desire to be morally good and develop a sense of belonging. Naturally, confession and self-criticism elicited collaboration from those who willingly engaged in them.

Self-criticism was considered an important means of self-cultivation toward moral goodness in Chinese tradition. Confucius, for example, considered self-criticism as an distinct moral attribute of a gentleman. In his *Analects,* Confucius praised several times those who willingly admitted their faults and mistakes, exhibited a high level of self-knowledge, and constantly examined and reflected on their own speech and action (Leys 1997, 1.4, 2.17, 5.27, 19.21, 19.25). Confucius regarded this process of understanding and exposing oneself to be a valuable experience of learning and growth. Communist leaders appropriated this Confucian approach to the process of thought reform in ridding people of bourgeois influence and traditional ways of thinking. Mao ([1943] 1975) demarcated the ability to self-criticize as an indicator of a good or a bad Communist. For this reason he asserted, "Self-criticism is imperative and wrong tendencies must be squarely faced and conscientiously corrected" (159). In another article Mao ([1945] 1977) reiterated, "Conscientious practice of self-criticism is still another hallmark distinguishing our Party from all other political parties" (266). It was, in Mao's words, "the only effective way to prevent all kinds of political dust and germs from contaminating the minds of our comrades and the body of our Party" (267).

Before the Cultural Revolution, Liu Shaoqi, the second in command, wrote *How to Be a Good Communist,* which became required reading for all Communist Party members. In this book Liu made a reference to Confucian teaching of self-cultivation and indoctrinated party members with communist morality. One aspect of such morality is self-criticism. Liu advised party members on the benefits of self-criticism: "Experience proves that whenever a comrade in a responsible position seriously practices sincere and necessary self-criticism before the Party membership and the masses, . . . their internal solidarity will develop, their work will improve, and their defects will be overcome, while the prestige of the responsible comrade will increase instead of being undermined" (Dittmer 1998, 262). Various forms of confession and self-criticism were pervasive prior to and during the Cultural Revolution. No one was exempt from this ritualistic and politicized practice.

Political study sessions. Political study sessions have been indispensable features of political education and thought reform in China since the 1950s. They took place in small groups that were usually formed based on school or work affiliations. The groups met regularly to study and discuss political documents that usually consisted of writings from higher levels of party organizations or articles published in the *People's Daily* or the *Red Flag,* the two major communist mouthpieces. The general purpose of these sessions had been to unify beliefs and persuade participants of the necessity of various policies and procedures sanctioned by the Communist Party. These small-group political study sessions had been ritualized with fixed agendas and unwritten norms. At each study session the group head, usually the local branch party secretary, would read the documents and then facilitate group discussion in sharing an understanding of the study materials. Winance (1959) described his own experience of these study sessions while he was in China: "For a year and a half I personally had to submit to Hsueh-Hsi [study session] three times a week, and the meetings lasted four hours each. Added to that were the extraordinary meetings, parades, and popular trials. In 1951, the professors at Szechwan University submitted to Hsueh-Hsi every morning from 7:30–9:30" (19). At the end of each session the group leader was responsible for reporting to party supervisors on how well the study sessions proceeded and how group members absorbed the materials.

Moreover, group members were expected to examine their own thoughts and behaviors in comparison with the directives and viewpoints expressed in the study of materials. In doing so, they were expected to engage in criticism and self-criticism of thoughts and behaviors that deviated from the party's preaching. The group member being criticized was singled out and experienced alienation by the other group members. The group member being criticized faced formidable pressure to make a public statement admitting his or her wrongdoings, expressing acceptance of the party's views, and pledging allegiance to the party. Under such circumstances, as pointed out by Whyte (1979), "The result is often that group members carefully search for cues about what public statements are required of them and make them, no matter what their private views and reservations are. Such sessions can become a charade that group members feel they must engage in" (117).

Political study sessions have functioned as places for downward communication in terms of transmitting party policies and messages, places that had provided powerful force for attitude change and thought control. As Townsend (1972) observed, "The Chinese Communists capitalize on pressures for associational conformity, which are particularly strong in the Chinese tradition, to enhance the persuasiveness of their doctrine and reinforce their demands for political unanimity" (263). Indeed, political study sessions have been sophisticated and effective means of political communication and persuasion and have been in operation to this day.

In addition to the forms mentioned above, the Communist Party employed a variety of other communication strategies to disseminate party propaganda and Mao's directives aiming at ideological transformation and thought reform. These forms included blackboard writing, wall posters, street-corner plays, folk dances, poetry reciting, and newspaper articles celebrating the cardinal principles of the party line. During the Cultural Revolution several new forms were added to this list, such as flyers, leaflets, pamphlets, Red Guard tabloids, denunciation rallies, and "everyday readings," to name a few.

Characteristics of Chinese Political Rhetoric Prior to the Cultural Revolution
China's political reality since 1949 has been shaped by constant exposure to political language formulated at the highest levels of institutional power. Unification of thought and collective commitment to the communist cause have been achieved through at least four rhetorical tactics: (1) ideological correctness; (2) private morality and self-cultivation; (3) agitation and hatred; and (4) formalized and obscure language. These methods were common prior to the Cultural Revolution and continued during its ten-year history.

Ideological correctness. Communist propaganda since the 1950s has been characterized by a strong emphasis on ideological conversion, based on the assumption that correct ideology and consciousness were fundamental to the moral well-being of the individual. According to Leshan Dong (1999), a Chinese communist view of what constitutes moral well-being would necessarily include a proletarian family background and active participation in all political campaigns. Active campaigning would include demonstrating loyalty to Mao and the party, confessing one's inner selfish thoughts and motives, and exposing other people's wrongdoings.

Ideological correctness was enforced through repeated exposure to the party's propaganda at various levels. Thought reform, with the techniques of confession, self-criticism, and political study sessions, had been effective means to ensure ideological conformity. From early ages children were taught that they were successors of the communist cause and that their mission was to attack the bourgeois class and to defend socialist revolution. All types of social discourse and the focus of school learning were centered around reinforcing Marxist-Maoist ideology and correct thought. Anyone who deviated from this centrality would be alienated and punished.

Recalling Wander's (1984) assertion that a nation's ideology is inextricably interwoven with its culture, sinologists have noted the striking similarity between Maoism and Confucianism in that both emphasize the role of ideology conformity and the moral integrity of the individual (for example, Chu 1977; Fairbank 1976; Pye 1968). While Confucius advocated moral instruction and ritualistic practices as means of cultivating *junzi* 君子 (gentleman), Chinese Communists promoted conformity to Mao's brand of Marxist ideology and the cultivation of a new moral exemplar, the new Communist person. In this sense Confucius and Mao seemed to find agreement in the notion that a perfect society requires the perfection of its people. Fairbank (1976) said it well: "[T]here are Confucian overtones in the Marxist-Maoist orchestration. The crucial role of ideology under communism lends particular interest to China's ideological past" (59).

Private morality and self-cultivation. While a moral person in traditional Chinese society would exhibit traces of Confucian ideals, a moral person in Mao's China must first and foremost have a correct ideology. Further, a moral person must have proletarian consciousness demonstrated through total devotion to the state, loyalty to the party and Mao Zedong, sacrifice for the collective good, willingness to endure hardship, and constant self-examination of one's inner thought. Ironically, these attributes of private morality were largely obtained through one's willingness to engage in self-cultivation that is deeply rooted in traditional Chinese culture.

Sinologists generally agree that Chinese communism consciously or unconsciously adopted and appropriated traditional rhetorical techniques in order to further its cause. For example, as Pye (1968) pointed out, "The entire structure of both imperial and Communist politics has rested on self-cultivation as the ultimate rationale for legitimizing high office and the manipulations of political power" (13). In Confucian society the educated elites were expected to engage in strenuous self-examination regarding their own thinking and behavior. The path to becoming a moral exemplar involved constant learning both from books and from the people one came in contact with, as well as from real life experiences. Likewise, Mao's new Communist person was to be both "red and expert," whose thinking and actions were guided by Marxist-Maoist ideology and who was also well versed in technical areas.

To accomplish this ambitious goal it was necessary to constantly engage in self-examination, checking one's thinking and behavior against Mao's sayings and the party's guidelines. Emphasis on private morality was intensified through the nationwide campaign known as "Learning from Lei Feng." Lei was a soldier from a poor family who was always ready to help others and was totally devoted to the communist cause. His diary was published as a model of high proletarian consciousness due to the way he described his loyalty to Mao and his determination to apply Mao's teachings to his everyday life. Diary writing was a popular way to accomplish this type of private morality. Ironically, many diaries of moral exemplars were published and subsequently plagiarized by millions of others.

Agitation and hatred. In characterizing Chinese political themes Pye (1968) asserted that "the dominant emotion of modern Chinese politics has been a preoccupation with hatred coupled with an enthusiasm for singling out enemies" (67). The Chinese people were encouraged to identify themselves by class background and then to demonize those associated with the exploitive class. As early as the land reform period peasants were mobilized to "spit bitter water" and given free rein to express their hatred of the landlords. Aggression in the form of profanity and beating was allowed. The same pattern of agitation and hatred escalated during the anti-rightist movement and finally reached its climax during the Cultural Revolution, resulting in widespread cruelty and violence and causing millions of deaths and suicides.

The rhetoric of agitation and hatred is not part of the ancient rhetorical tradition in China, which emphasized humaneness and harmony. This new rhetoric was in marked contrast to Confucian values of emotional restraint and social etiquette. In Chinese Communist political activities, such as political meetings and rallies, however, one would see constant bickering, arguing, and expressions of anger and agitation. As Solomon (1998) observed, unlike the Confucian code of ethics, Mao "saw resentment and hatred as the motivational basis of mass political participation" (514). Ironically, rhetorical acts characterized by agitation and hatred were justified on moralistic grounds, in particular, as expressions of class struggle. Contrasting these tactics with traditional Chinese politics, Pye (1968) lamented, "In modern times, however, hate and hostility are not only more openly acknowledged but they are extolled as positive virtues of the political activist" (68). The most popular word in Communist terminology was *douzheng* 鬥爭, meaning "to struggle, to fight," or to "make war." This term is used in expressions such as *sixiang douzheng* 思想鬥爭 (thought struggle), *luxian douzheng* 路线鬥爭 (line struggle), and *jieji douzheng* 階級鬥爭 (class struggle) prior to and during the Cultural Revolution. It evokes emotions of attack, combat, violent struggle, and bitter infighting.

Formalized and obscure language. Instead of employing a variety of stylistic devices that are found in abundance in the Chinese language, Chinese political discourse was characterized by what Schoenhals (1992) calls "formalized language." This restricted code was deemed politically appropriate and used primarily by party officials beginning in 1949. Some examples of such language are: "[We] are determined to carry out and execute the Party's policy and lines"; [We] must continue the revolution until its end"; "[We] must closely unite with Chairman Mao and the Party Central Committee"; and "[We] must strive for the communist cause." The uniformity in the use of such language by China's Communist leaders indicated that Chinese political discourse had its fixed forms, which were required by the political structure and in keeping with the aims of the government. What is worse, as the formalized language was plagiarized in every political speech, it deteriorated into dry and cumbersome clichés, which led to linguistic impoverishment and thought-deprivation. In the description of Lifton (1989), such a language system "is repetitiously centered on all-encompassing jargon, prematurely abstract, highly categorical, relentlessly judging" (429). Needless to say, a person's thinking and feeling will be immensely narrowed and deprived by speaking and being exposed to such a language system.

In contrast to the view expressed by Schoenhals, Pye (1979) characterized Chinese political language as "Aesopian language," emphasizing the leaders' use of "historical allegory and code words to make their points in public" (158). He considered Mao's writings effective in reaching the less educated Chinese. In Pye's view, "There are numerous examples in which Mao, in particular, used historical and other allegorical forms, not for clear and simple instruction of the masses but to make points that are at times highly obscure" (158–59). Winance (1959) concurs that Chinese communist language is obscure and unclear but seemingly effective. The use of obscure language has been a common rhetorical strategy across cultures—for example, by the Church fathers in their efforts to convert pagans to Christianity; the technique was much favored by Saint Augustine in the Middle Ages as it created an air of mystery so that people were free to fill in their own meanings. Terms in Chinese political discourse, such as "revolution," "proletarian," "bourgeois," and "class enemies," were abstract and ambiguous. Their meanings were never clearly defined, and perhaps for this reason they were effective in creating the idols of the marketplace.

In this chapter I reviewed theories on the relationship between language, thought, perceptions of reality, and culture from anthropological, philosophical, critical, and rhetorical perspectives. The anthropological perspective sheds light on the ways in which language structure and word choice affect thought patterns and prevailing worldviews. The philosophical perspective addresses how language relates to truth and knowledge and how it can simultaneously create and distort social reality. The critical perspective deals with the impact of institutional power and discursive force in shaping new consciousness and thought patterns. The rhetorical perspective examines how the use of symbols and forms of communication create identification and induce changes in attitude and behavior, as well as how political discourse is rooted in historical and cultural contexts. All these perspectives contribute to a well-rounded, in-depth understanding of the rhetoric of the Cultural Revolution by providing the necessary theoretical frameworks and analytic tools for making sense of the data. A review of the

Chinese Communist strategies of persuasion places these theoretical perspectives in context and provides background information on the rhetorical situation and political milieu prior to the Cultural Revolution. It also helps to illuminate the ways in which political rhetoric and the means of ideological transformation are rooted in Chinese culture and shared by the former Soviet Union.

Three

A Rhetorical Analysis
of Political Slogans

Through the use of slogans, China experienced a glorious victory as well as drastic chaos. Behind every slogan, there is an unforgettable national history as well as a personal story.

Wenhe Zhang and Yan Li, *Kouhao yu zhongguo* (Slogan and China)

Through the use of political slogans, a person's evil side was evoked, leading to actions of beating, smashing, and ransacking. I witnessed with my own eyes Red Guards shouting political slogans and singing revolutionary songs while mercilessly beating our landlord, an old man, to death.

Account from an interview

There is nothing all that new or culture-specific about the use of slogans; they have been in existence as long as language has been around and are generally employed "as a means of focusing attention and exhorting to action" (Urdang and Robbins 1984, 17). The word "slogan,"according to Sharp (1984), "is an Anglicization of the Gaelic 'slaughghairm' which means 'army cry' or 'war cry,' formerly used by the Scottish clans. Its purpose was then to inspire the members of the clan to fight fiercely for its protection or the extension of its glory" (v). In the context of sacred texts such as the Bible and the Qur'an, slogans are used as means of moral persuasion. They also are used as powerful tools in the dissemination of propaganda during times of war. Today in most industrialized and democratic countries slogans function as instruments of popular persuasion in advertising and political campaigns.

Political Functions of Slogans

For Shankel (1941), slogans are "significant symbols" of a society inasmuch as they are carefully crafted phrases or expressions that suggest actions, evoke emotional responses, and perform persuasive functions. Any given symbol can be shared by certain groups or cultures or it can be entirely unique to a particular group or culture, shedding light on its ideological formation. In this regard, in their study of the persuasive function of slogans, Stewart, Smith, and Denton (1995) maintain that "the slogans a group uses to evoke specific responses may provide us with an index of the group's norms, values, and conceptual rationale for its claims" (403). Slogans are easy to remember. They facilitate the release of pent-up feelings and allow us to engage in polarized thinking. According to Denton (1980), political slogans also function to simplify complicated ideas, express group ideology and goals, create identification, provoke violent confrontations, and provide hope for the future. In such circumstances slogans should be considered particular forms of public discourse that aim to unify public thought and agitate for various actions and reactions in the public sphere.

In her book *Totalitarianism* (1951), Hannah Arendt explores the topic of the use of language in legitimizing the goals of totalitarian states such as Nazi Germany and the former Soviet Union. One of the central features of Nazi propaganda, according to Arendt, was the "ingenious application of slogans" (55) in the justification of anti-Semitism and the extermination of six million Jews. Political slogans were also a powerful means of mass mobilization in the former Soviet Union. As described by Vaclav Havel (1985), they were seen everywhere and formed "part of the panorama of everyday life" (35); so pervasive were these slogans that they were embraced "by the entire society as an important feature of its life" and "seemed impossible to grasp or define" (37). Slogans were clearly instrumental in shaping class consciousness under Lenin's regime and in the legitimization of the "Great Purge"[1] of the Stalin era.

Throughout China's history slogans were used in peasant rebellions to further the cause of social justice. For example, as early as 209 B.C.E. a Chinese peasant rebellion raised the slogan "condemning no-virtue and denouncing the cruelty of Qin" in an attempt to overthrow the Qin dynasty (221–201 B.C.E.). During the "Yellow Banner" rebellion of 184 C.E. the slogan "The current regime has died; Yellow power will take over" helped focus resistance to the Eastern Han dynasty (25 B.C.E.–220 C.E.). During the May Fourth movement in 1919 the slogan "Down with Confucianism; promote democracy and science" played a seminal role in transforming the Chinese thought toward modernization and westernization.[2] Since 1949 and the establishment of the People's Republic of China, nearly every political movement has been initiated and facilitated by political slogans.[3]

While ideology is generally defined as "a pattern or set of ideas, assumptions, beliefs, values, or interpretations of the world by which a culture or group operates" (Foss 1996, 291), particular manifestation and expression of ideology are often revealed in the form of "ideographs," a highly politicized subcategory of slogans. Ideographs are ordinary and abstract terms infused with moral and constitutional value and used in political discourse to represent the ideals of a culture and to call for collective commitment to a normative goal (Condit and Lucaites 1993; MacIntyre 1981; McGee 1980). Terms such as "freedom," "liberty," and "democracy" are examples of common ideographs in American society. Condit and Lucaites (1993) identify three ways that ideographs are typically used: (1) as a justification for action; (2) as a shared symbol for participation in a rhetorical culture; and (3) as a means of persuasion. Political slogans share these functions in controlling and changing the public mind. They are the building blocks of ideology and are used to raise political consciousness and organize certain cultural attitudes as well as to further political goals and shape individuals' sense of reality (Denton 1980; McGee 1980). In this sense an ideograph as understood in the Western rhetorical tradition is closely associated with the ideological formation and the social construction of meaning that can be applied to any society.[4]

Wander (1983), in his examination of ideological/cultural criticism, highlights two elements that are relevant to our discussion: (1) fact, defined as what is present in the text and its medium; and (2) negation, defined as what is absent in the text and its medium. The former includes any rhetorical acts, artifacts, or mediums used to communicate messages that have significance. The latter refers to the identification of elements, people, or issues that are muted or objectified into what Wander referred to as a "third persona." In other words, negation has to do with the avoidance and dehumanization of certain characteristics such as animals and disease. According to Wander (1984), "The potentiality of language to commend being [as acceptable, desirable, and significant] carries with it the potential to spell out being unacceptable, undesirable, insignificant" (209).

Political slogans permeated every aspect of Chinese culture during the Cultural Revolution. They were the primary rhetorical symbols used to justify violent behavior, dehumanize class enemies, encourage antitraditional acts, and elevate the cult of Mao. The primary source of such slogans were the government-controlled media, Mao's quotations, and Lin Biao's speeches.[5] Some slogans were coined by the Red Guards and the Rebels. Political slogans were disseminated throughout the country via the electronic media as well as wall posters, rally speeches, leaflets, and loudspeakers. Certain slogans were used intensively during the Cultural Revolution and carried diachronic and synchronic meanings. Testimonies taken from memoirs and interviews by the author illustrate how political slogans served to mold certain ways of thinking and justify various actions.

Numerous political slogans appeared in a wide variety of official and unofficial mediums throughout China during the ten years of the Cultural Revolution.[6] Slogans of high intensity are defined as those that conveyed central ideological and political meaning, while slogans of high frequency were those widely and repeatedly disseminated through the propaganda machine. The most authoritative communist mouthpieces were government-controlled newspapers such as the *People's Daily* and the *Red Flag*. All ideological discourse in the public arena was molded after these primary sources.

Types of Political Slogans and Their Functions

"Never Forget the Class Struggle"

In *The Communist Manifesto* ([1848] 1965) Karl Marx and Frederick Engels assert that "the history of all hitherto existing society is the history of class struggle" (57). According to Marxist theory, class status is determined by an individual's relationship to the means of production, which also profoundly influences one's attitudes and actions. Adopting Marx's view of social change, Mao came to view the history of China as a class struggle between the ruling and the ruled classes, which was a generating force for social development. In his view, "In class society everyone lives as a member of a particular class, and every kind of thinking, without exception, is stamped with the brand of a class" (Mao [1937] 1975, 296). The goal of the Chinese Communist revolution was to elevate the proletariat to the status of ruling class. However, Mao was keenly aware that a Chinese Communist Party (CCP) victory did not guarantee the elimination of the opposing class. He recognized that class struggle would continue since the thoughts and behaviors of the bourgeois class would still exist and would pose a threat to the new order.

In the first decade after the Communist takeover of China the notion of class struggle took a backseat to economic development and the purging of party officials.[7] However, two major events took place in the late 1950s that caused Mao to identity class struggle as the core ideology of the CCP. The first event was the violent uprising of the Polish and Hungarian people against their respective Communist governments in 1956.[8] The second was the anti-rightist movement in 1957, when Mao discovered that there was strong opposition within and outside the Communist Party to his approach of socialism.[9] Concerned about losing both international and domestic support for his Communist regime and control of the "correct ideology," Mao introduced his "Never forget the class struggle" edict in 1962 at the second session of the Eighth Chinese Communist Party Assembly. At that time he reasserted the notion that proletarian and bourgeois classes were social enemies with antithetical economic goals and ideological interests, and that, as a result, constant struggle between the proletarian and bourgeois classes was inevitable. In his words, "Such a class struggle takes a long time, is complicated, and sometimes can be intensified" (Mao [1937] 1975, 13). In his view, the proletariat could strengthen its ruling-class status only by exercising dictatorial force over the bourgeois class. Otherwise the bourgeois class would attempt to reinstate capitalism.

The slogan "Never forget the class struggle" first appeared as the title of a commentary in the *People's Liberation Army Daily* on 4 May 1966, at the outset of the Cultural Revolution. Soon other official newspapers and magazines followed suit, filling their pages with the slogan. In a series of articles published in the *Red Flag* during 1966,[10] class struggle was the primary topic of political sloganeering. Readers were bombarded with headlines such as "Never Forget the Class Struggle" (*Red Flag*, vol. 7, 1966); "Thoroughly Bury the Doctrine That Class Struggle Is Nonexistent" (vol. 4, 1968); "Always Grasp the Canon of Class Struggle" (vols. 3, 4, 1969); and "Class Struggle Must Be Talked about Daily, Monthly, and Annually" (vol. 12, 1971). Moreover, during this time everything from academic research to political upheaval was made an issue of class struggle. Consider the following two headlines in this regard: "The Study of History Is a Class Struggle" (vol. 4, 1966); and "The Cultural Revolution Is a Struggle between Two Classes and Two Paths" (vol. 11, 1966).

Such slogans were soon widely used in public discourse, such as in political speeches, at group meetings, and on wall posters. For example, when asked to give a speech on behalf of the Red Guards, Xiaosheng Liang reportedly at first did not know what to say. Then, drawing on articles in the *Red Flag* and the *People's Daily*, he quickly composed a speech: "We revolutionary students fight with determination at the forefront of class struggle. We pledge to Chairman Mao to be the dare-to-die corps on the front lines of the class struggle. . . . Victory belongs to us, because we have the sharp weapon of class struggle from Mao Zedong's Thought. We will crush the black gangs who endanger our Party and socialism to death in the same way that parasites are annihilated" (Liang 1998, 27).

During the Cultural Revolution one's class status became the criterion for drawing lines between enemies and friends and, indeed, between good and evil. People were taught that class struggle existed everywhere, within and outside of the party, in society as well as in the family. Social relationships were delineated along class lines, and class enemies were identified on the basis of one's words and actions. As a result the Chinese people became increasingly class-conscious and highly politicized. In schools children were taught to hate their teachers who were labeled "class enemies." Luowen Yu (2000) recalls, "At the time, the only talk at the school was 'class struggle.' Students and teachers were expected to fill their speeches with the term 'class struggle.' The more frequently a person used the slogan, the more revolutionary the person appears to be" (49).

Class lines were drawn along two general categories: the five red categories and the five black categories. The five red categories included revolutionary cadres, revolutionary martyrs, revolutionary soldiers, workers, and poor and lower-middle peasants; the five black categories consisted of landlords, rich peasants, counterrevolutionaries, criminals, and rightists. It was believed that children born to these family backgrounds, whether red or black, would carry the indelible imprint of their classes. As a popular couplet declared, "The son is a hero if the father is a revolutionary. The son is a rotten egg if the father is a counter-revolutionary." This so-called theory of revolutionary inheritance had cast those born into the five black family backgrounds as enemies. Children of such backgrounds were considered guilty of the "sins" of their parents and grandparents. They were typically referred to as "bastards" or "sons of bitches." One person interviewed by the author shared his experience of being ostracized by his high school peers as the son of a "class enemy." He was constantly watched and ordered to confess the "bad influence" he received from his parents, alleged counterrevolutionaries. On the other hand, it was taken for granted that children from the five red-category backgrounds would feel unfailing love and loyalty to the party just as their parents were grateful to and had fought for the party. One interviewee, a former member of the Revolutionary Committee in charge of assigning jobs to high school graduates, revealed that the only criterion looked at was "family background." The children of the five red categories were assigned jobs in the cities, while the children of the five black categories were sent to remote areas.

Not all Chinese passively accepted the theory of blood line as the determining factor with regard to class enemies. Yu Luoke, a worker from Beijing who was twice denied entrance to college because of his parents' exploitive class background, wrote an article titled "On the Discussion of Blood Line." He distributed his article through-out the country with the help of his brothers. Yu argued that the influence children received from their teachers far outweighed the influence from their families. Friends, public discourse, and the work environment were significant factors in shaping one's worldview as well. He called for critical reflection on the theory of blood line and the equal treatment of all children (Yu 2000). Tragically, Yu was arrested for his dissenting views and was tortured while in prison. He refused to recant and was sentenced to death. He was executed on 5 March 1970 at the age of twenty-eight in the Beijing Workers' Stadium, a place filled with hateful slogans targeting class enemies.

In the climate created by the slogan "Never forget the class struggle," many party officials and administrators were accused of being "capitalist roaders" whose crimes were attempting to restore capitalism and subvert the course of socialism in China. Worse still, a class enemy could be anybody anywhere, including a family member. It was not uncommon for siblings to become estranged and embattled because they belonged to different factions of the Red Guards, each accusing the other of being a class enemy. Some children even brought home members of the Red Guards to search their own homes and beat their parents, having become convinced that their parents were class enemies. In fact, people were required to be constantly on the lookout for class enemies. One interviewee shared that after being taught that anyone around her could be a class enemy if he or she came from the exploitive class, she began to watch her mother's daily activities simply because her mother had been born into a landlord family. What is more, every time her mother shut herself in her room, the interviewee would suspect that she was sending telegrams to other class enemies overseas.

Since the ability to identify a case of class struggle was considered an indication of high-level revolutionary consciousness, people went out of their way to ferret out anyone who was suspicious of a class enemy. For example, dishonesty in business deal-ings could cause one to be labeled a class enemy. Gao Yuan (1987) recounts the fol-lowing scenario: "Several classmates and I managed to find a class enemy right outside the school's main gate. We came upon a peddler soliciting orders for name seals carved from pear wood. He was charging only three *mao* a seal, so we eagerly placed orders and paid him in advance. He said the seals would be ready that afternoon, but when we came back he had disappeared. We introduced the swindle in politics class as a real-life example of class struggle" (25–26).

Scrutinizing a person's speech or choice of words was also an approach to identify-ing class enemies. The following example, taken from interviews, shows how one man, Liu Shaoqi, was condemned for his use of the term *Daqing ren* 大慶人 (people from Daqing).[11] This interviewee's argument was that Liu's use of the term blurred class distinctions. There was no such thing as *Daqing ren*. There were only the proletar-ian *Daqing ren* and the bourgeois *Daqing ren*. He then charged Liu with embracing an anti-Maoist understanding of class struggle by his choice of words. In those days many formerly well-respected intellectuals and party officials were accused of being class ene-mies overnight. Ironically, these "class enemies" had been involved in the revolution for many years and were, in fact, thoroughly committed to the cause of overthrowing the exploiting class in China. Now they had become the target of the revolution.

Under the slogan "Never forget the class struggle," a person was judged primarily by the class category to which he or she belonged or alleged. What is more, violence against persons who were labeled class enemies was legitimized. Zhai (1992) offered a personal experience of an act of violence engendered by the concept of class struggle." This example pertains to a former landlord, Xiuying, whose death the author may have caused: "Xiuying's death would hardly have been news, but the thought that I might have killed her weighed heavily upon me for days. Still, eventually I managed to persuade myself it was all right. We were in a war and there are always casualties on battlefields. [I told myself] I shouldn't be intimidated by the death of one class enemy" (98). Indeed, many Red Guards believed that Chairman Mao wanted them to eliminate the bourgeoisie; thus beating was considered a revolutionary act that was justified in the name of a good cause. Many felt that it was their duty and obligation to use violent means against class enemies and to show no mercy in the face of the human suffering they inflicted on such enemies. As observed by Jing Lin (1991), members of the Red Guards "associated their acts with taking a class stand and conducting revolution to 'liberate' the proletariat and to uphold their great leader, Chairman Mao" (28).

In sum, the slogan "Never forget the class struggle" and other related ideographs divided the Chinese people and polarized proletariat and bourgeois classes. In fact, class became the only lens through which social relations were filtered and actions guided. In the United States critical scholars have pointed out the danger of categorizing and judging people according to race (for example, Asante 1998; Jackson and Garner 1998). Likewise, during the Cultural Revolution classifying people by their family backgrounds led to a narrow view of reality and much cruelty and suffering.

"To Rebel Is Justified"

With the encouragement of Mao and his trusted followers, high school and college students became passionately and enthusiastically involved in the Cultural Revolution. On 29 May 1966 a group of Tsinghua High School students gathered together to discuss how best to demonstrate their loyalty to Mao, and out of this meeting came the establishment of the Red Guards[12] (Zhang and Li 1998, 397). The color red symbolized the revolution, and the word "guards" represented their intention to protect Chairman Mao in his fight against class enemies. The Red Guards student organization soon spread throughout the country.

On 5 June 1966 the *People's Daily* quoted Mao's new directive: "All the doctrines of Marxism, with its many theories and postulates, can be summed up in one sentence: To rebel is justified."[13] This new assertion set the tone and focused the energy of the Red Guards. "To rebel is justified" became the watch phrase, the legitimating slogan, for the entire Cultural Revolution. Encouraged by Mao's endorsement, the Red Guards from Tsinghua High School issued a wall poster elaborating Mao's directive and declaring their position: "Revolution is rebellion. The soul of Mao Zedong's Thought is rebellion. When we say we are making more efforts in 'application,' we mean we are making more efforts to rebel. Daring to think, to speak, to act, to engage in adventures and to participate in the revolution can be encapsulated in one phrase: 'dare to rebel.' This is the most fundamental and most noble qualification for proletarian revolutionaries. This is the fundamental principle of the proletarian Party. Refusing to rebel illustrates one hundred percent revisionism. . . . Long live the spirit of revolutionary rebellion!" (Zhang and Li 1998, 397–98). Subsequently the slogan "To rebel is justified" was ritualized. For example, when someone was recruited to a Red Guards organization, a ceremony was staged in which the old Red Guards shook hands with the newcomers. Simultaneously both sides would chant "To rebel is justified" (Liang 1998, 143). This ritual is similar to the Nazis' practice of exchanging "Heil Hitlers" in greeting each other as a way of indicating their shared political identity.

In another wall poster two months later the Red Guards reiterated their central tenet. One paragraph of the poster said, "Rebellion is the tradition of our proletarian revolutionaries. It is a tradition we Red Guards must carry on. We rebelled in the past, are rebelling in the present and will rebel in the future. We need the spirit of rebellion for the next 100 years, 1,000 years, one million years, and ten million years" (Zhang and Li 1998, 399). Soon the slogan "Revolution is not a crime; to rebel is justified" swept the country, inciting revolutionary fervor. The "five dares" (dare to think, to speak, to act, to make revolution, and to rebel) and "four unafraids" (unafraid of heaven, of earth, of gods, and of ghosts) became the ideological foundation of thought and action for the Red Guards during the Cultural Revolution. To boost the spirit of rebellion Mao's poems were widely disseminated as slogans. The most common one was "Dare to clasp the moon in the Ninth Heaven; dare to catch turtles deep down in the five seas" (Mao 1976, 101). Such slogans stirred deep emotions, promoted a crusading spirit, and granted the Red Guards and the Rebels a license to insult, torture, and even kill class enemies.

In the traditional Chinese family there had long been an emphasis on hierarchy and respect for one's elders. However, under the slogan "To rebel is justified" and another related slogan that conveyed the rebellious spirit of the times, "Be willing to sacrifice and dare to drag down the emperor from the throne," many young people were so caught up in the revolutionary fervor of the times that they began to rebel against their own family members. For example, after being reproached by his father for a disciplinary problem, Chihua Wen (1995) recalls shouting at his father: "You get out of here instantly, or prepare to die!" He then pulled out his pistol and pointed it at his father's head, saying, "Listen carefully! Chairman Mao has already urged us to rebel. How dare you try to restrain and discipline me! You are right. I am not your son anymore. I belong to Chairman Mao and to the Revolution" (60). Three interviewees shared with me that they used this slogan to challenge and threaten their parents in similar situations. Rebellion against authority was considered the ultimate revolutionary act, an end in itself. As Wen recalls, "I kept making revolution—rebelling against anything, anyone labeled counterrevolutionary and doing what I thought was guarding Chairman Mao" (60).

In the name of "To rebel is justified" families were torn apart, classrooms were disrupted, teachers were tortured, property was damaged, and homes were looted. Rebellion against authority and against traditional cultural values was pervasive and rampant, causing general chaos, countless violations of human rights and dignity, and the wholesale defiance of laws. One interviewee described the cruelty inflicted on his elementary school principal: "He was made to bend his body. A big heavy placard was hung around his neck. He was kicked and slapped on the stage while we were shouting slogans: 'To Rebel Is Justified.' I heard he became sick after a few denunciation rallies. But the Little Red Guards would not let him go to the doctor and continued to beat him in subsequent rallies. Later I learned that he committed suicide. I did not think much of it except that he deserved to die because he had promoted bourgeois educational values and ideas." Another interviewee witnessed a group of Red Guards whipping their high school principal to death. Though many years have passed since that tragedy took place, he still remembers clearly the image of a few female Red Guards holding whips soaked with blood and the image of the dead body of the principal lying on the ground. In the climate created by the slogan "To rebel is justified," students relentlessly tortured and tormented their teachers and principals.

"Sweeping Away All the Monsters and Demons"

The phrase *niu gui she shen* 牛鬼蛇神 literally means "cow ghosts and snake spirits." Metaphorically it refers to monsters and demons. The term first appeared in an ancient Chinese poem by Du Mu of the Tang Dynasty (618–709 C.E.) describing the mystical and absurd style of another poet. The phrase also relates to supernatural creatures from ancient Chinese mythology in that cow ghosts and snake spirits were said to commit evil deeds while disguised as human beings. Thus the phrase was extended to refer to the force of evil in camouflage. During the anti-rightist campaign Mao Zedong used the words to describe those intellectuals whom he believed attacked the party through their speeches and literary works while pretending to be loyal to the party. Since cow ghosts and snake spirits were said to lose their evil powers once they were recognized, Mao decided to expose the "evil motives" of the intellectuals by allowing them to speak their minds in the "Double Hundreds Campaign" (Let one hundred flowers bloom and let one hundred schools contend). In Mao's ([1957b] 1977) words, "Letting cow ghosts and snake spirits come out of their hiding places makes it easier to annihilate them. Letting poisonous weeds break though the earth makes it more convenient to wipe them out" (437).

During the Cultural Revolution "monsters and demons" came to refer to all class enemies. The slogan "Sweeping away all the monsters and demons" first appeared as the title of a commentary in the *People's Daily* on 1 June 1966 in reference to those who promoted bourgeois ideas and revisionism within the party, in the government, in the army, and among intellectuals. It was also extended to refer to anyone who came from an exploitive family background or belonged to one of the five black categories.[14] Once someone was labeled as monster and demon, that person was automatically a class enemy.

Other related dehumanizing slogans soon filled the arena of public discourse. Many party administrators were labeled "capitalist running dogs" and removed from office. The *Red Flag* published an article titled "Clean Up All the Parasites" (vol. 11, 1966). Soon slogans such as "Down with monsters and demons" and "Sweeping away all the monsters and demons" were everywhere: on wall posters, in official newspapers, in the Red Guards' leaflets, and in rallying cries. Concerning denunciation rallies, the stage where the person was denounced was called *dou gui tai* 鬥鬼台 (the stage of ghost). Those being denounced were made into monsters by cutting their hair into *gui tou* 鬼頭 (ghost heads) and painting their faces with black paint. Some innocent people were virtually turned into "ghosts" overnight. For example, Wang Huo, a well-respected high school principal, was suddenly and without warning reduced to the category of "monsters and demons." The experience was devastating for him. Wang (1998) recalls, "At the denunciation rally, I was cursed and humiliated. The Rebels pledged to knock me to the ground, step on me with ten thousand feet, and fight the bloody battle with me till death" (46).

In the May Seventh Cadre School a common feature was the "struggle session in the field" where "monsters and demons were denounced." In Feng Zhao's (1999) description, "The sessions usually took place during a break from labor. They began with peasants' denunciation of the old society, followed by harsh reproach of the 'monsters and demons' by workers. One or two of the 'monsters' would be pulled in front of the workers and forced to confess their crimes. The sessions would end with slogan shouting" (72). Those regarded as monsters and demons usually fell under the strict surveillance of the Rebels. For example, the mother of one interviewee was accused of being a counterrevolutionary. For ten years she was closely watched by the Neighborhood Revolutionary Committee; she was constantly required to write reports confessing her "crimes" and had no personal freedom.

Worse, in order to demonstrate their revolutionary spirit, some Red Guards and even children went on the attack against individuals identified as "monsters and demons." Wen's story illustrates how the slogan inspired acts of violence, even among family members: "In the field the children of the prisoners followed the example of the Rebels and began beating their own fathers. One of them, a fourteen-year-old boy, carried a metal rod in his hand. He ordered the prisoners to stretch out their hands. One by one he slapped their palms with the rod while accusing them of being bourgeois because their hands were so smooth. This boy's father received his beating in turn. When I asked the boy later how he could strike his own father, he replied that he was only beating 'cow ghosts and snake spirits'" (Wen 1995, 15).

Ironically, when a person was labeled a "ghost" or "monster" and forced to undergo a series of physical and mental abuses, often he or she came to believe the charges and internalized them. For example, one interviewee told me that right before her mother committed suicide she announced to the whole family that she was, indeed, a monster and demon. In her will she advised her children to disown her for good, for she believed that she had done much wrong in her life. In a related account, Ji Xianlin, a well-known scholar and professor from Beijing University, recalls his experience in the "cowshed" (a place where the monsters and demons were incarcerated): "After being detained in the cowshed for a while, my brain began to be muddled and my mood was numbed. This is not a hell, but more than a hell. I am not a vicious ghost, but more than a vicious ghost. I feel like I am neither a human, nor a ghost" (Ji 1998, 176). Millions of innocent people were so physically and psychologically traumatized by torture and persecution that they lost their grip on reality and sense of who they really were.

As was the case with my father and countless others, the experience of being labeled "monsters and demons" was appalling and horrifying. Human beings were treated like animals and evildoers. In the process they were alienated and dehumanized. The slogan "Sweeping away all the monsters and demons" called for radical actions and left no room for sympathy or compassion for the accused.

"Destroy the Four Olds and Establish the Four News"
Slogans condemning traditional Chinese culture reached their apex during the Cultural Revolution. Any ideology or perception associated with traditional Chinese values was dismissed as a product of the "four olds" (old ideology, old culture, old customs, and old habits) and replaced with an ideology or perception associated with the "four news" (new ideology, new culture, new customs, and new habits). The slogan "Destroy the four olds; establish the four news" first appeared in a commentary in the *People's Daily* on 1 June 1966. In a speech at the assembly in celebration of the Cultural Revolution on 18 August 1966 Lin Biao repeated this theme, saying: "We must thoroughly strike down the old ideology, old culture, old customs, and old habits left by the exploitive class. We must reform any superstructures not suited to the socialist economic base. We must establish the authority of the proletariat, as well as establishing the new proletarian ideology, new culture, new customs, and new habits" (cited in Zhang and Li 1998, 402). Similar slogans soon appeared in the *Red Flag* attacking traditional Chinese values and practices with headlines such as: "Break Away from Old Ideology, Old Culture, Old Custom, and Old Habit" (vol. 11, 1966); "A New World Will Be Created by Condemning the Old World" (vol. 11, 1965); "Create a New World with a Proletarian World View" (vol. 11, 1965); "Establish with Great Effort Proletarian Power, Establish with Great Effort New Proletarian Ideology, Culture, Customs, and Habits" (vol. 11, 1966). With great frequency and intensity such slogans were disseminated throughout China, causing traditional Chinese values to give way to new cultural values aligned with "correct " political thought and class consciousness.

Like the slogan "To rebel is justified," the slogan "Destroy the four olds and establish the four news" was embraced with revolutionary zeal by the Red Guards. One wall poster from the Beijing No. 26 Middle School Red Guards made this clear:

> The present Great Proletarian Cultural Revolution must overthrow the old ideology, the old culture, the old customs, and the old habits: To rebel all out against the bourgeoisie is to completely smash the bourgeoisie, to establish the proletariat on a grand scale, to make the radiance of great Mao Zedong Thought to illuminate the

entire capital, the entire nation, the entire world. Armed with great Mao Zedong thought we are the most militant troops, the mortal enemy of the "four olds"; we are the destroyers of the old world; we are the creators of the new world. We must raise high the great red banner of Mao Zedong Thought, open savage fire on the "four olds," smash to bits imperialist, revisionist, and bourgeois goods and all things not in accord with Chairman Mao's Thought. (Schoenhals 1996, 212)

The slogan "Destroy the four olds and establish the four news" legitimized countless acts of destruction. Under this banner traditional Chinese signs, symbols, relics, and works of art were swept away. The destruction included changing old names, cutting hair and pants, ransacking homes, vandalizing cultural treasures, and desecrating temples.

The first symbols of traditional China to fall by the wayside were place names and family names. For example, in Bejing, *Changan* 長安 (Forever Peaceful) Avenue was changed to *Dongfang Hong Dajie* 東方紅大街 (Red Sun from the East Road); *Xiehe* 協和 (Peking Union Medical College) Hospital became *Fandi* 反帝 (Anti-Imperialist) Hospital; *Lantian* 藍天 (Blue Sky) clothes store turned into *Weidong* 衛東 (Defending Mao Zedong) clothes store. The same name-change fever continued in other cities. For example, as Liang Heng witnessed in Changsha, "Suddenly, 'Heaven and Heart Park' became 'People's Park,' 'Cai E Road,' named for a hero of the Revolution of 1911, became 'Red Guard Road.' The Northern Station where I had pushed carts for a day was now to be found on 'Combat Revisionism Street,' and a shop named after its pre-liberation capitalist proprietor became 'The East Is Red Food Store'" (Heng and Shapiro 1983, 68). According to Wen Zengde's description of Shanghai, "Students covered windows and walls with big-character posters and portraits of Mao. They tore down shop signs and street signs with old fashioned names. (For example, 'Prosperity Road' became 'Antirevisionist Street'; overnight, hundreds of stores formerly named 'Fortune' and 'Lucky' changed their names to 'East Is Red' and 'Revolution')" (Ross 1994, 86). Some people even changed their given names to demonstrate their revolutionary spirit. Typical revolutionary names were Wei Dong 衛東 (defending Mao Zedong), Zhong Dong 忠東 (loyalty to Mao Zedong), Wei Hong 衛紅 (defending the red), Xiang Dong 向東 (toward the East), Xiao Bing 小兵 (little guard), Ji Hong 繼紅 (inherit red), Zhi Hong 志紅 (determined red), and Ji Ge 繼革 (carrying on the revolution). Many children who were born during the Cultural Revolution were given these names as well.

The slogan "Destroy the four olds and establish the four news" was vague and ambiguous. No clear criteria were articulated regarding what constituted the four olds and what should be established as new. Even indoor plants and pet birds fell under scrutiny and were considered threats to the new order. One's physical appearance and attire also fell under the knife of revolutionary zeal. Women with long braids cut their hair short. The new style was known as "three-eighth style." It symbolized women's independence under communism, as 8 March was celebrated as International Women's Day. High-heeled shoes, skirts, and dresses, considered remnants of precommunist decadence and false consciousness, were outlawed. Men were not allowed to wear jeans or long hair. Some Red Guards enthusiastically participated in eradicating any trace of the old fours as reflected in dress and appearance. As Zhai remembers, "They stood on streets and stopped passersby to cut their narrow-legged pants and destroy their sharp-toed or high-heeled shoes. Girls' long braids were deemed feudal remnants and were cut by force" (1992, 92). For the ten years of the Cultural Revolution, Chinese men and women wore nothing but blue-colored Mao jackets or dark green army uniforms. Young women with long braids were rare. Femininity was considered bourgeois, and women were encouraged to dress as soldiers rather than as females.

In the interest of "Destroying the four olds," it was not uncommon for homes to be searched and ransacked. The Red Guards broke into wealthy family homes and confiscated or destroyed anything of value. Wang (1998) describes the scene inside his home during a Red Guard search: "Vases and other art pieces were smashed to pieces. All my diaries were taken away. . . . Most of my books of classics were taken away. Even my western suits, ties, my wife's traditional Chinese dress, and our photo albums were all taken away" (32). Some homes were searched repeatedly by different groups of Red Guards. In the name of destroying the old, the Red Guards burned books and traditional operatic costumes; destroyed temples, statues of the Buddha, and religious and cultural monuments; and looted family cemeteries of antiques and jewelry. As James Ross (1994) accurately observes, "The Cultural Revolution was driven by far more than Mao's thoughts and proclamations. It explored deep cleavages in Chinese society, and set off power struggle that virtually spread anarchy and destruction" (71).

Efforts to repudiate the old ideas continued and intensified with the official launching of the anti-Confucian campaign by the Gang of Four in 1974, two years before the end of the Cultural Revolution.[15] At that time the *Red Flag* began publishing articles denouncing Confucius and Confucian concepts. The assault on Confucianism in the pages of the *Red Flag* was unprecedented. The attacks were typically reduced to the form of CCP slogans and propaganda. Confucius and Mencius, once heralded as the great sages of ancient China, were demoted to the status of hypocrites and murderers, their philosophy equated with poison and deception. Examples of such slogans were: "Confucius and Lin Biao were both political swindlers" (vol. 3, 1974);[16] "Mencius is the trumpeter of the slave system" (vol. 7, 1974); and "Confucianists are bloody executioners" (vol. 12, 1974). The campaign not only targeted Confucius as counterrevolutionary but also attacked major Confucian doctrines, calling Confucius's "Golden Mean" notion "the philosophy of a political swindler" (vol. 2, 1974) and the concept of *ren* 仁 (loving, benevolence) "the fraud of hypocritical humanism" (vol. 2, 1974). Confucian teachings regarding self-restraint and the restoration of traditional values were identified as examples of "pulling history backward" (vol. 2, 1974). In the early stages of the Cultural Revolution the Red Guards had smashed Confucius's tomb and his statue in Qu Fu, his hometown. Such slogans oversimplified and effectively demonized Confucian ideology and traditional culture. Confucianism, once the standard for judging the merits of one's conduct in

Chinese society, had come under attack by Marxist revolutionaries as representing the epitome of class oppression.[17]

The slogan "Destroy the four olds and establish the four news" called for a radical transformation of Chinese culture and attempted to eradicate the traditional ways of thinking and doing things. As Markham (1967) asserts, "They [Chinese Communists] took the dichotomous view that the old and the new were locked in a death struggle and that one must die so that the other could live, rather than attempting to fuse the better features of the two" (438). Indeed, the damage done to Chinese culture and society under the weight of this slogan was unprecedented. In addition to the considerable violence and destruction wrought in its wake, the children of China who grew up during the Cultural Revolution know virtually nothing about traditional cultural values and ancient Chinese philosophy. The Cultural Revolution was indeed a cultural destruction and a national tragedy.

Slogans Eulogizing Mao Zedong
With the Communist takeover of China in 1949, Mao became more than the leader of China; he was elevated to the status of a savior of the Chinese people. Through Communist propaganda eulogizing Mao's character as well as his contribution to the overthrow of the old China and the founding of a new China, the cult of Mao was constantly reinforced. During the Cultural Revolution the glorification and mystification of Mao reached its apex.

Sources indicate that early on, the CCP had issued documents restricting any speech or action promoting leader worship (Li 1992, 355). In the first fifteen years of Mao's leadership he was recognized as a savior of the new China but was not worshiped as a god. However, during the first few years of the Cultural Revolution a series of articles published in the high-profile, government-sponsored media eulogized Mao as the "Red Sun of the Chinese people" and established him as the absolute, infallible authority of China (Yan and Gao 1986). According to Yan and Gao's account, Chen Boda 陳伯達 first coined the notion of the "Four Greatests," identifying Mao as the greatest teacher, the greatest leader, the greatest commander, and the greatest helmsman in his speech on 18 August 1966 at Tiananmen Square, when for the first time Mao received millions of Red Guards. Lin Biao and other trusted Mao followers subsequently began using the slogan in their speeches to promote Mao's cult status. Other popular slogans eulogizing Mao were the "Three Loyalties" (loyalty to Chairman Mao, loyalty to Mao Zedong's thought, and loyalty to Chairman Mao's proletarian revolutionary line) and the "Four Boundlessnesses" (boundless love, boundless loyalty, boundless faith, and boundless adoration for Chairman Mao). These slogans were shouted in public rallies by political leaders and the Red Guards, printed in all published media, and used frequently in public discourse. Similar slogans promoting the worship of Mao were "Establish Chairman Mao's absolute authority"; "Chairman Mao is the reddest sun in our hearts"; "Mao Zedong's Thought is our life root"; and "People all over the world love Chairman Mao." The most popular slogans of this type were "Long live Chairman Mao" and "Wish Chairman Mao ten thousand years of life." These two slogans were shouted at rallies and interjected at the ends of oral and written speeches. The first sentence Chinese first-graders were taught to write was "Wishing Chairman Mao ten thousand years of life." The first English sentence all middle-school students learned was "Long live Chairman Mao." One interviewee remembers a top news item of the time about a mute person whose first sentence uttered after being cured by acupuncture was "Long live Chairman Mao."

Chinese devotion to a great leader is deeply rooted in Chinese history and culture. The expressions *wan shou wu jiang* 萬壽無疆 (a thousand years of life) and *wan nian* 万年 (long life) first appeared in *Shi Jing* 詩經 (*The Book of Odes*). Composed around 700 B.C.E., it was one of the Chinese classics, sung as devotional lyrics during ancestor worship ceremonies for the king of Zhou dynasty (1027–770 B.C.E.)[18] as well as for every subsequent emperor throughout Chinese history, both in public and in private ceremonies.

During the Cultural Revolution the slogan "Long live Chairman Mao" was proclaimed in every part of China. One interviewee explained that when Mao's cult first began to develop he was critical of it and reluctant to use the slogans associated with it. However, he recalled, "after repeated exposure to the same slogans and images, I began to be convinced that Mao was the greatest and would live forever. I considered myself very lucky to live at this time in history." Another interviewee provided a different perspective: "I never believed that Mao would live ten thousand years and I don't think people around me believed it either. But we followed others and shouted the slogan anyway." Many people shouted these slogans, not because they believed in them but simply for the sake of protecting themselves from being accused of disloyalty to Mao Zedong.

Slogans of Mao's Quotations

The worshipful mythology surrounding Mao was more than merely a personality cult; it was also fed by devotion to his works and ideas. Mao's thought was propagated as an extension of Marxism and Leninism, applied to the Chinese situation through Mao's unique cultural and political lens. His theory was considered "invincible," "infallible" and of "boundless radiance" in its potential to transform every aspect of life. For example, the commentary in volume 11 of the *Red Flag* (1967) was titled "Mao Zedong's Thought Illuminates the Victorious Path of Our Party." Slogans in later issues of the *Red Flag* openly proclaimed Mao's omnipotence as well as his omniscience. Some examples are "Establish with greatest effort the absolute authority of the great leader Chairman Mao; establish with utmost effort the absolute authority of the great Mao Zedong's Thought" (vol. 16, 1967) and "Let Mao Zedong's Thought control everything" (vol. 1, 1969). Similar to Hitler's position in Nazi Germany, Mao was revered as a living god. His words were regarded as law and his Little Red Book as the sacred scripture.[19]

As soon as he was appointed the new defense minister replacing Peng Dehuai 彭德懷, who had been purged from the position because of his open criticism of Mao, Lin Biao launched a campaign within the army to "study and apply Mao Zedong's

Thought." In his speech to high-ranking army officials Lin Biao asserted the supremacy of Maoist ideology. In his words, "Studying the works of Mao Zedong is a shortcut to the understanding of Marxism" (Zhang and Li 1998, 358). In a later speech he reiterated, "We must raise highly the banner of Mao Zedong's Thought and take a further step in arming all soldiers with Mao Zedong's Thought and let Mao Zedong's Thought control everything" (360). To this end Lin Biao ordered the compilation and publication of the *Quotations from Chairman Mao,* which has become known as the Little Red Book. The book consists of excerpts from the five volumes of *The Selected Works of Mao Zedong.* During the Cultural Revolution it was circulated first in the army and then to the whole country. According to Zhang and Li (1998), between 1966 and 1968, 740 million copies of Mao's Little Red Book were published (367). The Chinese population at the time was 800 million. Thus, nearly every citizen carried a copy of the book. It became the bible of the nation, and Mao's words were often lifted out of context and made into slogans. Lin Biao told the nation, "Every word of Chairman Mao is truth; one sentence is worth a thousand sentences." He characterized Mao's words as *zui gao zhishi* 最高指示 (the highest directives), asserting that they "must be carried out whether one understands them or not" (361). Mao's utterances were printed on the front pages of all the newspapers, in school textbooks, on billboards, and on the Red Guards' leaflets. Further, they were recited by the Red Guards on streets, in stores, and on trains and buses.

One person I interviewed was in the second grade when the Cultural Revolution started. In order to help "disseminate Mao Zedong's Thoughts," he and a few others volunteered to read quotations from the Little Red Book on the bus. They started at one end of the bus route and took turns reading quotations to the passengers until the bus reached the opposite end. After a while these second-graders could easily recite many passages and could even identify the page numbers of certain quotations. Mao's words were often recited by a single person or a group as slogans to justify their actions. As Wang (1998) witnessed:

> If they [the Rebels] wanted to give a person a hard time, they would say, "Our great leader Chairman Mao teaches us that the most miserable moment of the counterrevolutionaries is the happiest moment of the people." If they wanted to justify beating upon a person, they would read [from Mao's quotations] that "Revolution is not a dinner party." If they wanted to apply a certain policy, they would read [from Mao's quotations] that "policies and strategies are the life lines of the Party." If they did not want others to use violence, they would say "Use words, not force." If someone from their own faction died of violence, they would recite Mao's saying "There is sacrifice in struggle; death is a common occurrence" (118).

Sometimes the use of Mao's quotations became absurdly nonsensical. For example, according to Feng Zhao's (1999) account, a "class enemy" once gave six ears of corn to six hungry women who were participants in the May Seventh Cadre School. The initial responses of these women to the man's kind gesture was to ask, "why has this class enemy sent us food? Is he trying to bribe us?" They went to the man with the Little Red

Books in their hands, threw the ears of corn back at him, and started reading a quotation from Mao: "Make trouble, fail, make trouble again, fail again . . . till their doom; that is the logic of the imperialists and all reactionaries the world over in dealing with the people's cause, and they will never go against this logic" (59). Through the lens of Mao's quotations the man's generosity was seen as an attempt to corrupt the revolutionaries.

Slogans eulogizing Mao elevated him to the status of a god, resulting in mass hysteria, blind faith, absolute obedience, and cultish behavior of all kinds. Fervent devotion to his words only and the absence of any alternative views made Mao the final arbiter of truth and knowledge and led to terrible acts of destruction and cruelty in his name.

A Rhetorical Analysis of Slogans

The slogans thus far identified served to raise class-consciousness, express the political goals of the CCP, and call for collective commitment in the furtherance of moralistic ideals. In addition these political slogans stirred the masses to radical thinking and action, dehumanized "class enemies," attacked traditional Chinese culture, and promoted the cult of Mao. Ironically, many of the slogans under consideration can be traced to traditional Chinese culture, yet they were used effectively in Communist China to dismantle traditional values, customs, and social relations.

Rhetorical Themes

From the previous exploration of types and functions of slogans, four rhetorical themes can be delineated. They are (1) radicalization, (2) alienation, (3) negation, and (4) mythmaking.

Radicalization. According to Ying-shih Yu (1994), "From the very beginning, Chinese Marxism was cast in the negative mold of May Fourth iconoclastic anti-traditionalism. Thus, it generated a radicalism of a highly destructive nature" (134–35). The destruction of traditional Chinese culture was gradually accomplished through the ideological campaigns of the 1950s and early 1960s, culminating in the Cultural Revolution. Mao (1940) believed that change in political and economic structures must coincide with the transformation of cultural norms and practices, and further, that a new culture could not be built without the total demolition of the old.

Radical thinking and action were promoted through such slogans as "To rebel is justified," "Sweep away all the monsters and demons," and "Destroy the four olds and establish the four news." These slogans inspired the Red Guards to ruthlessly attack anyone perceived as a class enemy while they relentlessly destroyed Chinese traditions. These slogans simplified theories related to social change, polarized reality into good and evil, and radicalized one's understanding of the old and the new. They provoked intense emotional responses and violent actions against anyone or anything considered a threat to the new communist order. In fact, the Cultural Revolution was nothing short of a cultural holocaust, in the wake of which China was left economically devastated and culturally deprived. While the "old fours" were systematically eliminated, nothing new rose to take their place.

Radical thinking and action were evoked through the use of war metaphors. Lakoff and Johnson (1980) discuss the use of war metaphor in the structure of an argument such as "attack," "defense," or "counterattack." They contend that such use of metaphor is emotionally loaded and has direct effect on thought and action. During the Cultural Revolution the use of war metaphor was pervasive; China became an ideological battleground where tactics and strategies were employed in fighting the enemies of the people. The battle required courage, determination, and sacrifice. Slogans such as "Never forget the class struggle," "To rebel is justified," and "Destroy the four olds and establish the four news" served to identify who the enemies were, what action should be taken against them, and why this action should be taken.

Alienation. The slogan "Never forget the class struggle" and other related catch phrases identified class as the sole criterion for organizing political reality, making moral judgments, and relating with other human beings. In traditional Chinese culture divisions were demarcated by wealth, education, and social status, while human relations were generally characterized by a high degree of harmony, tolerance, and respect for authority. Within the context of a Marxist analysis of class struggle each individual became identified with a particular class. The prevailing slogans of the time labeled the bourgeois class the evil enemy and the proletariat class the most revolutionary. Aspects of one's identity other than class status were totally denied. In this sense slogans related to class struggle created, in Burke's view (1969b), both a sense of being united in a common cause and, conversely, the experience of disassociation, alienation, and ostracism. In Havel's (1985) opinion, such slogans functioned as subliminal cues to acceptable conduct and values. They offered a panoramic view, reminding "where they are living and what is expected of them. [They tell] them what everyone else is doing, and indicate to them what they must do as well, if they don't want to be excluded, to fall into isolation, alienate themselves from society, break the rules of the game, and risk the loss of their peace and tranquility and security" (35–36). On the other hand, such slogans were also vague and ambiguous in meanings and definitions. Class enemies were identified in broad, ideological strokes or by subjective criteria. The notion of the four olds and four news left a lot of room for interpretation, as did the concept of rebellion. Out of fear people became willing to do whatever was necessary to prove themselves worthy members of the proletariat. Some even accused their friends, family members, and teachers of bourgeois or counterrevolutionary affiliations in order to establish their own political credibility.

Negation. Up to this point in the discussion we have looked at the elements of a text or medium that are considered significant. In Wander's (1983) terms, these are the "facts" of what is presented. The other side of the coin in the examination of rhetorical texts is "negation," or what is absent or being muted and objectified in the text or medium. Three aspects of negation can be identified from the slogans under consideration.

The first aspect is the negation of alternative ideological views. Chinese cultural and philosophical traditions are represented by several schools of thought, including

Confucianism, Daoism, Mohism, and legalism, with Confucianism as the dominant cultural ideology. Although Confucianism had been the target of bitter attack since the May Fourth movement in 1911, by Chinese intellectuals who considered its more conservative aspects obstacles to modernization, it was not completely condemned and censured until the Cultural Revolution. Chinese students who grew up during the Cultural Revolution were not taught Confucian philosophy in schools, nor were they exposed to it through social and public discourse. Instead they were taught an incomplete version of Western Marxism, combined with Mao's revolutionary ideas and the heroic mythology surrounding Mao's life and deeds.

Another aspect of negation was the suppression of diverse political views. Marxist-Maoist ideology was regarded as the only source of truth. Western ideas (with the exception of Marxism) were either considered not applicable to the Chinese situation or dismissed as bourgeois. This narrow interpretation of Western thought engendered dogmatism and isolationism on the part of the Chinese government and stifled the freedom of thought of the Chinese people. According to Dun Li (1978), an ideological commitment to a single doctrine or ideology is a form of imprisonment. The greater the commitment, the more imprisoned and dogmatic an individual, a group, or a nation will become. An interviewee offered an apt example of this: "The head of our department in the Chinese Academy of Social Science said to me after I told him that I was going to the United States to study ethnography, 'We are the best place for studying ethnography in the world and Marxist theories on ethnography are the best theories. What more do you need to learn? Why do you have to go overseas to study it?' I was very shocked at his arrogance and ignorance." Another interviewee lamented, "The Cultural Revolution taught us nothing but a bunch of Mao's sayings. We knew nothing about Western culture. I never learned who Einstein was, let alone other thinkers and theories. We were so ignorant and narrow-minded."

The third form of negation, according to Wander (1984), is dehumanization. The slogans centered around "Sweep away all the monsters and demons," effectively dehumanizing class enemies while legitimizing violent actions against them. Once people were labeled "cow ghosts and snakes spirits," they were treated like animals and evil creatures. The Chinese people were thoroughly indoctrinated with the notion that members of the bourgeoisie were poisonous to the revolutionary masses; the bourgeoisie were "parasites," "blood suckers," "vermin," and "stumbling blocks." By using these terms China's class enemies were treated as less than human and the extreme measures taken against them were deemed morally justified. Many people identified as inhuman members of the bourgeoisie were beaten, some to death, forced to commit suicide, or driven to labor camps. Their private property was confiscated, and family members were humiliated or executed. In sum, dehumanizing slogans legitimized violent actions and allowed one human group to demonize other human groups.

This rhetorical feature is reminiscent of Hitler's rhetoric used to justify the killing of the Jews by the Nazis. According to Koenigsberg's (1975) study of Hitler's *Mein Kampf* and his speeches, Jewish people were referred to as "parasites," "poison in the national body," and "noxious bacillus." They were considered "parasites" and "organic infesta-tion" on the body of Germany that must be removed. As Steven Perry (1983) points out, "The strategy of rhetorically renaming one's enemies in a conflict situation is a common one. It is done in order to depersonalize the enemy, to de-humanize him or her, and thus to ameliorate the prospect of extreme action against that enemy" (221). Just as the logic of disease metaphors justified the elimination of Jews, so the monster metaphors justified the beating and killing of class enemies in Communist China.

Mythmaking. According to Ernst Cassirer (1946), language can be divided into two functions, mythmaking and rationalizing, with mythmaking being more prevalent among humans. Myth, in Rowland and Frank's view (2002), has a transcendent fun-tion for a society and an individual. However, they also recognize that "Myth is often the [rhetorical] force motivating extreme actions, including terror" (297). Slo-gans related to the worship of Mao Zedong were mythmaking in the extreme that had induced hatred and violence. In the context of China's Cultural Revolution, the rhetoric of mythmaking was an appropriation of the traditional Chinese belief that the appearance of every great man was mandated by heaven. Thus, Mao's legitimate and absolute power should be granted without doubt. The purpose of such propa-ganda was to cultivate an attitude of absolute loyalty and obedience to Mao on the part of the Chinese people. Throughout Chinese history loyalty and obedience to authority have been considered the highest virtues. Like Mao, Chinese emperors of the past were typically the objects of cultlike devotion. While the "facts" or the syn-chronic ideographs used during the period under investigation established the cult of Mao, what was tragically negated was the critical-thinking ability of the Chinese people. Out of loyalty and devotion to Mao, and in defense of his teachings, millions of Red Guards burned cultural relics, looted stores, searched people's homes without warrants, and beat those considered members of the bourgeoisie, traitors, and counter-revolutionaries. As Stanley Milgram (1969) has pointed out, when obedience to authority "serves a malevolent cause, far from appearing as a virtue, it is transformed into a heinous sin" (2).

Slogans aggrandizing Mao, along with the phenomenon of sloganizing Mao's quo-tations, played out in what Burke (1966) would call "a living drama," involving actors whose motives were consciously or unconsciously communicated. According to Ernest Bormann (1972), a group fantasy is created through the communication pro-cess in a dramatic setting, which leads to a rhetorical vision that provides a coherent and mythic view to hold the public together. Slogans eulogizing Mao and sloganized Maoist quotations functioned in this way. While Mao worship resembled the mass mobilization and personality cults of other totalitarian societies such as Nazi Germany and Stalin's Russia, it can also be traced to the Chinese tradition of emperor-veneration, although the scale of mass hypnosis during the Cultural Revolution was unprece-dented in Chinese history. Similarly, the practice of memorizing and reciting Mao's quotations is akin to the way Confucian classics were learned in the past.[20] As Lucian

Pye (1985) points out, the great man ideal "is an amplification of the Confucian model of the father as the ultimate authority in the family" (185). The cult of Mao was in many ways consistent with traditional Chinese culture rather than a radical departure from it. Typically, slogans eulogizing Mao are characterized by frequent use of superlatives, parallel structures, and number abbreviations such as "three loyalties" and "four boundlessnesses." These linguistic features help facilitate memorization, allow group chanting practices, and intensify myth and mass hysteria.

Impacts on Thought and Action

Ideological indoctrination through the use of slogans in political discourse does not simply reflect but also shapes thought and culture. Slogans that promoted imported Marxist ideology in public discourse during the Cultural Revolution effectively altered Chinese thought and destroyed traditional Chinese culture. Slogans promoting class struggle, rebellion, and destruction were in open defiance of traditional Chinese regard for holistic thinking, social stability, and harmonious relationships. For example, the hallmark of the traditional Chinese way of life is *zhongyong* 中庸 (the mean or middle way). Confucius considered *zhong yong* the highest virtue, both in running the government and in interpersonal relationships (Confucius, *Lun Yu* 6.29.66). The concept of *zhong yong* puts a high value on keeping one's equilibrium and avoiding extremes in perceiving reality and making judgments. Class distinctions, characterized by dualistic categorization and dichotomized thinking, forced the Chinese people to bifurcate themselves into proletarian and bourgeois classes and relate to one another either as political comrades or enemies. With sole emphasis on the Marxist-Maoist theory of class struggle, Chinese thinking became increasingly politicized and polarized. Mao's popular quotation "Either the east wind prevails over the west wind or vise versa. There is no compromise in the path we take" was the guiding principle. "There is no middle way" was a commonly heard expression during the Cultural Revolution.

The Confucian notion of obedience to authority was successfully exploited by Mao and his followers. Slogans deifying Mao and idolizing his words led the Chinese people to place absolute faith in Mao and his ideology. The most alarming persuasive effects of such rhetoric were thought-deprivation and the loss of conscience, which allowed Mao's followers to believe that their actions, such as treating political enemies as less than humans, were justified and that the political reality (class struggle) they were facing was real. One interviewee remarked, "I felt so lucky at the time that I did not have to think. Chairman Mao had thought out everything for us. I had complete faith in him in directing China into a bright future." Another interviewee shared this story: "When my grandma saw our neighbor, a so-called class enemy, being tortured, she could not bear it and told us that it was a sin. We children immediately shut her up and accused her of lacking the proletarian consciousness." In examining his own thinking process during the Cultural Revolution, Ba Jin (1987) admitted, "I had developed a habit of listening to the authority; I had been used to disseminating and inculcating the words of the authority" (255). He lamented, "I have been enslaved for ten years" (377). "I never used my own mind to think" (379).

Another core value in traditional Chinese culture is *he* 和 (harmony), and the guiding norm in interpersonal relationships has traditionally been *yi he wei gui* 以和爲貴 (valuing harmony). Compromise had historically been the strategy for managing interpersonal conflicts. However, slogans such as "Down with class enemies," "Sweep away all the monsters and demons," and "To rebel is justified" fanned the flames of interpersonal tension, hostility, and hatred among the Chinese people, making compromise a thing of the past. As Feng Zhao (1999) observed, "That was the time period when hatred was cultivated. People set up enemies and made every effort to annihilate them. This could happen between strangers as well as between family members" (19). An interviewee revealed, "The word that was engraved in my mind during the Cultural Revolution was *dou* 鬥 (fight, contend). The phrase I remember the best was 'You gain great happiness by fighting against heaven, against earth, and against other human beings.' It was my motto during those chaotic years. I never learned how to get along with other people. Even to this day, I often find myself picking a fight quickly and being enraged easily. It could be my personality, but this *dou* mentality has greatly affected my personal life and professional career."

According to Arendt (1963), when language becomes banal and commonplace one's ability to think is impoverished. Further, the lack of conceptual clarity leads directly to the "banality of evil" on a broad scale. In the Chinese context, the heavy-handed and pervasive use of political slogans in both public and private settings has contributed significantly to a general thoughtlessness still evident in today's China. In my opinion, repeated exposure to slogans such as those examined in this chapter, coupled with absolute obedience to authority, served to create mystification, blind faith, and polarized thinking; they induced thoughtless actions, making evil a "banal" act easily performed at a nationwide scale.

A Rhetorical Analysis
of Wall Posters

As a medium of conflict there can be little doubt of the utility of tatzepao [dazibao, or wall posters]. Millions of youths were mobilized and tens of millions of tatzepao were produced promoting the Cultural Revolution.

Barry Broman, "Tatzepao: Medium of Conflict
in China's Cultural Revolution," *Journalism Quarterly*

The Chinese language has its long tradition and is rich and colorful, but during the CRM [Cultural Revolution movement], it was reduced to the polemical vocabulary and a set of dogmatic clichés. This language created, advocated, and greatly appreciated by the CRM rhetoric played an important role in mobilizing the masses, arousing the rebellion, and enhancing the morale of the revolutionary fighters.

Shaorong Huang, "Power to Move the Masses in a Mass Movement,"
in *Chinese Perspectives in Rhetoric and Communication*

Dazibao 大字报, literally "big character poster," was the most popular means of written communication during the Cultural Revolution. In fact, the Cultural Revolution was both ignited and prolonged by the practice of making *dazibao*. Participation in reading and writing *dazibao* became a national showcase and an integral part of the rhetorical experience to millions. These posters were generally three feet wide by eight feet high and were printed in stylized calligraphy. During the Cultural Revolution many individuals and families were adversely affected by wall posters. In the course of conducting my interviews some informants shared with me their memories of the ubiquity of wall posters and their devastating impacts. One interviewee witnessed members of the Red Guards posting *dazibao* all over his school principal's body. Others told stories recounting how shocked and scared they were at the sight of wall posters containing charges against their parents, and how their lives were forever changed by those experiences. In tracing the history of *dazibao,* identifying their rhetorical themes and features, and discussing their impact on Chinese thought and culture I use the English translation "wall posters" and the Chinese term *dazibao* interchangeably.

History of *Dazibao*

To create a wall poster all one needs is a big piece of paper, a brush, and ink. Wall posters can be authored by a single person or a group of people. Some are signed by the authors, and others remain anonymous. They can be drafted onto smaller papers first and then copied onto big posters or written directly on poster-size paper. Wall posters are usually posted in specially designated areas of schools, institutions, factories, or farms. However, at the peak of the Cultural Revolution *dazibao* could be found almost everywhere. A wall poster can take the form of a proclamation, announcement, denunciation, congratulation, satirical prose, comic strip, cartoon, confession, letter of accusation, or news report. The two most widely used forms during the Cultural Revolution were accusation and denunciation.

The use of wall posters in China for public communication was not an invention of the Communist Party. Records show that as early as the fifth century B.C.E., Deng Xi 鄧析, an innovative thinker and the best-known lawyer in ancient China, carved his views on judicial issues and his challenges to the orthodoxy of the Zhou dynasty (eleventh century B.C.E.–770 B.C.E.) on bamboo slips and hung them on walls for the public to read. In ancient China people were not allowed to see the emperor in person or to hear his voice directly. Wall posters were the only means of communicating royal edicts, pronouncements, and orders between the emperor and his people. Wall posters could also be used by local governments to make announcements, disseminate information, or describe the appearance of criminals at large. It is not surprising that Mao Zedong was a strong advocate of the use of wall posters. He reportedly wrote his first poster when he was seventeen years old expressing his political views in support of Sun Yat-sen.[1] *Dazibao* served as an effective instrument in the Chinese Red Army for the dissemination of communist propaganda and for purging party officials during the 1942 rectification campaign. Poon (1978) contends that Soviet methods for disseminating propaganda had heavily influenced China's widespread use of wall posters. According to Poon, "In Soviet Russia, posters in hand or typewritten form were tacked up on the walls of clubs, factories, institutions, or collective farms" (185).

Since the beginning of Communist rule in 1949 wall posters functioned as an efficient medium of mass persuasion. In fact, Mao asserted in 1958 that *dazibao* was "an extremely effective new weapon. It can be used in cities, the countryside, factories, cooperatives, stores, government offices, schools, army units, and in the streets. In short, it can be used wherever there are masses. It has been widely used [in the past] and should be used consistently [in the future]" (190–91). By 1957 Mao had endorsed the use of *dazibao* along with *da ming* 大鸣 (speaking out loudly), *da fang* 大放 (voicing one's views freely), and *da bianlun* 大辩论 (holding great debates). He advocated that these practices be adopted by ordinary people as means of criticizing party officials and encouraging participation in political activities. Intellectuals in particular were urged to speak out and voice their opinions regarding the party's weaknesses. They were told that their criticism of the party would be genuinely welcomed and would help further the cause of China's economic development.

However, when many intellectuals and non-Communists used this public medium to criticize party policies and express their dissenting views, Mao began to fear that the party would lose control and that there would be a political uprising against the party similar to uprisings in Hungary and Poland at that time. Soon Mao launched the anti-rightist campaign. Those who had voiced dissenting views were identified as rightists and arrested and imprisoned or sent to remote areas to do hard labor. The criteria for defining a rightist were not clear. However, in a speech on the steps and strategies of the anti-rightist movement Mao estimated that 10 percent of intellectuals would fall into the rightist category. In order to ferret out these rightists, institutions and organizations applied the 10 percent ratio to their faculty or staff. As a result 552,877 people were accused of being rightists; 99 percent of those were wrongfully charged when the constructive criticism they offered was interpreted as having antiparty motives (Fu Jin 1998). For example, Liang Heng's mother was labeled a rightist simply because she criticized her boss's unfair administrative behavior. She was sent to a labor camp in a remote area, lost her job, was ostracized by her colleagues, and was divorced by her husband (Heng and Shapiro 1983).

The first wall poster of the Cultural Revolution appeared on the campus of Beijing University on 25 May 1966. The poster was signed by six faculty members from that university; the primary author was Nie Yuanzi, from the philosophy department. A week later the text of the poster was published in the *People's Daily*. The poster questioned the motives of three university administrators for not encouraging students and faculty members to participate in the Cultural Revolution. Charging the administrators with "repressing the masses and the revolution," the poster further accused them of "acting entirely against the Party's Central Committee and Mao Zedong's Thought" (Tan and Zhao 1996, 22–24). The poster characterized the Cultural Revolution as an "ideological struggle" and accused the administrators of being the "obstacles to the revolutionary cause." The language was harsh, provocative, and emotionally charged. At the end the authors expressed their commitment to the Cultural Revolution and made an impassioned call to action: "To all revolutionary intellectuals, now is the time to fight. Let us unite and raise high the great flag of Mao Zedong's Thought. Let us unite under the leadership of the Central Party Committee and Chairman Mao. [Let us] expose all kinds of plots and monstrous tactics and controls. [Let us] annihilate all the monsters and demons completely, thoroughly, and entirely; annihilate all Khrushchev-like revisionists, and carry out until the end the socialist revolution! Defend the Party Central Committee; Defend Mao Zedong's Thought! Defend the proletarian dictatorship!" (24).

This first poster not only ignited the fires of the Cultural Revolution but also established the tone, the structure, and the use of language for all subsequent wall posters. Sloganeering and the rhetoric of agitation became the main features of wall posters during the Cultural Revolution, and the antagonistic and polarizing language of the first one was repeated in many that followed. Wall posters were heralded as the best fighting form for the revolutionary masses and a major manifestation of political struggle. Whoever is against using them is against the revolutionary masses, the authors of the first poster asserted (Nie et al. in Tan and Zhao 1996, 23). Xizhe Wang (1996) recalls that when he and his high school classmates first heard the reading of Nie's *dazibao* over the radio they immediately began organizing themselves and writing their own wall posters. In his words, "That was a sleepless night. The campus was filled with *dazibao* the next day. I wrote my own *dazibao* entitled 'There Is No Quiet Desk in the Number Seventeen School' [Wang's school] and posted it in front of the gate of the school" (3).

While some doubts had been expressed by intellectuals and party officials regarding Nie's argument and her use of *dazibao,* Mao responded to this poster with great enthusiasm and support in his "Bombard the Capitalist Headquarters: My Big-Character Poster": "How well written was the nation's first Marxist-Leninist wall poster and the commentary from the *People's Daily!* Comrades, please read this poster and the commentary again." Mao further asserted: "They [the administrators from Beijing University] are on the side of the bourgeois, favored capitalist dictatorship, which has pushed down the fervent movement of the proletarian Cultural Revolution. [They] turned right to wrong, confused black and white, encircled the revolutionaries, suppressed different views, and executed 'white terror'" (Tan and Zhao 1996, 28).

Mao's poster was displayed in the Zhong Nanhai compound (the residential and office area of China's top-ranking officials) on 5 August 1966 and was broadcast the next day. It effectively fanned the flames of revolutionary zeal and encouraged the use of *dazibao* as a powerful weapon against class enemies. Three days after Mao's *dazibao* was first broadcast, a proclamation known as "The Sixteen Directives" was ratified at the eleventh plenum of the Eighth CCP Central Committee. The fourth of the sixteen directives stated: "Make the fullest use of big-character posters and great debates to argue matters out, so that the masses can clarify the corrective views, criticize the wrong views, and expose all the ghosts and monsters. In this way the masses will be able to raise their political consciousness in the course of the struggle, enhance their abilities and talents, distinguish right from wrong and draw a clear line between the enemy and ourselves" (Schoenhals 1996, 36). The entire document was published in the *People's Daily* on 9 August 1966, heralding the official start of the "Great Proletarian Cultural Revolution." In this way *dazibao* was officially sanctioned as the most effective means of achieving the goals of the movement. Subsequently the use of wall posters became widespread. The scale of production was unprecedented, far surpassing that of Soviet Russia. On 17 January 1975 at the Fourth People's Congress the practice of making wall posters, in combination with *da ming* (speaking out loudly), *da fang* (voicing one's views freely), and *da bianlun* (holding great debates), was established as a constitutional right granted to all citizens of the People's Republic of China.

Such official sanctions generated a flurry of wall-postering activity, and soon wall posters covered campuses in Beijing and filled public wall space throughout the country. Chu, Cheng, and Chu (1972) described the massive scale of the phenomenon:

"Soon after Chairman Mao Tse-tung [Mao Zedong] posted his famous tatzepao [*dazibao*] . . . mainland China was literally covered by the Big-Character Posters. They were posted in schools, factories, dormitories, on walls and buildings so high that the Red Guards had to use ladders to reach them, in population centers like Peking and Shanghai, as well as in remote villages close to the border of Burma. Millions of Chinese took part in writing them. Millions more read them, studied them, discussed them, and criticized them. The extent of participation and the intensity of involvement in this mass movement seems to have had no parallel" (1).

During her 1967 trip to China, Barcata (1967) observed that "these messages [on wall posters] are mainly exhortations to follow the sublime thoughts of Mao" and that wall posters merely "act as circulars which inform, advise, urge, and criticize" (31). However, as political struggles among factions intensified and as the Red Guards became more fanatical, the function of wall posters was increasingly to humiliate and denounce party officials and humiliate the accused rather than simply to share information. They began to be used to spread rumors, intensify conflicts, evoke hatred, and threaten and bully people into submission. Wall posters were also used for confession or self-criticism, in response to charges or as a way to demonstrate one's "true revolutionary spirit." In essence reading, writing, and quoting from wall posters became national pastimes and political obligations during the Cultural Revolution, to the great detriment of the Chinese people and nation. *Dazibao* was indeed a powerful weapon on the battleground of the Cultural Revolution from which no one emerged unscathed and many lost their lives, their loved ones, or their sanity.

Rhetorical Themes of *Dazibao*

Although wall posters were everywhere during the Cultural Revolution, not many of them have been preserved. Consequently the main source of posters for this analysis is a collection of *dazibao* compiled by Fan Tan and Wumian Zhao and published in Hong Kong in 1996. Other examples were taken from Red Guard publications issued during the Cultural Revolution. The third source is memoirs and interviews. In the course of examining many examples of wall posters from these sources, three rhetorical themes emerged: (1) moral/ethical appeals; (2) Mao cultism; and (3) conspiracy theory.

Moral/Ethical Appeals

Nearly all wall posters have clear themes and goals. One common theme is the condemnation of class enemies, typically pointing out their evil motives and condemning their wrongdoings. For example, in a Red Guard wall poster addressing the nation Liu Shaoqi and Deng Xiaoping were identified as the most dangerous of all class enemies. The poster claimed, "For a long time, they [Liu and Deng] held important posts in the Party and nation, but they formed their own bourgeois headquarters in order to fulfill their own wicked ambitions. They are always hostile to Mao Zedong's Thought, have attempted to prevent the study of Mao's work, and have plotted against Chairman Mao, the reddest sun in our hearts" (Tan and Zhao 1996, 69). Once charges were leveled and accusations made, any words used to humiliate and curse the perpetrators were considered justified. This moral justification, through the legitimizing agency of language, was replicated in countless wall posters. For example, when students were encouraged to create wall posters denouncing their teachers, many were not sure at first what "crimes" to accuse their teachers of. However, once they were indoctrinated to think in terms of polarized categories of good versus evil, proletarian versus bourgeois, and Marxist-Leninist versus revisionist, students became confident of their ability to write *dazibao*. A former Red Guard recalls one of her experiences:

> I proposed to several students that we write a big-character poster about Yuying [the teacher]. They all supported the idea and gave me the job of drafting it. I thought for a long time about what "cap" [charge] would be proper for her. What counted as proletarian and capitalist? What was Marxist-Leninist and revisionist? I was never too sure. By watching others, though, I concluded that all the good things, such as loving our country and its people, doing one's job well, and being selfless and progressive were proletarian or Marxist-Leninist, and all the bad things one could think of were capitalist or revisionist. Thus, to denounce Yuying's capitalist and revisionist behavior, all I needed was to find a few of her previous faults. (Zhai 1992, 63)

On the basis of these "previous faults," the student accused her teacher of "teaching in a capitalist way" and "being anti-proletarian-democratic."

The cornerstone of the Cultural Revolution was the shared political understanding that everything deemed proletarian was moral and ethical while everything deemed nonproletarian was evil and harmful. This formula could even be applied to a person's hairstyle. Hairstyles considered bourgeois or revisionist were regarded as harmful to society and strictly prohibited. Liang (1998) recounts the following example of a wall poster seen in front of a barbershop: "'Only heroes can quell tigers and leopards / wild bears never daunt the brave' [Mao's poem]. For the cause of the Cultural Revolution, this shop will not cut hair that parts from behind, or in the middle, or that is less than one inch short, as these hair styles are nonproletarian. The shop does not provide hair oil, gel, or cream. The shop does not provide hair blowing or temple shaving services for male comrades, nor perms or curling hair services for female comrades" (125). The practice of starting a poster with one of Mao's poem was a common feature of poster writing, employed both as a stylistic device and as a justification to legitimize the action.

Moral/ethical appeals were a primary rhetorical theme in classical Chinese rhetoric, especially within the school of Confucianism. From the beginning of the Communist takeover of China in 1949, communist propaganda attempted to eradicate the influence of Confucianism. During the Cultural Revolution, Confucianism was severely condemned and bitterly attacked since it represented the four olds. Ironically, Maoist propaganda co-opted the Confucian model of moral/ethical appeals in an effort to mold the Chinese masses into selfless members of the communist state capable of sacrifice and devotion to the cause of communism. While the Confucian moral standard was *ren* (loving, benevolent), the communist moral standard was belief in and conformity to communist ideology. To meet this standard one had to be loyal to Mao and think and act in strict accordance with Mao's dictates. Any sign of disloyalty in thought or deed caused one to be labeled a "class enemy."

Mao's version of communism was articulated in many wall posters. For example, a poster criticizing Deng Xiaoping said the following: "It is the belief of the Communist Party headed by Chairman Mao that the goal of communism is to eradicate all the classes and societies with class differences. Mao's communist society is one in which all people have communist consciousness and quality; it is a society with advanced production methods. To reach these goals, [we] must strengthen the proletarian dictatorship, widely engage in class struggle, and develop the people's revolutionary thinking." Deng's version of communism, on the other hand, emphasized a better material life, symbolized by "a dish of stewed beef with potatoes" (Tan and Zhao 1996, 162). According to the authors of another wall poster (Red Guards from Beijing), "These are two drastically different views, just like the difference between water and fire. This is the struggle between two classes, two roads, and two ideologies. One [Deng's version] is to return to the capitalist road, toward the darkness, and the other [Mao's version] is the road to communism, leading to brightness" (162).

This type of moral absoluteness required conformity to Mao's version of truth, loyalty to Mao, and actions in accordance with proletarian ideology. Nearly all wall posters established such criteria for drawing lines between friends and enemies and between good and evil. In his book *A Rhetoric of Motives* (1969b) Kenneth Burke dissects the "moralizing process" of rhetoric in all socialization discourse (39). Through Burke's scrutiny of such moralizing processes in the rhetoric of Nazi Germany (1941) and in the context of Christian conversion (1961), he identified common ground in the practice of "foretelling the future" or promising a good life. Burke argues that the moralistic/prophetic appeal offers a compelling persuasive power for conversion to new beliefs. Similarly, in classical Chinese rhetoric the moralistic/prophetic appeal was employed with great effect in public and private persuasion. *Tian Ming* 天命 (the Mandate of Heaven) has been used in every dynasty of Chinese history to legitimize a new rule and justify the overthrow of the previous regime. In Communist China the notion of the "Mandate of Heaven" was replaced by the notion of "inevitable outcome of history." Speaking and acting according to proletarian ideology was believed to further the progressive force of society. This would automatically lead to a prosperous nation and a better life. Wall posters employed moralistic and prophetic language to defend the proletarian cause and denounce the bourgeoisie. To disagree with the Marxist-Maoist version of reality was to run the risk of having one's motives called into question. One would be accused of trying to "pull history backward." On the other hand, it was taken for granted that Mao's version of communism was mandated by human destiny and that following Mao's directive was to conform to the proletarian ideology. In this sense Mao successfully appropriated the traditional concept of *tian ming* in promoting his own ideological agenda.

Mao Cultism

Accusations or charges made in wall posters were often accompanied by sentiments eulogizing Mao as a savior, expressions of extreme loyalty to Mao, and fanatical pledges to carry on the revolutionary cause at all cost. For example, a group of Red Guards wrote:

> We, the Red Guards, are one of those rebellious, revolutionary organizations. When the black gangs of Liu Shaoqi cracked down on us, Chairman Mao saved us and supported us. In the critical moment when Liu and Deng's revisionism harmed us, Chairman Mao again rescued and liberated us. We have made serious mistakes. But we have boundless love for Chairman Mao, boundless loyalty to Chairman Mao. . . . Since Chairman Mao has called upon us to pick up our courage and fight again, we are determined to unite with many other revolutionary rebels. . . .We do so to make Chairman Mao proud of us. We must complete the task Chairman Mao has set for us. (Tan and Zhao 1996, 40)

Rhetorical flourishes such as the above appeared in millions of other wall posters. In such posters Mao was portrayed as a living god. His words were regarded as commandments for a noble cause. Faith in him could not be questioned. The Red Guards conducted themselves like crusaders, knocking down any heresy that did not conform to Mao's ideology.

Moreover, nearly every wall poster used Mao's quotations, poems, and new directives as justification for their accusations and action. For example, a wall poster attacking Peng Zhen, the former mayor of Beijing, began: "Our beloved Chairman Mao taught us, 'Whenever overthrowing a power, the first thing to do is to create public opinion to pave the way for the new ideology. The revolutionary class follows this rule; the counterrevolutionary class does the same.' The counterrevolutionary revisionist clique headed by black gang Peng Zhen was supported by Liu Shaoqi behind the scenes. They had plotted counterrevolutionary coup d'etat, aimed at subverting the proletarian dictatorship and restoring capitalism to China" (Tan and Zhao 1996, 288). The poster then listed the publications that were once under the control of the municipal government, describing these publications as poisonous arrows aimed at the heart of the party and Mao. In this case Mao's quotations and directives were used as major premises from which to draw conclusions.

As mentioned previously, Mao's poetry also appeared on wall posters. The poem most often cited was "With power to spare we must pursue the tottering foe. Do not copy Xiang Yu [who did not kill all the enemies and finally was killed by them], and do not seek idle fame." Mao wrote the poem in 1949 when the People's Liberation Army (PLA) occupied Nanjing, the headquarters of the Nationalists who were defeated by Mao's army. The poem called on the PLA to crush the Nationalist government completely and without mercy. It was appropriated in reference to the struggle against class enemies during the Cultural Revolution. At the beginning of the wall poster attacking Zhao Ziyang, the former head of Guangdong Province, this popular poem was quoted. It was often followed by cultish expressions of unqualified devotion to Mao, such as the following: "The boundless radiance of Mao Zedong's Thought lightens the revolutionary masses who have been mobilized. After over a year of battle, we finally overthrew the capitalist headquarters, headed by China's Khrushchev, smashed through the bourgeois counterrevolutionary lines and ferreted out Zhao Ziyang, the biggest capitalist roader in Guangdong Province. Zhao has become as filthy and contemptible as dog's dung. We need to raise even higher the great flag of Mao Zedong's Thought, and follow closely Chairman Mao's great strategic plan. . . . Let Guangdong become a scarlet Guandong under the guidance of Mao Zedong's Thought" (Hong Dong in Tan and Zhao 1996, 383). Here the action of completely knocking down Zhao Ziyang fulfilled Mao's call for "thorough annihilation" of the enemy. In all the posters of the time Mao's words were worshiped as absolute truth and infallible guidance in every aspect of life. For example, a poster titled "Fight for Bringing the Natural Sciences into the Era of Mao's Thought" began: "The people's revolution under the guidance of Mao Zedong is the locomotive of history's progression! The unprecedented Chinese Proletarian Cultural Revolution heralds a new era in the history of humankind. The world has entered a great new era of the Shining Flag with Mao Zedong's Thought. The sun rises from the East, sending a myriad of rays. Mao Zedong's Thought has illuminated the direction of the Natural Sciences with rays of sunlight, providing a radiant shining prospect" (Announcement of Scientific Revolution 1967, 1). Here, Mao is compared with the sun and his thought equated with a radiant sunshine covering and directing all aspects of human life. Cultish sentiments related to Mao were intensified through slogans written at the ends of wall posters. Typical slogans of this type were "Long live invincible Mao Zedong's Thought! Long live Chairman Mao" and "Long live and long long live Chairman Mao!" Slogans of this nature further escalated the revolutionary frenzy while reinforcing blind faith in Mao.

According to Hsia (1972), the cult of Mao was established in an ideological, as opposed to a religious, context because the deification of Mao was based on the belief that his thought represented the most advanced ideology and best served the interests of the proletarian. Wall posters such as those already examined effectively established Maoist ideology as the authoritative and invincible truth. Conversely, any deviance from Mao's thought would be ferreted out and severely punished. In the interest of defending Mao and furthering the cause of his revolution, wall posters functioned as powerful weapons on the ideological battleground. Words were used as bayonets to pierce through the hearts of class enemies. Innocent people were attacked, human rights were consistently violated, and a nation was destroyed.

Conspiracy Theory

One of the most destructive purposes of wall posters was to expose the "ulterior motives" and "unknown crimes" of those who disguised themselves as true revolutionaries. By this means class enemies were identified, denounced, and punished. For instance, one of Liu Shaoqi's daughters wrote a wall poster denouncing her own father as a liar and a person of "wicked ambition." She cited historical examples of Liu blocking the advocacy of Mao Zedong's Thought and attempting to elevate his own image above Mao's. She accused her father of using a "rightist line" while pretending to be a leftist. In one paragraph in which she accused her father of being "an absolute hypocrite," she charged: "Liu [referring to her father by his proper name] always thinks of himself first. He is extremely selfish and self-serving. However, in front of his comrades, he pretends that he lives a plain life" (Tan and Zhao 1996, 77). Typically the person who did the exposing was close to the accused either through family ties or a working relationship. It was expected that such a person would know "the truth" behind the revolutionary facade and thus would be credible in presenting the evidence. The practice of exposing one's own family members, friends, or colleagues through wall posters was common during the Cultural Revolution. The wall posters my mother received were written by her family members and friends. One interviewee recalled how her best friend exposed and denounced her own father (the head of a province) as a capitalist roader by means of a wall poster and then read the poster at a denunciation rally. Exposing family members and friends as class enemies served to prove one's loyalty to Mao and the party as well as to proclaim one's innocence. Sometimes the exposer was anonymous, signing the wall poster *geming qunzhong* 革命 群众 (revolutionary masses). This practice was accepted as a means of protecting the accuser from retaliation on the part of the accused. It also created a climate in which accusers were not held accountable for the accuracy of their accusations. This practice left ample room for the fabrication of charges or unfounded indictments.

In a manner reminiscent of what happened to my father, overnight party officials, formerly in good standing and with impeccable communist credentials, were identified as "hidden enemies" within the revolutionary movement and accused of waiting for an opportunity to restore capitalism to China. To persuade the public that the accused were hidden class enemies and to justify the denunciations, phrases such as "the most hidden peril" and "the worst potential plague" were employed in wall posters against them. The accused were described as "acting against the red flag by holding a red flag" or as being "the most dangerous enemy under the proletarian dictatorship." They were charged with "engaging in double-dealings, overtly agreeing but covertly opposing, forming their own Party, attempting to establish their own independent state, and pulling away from the proletarian revolutionary headquarters led by Chairman Mao" (Tan and Zhao 1996, 69). For example, Tao Zhu, a former member of the standing committee of the Political Bureau of the CCP, was accused of being a "typical counterrevolutionary double-dealer, always playing double-faced tricks, speaking one thing and thinking another, and appearing to be a human in day light while turning into a ghost in the darkness." Further, "He speaks in a human voice in public and talks in a ghost tongue in private. He always plays political trickery and seeks personal gains" (201). Party officials such as Tao Zhu were labeled "big careerists" and "big conspirators." Many wall posters bore these epithets or similar slogans. Some examples include "Look Closely at the Ugly Soul of [the accused]," "Uncover the Skin of [the accused]," and "The Ugly Scandal of [the accused]." Wall posters of this nature

enjoined readers to open their eyes and learn to recognize the true faces of these enemies. Once they were identified, it was legitimate and justified to denounce them
thoroughly and completely. The common exhortation was "to smash them into the
ground, step one thousand feet on their bodies and never let them stand up again as
long as they live."

The examples of posters cited above were mostly targeted at high-ranking officials.
However, similar conspiracy-theory-inspired posters could be found at the lower
levels. For example, one of the false charges leveled against my father was that he concealed his despotic, landlord family background, and because of this he was considered
the "most dangerous enemy." Liang Heng and Judith Shapiro (1983) offer a similar
wall poster denunciating another "hidden enemy":

> Although Li Xiao-Xiong is an old Party member, he wears his Party cloth to dis-
> guise his true mission. Before Liberation, he was an active reporter for the KMT's
> [the Nationalists] *Central Daily,* and he volunteered to stay behind as a spy when
> we routed Chiang Kai-shek's dogs and they fled to Taiwan. Every day he gathers
> information for them and works against us from within. As a proofreader, he has
> had many opportunities to show his hatred of the Party, as on the occasion when
> he deliberately turned the character "ten thousand" upside down. But our Great
> Leader Chairman Mao will live ten thousand and ten thousand years despite such
> pernicious spies. Down with Li Xiao-Xiong!!! (52)

Liang Heng was shocked when he read the poster, for he had always believed that the
man being accused had a glorious career as an underground party member and was
dedicated to the party's cause.

Many children growing up during the Cultural Revolution had to read *dazibao*
denouncing their own parents and were traumatized by the experiences. For example,
Liang Heng described his feelings after reading a *dazibao* calling his father a "hidden
enemy": "[E]very word engraved itself on my heart with a blazing knife, every phrase
struck me with a blow that was even greater than terror. I would never believe the
ground was steady again" (Heng and Shapiro 1983, 53). One interviewee recounted a
similar experience: "After I finished posting a *dazibao* denouncing our teacher with a
group of Red Guards at school, I went to my mother's work place to see her on my
way home, only to find that the entire building was covered with posters charging my
mother with various crimes. She was accused of being a traitor and a criminal. I was so
terrified and could not believe my own eyes. At that point, Mother came over to me
and asked me to go home. She was crying and telling me that she was not a true revolutionary and that I should never come to see her again. She was quickly pulled away
by the Rebels. A few weeks later, she committed suicide."

The children of people identified as class enemies carried psychological wounds of
a deep and pervasive nature. One minute their parents were beloved and respected;
the next they were vicious and evil enemies of the people. These children typically felt
betrayed by their parents, but at the same time they were confused, humiliated, and
grief-stricken. Some even wrote wall posters against their own parents. Some were

overburdened by their parents' alleged "crimes." Their self-esteem plummeted, and they became bitter toward their parents and society. Many were ostracized by their peers and the community, and suffered physically and mentally in subsequent years.[2] For example, the traumatic experiences of my family during the Cultural Revolution continue to haunt me in my dreams to this day.

In the climate in which conspiracy theories flourished, many party officials and innocent individuals were identified as enemies of the revolution. Unsubstantiated rumors, unwarranted charges, personal attacks, and relentless persecutions were commonplace. Similar conditions existed in Stalin's Russia and Nazi Germany, also with devastating effects. Fitzpatrick (1999) notes that a conspiratorial mentality had always characterized the Soviet Communist Party. Party members were relentlessly required to "be vigilant not only against the enemies without, but also the enemy within" (194) who had secretly penetrated the party. They were constantly encouraged to be suspicious of their fellow citizens, in particular fellow party members. According to Fitzpatrick, it was this mentality along with other factors and events that led to the Great Purge of 1937–38. The hunt for hidden "enemies of people" and "spies" focused primarily on the Communist elite and led to millions of executions and wrongful persecutions. In the case of the Nazis, Burke (1941) describes the process by which Hitler rationalized the extermination of Jews. According to Burke, Hitler first "essentialized his enemy" and then charged them with being cunning and seducing the Aryans. He made constant reference to the "Jewish plot" and "conspiratorial Jews" (167).

Rhetorical Styles of *Dazibao*

General Characteristics

As both a traditional and a modern medium of public communication in China, the wall posters in evidence during the Cultural Revolution had four characteristics. First, they were an easy and convenient way of voicing private views, complaints, blame, and accusations in the public arena. The issue of whether such accusations were true or false was totally left to the judgment of the reader. Second, the language used in wall posters tended to be harsh, provocative, and aggressive. The writing of wall posters was compared with engaging in a battle in which pens and ink were the weapons. For example, in a proclamation by a Red Guard group known as *weidong* (Protecting Mao Zedong), the authors describe themselves as "The weidong fighters, wielding their pens like knives, like rifles, and poised as if to command the wind and the clouds." These "weidong fighters" announced that they were launching "an all-out expose, all-out denunciation, and all-out settling of accounts with the heinous crimes and filthy counter-revolutionary revisionist trash" (Schoenhals 1996, 207–8). Third, since anyone could write a wall poster against anyone else, public discourse was no longer the monopoly of a few intellectual elites. Ordinary people and intellectuals alike used similar argumentative styles, played the same language games, and employed similar linguistic devices. According to Bredeck (1992), language establishes the rules of the game in the creation of social reality; "[a]s the number of 'players' grows, the 'rules' become increasingly compelling" (65). During the

Cultural Revolution every literate member of Chinese society became a participant in this language game. Anyone who could read and write could follow the rules of engagement and be part of the collective orgy of self-expression. Finally, virtually everyone could participate in the writing and plagiarizing of wall posters and took no legal or ethical responsibility for what they wrote. The authors of wall posters could say anything in attacking others. The use of wall posters to spread unsubstantiated rumors, assault a person's character, and ruin a person's reputation was common, and those who were targeted by wall posters received no legal protection.

A common political activity during the Cultural Revolution was the copying of wall posters. This was done in the name of learning how to be a revolutionary. As a result the format for writing *dazibao* became standardized in terms of structure and use of language. Three specific rhetorical features evident in selected wall posters can be identified: (1) organizational structure; (2) expressions of emotion, aggression, and profanity; and (3) the use of metaphors.

Organizational Structure

A common type of reasoning found in wall posters is syllogistic reasoning, with the implied or stated premise being "those who follow Mao are good people and those who disagree with Mao are bad people." The rhetorical devices for introducing the general (oftentimes moral) principles or premises used in *dazibao* range from the quotations and poems of Mao Zedong to abstract notions of class struggle and ideological justification. The minor premise could be the various political crimes a person committed in defiance of Mao or various accusations ranging from an "unrepentant capitalist roader" to a "hidden spy and traitor," a "counterrevolutionary," a "conspirator and plotter," or a "revisionist" and beyond. These charges could be newly invented or could stem from derogatory labels used by the official media. The reader could easily draw a conclusion that the person is guilty based on the moral criteria. To justify the charges or accusations, wall posters also employed an inductive reasoning process that entailed listing "evidence," "crimes," "conspiratorial behavior," and "evil motives." The purpose of presenting the evidence was never to question the major premise but rather always to confirm or verify it. The most elaborate and impressive wall posters were those that claimed to present new evidence and uncover the "ulterior motives" and "political crimes" of the accused, in order to justify the accusations leveled against them.

For example, in a wall poster attacking Zhu De, the president of the People's Congress, Zhu De was first labeled a "counterrevolutionary revisionist." He was then charged with "plotting to usurp the party and the army, and being a time bomb hidden at Mao's side." Zhu De was further accused of "constantly opposing Mao's correct path, promoting a bourgeois military, exuding a lasting poison, and committing heinous crimes" (Tan and Zhao 1996, 387). To prove these charges and accusations, the authors of the poster proceeded with evidence listed in chronological order: from 1928 when Mao and Zhu first joined each other in the Jinggangshan Mountains, where Zhu did not listen to Mao's advice, to 1961 when Zhu endorsed an open door policy and supported a free market economy. Zhu was portrayed as always "singing a different tune" from Mao. The term *yongyuan* 永遠 (always) was a frequently used term in *dazibao* of this sort. The alleged opposition to Mao could have been in reference to a mere disagreement with Mao, while the charge of plotting to subvert the party and Mao's authority may have been mere fabrication. Such exaggerations and outright fabrications were not uncommon.

Furthermore, a target person's family background could be considered "proof" for the person's "counterrevolutionary motives." Most high-ranking officials came from wealthy family backgrounds. Commonly wall posters written against them exposed these backgrounds or personal histories in order to discredit them. For example, a wall poster denouncing Deng Xiaoping began with: "The ghost, Deng Xiaoping, was born into a family of bureaucrats going back many generations, the family of a local tyrant, and the family of a feudal landlord." The poster then traced Deng's family three generations back and exposed the wrongdoings of each generation. The poster even named his wife, his cousin, and his brother and accused them of various "crimes" as well. The poster concluded with: "Comrades! Deng Xiaoping, the number one capitalist roader within the party, came from a reactionary family background of bureaucrats, local tyrants, and feudal landlords. He has long been in opposition to Chairman Mao and to the party and has been engaging in evil activities of counter-socialism. The cause for such action can be traced to his social and class roots" (Tan and Zhao 1996, 154). According to this syllogistic reasoning process, one's political stand is determined by one's social and family background, despite any and all appearances to the contrary. Liang Heng offered an example of a wall poster targeting his father with an argument presented in this fashion:

> That Liang Shan opposes the Party and Socialism is only natural. Let's investigate his history. His father was a doctor who came from Zhejiang to Hunan through tricking his "private patients" out of their money. So Liang Shan learned this skill from his family. When he was young, he eagerly entered the KMT's [the Nationalist Party] Youth League. His ex-wife is a Rightist, and she certainly became a Rightist under his influence. Then he saw by what happened to her that it won't do to oppose the Party openly, and he used articles and poetry to try to undermine it secretly. So his injury to the Revolution is even greater than his wife's. Chairman Mao teaches us, "Sham is sham, and the mask must be stripped off." Now the Great Proletarian Cultural Revolution is stripping off Liang Shan's skin to reveal his true appearance!!!!! (Heng and Shapiro 1983, 53)

Even though at times the "evidence" presented appeared to be far-fetched in confirming the charges, it was worded in such a way as to connect the person in question to the "high crime" of antiparty and anti–Chairman Mao affiliations. Obviously in these cases inductive reasoning based on evidence and examples was used to explain and reinforce deductive reasoning (the premise), rather than to draw conclusions or testify the general principles. This rhetorical feature can also be identified in persuasive activities of the ancient Chinese (Kroll 1985–87; Lu 1998b).

In sum, a common structure of the wall poster typically involves three primary components. The first component generally described the political situation as positive, glorified Mao, and expressed assurance in the success and moral justification of the Cultural Revolution. Rhetorical devices might have included a quotation from Mao, an excerpt from one of Mao's poems, a proverb, or simply extravagant expressions of praise. The second part lists charges and accusations against those identified as class enemies. This part employs a deductive reasoning process, which starts with subheadings enumerating the alleged "crimes" ranging from a counterrevolutionary activity to being a traitor, a revisionist, or a capitalistic roader. Each heading was followed by a presentation of the evidence, typically a combination of historical examples, narratives, and testimonies. If the person being accused was from a rich and exploitative family background, it was assumed that he or she had evil motives and was undoubtedly a class enemy. The third component of wall posters reinforces the absolute correctness of Mao's thought, expressing absolute loyalty to Mao, effusive wishes for his longevity, and hatred for all "class enemies."

Expressions of Emotion, Aggression, and Profanity
While moral appeals and rational arguments appear to be major rhetorical devices in wall posters, the use of emotional appeals, or pathos, cannot go unnoticed. In fact, because the poster was not an official medium, the expression of emotions was unrestricted. Emotional appeals were made through slogans professing boundless love and absolute loyalty to Mao. Such appeals were in sharp contrast to slogans expressing deep hatred for the target person, class enemies, and the capitalist system in general. The desired rhetorical effect was achieved through the use of high-sounding words, the repetition of certain phrases, and the generous use of exclamation marks. Here is an example of a *dazibao* that evokes emotion and hatred:

> Tao Zhu, the most heinous counterrevolutionary and revisionist, has been ferreted out by the revolutionary Rebels and masses. This is a matter of immense satisfaction. This is a great victory for the invincible Mao Zedong's Thought! This is a great victory for the proletarian revolutionary line headed by Chairman Mao! This is a great victory for the Proletarian Cultural Revolution! Let us raise highly the great flag of Mao Zedong's thought, waving the magic emblem in denouncing the revolutionary revisionist Tao Zhu. Let's knock him down, make him collapse and step on his body. We will never let him turn around in this lifetime!" (Tan and Zhao 1996, 184)

Emotionally charged expressions, as in the example above, typically appeared at the beginning and end of a wall poster. Posters tended to begin with Mao's poem and emotive expression of the political situation. For example, a wall poster denouncing three party officials began with "The four seas are rising with clouds and waters raging. The five continents are rocking with wind and roaring with thunder [Mao's poem]. Under the talented leadership of our great commander, Chairman Mao, the first Proletarian Cultural Revolution in human history is breaking through the wind and waves and advancing to victory. The roar of guns saluting undisputed victory vibrate throughout the universe. Red flags are waving all over the motherland. The situation is better and better!" (Tan and Zhao 1996, 466). This kind of language and format are still all too familiar to many interviewees. They recalled their own rhetorical experiences of using Mao's poetic verses to extol the virtues of the Chinese Communist nation, cities, and schools in the format illustrated above.

Linguistically the use of superlatives permeated the practice of wall-postering. Nearly all posters contained expressions such as "Chairman Mao is the reddest and reddest sun in our heart. We have absolute belief and admiration for Chairman Mao. Whoever is against Chairman Mao, we will smash them into pieces" (Tan and Zhao 1996, 400). Common types of superlatives are *da* 大 (big) and *zui* 最 (absolute, most). When *zui* combines with *da* or other adjectives, a higher level of superlative is created in order to enhance the expression of loyalty to Mao and aggravate condemnation of class enemies. Condemned high-ranking officials were often described as "*zui weixian* (the most dangerous) class enemies" and "*zui da* 最大 (the biggest) capitalist roaders within the Party." Chairman Mao is worshiped as "*zui hong* 最紅 (the reddest) sun in our hearts." Mao's quotations were considered *zui gao zhishi* 最高指示 (the highest commands). These expressions were often repeated in order to further intensify the feelings of love for Mao and hatred for class enemies.

John Locke ([1894] 1959) contended that humans create their own meanings of words in efforts to persuade others. Moral words, in particular, can be easily misconstrued by readers as they carry different meanings to different groups of people (106–7). Distortion of meanings by switching neutral terms to negative expressions permeated wall posters. For example, in a poster targeting a person's membership in an organization, the person was accused of "sneaking into" rather than "joining" the organization. In another example, a critique of Mao's status as infallible of truth was labeled "heresy" rather than a different view (Tan and Zhao 1996, 235). A comment on Mao's old age and critique of his cult status were labeled "counterrevolutionary speech" rather than honest opinions (361). Views on military strategies different from Mao's were dismissed as "historical mistakes" (388). A formal appearance, in a diplomatic context, was described as "base" and "coy" (532). According to Van Dijk (1995), the use of negative terms to describe political enemies was not "merely the nominal result of an evaluative categorization and identification, but also an ideological decision, given the political position of the speaker and her or his group" (259). Since the person targeted in a wall poster was by definition a "class enemy," it was ideologically congruent to switch the meanings of words in order to frame the enemy in a negative light.

Expressions of verbal aggression through politicized and polarized language were common in wall posters, intensifying the feelings of anger, hatred, and fear. For example, one poster charged that Deng Xiaoping "committed monstrous crimes against the Party and the Chinese people and deserves to be cut into thousands of pieces and burned in boiling oil" (Tan and Zhao 1996, 159). In another, Luo Ruiqing "must be knocked to the ground with a foot stepping on his body; never let him rise up again" (317). At the end of the *dazibao* condemning Peng Zhen, the former mayor of Beijing, the authors wrote, "Let us cast the most condensed bullets and melt the hottest flame through the accumulation of our thousands and thousands of streams of hatred, and fire them at counterrevolutionary, revisionist cliques and their behind the scenes supporters, Liu Shaoqi and Deng Xiaoping, and burn them to ashes!" (507). Such violent language filled the pages of *dazibao*. At the end of a wall poster titled "Severe Punishment for the Soviet Revisionist Bastards" the authors wrote: "Heavily punish the Soviet revisionist bastards! Down with the Soviet revisionists! Hang Brezhnev! Smash to pieces the dog head of Kosygin!" (297). These incendiary words helped spread "Red Terror" at the time and accelerated the use of violence in general. In his memoir of the Cultural Revolution, Ji (1998) commented ironically in this regard, "I have read thousands of wall posters. They are all the same. However, some are 'vivid' and 'fresh' to the eyes. For example, reference to 'chopping someone to pieces' or 'burning someone in hot oil'" (39). The wall poster that condemned my father cursed him with many dreadful varieties of death. Unfortunately, the experience of being on the receiving end of this kind of violent rhetoric was extremely common during the Cultural Revolution.

Clearly, the use of violent language leads to violent action. In the context of the Cultural Revolution the causal relationship between violent language and violent actions is not difficult to demonstrate. For example, Youqin Wang (1986) has recorded the persecution and death of Bian Zhongyun, the principal of a girls' high school in Beijing. The persecution started with posters accusing Bian of various kinds of counterrevolutionary crimes. One poster, which was placed on the door of her home, said, "Bian was a Rightist who slipped through the net. She has a close relationship with the former, corrupt, municipal government. She is a member of a big black gang, a member of the daring, anti-Party vanguard. She is a big bastard of the bourgeois dictatorship of revolutionary teachers and students, a big despot. Damn you! Behave yourself. Otherwise we will not let you off!" Another poster was pasted in her bedroom and said: "Dog despot, snake Bian. Damn you, Listen! If you dare to swagger around and lord it over the working people, we will beat your dog muscle, dig out your dog heart, and chop off your dog head. Damn you if you want to rise again! We will kill your grandchildren, wipe out your family root, and smash you to pieces." Agitated by such violent use of language, the Red Guards beat and tortured Bian to death. In the letter Bian wrote to the party leaders before her death she gave a more detailed description of the torture she received: "Out of the extreme anger and hatred, I was beaten and tortured for four to five hours. I was made to wear a dunce cap, bend my body to ninety degrees and kneel down. I was beaten with fists, kicked with feet, and pinched with fingers. I was tied up with ropes. They poked my back with rifles, filled my mouth with mud, covered my face with mud and spit all over my face and body" (Youqin Wang 1996, 22).

Curse words and taboo language had became hallmarks of revolutionary phraseology and were frequently used in *dazibao*. The term *hundan* 混蛋 (bastard) was widely used during the Cultural Revolution in reference to class enemies. The curses *jiangui* 見鬼 (go to hell), *jian yanwang* 見閻王 (meet your death), and *Ta ma de* 他媽的 (damn you) were commonly used against class enemies. Female Red Guards were especially prone to cursing as a way of demonstrating their revolutionary spirit. Frequent use of such language had become part of their public discourse symbolizing masculinity and toughness. One interviewee recalled an occasion when a group of female Red Guards got on the bus she was riding and started reading an announcement. In her words, "They ended every sentence with '*ta ma de*.' In the end, I could not remember anything they announced but the pounding sound of '*ta ma de*.'" Another interviewee described a situation in which her revolutionary comrades were using profane terms but she had trouble uttering them. She recalled the moment: "I was very nervous. On the one hand, I was afraid that I would be perceived as not revolutionary enough if I did not join the crowed. On the other hand, I had never used such words in my life and I just could not utter them. I accused myself of lacking revolutionary feelings for the proletariat and of not having enough hatred of 'class enemies.'" On a similar note, a male interviewee expressed his struggle with the use of violent language and profanity: "I was brought up to use mild and polite language in my speech. When I first saw the violent and profane language used in wall posters, I was very uncomfortable and could not accept it. For a long time I remained silent and had trouble writing *dazibao* using such language. It was the norm at the time. I always thought that the reason I could not come up with such language was that I lacked the proletarian sentiments and needed to examine myself closely."

In response to the concern that such aggressive use of language and violent actions, on the part of the Red Guards, was a violation of basic human dignity and decency, a commentary from the *Red Flag* offered the following justification: "The Red Guards have ruthlessly castigated, criticized, repudiated and exposed the decadent, reactionary culture of the bourgeois Rightists to the bright light of day, landing them in the position of rats running across the street and being chased by all. So they shout: 'this violates human dignity.' To speak frankly, we should not only violate their 'dignity' but knock them down so that they can never rise up again" (in Schoenhals 1996, 47). Thus the use of aggressive language and profanity was praised, sanctioned, and indirectly endorsed by Mao. Actually, Mao sometimes used profane language in his poems and writings, and profanity sometimes appeared in the official media denouncing "enemies of the people." Consequently, the Red Guards were conditioned to believe that class enemies deserved to be verbally abused and humiliated; violence done to class enemies was justified in the name of furthering the revolution. As Dittmer (1979) observes, through acts of violence "the young rebels experienced a sense of euphoria and omnipotence" (217).

The Use of Metaphors

The use of metaphors is a recurring rhetorical technique in classical Chinese literary and historical texts. War metaphors and animal metaphors are particularly popular in *Zhan Guoce* 戰國策 (Intrigues). The concept of *pi* 譬 (metaphor) was coined by Hui Shi 惠施 (380–20 B.C.E.), who defined the use of metaphor as "using what people know to convey and explain what people do not know" (SY 11.8.471). While metaphor was an effective persuasive device in the social and political context of ancient

China, metaphor used in wall posters during the Cultural Revolution mainly served to dehumanize and objectify class enemies, to intensify hatred, and to provoke violent acts. War metaphors and animal metaphors were common in wall posters during the Cultural Revolution, just as they had been in classical times. For example, members of the CCP were instructed to "use pens as knives and guns" to "fire at the capitalistic headquarters" and "hold on to the revolutionary front line." In addition, the Cultural Revolution was described as "the fifth campaign" launched by Mao, following other campaigns in the history of the CCP against the Japanese and the Nationalists. The difference in ideology between Maoists and anti-Maoists was characterized as a "battle" between true revolutionaries and capitalists or revisionists. True revolutionaries must "attack and aim at revisionists" (Tan and Zhao 1996, 330). "If enemies do not surrender, we will annihilate them all" (331). Further, Mao's directives were characterized as "strategic plans" capable of "smashing class enemies to pieces" and "tearing up the enemy's front line" (410). The ultimate aim of the Cultural Revolution was to "gain a thorough victory" over counterrevolutionary forces. Toward this end, the Red Guards must "bravely and tenaciously fight against class enemies" and "pledge to fight to the death in defending Chairman Mao and the proletarian headquarters" (411). In this ideological battlefield, "There will be no withdrawal of soldiers in winning a thorough victory" (172).

The pervasiveness in the use of militaristic terms during the Cultural Revolution was largely attributed to Lin Biao, who was credited for coining war metaphors in the following passage from a speech: "The battlefield of the Cultural Revolution cannot call a cease-fire. This is a war without that option. There may be a cease-fire in a regular war, but not in an ideological battle. The approach to this ideological war is different. Sometimes it is a huge battle; sometimes, it is a small fight. At certain times, there must be huge battles; at other times, there can be small fights. Regardless of whether we are engaged in a huge battle or a small fight, [we] must fight on until the end" (Huo Wang 1998, 269). These metaphors have served to add force and violence to the drama of the Cultural Revolution. Lakoff and Johnson (1980) discussed the use of war metaphors by U.S. presidents to distort realities and constitute a license for policy change. War metaphors used by Lin Biao served to direct thoughts and actions of sacrifice and martyrdom in the ideological battle and granted a license for violence and brutality.

War metaphors used in wall posters have made their way into everyday discourse. For example, the phrase "strategies and tactics" was commonly used in reference to completing a task and in the context of foreign relations. A close friend was referred to as "a buddy in the same battlefield." The act of finishing a task was considered "a battle of fortification." Metaphors of war even made their way to the dinner table. For example, it was common to hear people say "annihilate all the dishes" when encouraging others to finish all their food. According to Perry Link (1999), no ruler had been as successful as Mao in transferring public language into private life and, by so doing, accomplishing the unification of language and thought.

The second classification of metaphors dehumanizes class enemies by calling them "cow ghosts and snakes spirits." For example, Wang Guangmei, wife of Liu Shaoqi, was described as a "monster" and a "snake" (Tan and Zhao 1996, 239) and "a dog drowning in the water" (86). Those who had different views from Mao were labeled "members of a dog pack" (153). Terms such as *gou* 狗 (dog), *zhu* 猪 (pig), and *du she* 毒蛇 (poisonous snake) were commonly used against class enemies. In fact, some Red Guards identified their organization as *da gou dui* 打狗队 (the dog beating team) and called the children of class enemies *gou zaizi* 狗崽子 (sons of bitches).

Sometimes war metaphors and animal metaphors were combined in a single directive. For example, one of the announcements put out by the Red Guards said the following: "Now we must fire at the capitalistic running dogs, monsters and demons. We must target the residue of old ideology, old culture, old custom, and old habit. We must smash anything that does not conform to Mao Zedong's Thought" (Tan and Zhao 1996, 36). The use of these dehumanizing metaphors had the effect of justifying the violence done to class enemies. Zi-Ping Luo (1990) provides an account in her memoir that illustrates this point: "It was still late August, when one day the door to the Spanish house was flung open and the two spinsters were forced to kneel in front of it. Dragged from her wheelchair, the old mother was told to join them, but she was so feeble that she collapsed into a heap on the terrace. A mob yelled and screamed, banging their fists on every available surface. The old women were called 'bloodsucking leeches,' 'maggots,' and 'intestinal parasites'" (28). In her examination and analysis of metaphors used to dehumanize migrant workers in hundreds of *Los Angeles Times* articles, Ana (1999) concludes that metaphors employed in political discourse facilitate conceptual change, embody the worldview of the users, and reveal the dominant mapping of political issues. Indeed, the metaphors used in Chinese wall posters defined the political reality in China as a life-or-death struggle between the forces of good (proletariats) and evil (class enemies). War metaphors set the stage for bloody battles, gave license to torture and kill, and inflamed the soldiers' fighting spirits. Animal metaphors disparaged human beings, legitimized cruelty, and allowed for the ruthless treatment of innocent individuals.

Effects of *Dazibao* on Chinese Thought, Culture, and Discursive Practices

The scale of the use of wall posters as means of mass communication and political mobilization during the Cultural Revolution is unprecedented in human history. The practice provoked revolutionary frenzy, encouraged lying and the spreading of rumors, and ruined the lives of many innocent people. Moreover, it gave rise to a new way of thinking, a new culture, and a new language in China; its influence can be easily recognized to this day.

Thought patterns. The traditional Chinese character, according to Lin Yutang (1936), consisted of the qualities of serenity, patience, pacifism, and conservatism, among others. Influenced by a combination of Confucian, Taoist, and Buddhist elements, an educated Chinese person was "always characterized by his common sense, his love of moderation and restraint, and his hatred of abstract theories and logical extremes" (104). The traditional Chinese mind was considered intuitive, holistic, and generally nonreactive, having been influenced by Daoist philosophy and Buddhist religion (Nakamura 1964). However, communist propaganda, with its discursive forms of deductive reasoning and moral absoluteness, had effectively altered the way Chinese people thought: from holism to polarization; from valuing practical wisdom to idealistic abstraction; and from a commonsense orientation to dogmatic adherence to communist ideology. Both Western influence (except Marxism) and traditional Chinese culture were considered harmful. They therefore had to be totally eradicated. Views and opinions were to conform to Mao's teachings, which were regarded as the absolute moral truth. Any deviance from Maoist ideology was considered bourgeois, evil, and absolutely wrong. The average laid-back, patient, peaceful, and conservative Chinese as described by Lin Yutang was turned into an aggressive, irritable, hostile, and radical version of his or her former self. A sleeping giant (as Napoleon referred to China) had in the twentieth century awakened to a kind of mass hysteria, following the examples of Soviet Russia and Nazi Germany.

The moral appeals characteristic of Chinese wall posters created a thought pattern of absolute certainty. Although *dazibao* was a communication medium employed by the Red Guards and embraced by the masses, the discursive style was copied from that of the official communist media. As in the discourse of the official media, all wall posters started with presuppositions (counterrevolutionary charges, abstract and high-sounding statements, or expressions of loyalty to Mao) that were taken as truth and never questioned. With the emphasis in the writing of wall posters on moral absoluteness and blind acceptance of the major premise, Chinese thinking became increasingly dogmatic, essentializing, and polarized. One interviewee put it this way: "The language of the Cultural Revolution created polarization, narrow-mindedness, and dogmatism caused by a combination of Utopianism and feudalism. This was the result of long term isolation and closed-mindedness. All we knew at the time was 'class struggle.' We were so ignorant and arrogant, just like frogs trapped in a well, naively believing that the size of the sky is just as big as the size of the well." In other words, the Chinese people were deprived of their critical-thinking abilities as their linguistic options were severely curtailed by the force of the dominant ideology. Woodward and Denton (2000) put it well: "Power in language is exhibited in many ways: arguments grounded in language that legitimates the rule of those who govern, appeals to moral authority, or narratives of preferred behavior" (74). Here the authors highlight the importance of taking note not only of what is said but also of how it is said. They also point out the interrelatedness of power and language.

Wall posters were also used by political dissidents, such as Zhang Zhixin, Yu Luoke, and Wei Jingsheng, to express their disagreement, defiance, resistance, and critical views. Dissidents were severely punished by being tortured, put into prison, or even sentenced to death. Zhang Zhixin, who questioned Mao's and Lin Biao's theories of class struggle, was literally muted and then executed. Yu Luoke, who challenged the theory of "blood lines," was imprisoned and finally put to death.

Social relations. The original intention in allowing the use of wall posters was to express different views as means of preventing corruption and the abuse of power. This intention was lost, however, in the face of mass hysteria and an authoritarian state that required its citizens to listen and obey one voice and one version of the truth. Instead *dazibao* was used as a weapon of personal attack, causing chaos and ruining people's lives. Even though the practice of *dazibao* was banned after the Cultural Revolution, it is still commonplace today to take revenge or deliberately ruin someone's future through the writing of an anonymous letter. One interviewee offered such an example: "During the election of representatives for the People's Congress in Harbin, the office of Internal Discipline received many anonymous letters exposing the 'corporate crimes' of the candidates. Then the office of Internal Discipline took a long time to investigate the case and prove the person's innocence. However, the date for the election was already passed by the time the investigation was concluded and the candidate missed an opportunity for a promising political career." Anonymous letters, an offshoot of wall-postering, have engendered suspicion and distrust, wounded colleagues and friends, ruined relationships, and destroyed many lives.

Confucianism emphasizes the moral well-being of the individual, understood as the basis for the moral well-being of the family and society. Confucius categorized people into one of two categories: *junzi* 君子 (gentlemen) or *xiaoren* 小人 (base persons). However, Confucian doctrine instructs the individual on how to become a cultivated, loving, mature, and responsible person; it does not teach hatred of those who held different views. Further, Confucianism advocates scholarly achievement, respect for authority, and filial piety; it counsels against cultish behavior of any sort. Chinese communist discourse co-opted various elements of Confucian doctrines, such as respect for authority in the interest of furthering its goals. At the same time communist discourse violated many Confucian principles, especially those related to maintaining harmonious human relationships through tolerance and respect.

Cultural and linguistic behavior. In a sense *dazibao* of the Cultural Revolution embodied the spirit of Lu Xun 魯迅, with an essay style characterized by its brevity and sharp, aggressive language. In his "Talks at the Yan'an Forum on Literature and Art," Mao ([1942] 1965) praised Lu Xun for his skillful use of "burning satire and freezing irony, cast in the form of an essay, to do battle" (92).[3] Indeed, Lu Xun, a writer and literary critic in the 1930s, represented the epitome of the antitraditionalism that emerged after the May Fourth movement in 1919. In Lu Xun's (1970) view, an influential essay should function like a javelin or dagger, piercing into the soul of humanity and the dark side of society (36). For him, writing literature meant taking part in a battle, with the writer as a fighter against the feudal tradition. According to Zhao, "Lu Xun had promoted the spirit of 'cutting to the bone' and 'flogging the cur that's fallen into the water.' He encouraged a soldier's mentality of facing the cruelty of life and not being afraid of blood. He embraced the spirit of criticism with cold eyes and was not afraid of fighting alone in a battle" (Tan and Zhao 1996, 19). An admirer of Lu Xun, Mao regarded him as a national hero and exemplary fighter of the pen. In Mao's ([1940] 1965) words, "Lu Xun breached and stormed the enemy citadel; on the cultural front he was the bravest and most correct, the firmest, the most loyal and the most ardent national hero" (372). Lu Xun's militant style of writing had its artistic merits but also played a significant role in radicalizing the Chinese mind to its greatest extent since the second part of the twentieth century. His influence contributed to the destruction of Chinese culture during the years of the Cultural Revolution.

Traditional Chinese culture values harmonious and loving relationships. From an early age children were taught to avoid direct confrontation with others, be polite and save face at all costs and help others to do the same, and practice restraint in expressing emotions. Children learned to follow a set standard of etiquette in their use of language. Aggressive tendencies and profanity would be frowned on and socially sanctioned. Unfortunately, the Marxist/Leninist/Maoist rhetoric of the Cultural Revolution created a public discourse that placed high values on confrontation, expressions of hatred, and a general rebelliousness of spirit. This value orientation was reflected in the writing of wall posters and became an important part of the socialization process for Chinese children, especially those growing up during the Cultural Revolution. Many interviewees reflected on their current use of language and communication style at home and in the workplace, acknowledging a lingering tendency to be confrontational and argumentative. While working in U.S. companies they often find themselves being perceived as uncompromising and militant when dealing with conflict and interpersonal issues.

In his study of contemporary Chinese political behavior, Lucian Pye (1992) notes that "the dominant emotion of modern Chinese politics has been a preoccupation with hatred coupled with an enthusiasm for singling out enemies" (67). Pye's observation is, unfortunately, borne out by ample evidence. In my examination of the use of language in Chinese wall posters expressions of hatred, aggression, and profanity were common and ubiquitous. Attracted by the communist utopia and swayed by a crusading spirit, the Red Guards (most of them very young) waged personal attacks, humiliated political opponents, dehumanized "class enemies," and in general let out their pent-up feelings of hatred. Such political behavior was largely guided by the use of deductive reasoning, moralistic appeals, and the dehumanized language of wall posters. As Anita Chan (1985) points out, the climate engendered by the Cultural Revolution "created competitive aspirations to prove personal devotion, instilled exaggerated needs to conform to political orthodoxy, and encouraged strong prejudice against outcast groups" (2). In this context it is not surprising that the Red Guards treated class enemies with contempt, cruelty, and violence. The function of aggressive and violent language in Chinese wall posters resembled the function of hate speech in the United States in that it "seeks to move an audience by creating a symbolic code for violence" (Whillock 1995). It aims to "inflame the emotions of followers, denigrate the designated out-class, inflict permanent and irreparable harm to the opposition, and ultimately conquer" (Woodward and Denton 2000, 80).

From classical to modern times Chinese language has been rich and varied in its rhetorical and linguistic devices and aesthetic expressions, as reflected in numerous classical and contemporary works of history and literature. During the Cultural Revolution *dazibao* became a major means of political communication and dominating Chinese discursive practices. The pervasive use of wall posters in the political arena forced many people to conform to one style of communication in their development of arguments˙ and general use of language. The diverse language devices to convey profound and complex meanings in the Chinese literary tradition were tragically lost. Flowery exaggerations, combined with vulgar denunciations, and banal clichés became the dominant linguistic features of the time. The basic structure and linguistic features of wall posters were similar. From a critical and creative perspective, such lack of linguistic variety stifled Chinese thinking. In his article "Politics and the English Language," Orwell (1956) lamented the fact that all political publications in the England of the 1950s were alike in their use of words and styles. The danger of such discursive conformity, according to Orwell, was that it would lead to stagnation of thought and distortions of meaning. In his words, "You can shirk it [your responsibility] by simply throwing your mind open and letting the ready-made phrases come crowding in. They will construct your sentences for you—even think your thoughts for you, to a certain extent—and at need they will perform the important service of partially concealing your meaning even from yourself" (362). Orwell was concerned that this formulaic use of language would reduce the speaker to a machine and lead to political conformity. Similarly, the language of wall posters was characterized by formalized, set phrases with politicized and inflated meanings. This, in turn, produced a mind-set that was simplistic, reductionistic, and essentialistic. Worse still, one's private thoughts were diminished and made congruent with public thought in the process. One interviewee shared the following experience: "As the New Year of 1972 was approaching, someone in my dorm suggested four of us write a New Year's commentary separately. The New Year commentary was a popular form of political expression during the Cultural Revolution. The four of us, all Chinese majors and second-year college students, spent one hour writing it. When we finished, we compared the four versions. We discovered very little variation in the way we structured the essay and employed language and expressions. We looked at each other dumfounded." Such linguistic and political conformity can be found among the Chinese to this day, both in the official media and in personal speeches.

Since the end of the Cultural Revolution wall posters have been used to further a more democratic impulse. Ironically, when *dazibao* began to pose a threat to the legitimacy of the Communist government, it was discredited as the cause of chaos and social unrest. By 1980 the constitutional right of using wall posters was revoked by the People's Congress, and now anyone who engages in the practice to harm innocent people is in violation of the law. Even though the use of *dazibao* was banned in China, the extensive cultural damage left in its wake will take time to undo; wounds caused by the Cultural Revolution are slow to heal, and the linguistic/discursive behavior shaped during the Cultural Revolution will be unraveled only after much effort.

Five

A Rhetorical Analysis of Revolutionary Songs and Model Operas

Music and the other performing arts [in China] were to be used solely as tools for indoctrinating the ideology of proletarian dictatorship and advocating class struggle.

Mingyue Liang, Music of the Billion

Singing revolutionary songs has given me energy and boosted my spirits. They are the only songs I know and can remember. These songs still have an impact on me. They reminded me of those crazy and chaotic years. At the same time, I feel exhilarated; it warms my heart when I hear these songs.

Account from an interview

One striking rhetorical phenomenon during the Cultural Revolution was the production and popularization of revolutionary songs and the so-called model operas.[1] The rhetorical impact of these art forms went far beyond the functions of aesthetics and entertainment. They were important aspects of the political discourse, exerting powerful, persuasive appeals and inciting revolutionary fervor. Many interviewees distinctly remember the lyrics and music of these songs and operas.

Rhetorical Functions of Music in China

The transformative power of music with regard to human thought and behavior was long recognized in both ancient Greece and China. For example, in *The Republic,* Plato warned that the wrong kind of music could endanger the state. Similarly, the ancient Chinese regarded *yue* 樂 (music) as the crucial component in exercising *li* 禮 (rituals and rites), while *li,* in turn, taught people how to feel, think, and act and helped maintain the stability of the state (*Li Chi,* in Legge 1967). Confucius was a great fan of music. According to a legend, once he had heard the "Hymn of Shao" he was so overcome with its beauty that he forgot the flavor of meat for three months (Confucius, *Lun Yu* 7.14). However, for Confucius, "Music does not only mean the sound of bells and drums" (17.11). It can "penetrate into one's spirit" (3.23) and help one "achieve a sense of fulfillment" (8.8). Further, for Confucius, music was closely related to thinking.

For example, he considered the Chinese classic *Shi Jing* (the *Book of Odes*), consisting of 305 lyrics and dating back to 700 B.C.E., an "expression of correct thought" and advocated that it be required reading for all (2.2). So great was Confucius's regard for music that he included music education as one part of the six arts in his curriculum.[2] Further, he and his disciples held that the teaching of virtuous songs along with the use of correct musical instruments would help cultivate ethical conduct and establish a moral society. Music should therefore contain ethical lyrics and healthy melodies in order to induce socially desirable behavior. Traditionally art and music were not produced and performed purely for pleasure. They had didactic functions and served as means of political control. In imperial China music was an integral part of state rituals and ceremonies; the emperor of each dynasty had his own music bureau, with professional musicians providing ceremonial music for court rituals. Such music was intended to elicit proper conduct from the imperial subjects.[3]

Traditional ways of relating to music have been extended in modern China into a means of forging ideological bonds and creating new identities through mass singing. According to Wong (1984), the mass singing practice was first introduced to China by Protestant missionaries in the nineteenth century. It was used to imprint on the masses the state hymn of the Heavenly Kingdom, sung in homage to Hong Xiuquan 洪秀全 (1814–68), leader of the Taiping Rebellion (1851–64). Subsequently, German military instructors reinforced the practice of mass singing while training Chinese troops. In Wong's opinion, these Western influences set "precedents for the use of mass songs as a modern political and didactic tool" (114). Further, the introduction of Western music brought along pentatonic melodies. "For several generations, this type of westernized song has been a major ingredient in the musical diet of Chinese students" (116). For example, mass songs were used to promote patriotic sentiments in student protest movements in the 1920s and 1930s. Wasserstrom (1991) recorded that students used group singing as a propaganda technique in many of their patriotic marches, as well as in their protests against the Japanese invasion. Mass choral groups were organized and often gave public performances where patriotic songs were sung as means of mobilizing the masses. Such performances, in Wasserstrom's view, "provided a valuable medium for spreading ideas and embedding slogans in the mind of the general population," and further, "collective singing became an important way of expressing national and/or class solidarity" (212).

Songs and other art forms have been used as primary tools of propaganda in Yan'an, a small town in Shaanxi Province in northwest China that served as the headquarters for the Communist Party in the 1930s and 1940s. In fact, the Lu Xun Academy of Art and Literature was established in Yan'an to train professional musicians and performers with a clear ideological orientation toward communist ideals and proletarian values. Numerous *wengongtuan* 文工團 (performing teams) trained in this academy gave performances on the front lines, praising war heroes and eulogizing the success of the Red Army in order to boost the morale of soldiers. Perris (1985) contends that it was during this period that "the Liberation forces began the organized use of music for propaganda to the populace by broadcasting revolutionary songs and choruses over its 300-watt transmitter" (99). It was also at this time that Mao Zedong delivered his famous speech titled "Talks at the Yan'an Forum on Literature and Art" ([1942] 1965), in which he identified the goal and function of art as the propagation of Marxist-Leninist ideology in order to serve the interests of the proletariat. He shared with Lenin the view that art and literature must "fit into the whole revolutionary machine as a component part" and "that they operate as powerful weapons for uniting and educating the people and for attacking and destroying the enemy" (70). Also echoing Lenin, Mao asserted that art and literature must represent the life experiences of the proletarian class and edify the workers, peasants, soldiers, and cadres. In his words, "There is in fact no such thing as art for art's sake, art that stands above classes or art that is detached from or independent of politics. . . . Literature and art are subordinate to politics, but in their turn exert a great influence on politics" (86). This view of the relationship between art and politics led Mao to a rhetorical conceptualization: "What we demand is the unity of politics and art, the unity of content and form, the unity of revolutionary political content and the highest possible perfection of artistic form. Works of art which lack artistic quality have no force, however progressive they are politically. Therefore, we oppose both the tendency to produce works of art with a wrong political viewpoint and the tendency toward the 'poster and slogan style' which is correct in political viewpoint but lacking in artistic power" (90).

Mao's pronouncement on the integration of content and style resembles the viewpoint embodied in Roman rhetorician Quintilian's well-known saying "A good man speaks well." In fact, Mao's rhetorical stand is probably closer to that of Saint Augustine, who believed that persuasion/conversion only occurred through the eloquent articulation of ultimate Christian truth (*On Christine Doctrine*, book 4, 29). As Mao was anticipating the establishment of a communist government under his leadership with a new socialist economic structure, he was certainly well aware of the formidable task of ideological transformation from feudalism to his version of socialism and communism, or the proletarian consciousness. To assure the success of this transformation it was important to combine the elements of "wisdom and eloquence." Mao's seemingly "critical approach" (speaking for the common people and empowering the oppressed) to art and literature was appealing to many at the time when he delivered the speech. Ironically, eight years later when the Communists took power and became the new ruling class art, literature, and especially music began to take on the characteristics of totalitarianism. In other words, they sought to affirm state ideology and control the minds of the people. Mao encouraged artists and performers to turn to Chinese folk arts and popular songs for inspiration in artistic merits. This strategy was described as turning "inward to [one's] indigenous knowledge in order to make the alien ideology survive" (Mao [1942] 1965, 87), a rhetorical appropriation characteristic of Chinese communist propaganda.

The topics of the rhetorical songs have drawn the attention of Western scholars, among whom there is general agreement that songs are not written or sung for entertainment alone but also serve primary functions with regard to persuasion, reinforcement, and/or ideological expression (Irvine and Kirkpatrick 1972). In the words of Rybacki and Rybacki (1991), "Rhetorical songs describe social conditions, pose questions, express discontent, and attempt to influence public opinion" (277). American scholars have studied the rhetorical impact of songs in changing political attitudes and provoking political actions (for example, Branham 1999; Carter 1980; Gonzalez and Makay 1983; Kosokoff and Carmichael 1970). Indeed, songs often convey powerful rhetorical messages, address rhetorical exigencies, express ideological agendas, arouse emotions, and stimulate actions. Denisoff (1983) identifies such rhetorical songs as "propaganda" and describes their persuasive functions as reinforcing a system of values and promoting group unity. A song that exemplified these functions in the context of Chinese communism was "The Three Main Rules of Discipline and the Eight Points for Attention." The lyrics of the song were Mao's instructions on the proper conduct of the Red Army. The song served to reinforce Red Army norms and unify the peasant soldiers. With its simple rhythms, low tone, and point-by-point progression it was easy to sing and remember.

Rhetorical songs were used extensively in communist and totalitarian societies. In comparing the function of music in totalitarian societies Perris (1985) examined the persuasive feature of music in Nazi Germany in justifying and agitating anti-Semitic sentiments. He also examined the ways in which Soviet Russia and Communist China employed music as a state art in order to implant Marxist ideology, arguing that such an approach to music education worked well in China as "Chinese tradition supports the twin functions of aesthetic enjoyment and ideological instruction as a familiar condition of music" (108). During the Cultural Revolution, Mao's "Talks at the Yan'an Forum on Literature and Art" was extensively studied and widely cited in political discourse. In Minmin Wang's (2000) view, the speech "helped establish his [Mao's] political and ideological dominance in the Chinese Communist Party" (180). It was used not only to establish the criterion for drawing the line between revolutionary and bourgeois arts but also as an incentive to produce proletarian art. Subsequently numerous revolutionary songs were written to further the communist cause among workers, peasants, soldiers, and educated youths. These songs were sung en masse in schools, in workplaces, at rallies, and even in private homes.

In their discussion of the framework used for the rhetorical criticism of songs, Rybacki and Rybacki (1991) suggest taking a close look at songs that contain emotional appeals either in their lyrics alone or in the combination of lyrics and music. Irvine and Kirkpatrick (1972) contend that the rhetorical impact of songs is derived from the formation of "amplificative" meaning, defined as "a metaphoric process resulting from contrasting and complimentary associations of various musical elements" (273). These frameworks can be used to analyze songs and operas produced during the Cultural Revolution, with a focus on lyrics but also looking at musical components such as melody, chord progression, and rhythm.

A Rhetorical Analysis of Revolutionary Songs

I have examined over three hundred revolutionary songs produced and recorded in songbooks during the Cultural Revolution. I am familiar with most of them as I grew up singing these songs. The songs being analyzed fall mainly into three categories: (1) songs of eulogy; (2) songs of Mao's quotations and poems; and (3) songs of radicalization. Although there were other types of songs during the Cultural Revolution, such as those praising workers, peasants, and soldiers, these three types were most pervasive.

Songs of Eulogy

Songs of eulogy were disseminated through songbooks, over the airwaves of state-sanctioned radio programs, through loudspeakers, and on the pages of Red Guard pamphlets. They were sung in groups and performed in the streets and on stages during the Cultural Revolution. In fact, these songs were sung virtually everywhere, so that one could not pass a single day without hearing several of them. The subject of the eulogy was primarily Mao Zedong; other types of eulogies were aimed at glorifying the party and the nation.

The worship of Mao intensified to an unprecedented degree during the Cultural Revolution. Countless songs were written and sung constantly praising his personal wisdom and unfailing leadership. The most well known and frequently sung of these is "The East Is Red." It affirmed Mao as a savior and his leadership position as heavenly mandated. The first two verses of the lyrics are:

> The East is red; the sun rises.
> China has got a Mao Zedong.
> He seeks happiness for people
> and he is the people's savior.
>
> Chairman Mao loves people.
> He is our leader
> For building a new China
> And he is guiding us into the future.
>
> (*Eulogy of Mao Zedong* 1978, 1–9)

The melody for "The East Is Red" was taken from a folk song from Shaanxi Province. It was first sung in public at the musical epic of the same title prior to the Cultural Revolution. During the Cultural Revolution the song became the most popular in all of China. It was played at every significant public event, including the party's congregations, rallies, and celebrations. Every time Mao came out to meet the Red Guards in Tiananmen Square he would emerge accompanied by this song. In every songbook published during the Cultural Revolution the first song inevitably was "The East Is Red." Radio broadcasts were the main medium of communication during the Cultural Revolution, and the first tune played every morning from the official radio station was "The East Is Red." This song was sung at every important ceremonial occasion and through the loudspeakers of Red Guard organizations on campuses and in the streets.

A central element of Chinese mythology is the notion that emperors are mandated by heaven; thus they are the "Sons of Heaven." Songs such as "The East Is

Red" reinforced the myth that Mao was just such a deity sent by heaven to help the Chinese people live better lives. In this way Mao was established as the legitimate leader of China, a living god who would surely bring happiness to people. In fact, as described by Adrian Hsia (1972), "Mao is represented not only by heaven, but by mother earth as well, and the sun symbol is now also reserved exclusively for Mao" (230–31). Indeed, in almost all the songs eulogizing Mao he is symbolically associated with the red sun or golden sun with its infinite radiance that shines over China, bringing energy to human beings on earth. In many songs Mao was described as "the red sun in people's hearts" and "the dearest person on earth." The most popular song in this category composed by the Red Guards had the words:

> Beloved Chairman Mao,
> You are the red sun in our hearts.
> We have so much to tell you and
> We have so many songs to sing to you.
> Hundreds and thousands of red hearts are pumping excitedly;
> Hundreds and thousands of smiling faces face the red sun.
> We wish you, our leader Chairman Mao, a long long life,
> long long life!

(Eulogy of Mao Zedong 1978, 148–50)

Like "The East Is Red," the above song was sung everywhere and all the time, often accompanied by a "loyalty dance" as part of the ritual. While songs such as this one are emotionally charged, expressing loyalty and cultlike devotion to Mao, other songs eulogizing Mao tell stories of how he led the Chinese Revolution, established the Red Army, corrected the wrongdoings of certain party leaders, or defeated the enemies of communism prior to 1949. This narrative form had a powerful, persuasive effect as it was familiar to the audience and easy to remember. Of the 180 songs in *Eulogy of Mao Zedong,* about 50 of them tell the story of Mao's political career and heroic deeds. A large proportion of eulogy songs were sung from the viewpoints of minority groups or from workers, peasants, and soldiers. These songs describe Mao as "the sun with golden radiance," "the bright light," "the helmsman," "the biggest benefactor," and "the wise commander." The language used to eulogize Mao was effusive to a degree that far exceeded anything heard before, whether in reference to a man, a nation, or a cause.

Most songs of this type borrowed extensively from folk melodies characterized by spontaneity, simplicity, expressiveness, and beauty. In Chinese, folk songs are known as *min'ge* 民歌, or "layman's songs." During the Cultural Revolution they appealed to both the common people and the literati in that they allowed for the telling of a story in long, highly emotive sentences and stretched melodies. It was an effective form for promoting adoration and loyalty to Mao. In the words of one interviewee, "I learned Mao's greatness through singing these songs. Some of them were so beautiful that I still remember them after all these years. I no longer idolize Mao as I used to, but I still have deep respect for him. You have to admit that he was an extraordinary man." It is not surprising that many former members of the Red Guards kept a collection of odes extolling "the Red Sun" (referring to Mao Zedong).

Another popular song at the time was "Sailing the Sea Depends on the Helmsman." The lyrics are:

> A helmsman is needed for sailing in the ocean.
> The sun is needed for all things to grow.
> Plants grow stronger when nourished by morning dew.
> Mao Zedong's Thought is needed for the revolutionary cause.
> Fish cannot live without water;
> Melon cannot grow without vines.
> The revolutionary masses cannot survive without the Communist Party;
> Mao Zedong's Thought is the forever shining sun.
>
> (Xiaobing Wang 2001, 175)

While "The East Is Red" was usually sung or played at the beginning of an event, "Sailing the Sea Depends on the Helmsman" was always sung at the end of an event. Leaders such as Premier Chou En-lai were often seen conducting this song at rallies with the Red Guards. Like "The East Is Red," it legitimized the absolute authority of Mao Zedong's Thought, through a simple logic and metaphorical expressions that common people could easily identity with and be persuaded by. Essentially, such songs eulogizing Mao permeated the air of Communist China during this time. Liang (1998) described his experience while he was in Beijing waiting to be reviewed by Mao: "The whole of Beijing must have installed hundreds and thousands of loud-speakers playing 'The East Is Red' and 'Sailing the Sea Depends [on] the Helmsman,' songs of Chairman Mao's quotations and poems, and other revolutionary songs eulogizing Chairman Mao. They were played in a kind of frenzy for days and nights on the streets of Beijing" (255). In a sarcastic tone Liang remarked, "With the exception of Chairman Mao, no leader of any other country and no emperor of imperial China could have tolerated the sound of such loud and never-ending noise."

Mao's godlike image was elevated not only through songs eulogizing him as a savior but also through songs eulogizing his works. In such songs the use of metaphors was a common feature, and Mao's utterance and written words were considered the source of inspiration and life force. The following are examples of this type of song.

> Mao's works are like the sun.
> Every word and every sentence radiates with golden light.
> It brightens the soldier's heart;
> It gives direction to our work and study.
>
> (Eulogy of Mao Zedong 1978, 300)

The song that follows expressed the feelings of a reader:

> I love to read Mao's books the best.
> I read them hundreds and thousands of times.

I work hard to understand their profound meanings.
[I feel] as if a timely rain drops on a dry land and
Small plants are moistened by the morning dew.
The dew of Chairman Mao nourished me.
I am full of energy when doing revolutionary work.

(*Eulogy of Mao Zedong* 1978, 297)

In these two songs Mao's words are revered as "the sun," "a timely rain," and "morning dew" in providing nutrition for the revolutionary spirit and guiding the cause of revolutionary action. These nature metaphors are easy to understand and identify with, especially by the peasants, who comprised 80 percent of the Chinese population. Other metaphors found in songs eulogizing Mao's works included "the compass," "the telescope," "the microscope," "the train engine," "the demon-exposing mirror," and "a thousand-pound cudgel."

Other revolutionary songs popularized during the Cultural Revolution were songs in praise of the Chinese Communist Party and socialist system. In theory, decisions regarding national issues were made by the collective efforts of the CCP, the ruling party in the country. However, once Mao was deified and his writings elevated to the level of scripture, there was no longer any clear line of demarcation between Mao, Mao Zedong's Thought, the Communist Party, and the nation. Terms used in reference to the party, Chairman Mao, and China were often used synonymously. To act against Mao was to act against the party and interest of the nation. Conversely, to praise the party and the nation served as an equivalent of praising Mao and reinforcing his authority and cult status.

A popular song sung before, during, and after the Cultural Revolution is "There Will Be No New China without the Communist Party." In this song the party was not only praised for working hard for the nation and saving China but also was personalized in the form of a third person singular male:

He [the Party] directed the path for liberation;
He led China to a bright future;
He fought against the Japanese for eight years;
He improved people's lives;
He established a revolutionary basis;
And he practiced democracy.
There will be no new China without the Communist Party.
There will be no new China without the Communist Party.

(Xiaobing Wang 2001, 164)

In this song "he" can mean the collective party or can imply Mao Zedong, the leader of the party. The logic is simple: the new China was established by the Communist Party, which was under the leadership of Mao Zedong. If the party had saved the Chinese people in the past, it was also capable of leading the Chinese people in the present and into the future. If the party had been correct in making decisions and carrying out its mission in the past, it would not make mistakes in the present and the future. While some songs identified Mao as the father of China, other songs identified the Communist Party as the mother of China: she who gives love and protection, nurturing the country and generating energy for revolutionary causes.

In almost every song in praise of the party the message "there will be no new China without the Communist Party" was repeated. Repetition is a powerful means of persuasion in totalitarian societies. As Hitler stated in *Mein Kampf*, "The masses are slow to comprehend, they must be told the same thing a thousand times" (Yu 1964, 156). The more frequently a line was repeated, the more likely it was to be remembered and accepted as truth. Moreover, as Irvine and Kirkpatrick (1972) point out, that repetition causes the listener to be "bombarded by a fantastic array of stimuli, in collections constituting patterns capable of producing a feeling or an attitude" (276). Thus, instead of questioning the logic of the lyrics at the cognitive level, the musical experience was more likely to produce amplificative meaning that produced a change in attitude. The belief that the Communist Party was always great, glorious, and correct was never questioned. Even years later in 1989 during the Tiananmen Square student democratic revolt, students demanded the resignation of Deng Xiaoping but never questioned the authority of the Communist Party or even for a moment entertained the possibility of a political change to a two-party system.

Some Chinese songs were directly in praise of the nation and the Chinese people. These songs were sung even before the Cultural Revolution but popularized during the Cultural Revolution. Such songs would, for example, describe the vast waves of the Yangtze and Yellow Rivers or praise China's beautiful homeland and its heroic people. These songs always ended by looking to Mao or the Communist Party for guidance toward a bright future. One song, commonly known as "Singing for the Motherland," illustrates this well:

> A five star red flag is fluttering in the wind.
> Victory songs are loud and clear.
> [We are] singing for our beloved motherland.
> We walk into prosperity and wealth,
> Going through mountains and plains
> Cutting across the rolling Yellow River and Yangtze.
> This vast and beautiful land is our beloved homeland.
> Heroic people stand up and are unified as solid steel.
> We [Chinese] are industrious, we are brave,
> Independence and freedom are our ideals.
> We conquered many hardships and won liberation.
> We love peace, we love our homeland.
> Whoever dares to invade us would meet with death.
> The sun in the East is rising. The People's Republic is growing.
> Our leader, Mao Zedong, guides the direction.

Our life is better each day,
And our future is bright with thousands of points of radiance.

(Xiaobing Wang 2001, 299)

Songs such as this one promoted patriotic sentiments and national pride as well as strengthening the connection between Mao and the country. Some songs in this category incorporated high notes, long chords, and elements of folk songs. As this type of song integrated artistic/aesthetic components with spiritual/moral dimensions, it gave the listener a deep, heartfelt appreciation for the motherland, in addition to a sense of confidence and well-being. Through such songs Mao and the party were elevated to the status of saviors, while the Chinese were celebrated as the people most worthy of enjoying the best natural resources and social system in the world.

Through such typical songs of eulogy Mao, the party, and the socialist system were portrayed as the best, the brightest, and the most compassionate without exception. Anyone who dared challenge Mao, his teachings, his party, or his political system was the enemy. Consider the following peasant song, which was popular during the Cultural Revolution:

Heaven and earth are great, but greater still is the kindness of the Party.
Father and mother are dear, but dearer still is Chairman Mao.
Nothing is as good as socialism.
Rivers and oceans are deep, but still deeper is the comradeship of the
    proletarian class.
Mao Zedong's Thoughts are the revolutionary treasure;
Whoever is against those is our enemy.

This song did not appear in any songbooks, as it was not professionally composed. However, it is one of the most popular songs sung by the Red Guards all over China. The song illustrated well the revolutionary fervor, hero worship, and radicalization promoted by the songs in this category. In the words of one interviewee, "This song had a great impact on me. I always believed that the Party and Chairman Mao were above everything. My family would come second when it came to loyalty and faithfulness. When my father was accused of being a spy, I was so confused. I talked myself into trusting the Party and Chairman Mao more than my own parents by singing this song. In a way, I was forced to choose between my parents and Chairman Mao."

Songs of Mao's Quotations and Poems
In *Mao Tsetung and China,* FitzGerald (1976) argues, "The Thoughts of Mao Tsetung [Mao Zedong] have become to his own people in his own age what the Sayings of Confucius were to the Chinese people for the past two thousand years: the source of inspiration and guidance in matters social, political and moral" (1). While this observation gives the reader some idea of the importance of Mao's influence in contemporary China, it is still difficult for those who were not actually living in China during the Cultural Revolution to grasp just how pervasive and omnipresent Mao's teachings

were. Indeed, during the Cultural Revolution, *Quotations of Chairman Mao* was the bible for every Chinese person. Not only did everyone have a copy of the book, but most people, especially the young, could recite entire passages from it. It was a collection of Mao's sayings extracted from the five volumes of his writings and was certainly the best-seller at the time.[4] Lin Biao was at the forefront of this indoctrination campaign. In the preface of *Quotations from Chairman Mao,* Lin (1966) insisted, "In order to truly master Mao Zedong's Thought, we must repeatedly study Chairman Mao's many essential concepts. We must memorize adages, study them repeatedly and apply them repeatedly" (3).

To facilitate the memorization and indoctrination process, music was written for many of Mao's quotations. For example, from 1 October to 25 October 1966 the *People's Daily* published three groups of quotations in song form. The first group contained songs affirming the absolute authority of the party, such as "The Core of Leadership for Our Cause Is the Chinese Communist Party" (*Quotations from Chairman Mao,* 1), "We Must Have Faith in the Masses and We Must Have Faith in the Party" (3), and "Policy and Tactics Are the Life Force of the Party" (7). The second group consisted of songs expressing radical sentiments, such as "Revolution Is Not a Dinner Party" (11) and "He [the Enemy] Will Not Fall If You Do Not Beat Him" (10). The third group of songs included excerpts from Mao's three most well-studied articles set to music: "Serve the People"; "In Memory of Norman Bethune"; and "The Foolish Old Man Who Moved a Mountain." Subsequently the *People's Daily* and other newspapers regularly printed quotation songs complete with musical notes. These were taken directly from the paper and used as sheet music at rallies and celebrations.

Quotation songs soon were played through the loudspeakers at the National Day celebrations and at Mao's reviews of millions of Red Guards in Tiananmen Square. In this way the practice of singing Maoist quotation songs spread rapidly throughout the country. An article published in the fifth issue of *Songs of the Liberation Army* describes the atmosphere and scale of this phenomenon:

> Quotation songs received enthusiastic response from workers, peasants, soldiers, and the Red Guards when they emerged. From the city to the countryside, from inland to the borders, from army camps to factories, from rice fields to classrooms, quotation songs are heard everywhere. Quotation songs are known to every family. The old and young, men and women all sing quotation songs. The popularity of these songs is unprecedented not only in China, but in the history of world music. . . . [T]he singing of quotation songs not only promotes a new wave of workers, peasants, and soldiers studying Chairman Mao's works, but also marks a new level of musical development in our country. We have entered a new era. This is one of the great victories of the Proletarian Cultural Revolution." (1967, vol. 5, cited in He 2000)

Most quotation songs were composed by professional musicians, the best known among them being Li Jiefu (1913–76), president of the Shenyang Conservatory. Li Jiefu was known to have composed over one hundred quotation songs, along with many other types of songs.[5] Although writing music with long sentences and abstract political terms posed many artistic challenges, Li and a few other composers managed to combine indigenous melodies with features characteristic of Western mass songs, such as marchlike rhythms and steady progressions. According to Irvine and Kirkpatrick (1972), these musical features tend to induce a sense of confidence in the listener. When such features are combined with highly emotional responses, they engender profoundly persuasive effects almost beyond the control of the listener. Typical examples of such songs are "Make Up Your Mind" and "Rebellion Is Justified":

> Make up your mind.
> Do not be afraid of sacrifice.
> Overcome all obstacles.
> Strive for victory.
>
> *(Quotations from Chairman Mao, 157)*

> Marxist doctrines are many.
> All can be summarized in one sentence:
> Rebellion is justified.
>
> (Mao's new directive)

"Make Up Your Mind" was the song most familiar to the Chinese people. It encouraged a spirit of determination and fearlessness, and had direct application to any situation of hardship or difficulty. The second song, "Rebellion Is Justified," was the favorite of the Red Guards, who sang it virtually everywhere, especially in the first two years of the Cultural Revolution. They used it not only to inspire and indoctrinate themselves but also to popularize and disseminate Mao's teachings to the masses. One interviewee recalls: "Every time a new quotation song came out, we would practice and master it. My classmates and I organized a Mao Zedong's Thought propaganda team. We went to the Beijing Railway Station and sung new quotation songs to the travelers in the waiting rooms. Sometimes we used quotation songs to solve problems on the spot. For example, if we wanted the travelers to help each other, we would sing the quotation song, 'We all come from five lakes and four oceans [from everywhere] for the same revolutionary purpose.'" Many interviewees claimed that they still remember a lot of these quotation songs and have internalized some of them to such an extent that the songs guide their conduct to this day. In the process of singing these songs the Chinese people were transformed into true adherents of Mao's teachings, embracing his every utterance as sacred, infallible truth; they sincerely believed that Mao's pronouncements could apply to every individual and situation.

Quotation songs were also used to justify radical actions. For example, the Red Guards sang "Rebellion Is Justified" while raiding people's houses, denouncing their teachers and principals, and beating class enemies. Several interviewees had either participated in or witnessed people's homes being raided to the tune of songs such as "Rebellion Is Justified" and "Revolution Is Not a Dinner Party." One interviewee recalled how terrified she became each time she heard these two songs in particular because her family's home had been searched and ransacked by the Red Guards singing these songs and shouting political slogans.

In addition to Mao's prose pronouncements, many of his poems were made into songs. According to He (2000), the first song created from one of Mao's poems was published in the third issue of the *Red Flag* in 1965. A year later some of these poetry-derived songs were sung at the "Spring of Shanghai" concert. During the Cultural Revolution nearly all of Mao's published poems were made into songs.

Ironically, while Mao appeared to be antitraditional, his poems preserved many of China's traditional literary expressions and classical allusions. Unlike quotation songs that were linguistically unimaginative and combative in composition, Mao's poetry songs were lyrically expressive and melodious to the ears. Unlike quotation songs that can be sung anywhere and by anyone due to their simple language and music, poetry songs were typically sung by those who were musically gifted or by professionals onstage.

Like Mao's quotation songs, poetry songs were also used to incite revolutionary fervor and justify violent actions. The favorite poetry song of one member of the Red Guards was "Xi Jiang Yue: Jinggangshan" (Moon of West River: Jinggang Mountain):

> Below the hills fly our flags and banners,
> Above the hilltops sound our bugles and drums.
> The foe encircles us thousands strong,
> Steadfastly we stand our ground.
> Already our defense is iron-clad,
> Now our wills unite like a fortress.
> From Huangyangjie roars the thunder of guns,
> Word comes the enemy has fled into the night.
> (*Mao Tsetung [Mao Zedong] Poems* 1976, 8)

The above poem was written in 1928 after a battle in which the Fourth Regiment of the Red Army successfully repulsed the Nationalists' assault and defended the first communist base, Jinggangshan. This poetry song was also used widely by the Red Guards during factional infighting in which each side considered the other side the political enemy and themselves true revolutionaries. The song boosted their morale and fighting spirit while at the same time sanctioning and justifying violent actions against the enemy. So successful was the song that the term *jinggangshan* 井岡山 (Jinggang Mountain) became a revolutionary symbol in and of itself.[6] For example, a Red Guards organization from Tsinghua University called themselves the Jinggangshan Corps and their publication *Jinggangshan*. Two interviewees who are graduates of Beijing University witnessed firsthand the factional infighting between Red Guards groups on campus. This militant song and others like it were played during the heat of the battle that ensued.

A favorite poetry song of many female members of the Red Guards was "Seven Absolute: Militia Women," written by Mao in 1961 in praise of a female militia:

How bright and brave they look, shouldering five-foot rifles
On the parade ground lit up by the first gleams of day.
China's daughters have high-aspiring minds,
They love their battle array, not silks and satins.
(*Mao Tsetung [Mao Zedong] Poems* 1976, 76)

Female Red Guards presented themselves according to Mao's description of the female militia in this poem. It was a fashion at the time for women to dress in army uniforms bound at the waist with leather belts. They also wore soldier's caps and shoes and carried soldier's bags. They wore their hair short, wore no makeup, and were expected to hide any feminine features. Ruthless aggression and militancy were also the norm among female members of the Red Guards. An interviewee recalls that a group of female Red Guards came to search his home and beat his mother, who was accused of being counterrevolutionary. In his words, "They were all very good looking in their teenage years. One of them beat my mother with the leather belt yelling 'If you dare to resist, I will make you go to hell.' I was trying to stop her from beating my mother. She then turned around and started beating me. For many years, I could not understand why these good-looking young women had so much hatred. They did not even know us." Another interviewee described one of her female classmates as the most relentless and merciless individuals at denunciation rallies. In her account, "She was a model student, always nice to others. But she acted like a completely different person at denunciation rallies during the Cultural Revolution. She shouted the loudest revolutionary slogans and used a lot of swear words in denouncing the teachers. She was the first to beat the teachers with the leather belt and would constantly beat them and shout at them." Song Binbin, a female member of the Red Guards who had the honor to wrap Mao's arm with the Red Guard armband, was asked by Mao to change her name to *Yaowu* (Be Militant). She changed her name immediately and subsequently became one of those very militant Red Guards. She was alleged to have killed seven people during the Cultural Revolution (Xu 1999, 64). Perhaps not all female Red Guards turned into monsters, as in these examples; yet vulgarity, masculinity, militancy, and ruthlessness were encouraged in women and associated with a true revolutionary commitment.

Through the singing and hearing of songs derived from Mao's poems, certain lines became so familiar that they were repeated in wall posters, speeches, and Red Guard propaganda materials in order to enhance the artistic effect. Lines such as "The spring wind blows amid profuse willow wands, / Six hundred million in this land all equal Yao and Shun" (Mao 1976, 70) and "The Four Seas are rising, clouds and waters raging, / The Five Continents are rocking, wind and thunder roaring" (94) were used to capture the power, beauty, and excellence of the nation and its people. Poetic sentiments such as "Bitter sacrifice strengthens bold resolve, / Which dares to make the sun and moon shine in new skies" (72); "the Golden Monkey wrathfully swung his massive cudgel; / and the jade-like firmament was cleared of dust" (82); and "We can clasp the moon in the Ninth Heaven; / and seize turtles deep down in the Five Seas" (100) were used to boost morale, express resolve and godly power, and demonstrate martyrlike commitment. Ironically in those days, when public discourse was filled with clichés and dreary, politically correct speech, Mao's poems were the only artistically and aesthetically pleasing rhetorical device sanctioned by the government. Singing Mao's poetry songs therefore became the only form of entertainment available to the masses.

Through the singing of quotation and poetry songs Mao's teachings were disseminated and absorbed at a speed and scale unprecedented in human history. Newspapers constantly ran stories describing how workers, peasants, and soldiers successfully applied Mao's teachings in resolving their daily problems and exposing class enemies. Under the influence of these songs the Red Guards and Rebels became even more radical and violent proponents of the revolutionary cause. Indeed, they came to regard themselves not as mere messengers of Maoist ideology but as literal embodiments of the truth.

Songs of Radicalization

The call for a radical transformation of Chinese culture was first articulated by intellectuals during the May Fourth movement of 1919. In the wake of the overthrow of the Qing dynasty (1616–1911), China began its long trek toward modernization by reforming its language system from a classical form preserved by the literati to a simplified vernacular form accessible to ordinary people.[7] After the May Fourth movement all songs and written material in the public arena employed the vernacular style. In particular, protest songs expressing frustration and outrage toward Japanese invaders and European imperialists used short phrases and simple compositions. This strategy made it relatively simple for the masses to memorize and sing the songs. Recognizing the power of songs to unite the Chinese people, communist composers such as Nie Er (1912–35), Tian Han (1896–1968), and Xian Xinghai (1905–45) wrote many patriotic, anti-Japanese songs. Typically these songs served as an outlet for the intense indignation of the people while arousing them to militant action against the enemy. The well-known "Marching Song of the Courageous Army" epitomized the songs of that period:

> Rise up!
> Those who do not want to be slaves.
> Let's build our new Great Wall with our blood and flesh!
> China is at its most perilous moment.
> Everyone is forced to give the last roar.
> Rise up, rise up, rise up!
> Let's unite and march against the enemy's gunfire,
> Marching on, marching on!
>
> (Xiaobing Wang 2001, 29)

The music of this song was characterized by low notes, a steady progression of pitch, and a marchlike rhythm. The song was so effective in arousing patriotic sentiments that it was later selected as the national anthem of the People's Republic of China.

Another song popular among the Communists of the early twentieth century was "Internationale."[8] It was introduced to China in 1923 by Qu Qiubai, who also translated the song into Chinese from the original French. An English version of the first stanza goes:

> Rise up!
> Hungry and cold slaves.
> Rise up!
> The oppressed of the whole world.
> The blood in our bodies is boiling,
> Fight for the truth!
> The old world shall be utterly routed.
> Slaves, rise up, rise up
> Do not say we have nothing.
> We want to be the masters of the new world.
> This is the final battle.
> United for tomorrow.
> Internationale will be realized.
>
> (Xiaobing Wang 2001, 28)

The song articulated the glorious fight for communist ideals worldwide. It was sung and played at every important political occasion or protest in Communist China. During the Cultural Revolution the first song played on the radio every day was "The East Is Red," while the last song played at the end of each day was "Internationale." One interviewee related that her father (a veteran Communist) knew the song so well that he often sang it in his dreams. When the Rebels heard him singing the song in his sleep while incarcerated, they would beat him. Presumably the reasoning behind this was that an alleged traitor and capitalist roader had forfeited the right to sing revolutionary songs. "Internationale" was sung by the students involved in the 1989 Tiananmen Square student demonstration as a means of persuasive appeal as well as a way of protesting the government in a manner to which the government could not object. While songs of this nature exerted a positive influence during the anti-Japanese movement and in promoting communist ideals in general, the meanings of the lyrics were extended to target and assault new enemies of people by the Red Guards during the Cultural Revolution.

In her study of Red Guards' songs Vivian Wagner (1999) notes, "Predominant issues of Red Guard songs were struggle and rebellion, adoration and defense of Mao, the Party, the Cultural Revolution, and the Red Guard movement itself" (21). In addition Red Guard songs tended to be radical and militant. Unlike eulogy, poetry, and quotation songs, Red Guard songs were not composed by professionals. They incorporated the general features of protest songs, with lyrics designed to ignite revolutionary fervor and defy class enemies. The Red Guards also borrowed extensively from Chinese *minyao* 民謠 (folk verse) in that their songs were simple, had short rhythms, and could easily be chanted as well as sung. In this latter respect these songs bore a resemblance to African-American rap music. Most Red Guard songs were not included in published songbooks but were circulated in pamphlets or collections such as *The Red Guards' Fighting Songs*. A song familiar to most interviewees is:

> Take a pen and use it like a gun;
> Target the black gangs [metaphor for revisionists].
> Revolutionary teachers and students all rebel
> and become pioneers in the Cultural Revolution.
> Beat them, beat them, beat them, the sons of bitches!

> Praise Chairman Mao; eulogize the Party.
> The Party is my birth parents.
> Whoever dares to say a word against the Party
> Let him go to hell.
> Kill, kill, kill, Hee!

According to He (2000), this song was composed by a middle-school member of the Red Guards. It was never published, recorded, or broadcast through the official media. However, because of its simple tune and vehement, emotionally charged lyrics, it soon spread throughout the country, inciting countless acts of rebellion while deepening popular devotion to the party and Mao Zedong. Several interviewees sang the entire song to me by heart. Without exception they now believe that the song created a climate of violence and general reactivity during the Cultural Revolution, although at the time they felt ennobled by the song and filled with revolutionary idealism.

These songs, and others like them, sung by the Red Guards during the Cultural Revolution were typically aggressive, militant, and profane. Aesthetically they were coarse and nonmelodic. Stimulated by songs of this nature, the Red Guards became far more radical than Mao and his colleagues, in both their rhetoric and conduct.

A hallmark of radicalism was the song "Gui Jian Chou" 鬼見愁 (Making the Ghost Gloomy). The song was originally a *duilian* 對聯 (antithetical couplet) and was set to music by a member of the Red Guards while in the bathroom.[9] This song helped popularize the theory of blood lineage as the determining factor in distinguishing revolutionaries from class enemies. The lyrics are:

> If the father is a hero, the son is a good guy.
> If the father is a counterrevolutionary, the son is a scoundrel.
> Follow Chairman Mao if you are a revolutionary.
> Scram if you do not participate in the revolution!

The song is usually followed by violent slogans or profane expressions such as "Fuck him if he is against Chairman Mao" or "Smash his head to pieces." By means of this song and others like it, radical actions were justified against those who came from bourgeois or landlord families, families having any historical connection with foreigners or the Nationalist Party, and rightists. Family origin became the ultimate criterion for judging one's revolutionary credentials. It was not uncommon for children from such families to disown their parents or run away from home in order to show their loyalty to Mao and the revolutionary cause. Many of the children of "problem parents" were ill treated and tortured because of their blood lineage.

A third song characterized by the call to radical action was "hao ge" 嚎歌 (Howling Song), or "The Song of Cow Devils and Snake Spirits." One of the many ways that Red Guards and Rebels humiliated class enemies who were detained or imprisoned in cowsheds was by requiring them to sing the song. The first and second verses are as follows:

> I am a cow devil and snake spirit.
> I am the enemy of the people.
> I have committed a crime.
> I deserve the punishment of death.
> People should smash me into pieces.

> I am a cow devil and snake spirit.
> I need to confess my crime.
> I have committed crime.
> I must reform myself.
> I will meet death in the end if I do not confess [my crime].

> (He 2000, 12)

He (2000) documented the fact that even some famous artists were made to sing the song. He recounts how Ma Sicong, a well-known musician, gave a speech after defecting to the United States during the Cultural Revolution. In his speech Ma explained that he had fled his homeland because of the torture and humiliation he had been forced to endure, including singing the "Howling Song." The song was known to many children, who incorporated it into their play worlds in the form of a game called "Cow Ghosts and Snake Spirits." One interviewee recalled how she was made to sing the song repeatedly by other children in the game because her father was a class enemy. Singing the song was a kind of mental torture for the accused. Some were driven crazy by it; some even committed suicide because they could not stand the humiliation. For others the song became a tool of self-hypnosis and persuasion. An interviewee told the story of his boss being made to sing the song many times as punishment for the crime of being a class enemy. Finally he confessed that he had committed counterrevolutionary crimes and stated that he deserved to die. He (2000) laments, "The song was an unprecedented embodiment of human evil that reached its climax during the Cultural Revolution. No one has ever created a song for the self-humiliation of prisoners, not even the Nazis. This was the most shameful page in the history of Chinese music" (12).

A Rhetorical Analysis of Revolutionary Model Operas

One of the so-called achievements of the Cultural Revolution was the production of "model operas." These party-sanctioned operas were considered revolutionary and modern in terms of thematic and musical features when compared with traditional operas. Given Mao's view that art must serve the interests of the workers, peasants, and soldiers and must conform to proletarian ideology, traditional operas were considered feudalistic and bourgeois and were banned during the Cultural Revolution. Jiang Qing, Mao's wife, was the chief advocate and engineer of the transformation from traditional opera to revolutionary opera. She chose the Beijing opera as her laboratory experimentation for accomplishing this radical change in theater art.

Beijing opera established itself as an independent entity during the Qing dynasty (1644–1911) and was well liked by emperors and commoners alike. It embodied traditional skills related to singing, talking, dancing, acting, and the martial arts, reaching its peak in popularity and artistic refinement in the twentieth century, when it became the epitome of Chinese culture and the hallmark of the Chinese performing arts. During the Cultural Revolution, under the direct supervision of Jiang Qing, traditional Beijing opera was revolutionized in both form and content. Eight *yangban xi* 樣板戲, or model operas, were produced in the first three years. They included five Beijing operas, *The Red Lantern*, *Sha Jia Bang* (Sha Jia Village), *Taking Tiger Mountain by Strategies*, *Raid on the White Tiger Regiment*, and *On the Dock*; two ballets, *Red Detachment of Women* and *White-Haired Girl*; and one symphony, *Sha-jia-bang Symphony*. After 1969 several other model operas were produced, including *Azalea Mountain*, *Ode to the Dragon River*, *Battle in the Plains*, and *Bay of Panshi*, following the original model in content and form. These new revolutionary theatrical forms were praised as shining victories of the Cultural Revolution and Mao Zedong's Thought. An article published in the *Red Flag* under the pen name "Hong Cheng" (Red Town) states, "The glorious achievement of revolutionary operas marked a revolution in art by the proletariat. It is the major component of our country's proletarian cultural revolution. . . . In the series of revolutionary model operas nurtured by beloved Comrade Jiang Qing, the image of proletarian heroes is established; the stage that has been controlled by landlords and representatives of the bourgeoisie for the past thousand years is now gone. The real master of history has entered the field of art and started a new era in the history of art" (cited in *Relie zanyang geming yangbanxi zhiquweihushan* 1969, 32).

Model operas were performed on stages, broadcast on the radio, made into films, and sung by millions of people. They were the only available theatrical entertainment for 800 million people (the population of China at the time). As Huo Wang (1998) remembered, "Model operas are the only art form left in the whole of China. You cannot escape from listening to them. You hear them every time you turn on the radio. You hear them from loudspeakers every time you go outside" (202). Unlike European opera, which was essentially entertainment for the elite, modern Beijing opera had become a popular/political art. Many ordinary Chinese citizens were familiar with the arias in these model operas and would sing them at home or on the streets.

Guided by Mao's "Talks at Yan'an" and supervised by his wife, Jiang Qing, model operas aimed at achieving three goals. The first was to affirm the correctness of Mao's theory of "the armed struggle of the masses"; the second was to indoctrinate the masses with the notion that there had always been a class struggle between the proletarian and the bourgeoisie; and the third, and foremost, was to present a heroic characterization of workers, peasants, and soldiers. Only in this way can we "consolidate our socialist economy and serve the proletarian dictatorship," according to "Chu Lan," a pen name given to a writer in the *Red Flag* (*Wenyi pinglun ji* 1974, 95). These three goals had to be reflected in the content of the operas. In this way the theatrical art, similar to other art forms at the time, was politicized. According to Meng Wang (2001), "this feature of art being politicized is rooted in Chinese tradition, which has made the characteristics of Chinese politics as moral, sentimental, and instable" (334).

The musical feature of the modern Beijing opera was presented through Western musical instruments such as the violin and piano, combined with traditional Chinese musical instruments such as *jinghu* (Beijing operatic violin), *erhu* (Chinese violin), gongs, and drums. In addition, certain musical features of contemporary songs were added to traditional operatic melodies. An article in the *People's Daily* (11 November 1969, in *Relie zanyang*) raved that this intermingling of international styles "first successfully combined Eastern and Western musical accompaniment and marked a revolution in theatre art" (117). Although each model opera had its own story line, all shared some common themes. The analysis that follows focuses on two common themes, character portrayal and arias, in three important respects: depiction of revolutionary heroes, intense hatred and lack of personal feelings, and politically correct speech.

Depiction of Revolutionary Heroes

In each model opera a heroic lead plays the part of a real-life worker, a peasant, a soldier, or a low-level party official, with a keen sense of class consciousness and moral righteousness. For example, the character Fang Heizhen (in *On the Docks*), the party secretary of a Shanghai dock, was a middle-aged woman. She exposed the plot of a class enemy who mixed grains with dangerous chemicals in a sack of grain that was about to be shipped to Africa. Under her leadership the dockworkers successfully identified the sack in question and prevented a disaster in which people would have been poisoned and China's international reputation damaged. Fang Heizhen also educated Han Xiaoqiang, a young disgruntled dockworker, about the revolutionary history of the dock, persuading him to stay in the job. The proletarian heroes were always wiser, more intelligent, and better looking than their enemies. Yang Zirong (in *Taking Tiger Mountain by Strategies*), Aqing Sao (in *Sha Jia Village*), and Yan Weicai (in *Raid on the White Tiger Regiment*) easily outsmarted their enemies, wittily exposing their tactics and prevailing in the end. At Jiang Qing's request, their image had to be *gao* 高 (lofty), *da* 大 (glory), and *quan* 全 (complete) in the representation of the proletarian class. Meanwhile, in sharp contrast, the "bad guys" always looked base, shabby, ugly, and stupid.

DaizongYu (2001) offers the following example of such contrast in *Taking Tiger Mountain by Strategies*: "Yan Zirong (the heroic lead) emerged to majestic music, always taking center stage. He was singing and dancing, dragging Zuo Shandiao (the leader of the bandits) around by his nose on stage. When presenting a map, Yang stood in a majestic posture while Zuo Shandiao took the map with his body bending over" (3). This type of theatrical presentation followed the canon of the "Three Prominences" first proposed by Yu Huiyong, the minister of cultural affairs during the Cultural Revolution. It states: "In portraying all the characters, the positive figure must be prominent; In portraying the positive figures, the heroes must be prominent; In portraying heroes, the leading hero must be prominent" (Gucheng Li 1992, 60). This style of depiction aimed at diminishing bourgeois arrogance and enhancing proletarian self-esteem. However, this strategy created stereotypical images of "good guys" and "bad guys" based simply on appearance, with dire consequences for real Chinese people who had not been blessed with good looks. For example, one interviewee shared that when she and her classmates went to the Beijing railway station to read and sing Chairman Mao's pronouncements, they could always identify class enemies by the way they dressed and looked, based on the dictates of the model operas. American soldiers of the Korean War were the "bad guys" in *Raid on the White Tiger Regiment*. Consequently another interviewee confessed that she had always held the image of American soldiers as ferocious, hideous, and savage-looking. When years later she lived with a host family in the United States and discovered that her host had been a soldier during the Korean War, she was shocked at the contrast between the real person and her own preconceived image.

Intense Hatred and Lack of Personal Feelings
Hatred permeates every model opera. The hatred of class enemies was justified during the Cultural Revolution as they were perceived to be cruel, oppressive, and evil. The plots of the ballets *White-Haired Girl* and *Red Detachment of Women* each centered around a young woman who was exploited and oppressed by her vicious landlord. The young women escaped from their captives and were rescued by the communist army. In *Taking Tiger Mountain by Strategies* the heroic Chang Bao's grandmother was killed by a bandit and her mother forced to jump from a cliff. To avoid being captured, Chang Bao dressed up as a man and hid in the mountains. Li Tiemei, the young woman in *The Red Lantern,* learned from her adoptive grandmother that her parents had been killed by the Japanese. All three of these young women expressed extreme anger and hatred toward their enemies, along with a fierce determination to join the revolutionary force. These emotions intensified through the course of the opera as the music and singing became more and more passionate. The basic operatic message of these stories was that the villain or villains must be eliminated through the "armed struggle of the masses" so that a new society could be established. These operas also demonstrated that determination to sacrifice for the revolution must be motivated by deep hatred for all class enemies and love for the Communist Party. In the words of one interviewee, "After I repeatedly heard, saw, and sang along with model operas, I began to hate the old society and appreciate even more our new society. I felt so grateful to the party and Chairman Mao and was ready to fight any enemies and sacrifice my life to defend our country."

Class enemies did not always have their origins in the old society. In the model opera *On the Docks* the enemy emerged from within the new China and was therefore more difficult to identify. Through the evocative singing of the heroic party secretary, Fang Haizhen, the audience was moved to levels of intense hate for this new class enemy, shown engaging in acts of sabotage against Communist China. In this way the Maoist directive to "Never forget the class struggle" was reinforced and the masses were taught to be ever vigilant against the emergence of new class enemies. As Lu and Xiao (2000) observe in their analysis of model operas, "People are only presented in two fashions, friend or foe. If they belong to the same class, the proletarian class, then they are all class brothers and sisters. Otherwise, they are enemies" (245). ·

Furthermore, through model operas people were taught that there was no such thing as pure emotions and feelings toward others. All feelings and emotions were dictated by class identity. The heroic leads in these operas showed little personal feeling for others. Their concern for the poor and oppressed derived from their proletarian class consciousness, nothing more. Accordingly, the plot never involved any consideration for loving interpersonal relationships. One did not love a particular individual; one only loved communist ideology, the party, and Chairman Mao. All the heroic characters were single, middle-aged males or females, with the exception of Aqing Sao, who was married but whose husband never appeared onstage. There was absolutely no romance between male and female leads, and the only family that ever appeared in model opera was the ideologically based, rather than blood-related, family in *The Red Lantern*. The son, Li Yuhe, and the granddaughter, Li Tiemei, were from different families, and their own family members had died as revolutionary martyrs. They formed a new three-generational family for the revolutionary cause. Tellingly, some model operas, such as *Taking Tiger Mountain by Strategies, White-Haired Girl,* and *Red Detachment of Women,* contained romantic story lines in their original versions. However, the original versions were modified and these scenes removed. Love scenes were considered bourgeois, and sex was taboo; as in George Orwell's *1984,* sexual desire was considered a thought crime.

Politically Correct Speech

In traditional operas the lyrics typically consisted of emotionally expressive narratives. The language was poetic, exquisite, and classical. Such features were rare in model operas, which were characterized by politically correct speech and jargon, paralleling the rhetoric of the official media of the time. For example, in an aria in *Taking Tiger Mountain by Strategies* sung by Shao Jianbo, the political commissar of the Communist army, the following politically predictable explanation was given as to why his troop came to Tiger Mountain:

> We are the army of the workers and peasants.
> We came to the Mountain to annihilate reactionaries
> And change the world.
> For several decades, we fought from South to North.
> The Communist Party and Chairman Mao,

Guided us forward.
A Red Star is on our hat.
Two revolutionary flags are at our sides.
Dark clouds will be dispelled wherever there is a flag.
The people in the liberated zone have denounced the landlords;
And become the masters.
The people's army understands the misery of the people.
We come here to wipe out the bandits in Tiger Mountain.

An aria sung by Fang Haizhen in *On the Docks* was also filled with empty political utterances and clichés:

The whole world was changed by revolution.
Awakened people linked together through their hearts.
Mao Zedong's Thought spread like the east wind.
The fighting horn echoes over a whole new China.
Heroic soldiers emerged from fire:
Huang Jiguang, Luo Shengjiao, Yang Gensi, and Qiu Shaoyun [all war heroes]
Bravely marched in the battle against imperialism;
And exhibited the fighting spirit of internationalism.
There are thousands of heroes.
We must learn from their spirit of sacrifice to the world.
Participate in revolution for the whole of life.
Be a never-rusty screw for the revolutionary cause.

Such stylized wordplay appeared repeatedly in the official media of the time, serving the didactic purpose of raising proletarian consciousness and cultivating a love for Mao Zedong and the party. The incorporation of political jargon into the operatic format helped facilitate these aims. Members of the proletariat were portrayed as fearless heroes with undying loyalty and devotion to Mao Zedong and the party. In fact, the heroic leads in model operas were presented as real-life revolutionary role models in every thought, word, and deed. Because of the high moral tone of their speech they were considered above reproach and could not be challenged. They functioned as moral exemplars for the masses.

With all the efforts to promote model operas, not all of them achieved the desirable persuasive effect, however. For example, one interviewee told me that he never liked *On the Dock* and never appreciated the arias by Fang Haizhen, even though he knew she was a first-rate actress. On reflection he believes the main reason for his lack of appreciation is that he was put off by the political jargon and propaganda. Clearly, such operas failed to avoid the poster-and-slogan style of indoctrination and thus lacked genuine artistic merit, demonstrating the challenges inherent in achieving a true marriage of style and content. Further, because the lyrics in model operas deviated too much from traditional operatic content, the audience typically could not relate well to the perfect heroes of this new revolutionary form.

Impact of Revolutionary Songs and Operas

Impact on Culture

Songs became instruments of socialization, political control, and ideological persuasion in Communist China during the Cultural Revolution. They were part of a mechanism intended to remold the thought processes of almost one quarter of the human race. They were utilized in a campaign to mobilize the population to achieve specific goals such as disseminating radical ideas, eradicating class enemies, and maximizing cultlike devotion to Mao and the Communist Party. Although strategies of mass persuasion had been carefully orchestrated by the ruling party since 1949, these strategies were initiated and executed primarily by the masses during the Cultural Revolution. As Frederick T. C. Yu (1964) observed: "Ironically, perhaps, the Chinese Communists may be trapped by their own successful persuasion. By their incessant use of persuasive communications, the Communists have stirred up much of the old, traditional China; they have turned millions of unconcerned, conciliatory, and easy-going peasants and workers into aggressive, agitated, and vicious fighters and revolutionaries; they have introduced a type of political activity and a pattern of socialization that had never existed in the country" (158–59). Indeed, revolutionary songs and model operas have exerted powerful political force in agitating the masses and changing the face of Chinese culture.

In his examination of the changes in Chinese music Kraus (1989) remarked, "The music of the Cultural Revolution followed the trend established by 1964, although with greater violence and chaos. European classics were banned, but cultural revolutionaries propagated a music that was in fact highly Western in its technique, harmonic structure, instrumentation, and emphasis on choral singing. Music was an important part for the new art which Cultural Revolution leaders proposed to replace the old" (128). Mass songs, the violins and pianos used in model operas, and Marxist-Leninist ideology on art were certainly borrowed from the West and applied to the Chinese situation. Mao's wife, Jiang Qing, and the devoted Chinese masses helped him fulfill his mission of replacing old art forms with new. This in turn had a profound effect on Chinese culture, language, and communication. Ironically, when traditional art forms were written off as feudal and everything Western was dismissed as bourgeois, the guiding principle for the operatic revolution became Mao's teaching: "Make the past serve the present and foreign things serve China" (*Wenyi pinglun ji* 1974, 13).

In fact, the success of eulogy songs and quotation songs can be directly attributed to characteristics of traditional Chinese culture. Traditional Chinese culture emphasized *xiao* 孝 (filial piety) and *zhong* 忠 (loyalty). Filial piety was practiced with regard to family members, especially the elderly. Loyalty, on the other hand, was cultivated in relation to superiors, such as in the relationship between court ministers and the emperor. Having thoroughly embraced the Mandate of Heaven notion, the common people were typically in awe of the emperor. There were many literary and artistic expressions of this. For example, in the *Book of Odes* many passages profess loyalty and boundless love for the emperors of the Zhou dynasty (1027–770 B.C.E.). In traditional operas loyalty to the emperor and obedience to authority were highly praised. The Mandate of Heaven mythology of ancient China was naturally extended to adoration for Mao Zedong in modern times. When revolutionary songs equated Mao with the golden sun and his teachings with sunshine, the Chinese embraced such exaltation and took it in stride. Loyalty to the emperor was transferred to Mao and the party. Obedience to authority became obedience to Mao's teachings. Similarly, traditional Chinese values emphasized sacrifice for the community and state. The new revolutionary art forms celebrated sacrifice for the proletarian cause.

In Chinese language the two characters *guo* 國 (state) and *jia* (family) 家 are always used together, implying that the head of the country is also the head of the family. As China has had three thousand years of practicing filial piety in relation to the family, it was not difficult to extend the practice and apply it to the head of state. Though Mao presented himself as a radical reformer of Chinese society and was critical of traditional Chinese attitudes concerning filial piety and loyalty, he allowed the masses to worship him as another Chinese emperor.[10] The only difference was that no Chinese emperor before him had ever been elevated to such a grand scale of deification.

Several interviewees shared with me the processes they underwent in eventually coming to regard Mao as a living saint. Before the Cultural Revolution they already had great adoration for Mao, but not to the extent that Mao was even dearer to them than their own parents were. After singing and hearing many songs eulogizing Mao and his thought, these interviewees were convinced that Mao was the dearest, the wisest, and the greatest. They felt lucky to live during Mao's era and came to feel that they would not hesitate to sacrifice their lives to defend him. Toward the end of the Cultural Revolution the cult of Mao began to decline as many had become disillusioned. Interestingly, the worship for Mao has made a comeback in today's China. Many popular songs eulogizing Mao during the Cultural Revolution have regained their popularity and are available in the marketplace. It seems that the Chinese psyche needs a mythical figure like Mao. On the other hand, the practice of placing absolute faith in a godlike leader seems to have been shattered to a large degree by Mao's death. Deng Xiaoping and the current leaders (for example, Hu Jintao, Jiang Zemin) were never elevated to cult status as Mao was. No songs have been written eulogizing their deeds, and it is actually quite acceptable nowadays to criticize and even ridicule state leaders in private settings.

Impact on Thought

The singing of quotation songs helped with the memorization of Mao's instructions and sayings. Memorizing classics by heart has been a Chinese tradition. In imperial China children who could afford private tutoring would learn to recite and remember Confucian doctrines without understanding their meanings. Likewise many people, especially less educated workers and peasants, did not understand the meaning of Mao's words and sometimes applied them inappropriately as a consequence. Zealous members of the Red Guards, in particular, dogmatically applied Mao's pronouncements to meet their needs in defeating opponents or justifying violent conduct.

Traditionally the Chinese are known for their good common sense (Lin 1936), and Chinese thinking is characterized as synthetic and holistic (Kincaid 1987). This was not the case during the Cultural Revolution, when words were taken out of context and applied haphazardly as universal truths, fostering rigid thinking and blind faith. Through the promotion of popular revolutionary songs the Chinese people became increasingly more radical and polarized in their thinking. The lyrics of these songs were not known for their well-reasoned arguments but instead for their totally emotional and fanatical appeals. The songs did not address questions of injustice in concrete terms but rather provoked radical action through appeals to abstract doctrines and mythical figures. These songs not only totally negated alternative ideology and vigorously condemned indigenous cultural values, they also attacked any alternative views, in order to demonstrate their total allegiance to Mao. In this way participants were isolated from the outside world and deprived of critical abilities.

Singing songs of eulogy and songs of Mao's pronouncements promoted a sense of blind faith and acceptance of Mao as a living god and Mao's teachings as absolute truth. As blind faith in Mao increased, the ability to question and think critically diminished in inverse proportion. The irony was that few people had seriously studied Mao's works; most people could only sing or recite quotations out of context. Their speech became riddled with political clichés and jargon, in both the public and private spheres. George Orwell (1949) said it well half a century ago, in reference to a fictional totalitarian state: "In a way, the world-view of the Party imposed itself most successfully on people incapable of understanding it. They could be made to accept the most flagrant violation of reality, because they never fully grasped the enormity of what was demanded of them. . . . They simply swallowed everything" (157). The thought processes of the Chinese people were dictated by Mao's speech or by the official newspapers and media. This proved an effective way to enforce the uniformity of thought characteristic of other totalitarian societies. As the range of word choices became smaller and smaller, the Chinese worldview became narrower and narrower, to the point where the masses had no thoughts of their own. Especially when singing became automatic, lyrics and music exercised a hypnotic power to take away the ability to think.

Impact on Communication

Worse still, songs of radicalization and operas promoting hatred turned many Red Guards into monsters, warriors, and fanatics. Traditional Chinese culture taught people love and benevolence. Indeed, Confucius's concept of *ren* (benevolence) was based on love for the family and community. Further, the role model for the community was *junzi* (gentleman), who speaks and acts for the well-being of others and society. *Renai* 仁愛 (benevolence and love) had been the core value in governing and managing personal relationships. Traditional operas and performing arts emphasized compassion, love, and forgiveness. In contrast, the radical songs and model operas produced during the Cultural Revolution bred hatred, revenge, and violence. In their study of revolutionary children's songs Chu and Cheng (1978) discuss the fact that children's songs produced during the Cultural Revolution were militant and agitating. In their words, "In terms of militancy, revolutionary children's folk songs liberally apply such phrases as 'opening fire at,' 'smash them,' 'repudiate until they stink,' 'pierce through their black hearts" (39–40). Hatred of class enemies was promoted through the singing of revolutionary songs from an early age. Before the Cultural Revolution such hatred was targeted at American imperialism, Soviet revisionism, and the Nationalist Party. During the Cultural Revolution the hatred was turned toward capitalist roaders and the five black categories or class enemies. Love was reserved for Mao Zedong and the party alone. The hatred stirred up by inflammatory and polarized language provided the fuel for violence and mass hysteria, and it led to deficiencies in psychological development and deprivation of humanity. This mentality of hatred is still evident in China today. Influenced by official media rhetoric with regard to Sino-American relations, some young people freely express resentment and hatred toward Americans, as articulated in the 1996 best-seller *China Can Say No* (Song, Zhang, and Qian 1996a).

Moreover, the watching and singing of model operas engendered stereotypes and polarized thinking in categories of "good guys" versus "bad guys." This tendency is reminiscent of the American Hollywood style of storytelling except that in model operas "good guys" and "bad guys" were defined by their class affiliations and the class struggle was always the dominant theme in each opera. Heroes were always virtuous proletarians. The party secretary was always correct. Landlords and capitalists were always villains. There was always someone in a leadership position who needed help raising proletarian consciousness. An innocent family or individual was always exploited, abused, or killed by the bad guys. The same format and portrayal of characters was extended to other theatrical and literary forms. In these ways the performing arts were completely politicized and subordinated to the political agenda.

Another significant feature of model operas was their impact on perceptions of womanhood. Taught to model themselves after the heroines in the model operas, women growing up during the Cultural Revolution went through a major gender identity crisis. On the one hand, they were expected to embody traditional virtues of womanhood with feminine attributes and devotion to their husbands and children. On the other hand, they were expected to be masculine, tough, and ambitious. Several women interviewees expressed concern about their inability to present themselves in a feminine manner. For example, they claimed not to know how to dress themselves properly, to apply makeup, or to express their romantic feelings and sexual desires. They believe that the socializing influences they experienced during the Cultural Revolution have adversely affected the way they communicate with their male partners and colleagues, their choice of dates and decisions regarding marriage, their identity construction processes, and the way they raise their own children.

Interestingly, the singing of revolutionary songs and operatic arias did not come to an end with the close of the Cultural Revolution. In China today one can easily purchase songbooks and CDs eulogizing Mao Zedong as well as VCDs and DVDs of model operas. Further, one can easily hear such songs sung at karaoke bars or parties.

The songs no longer exert the degree of influence they did during the Cultural Revolution, however. Instead they have become historical records enjoyed purely for pleasure and nostalgia, and seemingly without any lingering negative association.[11] For example, one interviewee described how the parents of a student at a Chinese school in Chicago responded with enthusiasm when asked to sing songs from the Cultural Revolution, such as "On the Golden Mountain of Beijing" or "Red Lake Water," for the celebration of the Chinese New Year.

A Rhetorical Analysis
of Political Rituals

The Chinese people used to have a lot of emperors. When they did not have one in the CRM [Cultural Revolution movement], they made one up. They also used to have plenty of gods to worship. During a period when all the old gods were abolished, they had to create a new one. This was the principal cultural background for the emergence and practice of rituals during the Cultural Revolution Movement.

Shaorong Huang, *To Rebel Is Justified*

In the first three years of the Cultural Revolution, my mother made all family members follow the ritual of worshipping Mao in the morning. If we children did something wrong, she would ask us to write a self-criticism report, and either read it to the family or post it on the wall. . . . We had so many meetings at school and there were always various types of rallies, parades and debates on the street. I still have vivid memories of these events.

Account from an interview

Philipsen (1987) defines ritual as "a communication form in which there is a structured sequence of symbolic acts, the correct performance of which constitutes homage to a sacred object" (250). Put another way, through ritualistic practices symbols and behaviors are standardized, participants follow prescribed social rules and norms in their conduct, and activities are centered around paying reverence to a spiritual figure or domain. Rituals typically function to maintain social order, instill cultural values, and reinforce socially desired behavior. By observing and participating in rituals participants affirm a shared identity and achieve a sense of togetherness. According to Philipsen, ritualistic performance acts as a vehicle for the articulation of myth, defined as "a great symbolic narrative which holds together the imagination of a people" (251). Moreover, rituals provide occasions for social actors to express themselves dramatically. Religious ceremony is a common form of ritualistic drama. In this context participants pay homage to a supernatural being through a sequence of ritualistic acts, supernatural mythology is being communicated, and a social drama is played out following a prescribed set of procedures. Ideally, in the process participants are emotionally engaged in a catharsis of sacred dimensions.

While religious rituals are rooted in cultural traditions, they sometimes function as powerful means of political persuasion. For example, the Japanese military is known to have used religious rituals borrowed from the Shinto tradition to promote nationalistic sentiments and a sense of racial superiority in the furtherance of their expansionist policies during World War II. In addition, Fundamentalist Muslims have employed Islamic rituals to promote the spirit of jihad and unification of the Arab world. U.S. president George W. Bush has harnessed the emotive power of Christian mythology through his use of ritualized words such as "evil" and "crusade" in his speeches condemning terrorism and justifying U.S. military actions. As another example, Falun Gong practitioners in China expressed their demands for human rights through ritualistic demonstrations in Tiananmen Square and throughout the world.[1] Kenneth Burke (1969b) characterizes such persuasive activities, which take place through dramatic performance, ritual, and symbolic enactment for the purpose of affirming and creating a shared identity, as "pure persuasion."

Rituals, rites, and codes of propriety (*li* 禮) are essential elements of a Confucian society. For Confucius, only through the performance of certain rituals involving listening, speaking, singing, and dancing on occasions such as funerals, ancestor worship, and official ceremonies was it possible to learn proper social behavior and attain the mental state of benevolence. In these ways hierarchical relationships and social order could be maintained. Thus, Confucius regarded submission to rituals as a hallmark of human virtue, or *de* 德 (Confucius, *Lun Yu,* 12.1), and admonished his disciples to conform to the dictates of *li*. In this regard he counseled the state kings of his time to "lead the masses by virtue and restrain them by rituals so that they can develop a sense of shame and a sense of participation" (2.3). In the Confucian scheme of things, ritualistic performance was aimed at instilling social values, reinforcing social hierarchy and unity, and maintaining stability through repeated and carefully orchestrated procedures. For example, in the ritual of ancestor worship, family members traditionally sacrifice food and animals to their ancestors, kowtowing to them in chronological order from the oldest to the youngest family members.[2] Through this highly standardized ceremonial rite the value of filial piety is reinforced, family hierarchy is upheld, and family cohesiveness is strengthened.

Rituals have been manipulated and appropriated to achieve political goals in virtually every nation in the world. In the U.S. context, Bennett (1980) points out that political campaigns, elections, and public debates in American culture are examples of political rituals that affect public thinking and action. In his view, rituals of such nature "use dramatic themes and actions to attract attention, simplify problems, emphasize particular principles, and structure the responses of participants" (176). Hence public perceptions of reality are shaped through the dramatic enactment of the myths rather than through rational engagement. Chinese political communication is, likewise, characterized by participation in political rituals and the enactment of myths and legends related to Mao and the CCP. Echoing the Confucian model of China's ancient past, modern-day Chinese people typically respond to political pressure from their leaders with a set of desired behavioral and linguistic patterns. As Pye (1968) observes, "Once the correct responses are learned, they [the Chinese people] can be tireless in repeating what they feel is expected of them. The result is a widespread tendency to standardize and ritualize all forms of learned behavior" (187). While the standardized and ritualized practices of confession, self-criticism, and political study sessions continued to exist during the Cultural Revolution, more ritualistic forms were added and enacted at that time.

I am inclined to label the ritualistic practices of the Cultural Revolution "political rituals" as they were performed purely for the political purposes of mind control and to promote submission to authority. Various types of political rituals were practiced during the Cultural Revolution and had impact on Chinese thought, culture, and communication.

Types of Political Rituals

On the basis of published memoirs and interview findings, four types of political rituals practiced during the Cultural Revolution can be discerned. These involve: (1) self-criticism and fighting selfishness; (2) deification of Mao Zedong; (3) political activities; and (4) public debates.

Self-criticism and Fighting Selfishness

From the time of the Yan'an thought reform movement of 1942, confession, self-criticism, and political study sessions were the primary techniques for instilling class consciousness used by Mao and the Communist Party. These ritualistic forms, with their standardized procedures and expectations, had become part of the political landscape of Mao's China. Participants would first self-disclose their "sins," ranging from disagreement with the party to selfish thoughts or conduct. Next they would express the need to reform themselves in accordance with Marxist-Maoist ideology. At this point they would typically invite criticism from their communist comrades and engage in more self-criticism of their errant thoughts and actions. Then participants would share their experiences of coming into full revolutionary consciousness and describe how criticism and self-criticism had assisted them in this regard. During the Cultural Revolution this political ritual continued and was intensified with the issuance of Mao's new directive called *dou si pi xiu* 鬥私批修 (Fighting Selfishness and Denouncing Revisionism). Forums for self-criticism were subsequently referred to as "Fighting Selfishness and Denouncing Revisionism" sessions.

The new directive was announced in a speech by Lin Biao during the eighteenth anniversary celebration of the founding of the People's Republic of China. Lin Biao explained the meanings of this new directive: "Chairman Mao recently stated that '[We] must fight selfishness and denounce revisionism.' To 'fight selfishness' is to use Marxist-Leninist and Maoist Thought to fight against selfishness in one's head. To 'denounce revisionism' means using Marxist-Leninist and Maoist Thought to fight against revisionism and against a handful of capitalist roaders within the Party. The two objectives are interrelated. Only by doing well in fighting selfishness, can we carry out the task of repudiating revisionism" (*People's Daily,* 2 October 1976). According to this explanation, the fight against selfishness was closely linked to the ideological struggle against revisionism, which threatened to return China to its miserable past in the fashion of feudalism and capitalism. It was therefore the responsibility of every citizen to weed out even the slightest hint of selfishness in order to prevent China from becoming a capitalist society. The slogan "Fight Selfishness and Denounce Revisionism" soon permeated public discourse in China. In the minds of the Chinese masses it was left to the intellectuals and government officials to "denounce revisionism," but "fighting selfishness" was understood as a revolutionary activity that applied to everyone.

The fight against selfishness began with self-criticism, which was rooted in the Confucian tradition. Confucianism promoted self-contemplation and self-criticism as means of cultivating and acquiring virtue. In this regard Mencius, Confucian scholar of the highest ranking, believed that human nature was inherently good (Mencius 1992, 6a.6.257). However, in order to maintain one's goodness, one must constantly engage in self-cultivation and self-examination. In Mencius's view, humans are entirely capable of rectifying themselves and making moral decisions (6a.8.165). Further, the desired mental state of *ren* (benevolence) could be achieved through introspection and contemplation of one's own thoughts and deeds (4b.28.191). This belief in basic human ability has been co-opted for achieving communist morals, implicit in Mao's propaganda campaigns calling for ideological transformation as well as in the government's efforts to remold a new Communist person. For Mao, proletarian consciousness was characterized by a selfless mind-set that could be cultivated in individuals who were willing to engage in self-criticism and voluntarily abandon thoughts and behaviors not in alignment with communist ideology. As early as 1942 Mao advocated the use of self-criticism as a way of overcoming complacency and obtaining correct thought. In his words, "A person with truly good intentions must criticize the shortcomings and mistakes in his own work with utmost candor and resolve to correct them. This is precisely why Communists employ the method of self-criticism. This alone is the correct stand. Only in this process of serious and responsible practice is it possible gradually to understand what the correct stand is and gradually obtain a good grasp of it" (Mao [1942] 1975, 93). Thus, for Mao, it is possible to educate and reform oneself as long as a person is willing to expose his or her inner thoughts and engage in self-criticism. As Pye (1968) notes, moral persuasion and self-cultivation have been persistent features of Chinese political communication. Indeed, the desire to be a good, selfless person lies deep within the Chinese psyche. During the Cultural Revolution self-criticism was often presented in the form of confession, and this confessional language was ritualized and standardized.

Confession and self-criticism during the Cultural Revolution took different ritualistic forms. The first type concerns those intellectuals or party officials who were considered class enemies. In their confessions they were required to identify their "ideological errors," find the sources of their wrong thoughts, and express willingness to correct them. For example, Feng Zhao (1999) recorded the following confession by a high-ranking official:

> I joined the revolution over twenty years ago. I have never worked in a lower level position. I have never been an ordinary worker. I have been in a leadership position all these years. As I got promoted to a higher position, my desire for luxury became strong, and I was further removed from working-class people. I had reached the dangerous point [of becoming a class enemy]. . . . Since I came to the May Seventh Cadre School, I have worked as an ordinary person at the basic levels. From the experience of working with workers and peasants, I have become their student. I obey their orders and never ask for special treatment. This experience has helped me fight against my corrupt soul and rectify my bourgeois behavior. (20)

Confessions of this type would be read in public or posted in public forums. Willingly or unwillingly, the person under scrutiny would "disclose" his or her shortcomings, real or fabricated, as a demonstration of willingness to be reformed. Feng Zhao (1999) recorded a series of confessions by intellectuals and party officials in the May Seventh Cadre Schools. All of them admitted that at some point in their communist careers they had discontinued the effort of self-examination and thought reform, and that this had led to mistakes either in thought or action against the proletarian ideology. Without exception, they expressed gratitude to Mao Zedong and his teachings, as well as for their experiences of intimate association with workers and peasants.

These views of thought reform had been extended to the children of class enemies as well. Labeled "rectifiable," these children with family backgrounds in the five black categories were presumed to have been harmfully influenced by their parents and thus in need of self-efforts to repudiate such influence. Repeated exposure to this type of public discourse, in school and in the media, engendered a self-fulfilling prophecy for many "rectifiable children." Several interviewees who had been classified as such recollected how they had been taught and come to believe that they were infected with traces of bourgeois thought and behavior simply because they came from family backgrounds with little or no contact with workers and peasants. In order to improve themselves and repudiate their bourgeois habits of thought, they would constantly criticize themselves at school, engage in self-confession in their diaries, and in general do everything they could to reform themselves.

However, self-criticism alone could not accomplish these goals. It was also necessary to do hard physical labor and learn from workers and peasants in their daily lives. One interviewee described her feelings and behaviors at the time: "I wanted to show how I had abandoned my bourgeois family influence by wearing shabby clothes and shoes. Once my pants had a hole, I just patched it and put the pants on again. I refused to eat any good food and wear any new clothes. I always chose to do the dirtiest work and deliberately forced myself to endure hardship. I thought this would prove that I had truly reformed myself and transformed into a true proletariat." Another interviewee recalled:

I and a few other "rectifiable children" volunteered to clean public toilets after school as a way to reform ourselves and get closer to the experience of workers and peasants. I was born into an intellectual family. I was taught by the party and Chairman Mao that intellectuals were afraid of hardship and dirty work. I was convinced that I was born with some moral defects but I believed I could change myself by doing dirty work and engaging in self-criticism. It had become a ritual at home that when I had done or said something wrong, my mother would ask me to write a self-criticism report and post it on the wall. I constantly criticized myself at school and consciously chose to do work that would make me dirty, as a way of reforming myself.

Many "rectifiable children" chose to work in remote rural areas or the poorest parts of the country after high school graduation for the same reason.

Another type of self-criticism concerned the "ordinary people." It was presumed that everyone had selfish thoughts or engaged in selfish actions at one time or another. It was, therefore, imperative even for workers and peasants to constantly fight against selfishness. Schools and workplaces hosted criticism/self-criticism forums for Fighting Selfishness and Denouncing Revisionism. In order to prove their commitment to the guiding principles of the Cultural Revolution, many people went out of their way to find fault with themselves. Several interviewees recollected engaging in the revolutionary activity of "fighting selfishness." One interviewee recalled: "Once I saw one fen (one eighth of a U.S. penny) on the road. I picked it up and put in my pocket. Then I thought about Mao's teachings and realized I was being selfish. I then handed the penny over to a policeman. During a 'Fighting Selfishness and Denouncing Revisionism' session, I told this story to my class at school. I exaggerated the struggle I went through in making the decision to give back the penny. My teacher and classmates applauded my efforts. I felt good about myself." This rite of passage encouraged individuals to confess their moral defects and also exerted peer pressure on other participants to do the same. In this way one's sense of guilt was transformed into a moment of revolutionary redemption shared by all who witnessed it. Ross (1994) characterizes this process of public self-criticism as an effective "remolding system" for "becoming a new person" (9). Self-criticism sessions were similar to the religious ritual of "Bible Studies," whereby an individual discloses his or her sinful thoughts and acts and struggles to live a good Christian life, in accordance with the teachings of Jesus Christ. Through self-criticism and confession the person is redeemed and morally cleansed.

Not all self-criticism reports revealed the true thoughts and experiences of those composing them. In Fighting Selfishness and Denouncing Revisionism sessions all participants were expected to present their confessions or self-criticisms along the lines of the protocol mentioned above. However, out of fear of being ostracized, some individuals were pressured to fabricate stories. For example, one interviewee recounted:

When it was about my turn to share my selfish thought at the "Fighting Selfishness and Denouncing Revisionism" session, I was very nervous because I did not know what to say. I never had those transformative experiences that others described. I did not want to be perceived as arrogant so I made up a story. I told the class that I disliked the smell of a peasant while working in the field. After I studied Mao's works, I realized I was influenced by bourgeois thoughts which were detrimental to my spiritual well-being. I began to respect peasants and regard them as teachers. My teacher and classmates looked pleased after hearing my story. I was relieved.

Such forms of self-criticism exerted the pressure to lie and forced the participants to conform to the political and ritualized discourse expected of them. For example, Luo (1990) recorded a confession related to a poem written by a fifth grade student. The poem was found when Red Guards searched the student's apartment. It described his parents as "the light of the world" during a time when the student was sick. According to the Maoist mythology of the time, such expression of reverence could only be used in reference to Chairman Mao, so the student was forced to write a self-criticism report in strict conformance to the politically correct rhetoric of the communist ideology. The student wrote:

> First, let me salute and wish a long, long life to our Great Leader, Great Teacher, Great Commander, and Great Helmsman, the Reddest Sun burning in our hearts, Chairman Mao. I also wish Vice Chairman Lin Biao eternal health! Everlasting health to Lin Biao! This great, unprecedented Proletarian Cultural Revolution has washed the concealed filth and scum off the streets and into the sewer like a spring torrent. Just as a harsh, autumn wind blows away the dead and useless leaves, so has the Cultural Revolution dispersed the Four Obsolete Vestiges and the Ox Ghosts and Snake Devils. The Red Guards came to my house and helped me. Such actions are both just and revolutionary. . . . (47–48)

These are typical lines from the opening paragraphs of a self-criticism report during the Cultural Revolution. The remainder of the report would include confession of one's faults, an analysis of the roots of one's faults, and an indication of how to correct one's faults. In her memoir Niu-Niu (1995) provides an example of one such forced confession: "My shortcomings are very serious; they are unpardonable. I am ashamed, but I beg you nevertheless to continue helping me correct my faulty. My mistakes show that I have not understood the aim of the great Cultural Revolution and that I don't have enough love for Mao. All my life I must study Mao's sayings with determination and love the Party with all my heart" (102). Such confessions were read in public, posted on bulletin boards, or reviewed by Red Guard leaders. Some people took self-criticism very seriously and truly believed that they had indeed committed mistakes. Others said things they did not mean for fear of social ostracism and punishment. Willingly or unwillingly, virtually every member of Chinese society participated in the ritual of fighting selfishness through criticism and self-criticism.

The practice of keeping diaries was another method of voluntary thought reform and fighting against selfishness. The use of diaries as a public forum for exposing selfish thoughts and promoting correct ideology was inspired by Lei Feng, a government-sanctioned, revolutionary role model of mythic proportions. Lei Feng kept a diary of his attempts to live a truly exemplary life in strict adherence to the communist ideal, as espoused by Mao Zedong. After his death as a young soldier Lei Feng's diary was published. His example was followed by millions who began recording their own successes and failures at thought reform in their diaries. Though individual experiences of consciousness raising might differ, the language used in the diaries conformed to the highly formalized political discourse of the time. Some people kept diaries for the sole purpose of public review. As one interviewee explained: "I wrote several volumes of diaries during the Cultural Revolution. I used language that showed my loyalty to Mao and depicted myself as a selfless person. I imagined that my diaries would be published and read by many people as a source of inspiration after I had died a hero."

Indeed, diaries were considered hard evidence of people's degrees of loyalty to Mao and the revolutionary cause. Consequently many people were persecuted simply because they expressed politically incorrect views on the pages of their diaries, which were then stolen and read by someone else. For example, Yu Luojin and Yu Luoke were arrested simply because their diaries, in which they expressed doubts, confusion, questions, and disagreements with various aspects of the Cultural Revolution, were found and turned over to the police. Their views were considered counterrevolutionary and constituted political crimes. Yu Luojin was imprisoned and sent to a labor camp for many years. Her brother, Yu Luoke, was imprisoned and sentenced to death (Yu 2000). From examples like these, people learned to protect themselves by fabricating the contents of their diaries. One interviewee explained that prior to the Cultural Revolution he had written a diary expressing disillusionment and concern for his future under communist rule. Seeing how people were persecuted for the views expressed in their diaries, he destroyed this diary. Then out of fear that he would be asked what happened to it, he laboriously fabricated a politically correct diary to take its place.

Self-criticism was employed as a means of self-cultivation in Confucian China. Unfortunately this traditional practice was appropriated by the Communist Party in the interest of promoting political conformity throughout its ruling period. Those who participated in confession/self-criticism rituals during the Cultural Revolution bear deep psychological scars that may take years to heal. Such rituals had a huge impact on the Chinese communication behaviors.

Deification of Mao Zedong

Jowett and O'Donnell (1999) identified four ritualistic elements common to all religions: "1) charismatic figures; 2) heavy symbolism; 3) a simple and incessant moral philosophy; and 4) an understanding of the needs of one's audience" (54). Though communism is not a religion per se and Mao is not a supernatural deity, the rituals of the Cultural Revolution were characterized by all of these elements. In fact, during the Cultural Revolution one's daily life was permeated with ritualistic practices of a religious nature. For example, after arriving at work or school the day typically began with *san jing san zhu* 三敬三祝 (three respects and three wishes) to Chairman Mao. Everyone lined up before the portrait of Mao Zedong and waved the Little Red

Books, wishing Chairman Mao three times longevity and Lin Biao three times eternal health. The same ritual could also take place immediately after waking up, before the start of a meeting, and before every meal. It was then followed by singing "The East Is Red" and reciting Mao's quotations.

After the wishes and singing in front of Mao's portrait, a group leader would ask for guidance. This process was known as *zao qingshi* 早請示 (asking instructions in the morning). At the end of the day people gathered again in front of Mao's portrait to report what work they had accomplished during the day and what thought problems they had solved through studying Mao's pronouncements, confessing their selfish thoughts, and struggling to overcome them. This ritual was known as *wan huibao* 晚彙報 (reporting in the evening). For those labeled "class enemies," as Wang (1998) recorded, this was the time to confess one's crimes in front of Mao's portrait and recite the following words: "Beloved Chairman Mao, I have sinned, I am a criminal. I am ungrateful to you" (187). To be politically correct, in holding Mao's Little Red Book one must place the book over one's heart with the thumb in the front and other fingers behind, indicating absolute loyalty and boundless love for Mao. Several interviewees recalled that they observed this ritual within their families and neighborhoods as well.

The ritual of worshiping Mao was often accompanied by *zhong zi wu* 忠字舞 (the loyalty dance), which involved the simple movement of stretching one's arms from one's heart to Mao's portrait, symbolizing again absolute loyalty and boundless love for Mao. The steps of the dance had their origins in a Xinjiang folk dance, while the music derived from a popular eulogy song, "Beloved Chairman Mao." The lyrics were as follows:

> Beloved Chairman Mao,
> We have so much in our hearts to tell you;
> We have so many songs to sing to you.
> Hundreds and thousands of red hearts pump for you;
> Hundreds and thousands of red hearts face the red sun;
> We wish you a long life forever.

The loyalty dance was performed in classrooms, in workplaces, and on the streets throughout the country. At times passion for the loyalty dance rose to absurd levels. For example, Xiao Di (1993) recorded that a local official sang revolutionary songs and danced the loyalty dance, in utter devotion to Mao, all the way from the airport to his office after returning from a conference in Beijing (165). An interviewee recalled how a shop assistant had gathered all the customers together to do a loyalty dance at the start of the business day. Huang (1996) witnessed a grand performance of the loyalty dance by thousands of workers in the city of Xian: "The performers filled a very wide street for a length of nearly half a mile, following a truck with a huge portrait of Mao on it and two loudspeakers singing songs praising Mao. All the performers danced seriously, and people on sidewalks watched them with respect" (146).

The loyalty dance was most popular among students, workers, and peasants. Some embraced it as a form of entertainment since no other types of entertainment were available at the time. Many intellectuals disliked the dance, feeling that it was foolish and distasteful. In Wang's (1998) words, "It was disgusting, my skin felt itchy and my hair was standing on end when I saw people doing the loyalty dance. . . . This way of presenting loyalty is too artificial and hypocritical" (187). An interviewee recalled how, as a guest at a hotel, he had been called on, along with other guests, to participate in a loyalty dance. When he refused to participate, he was accused of not loving Chairman Mao enough. Under political pressure he reluctantly joined in. The fanaticism displayed with regard to the loyalty dance did not last long, possibly because of its seemingly ludicrous nature.

The zeal to deify Mao intensified as the Cultural Revolution unfolded. Slogans eulogizing Mao were repeated constantly throughout the country. Mao's portrait was posted on the streets, in workplaces, in classrooms, in every household, on trains and buses, and in stores. Further, it was posted alongside every one of Mao's pronouncements printed in official newspapers or Red Guard handbills. Every day people participated in political activities such as rallies and parades, shouting the slogans "We Wish Chairman Mao Thousands of Years of Life!" and "We Wish the Vice-Chairman Lin Biao Eternal Health!" To show their loyalty to Mao some people even painted the Chinese character *zhong* 忠 (loyalty) and wore it on their chests. The character was made in various art forms and different sizes. In addition traditional Chinese altars used for ancestor worship were converted into altars of loyalty to Mao. As observed by Hsia (1972), "Many Chinese villages have dedicated 'rooms of loyalty' to Chairman Mao and many peasant households have their own 'tablets of loyalty.' These are clearly derived from the ancestral temples and tablets of the old China; mornings and evenings the villagers gather, either in their communal room, or in front of their family tablets, to pay homage to Mao Tse-tung [Mao Zedong]" (233).

Another way of showing loyalty to Mao was to wear a Mao badge on one's chest. The making, collecting, and trading of Mao badges became a national pastime. Badges varied in size from as small as a penny coin to as large as a rice bowl. Everyone in China, from top officials to ordinary people, wore Mao badges. Badges were made of metal, glass, wood, or plastic in all kinds of designs, some elaborate and some simple. The badge symbolized being with Mao in spirit and being guided by him at all times. In his memoir Gao Yuan (1987) describes the transcendental experience of wearing a Mao badge: "I pinned one on my chest and the other inside my pocket. I was sure I could feel Chairman Mao's radiance burning into me" (120). In a Cultural Revolution photograph collection by Li Zhensheng (2003), a soldier is shown to wear 170 Mao badges on his cap and uniform as a way to express his loyalty and admiration for Mao. Many people pinned the badges they collected onto pieces of red cloth. Nearly every family had a large collection of such badges; my mother has collected over three hundred of them. An interviewee recalled that when Mao badges first appeared she and her family had to stand in line overnight in order to purchase them. By her account, "There were hundreds of people in line. There was a limit on how many a person could buy, so my whole family went. Whenever someone promised to get a new Mao badge for us, we were very grateful. We regarded these badges as family treasures." Mao's image and related symbols were omnipresent during the Cultural Revolution. Luo (1990) describes a typical wedding photo at the time: "[It] showed the bride and groom posing with red bags at their waists, Chairman Mao's picture pinned to their chests, Little Red Books held in one hand over their shoulders, and stacks of Chairman Mao's works in the other. A sunflower in the background represented their loyalty to the Red Sun" (114). Naturally, typical wedding gifts at the time were Little Red Books and Mao badges. While the country was on the verge of economic collapse the production, distribution, and trading of Mao badges escalated. Ironically, today these badges are considered valuable "antiques" and are sold at exorbitant prices. Bennett (1980) asserts, "The focus on powerful human image (whether they be heroic leaders or gods) is an element of many rituals in which private life concerns are translated into shared public images and formulations" (178). Indeed, during the Cultural Revolution participation in the rituals of deifying Mao revealed Chinese people's desire for protection and blessing from Mao, and public rituals had become significant forms to express such desire.

These ritualized practices were so politicized that anyone who dared to voice differing opinions would immediately be labeled a "counterrevolutionary." For example, one interviewee recalled the persecution of his colleague Mr. Chen for the following thought crime: "When we all lined up for the morning ritual of wishing Chairman Mao a long life, Teacher Chen uttered, 'this is like saying prayers to God.' His utterance was heard by someone standing next to him. He was immediately reported and charged with the crime of being a counterrevolutionary.[3] He was then denounced countless times at rallies, removed from his teaching position, and sent to a remote rural area. He worked as a peasant for eight years until the end of the Cultural Revolution." In addition graphic or photographic images of Mao were considered so sacred that any damage done to them was deemed an act of deliberate sabotage and open defiance against Mao. For example, an interviewee told the following story: "One of my classmates was trying to cover a statue of Mao on a rainy day. By accident, he knocked off part of the statue, which smashed to pieces. The next day, the boy was labeled a counterrevolutionary and denounced by the whole school. He was only twelve years old at the time. The ordeal was a huge humiliation to him and his family." There are countless such stories of innocent people accused of being counterrevolutionaries for committing purely accidental acts.

Political rituals also took the form of the Red Guards' travels around China and Mao's review of the Red Guards. These rituals further escalated the fanatical deification of Mao. In the first year of the Cultural Revolution the Red Guards traveled around the country free of charge, in the interest of sharing their revolutionary experiences. This practice was known as *Da Chuanlian* 大串聯 (the great exchange). *Da Chuanlian* was first encouraged by Mao Zedong, who in 1966 was quoted as saying:

"Students from all over the country want to come to Beijing. This request should be granted and they should not be charged for their traveling cost" (Xiao Di 1993, 80).[4] On 16 October, Chen Boda, the head of the Cultural Revolution Committee of the CCP, issued a document with the approval of Mao Zedong claiming that "*Da Chuanlian* and the Red Guards are the two great inventions of the Proletarian Cultural Revolution. Chairman Mao strongly supports *Da Chuanlian* and advocates further promotion of this revolutionary action" (81). Many Red Guards took advantage of this opportunity to visit places where Mao and the Communist Party had lived and worked. These places were revered as *geming shengdi* 革命圣地 (sacred revolutionary lands). Like the religious practice of pilgrimage to holy places for the purpose of gaining protection, inspiration, and enlightenment from saints or other holy figures who function as channels of the divine, travel by members of the Red Guards was conducted to "sacred revolutionary lands" in order to experience firsthand the glorious history of the Communist Party and bring themselves closer to the spirit of Chairman Mao. Some Red Guards visited universities and high schools across the country in the name of *qujing* 取經 (getting the script) and *shanfeng dianhuo* 煽風點火 (inflaming and agitating). They called on students and the masses to rebel against local administrators and party officials, thereby creating a chaotic situation. Such revolutionary ardor was further encouraged and inflamed by Mao's reviews of millions of impassioned Red Guards in Tiananmen Square.

On 18 August 1966 Mao Zedong made his first appearance at the Gate of Heavenly Peace in Tiananmen Square. Wearing an army uniform and a Red Guard armband, he received millions of Red Guards from all over the country. The *People's Daily* reported the scene the following day: "At five o'clock in the morning, the sun rose from the eastern horizon, sending a thousand rays of radiance. Chairman Mao greeted a sea of people and streamers in Tiananmen Square. . . . The square was boiling. Everyone raised both hands above their heads, jumping, cheering, clapping hands toward Chairman Mao. Many people's hands had turned red because of the constant clapping; tears of joy and adulation streamed down their cheeks. . . . The masses chanted over and over, 'Long live Chairman Mao! Long live, long, long live!.' Waves of chanting rose again and again, vibrating the air of the capital." Such public spectacles of epic proportions took place on eight separate occasions during a three-month period in the late summer and fall of 1966. Each time the same rituals were repeated. Each time the *People's Daily* reported the event with passionate and emotionally charged language. The reports were read through loudspeakers, over the radio, and in political meetings by people all over China.

Many of those who were present in Tiananmen Square during Mao's historical reviews of the Red Guard troops considered these the happiest moments of their lives. Such epiphanies were recorded in countless memoirs of that time. For example, Liang Heng, a Red Guard himself, described his feelings on seeing Chairman Mao: "I was bawling like a baby, crying out incoherently again and again: 'You are our hearts' reddest, reddest sun!' My tears blocked my vision, but I could do nothing to control myself" (Heng and Shapiro 1983, 124). Liang Heng then sent a telegraph to his family saying, "this evening at 9:15, I became the happiest person in the world" (125). Other Red Guards reported the opposite experience. After waiting for several hours and enduring heat, thirst, hunger, and fatigue, Quan Xie (1998) finally saw Mao Zedong standing in a jeep as he passed by the crowd. In Xie's words, "I saw him wearing a green army outfit. Maybe because he was too tired, he was expressionless. . . . I thought at such a moment I would have some wonderful feelings. However, I did not experience anything. I did not feel anything sacred. I was not even excited. . . . I then felt a sense of guilt" (150). Several interviewees reported not being able to see Mao's face clearly, either because he was too far away or because he went by too quickly. However, all vividly recalled the experience of patiently waiting in an atmosphere of extreme, emotionally charged anticipation for the arrival of Chairman Mao and then, when he finally did appear, the symbolic acts of Mao deification expressed through slogan shouting, hand shaking, jumping, and cheering.

Shaking hands with Chairman Mao was considered the ultimate honor. Those who were given this honor were expected to share the blessing with their comrades. Liang Heng describes how this was accomplished: "Those [hands] Chairman Mao had touched now became the focus of our fervor. Everyone surged toward them with outstretched arms in hopes of transferring the sacred touch to their own hands. If you couldn't get close enough for that, then shaking the hand of someone who had shaken hands with our Great Saving Star would have to do. So it went, down the line, until sometimes handshakes were removed as many as one hundred times from the original one, spreading outward in a vast circle like waves in a lake when a meteor crashes into its center" (Heng and Shapiro 1983, 123). After shaking hands with Chairman Mao one devoted member of the Red Guards reportedly would not let anyone touch his right hand and began using his left hand only. Eventually he covered the right hand with a white glove and embroidered on the glove the date he had been received by Chairman Mao (Xiao Di 1993, 162). Such rituals established the cult of Mao as perhaps the most fanatical in the history of the world, with millions of devout followers who had completely surrendered their own reason and will. In the words of one Red Guard who was received by Mao Zedong, "I am very lucky to have had such an experience . . . I have resolved to dedicate my whole life to Chairman Mao and the Great Proletarian Cultural Revolution. I will give every drop of blood in my body to work to liberate all of mankind" (Ji Li Jiang 1997, 107–8).

In traditional China the Chinese masses would never have had the opportunity to see the emperor in person. When the emperor had appeared in his imperial court, all those present would kneel down and kowtow, wishing him ten thousand years of life. The reaction of the Red Guards on seeing Mao bears close resemblance to rituals expressing loyalty, respect, and reverence for the emperors of China's ancient past, except that in the modern-day drama such rituals were enacted with a greater degree of enthusiasm and fanaticism. Mao's frequent appearances enhanced his deified image and reinforced his cultish appeal.

Political Activities

Political rituals during the Cultural Revolution also took the form of structured activities such as "Everyday Reading" of Mao's teachings, "Sharing Experience in Applying Mao's Teachings," "Remembering the Bitterness of the Past and Appreciating the Sweetness of the Present," and denunciation rallies.

"Everyday Reading." Known as *tiantian du* 天天讀 in Chinese, Everyday Reading was a ritual involving the reading and reciting of Mao's quotations and essays every morning. This ritual took place in schools, factories, government offices, and virtually every public place. Readings and recitations could be done by an entire group, or one individual might take the lead while others listened. The reading usually lasted one hour and was preceded by the three wishes for Mao's longevity and the singing of "The East Is Red." Many interviewees still clearly remember this ritualized experience. One interviewee recalled, "In the first two years of the Cultural Revolution, there was no school. When school resumed, all we learned at school were Chairman Mao's pronouncements. Every morning, we read Mao's quotations as a group. Sometimes, the teacher would appoint someone to read specific passages on specific pages. Over time I became very good at pinpointing certain quotations on certain pages." According to another account, "We did not quite understand the meanings of these quotations, but it was a fashion at the time to be able to recite as many quotations as possible. It was an indication of how loyal you were to Mao and how well you knew Mao's teachings. I remembered many of them and can still recite Mao's 'three old essays' ('Serving the People,' 'In Memory of Dr. Bethune' and 'The Foolish Old Man Who Moved a Mountain') with ease."[5] Everyday Reading became a measure of one's political consciousness. No one dared to be late for such readings, and missing even one of them was considered an indication of *sixiang wenti* 思想問題 (thought problem).

Everyday Reading also included the reading and recitation of Mao's new directives introduced during the Cultural Revolution. The issuance of a new directive was usually announced on the radio several hours before the new directive was actually read on the air, often after 8:00 P.M. Ritualistically, every time the advance notice was given, people would start preparing a parade or loyalty dance in celebration. As soon as the new directive was issued, people were expected to remember it and recite it by heart. During the ensuing celebration people would flood into the streets and parade around while reciting the new directive, singing songs eulogizing Mao, and dancing the loyalty dance. Such celebration rituals would last until midnight.

"Sharing Experience in Applying Mao's Teachings." This ritual, known as *jiangyong hui* 講用會, took the form of a small-group meeting, a seminar, or an assembly where one person or a group of people shared the ways in which they had applied Mao's teachings to their lives. They described how they and society as a whole had benefited from the application of Mao's teachings. "Role models" were chosen by the government and invited to various places to share their *xinde tihui* 心得體會 (reflections and experiences). The

origin of this ritual can be traced to Lei Feng, who was promoted by the government as a national hero. Official reports of Lei Feng's good deeds helped promote nation-wide reflections on Mao's teachings. During the Cultural Revolution the sharing of reflections and experiences related to Mao's teachings became ritualized and politicized. The reading of Mao's pronouncements and application of them to everyday life demonstrated one's loyalty and love for Mao. Engaging in these activities in public settings served to exert peer pressure and further the cause of thought control.

During the Cultural Revolution countless sessions and assemblies were held for this purpose. The speeches given by government-sanctioned role models were in a ritualized format. Speakers would first identify their own selfish thoughts or problems. They would then describe how they had recognized their own problems by recalling Mao's words. Then they would discuss how their proletarian consciousness had been raised as a result of their interactions with workers and peasants. Typical speeches would include the reading and reciting of Mao's quotations and demonstrate the application of Mao's teachings, which were regarded as serving the functions of nourishing one's soul, providing inspiration, and guiding one's life. Language usage conformed to the political rhetoric of official newspapers and publications. Speeches usually ended with the shouting of slogans such as "Long Live Mao Zedong Thought!" and "Long Live Chairman Mao!" Audience participation involved applauding and cheering the speakers in a routinized manner. Some of these speeches were published (for example, *Zuguo Renmin*, 1969; *Wenhua Da Geming Yu Xinren*, 1976) and read during required political study sessions at schools and in workplaces. At times the government promotion of revolutionary role models reached absurd levels. For example, a popular role model during the Cultural Revolution was Gu Atao, a female peasant who was illiterate but nevertheless traveled the entire country sharing her reflections and experiences by drawing pictures (Zhang and Li 1998, 370–71).

People experienced different feelings and struggles in the participation of this type of ritual. One interviewee commented, "At the time, we often listened to speeches given by heroes. They had done so many good deeds for people and their spirits were uplifted as a result of studying Mao's works. I was very touched by their deeds. I was convinced that Mao Zedong's Thought was very powerful and I believed in everything Chairman Mao said." Another interviewee recalled, "Many people gave speeches on how they had tasted so much sweetness [an expression of having benefited] from reading Chairman Mao's teachings. I tried to summon the same feelings by reading Mao's works and following their examples, but I never experienced the same taste as they did. I blamed myself for not having enough love for Chairman Mao." The use of role models to inspire desired social attitudes and behaviors is rooted in the Confucian tradition. The practice was adopted by the Chinese Communist Party in a quest to reinvent the new Communist person (Munro 1977; Mei Zhang 1999).

"Remembering the Bitterness of the Past and Appreciating the Sweetness of the Present." This ritual, known as *yiku sitian* 憶苦思甜, took the form of an organized public gathering.

The organizers chose one or a few persons to describe the harsh and miserable lives they led because of the exploitation or ill treatment by landlords or capitalists prior to the Communist takeover. The ritual began with the audience and speaker singing songs together. A typical song for such occasions was:

> The sky is covered with stars;
> The moon is shining.
> The production brigade is holding a meeting,
> Telling bitterness and redressing an injustice.

The song was followed by personal accounts of enduring hunger, beatings, rape, and torture. Some accounts even included descriptions of loved ones dying of starvation or being tortured to death. Each speaker would compare the bitter life of the past with the sweet life of the present and express gratitude to the party and Chairman Mao. Because the accounts were personal experiences they were believable and persuasive, and many people were moved to tears. A speaker would end a speech by shouting slogans condemning class enemies and wishing Chairman Mao a long life. These occasions were usually emotionally charged. If the person being condemned was present, as happened in some rural areas, hatred toward the target person could be easily inflamed and escalate to violence. Such ritualistic practices were held in workplaces, at schools, in neighborhoods, and on the streets. Combined with other forms of disseminating propaganda, the ritual of remembering the bitterness of the past and appreciating the sweetness of the present helped engender antagonism toward the past and hatred of class enemies. It also served to instill feelings of gratitude and loyalty toward Mao and the party.

In schools and some workplaces people were required to eat *yiku fan* 憶苦飯 (recalling bitterness meal), made of tree leaves or chaffs mixed with horse dung or dirt, as part of the ritualistic practice of remembering the past. Not surprising, the meal had a terrible taste and was hard to swallow. Schoolchildren who were too young to have firsthand experience of pre-Communist China were told that this was the type of food poor people ate before Chairman Mao liberated Chinese people from their misery. After a meal of bitter remembrance the children were required to participate in discussions in which they were expected to express their hatred for the old society, appreciation of the new society, loyalty to Mao, determination never to let the old days return, and dedication to the communist cause that promised a good life for all. One interviewee commented: "The ritual of remembering the bitterness of the past and appreciating the sweetness of the present had a big impact on me. I was convinced that the old society was bitter and miserable and that I was so fortunate to live in Mao Zedong's era. My father came from a poor family. Without the Party and Chairman Mao, I would have had to live such a life and eat such food or go hungry."

Denunciation rallies. Denunciation rallies were public spectacles where class enemies were criticized, condemned, humiliated, cursed, and attacked. Known as *pidou hui*

批鬥會, or struggle sessions, such rallies, which were held in workplaces, classrooms, auditoriums, on campuses, and in the streets, were highly ritualized during the Cultural Revolution. Some struggle sessions were attended by only a small group of people, while others drew crowds of thousands of people in huge stadiums. The rallies were decorated with banners and colored posters bearing slogans such as "Carry on the Cultural Revolution to the End!," "Condemn and Annihilate All Class Enemies!," and "Long Live Chairman Mao!" Mao's portrait was placed in the center of the denunciation platform. Audience members all wore Mao badges pinned to their chests and held the Little Red Books in their hands. Before the rallies officially began they sang revolutionary songs in unison.

In smaller sessions the audience members and speakers were typically colleagues, former students, subordinates, or friends of those being denounced. The denunciation rally was the arena in which students were pitted against their teachers, friends and spouses were pressured to betray one another, children were manipulated into exposing their parents, and subordinates were encouraged to condemn their superiors. All such actions were considered revolutionary. One interviewee reportedly witnessed a wife slapping her husband at a denunciation rally. The wife gave a speech exposing and denouncing her husband for counterrevolutionary conduct, after which she announced that she was ending their marriage. As Ross (1994) remarks, "The goal of the struggle session was not simply to humiliate or force confessions. It also was a way to force everyone to participate in the excesses of the revolution, to make them share responsibility" (104).

The person being denounced was made to wear a dunce cap three feet in height and a heavy iron placard on which the person's name and crime were written in black ink with a red cross superimposed across the writing. Female "criminals" were forced to shave half their hair off and leave the other half uncut. This humiliating tactic was known as *yinyang tou* 陰陽頭. Sometimes the denounced were paraded in trucks. They were made to stand with their heads down and bodies bent at a ninety-degree angle or to kneel down on the platform, depending on the seriousness of the accusations against them. The person who chaired the rally would announce its start and then shout out a series of ritualized slogans, including "Down with [name of the denounced]." Sometimes the rally leader would force the person being denounced to indict himself or herself, or to recite Mao's quotations.[6]

The rhetorical form of the typical denunciation speech was similar to that of wall posters. It started with a list of the person's alleged crimes, followed by a review of the charges or any new evidence against the person in question. The denunciation speech would incorporate Mao's quotations or poems, interspersed with coarse or vulgar language designed to humiliate and insult the person. It usually ended with slogans such as "Down with [name of the denounced]!," "Pledge to Defend Chairman Mao!," and "Long Live Chairman Mao!" Ji (1998) recounted his experience being on the receiving end of a denunciation rally: "Everything was ritualized. I first heard a loud chorus of 'Down with . . .' naming every condemned person. Then I heard the speaker read [Mao's] quotations like, 'Revolution is not a dinner party. . . .' Afterwards were the denunciation speeches. I could not hear clearly what was being said. In fact, I did not want to listen. I'd heard enough. All I heard was the speaker's pledge of loyalty to Mao and the hoarse shouting of slogans to the point of howling" (115). One interviewee recalled a rally denouncing her father: "A Red Guard pushed my father down to the ground and yelled at him, 'Who are you?' My father replied, 'I am a Communist Party member.' The Red Guard snapped, 'You are a spy; how dare you say you are a party member?' They then beat him all over." Many people I interviewed were in their preteen or teenage years during the Cultural Revolution. When I asked what they remembered most, invariably I was told "quotation songs, slogans, the loyalty dances, the parade of cow ghosts and snake devils and denunciation rallies." One interviewee shared the following: "I witnessed with my own eyes the parade and struggle session of a school principal. The Red Guards put a trash can over his head. He was made to hold a stick in one hand and a pail in the other hand. He was forced to hit the pail with the stick while shouting to the onlookers, 'I am a capitalist roader and I carried out a bourgeois educational line.' A group of kids followed behind him, spitting and throwing stones at him." Such humiliating and brutal scenes were not uncommon during the Cultural Revolution.

Political activities of all sorts aimed to promote Mao's teachings as absolute truth in guiding individual and social lives. Through repeated exposure to the reading and recitation of Mao's pronouncements in ritualistic settings, a sense of shared identity and unified belief was engendered. Ritualistic denunciation rallies and bitter recollections of the past served to generate hatred and dehumanize those identified as enemies. The atmosphere created during such rituals appealed to emotions rather than reason, to religious fanaticism rather than sound judgment.

Public Debates

Argumentation and public debates were common occurrences in the imperial courts and intellectual arenas of ancient China. Traditional Chinese philosophers such as Confucius (551–479 B.C.E.), Mencius (390–05 B.C.E.), Xunzi (298–38 B.C.E.), Mozi (475–390 B.C.E.), and Han Feizi (280–33) had all traveled widely to various kingdoms, propagating their political doctrines to heads of state. Often they were required to debate with their opponents and engage in persuasive activities in order to have their views accepted (Lu 1998b; Oliver 1971). Further, emperors were in the habit of calling on their ministers to contribute ideas on governing and would typically allow the ministers to debate among themselves in the imperial court before the final decision was made. Public debate activities can also be traced to the Jixia 稷下 Academy, where philosophers of various schools of thought hosted public debates over moral, political, and epistemological issues in the third century B.C.E. (Zhang 1991).

This ancient ritualistic practice continued during the Cultural Revolution and was encouraged by Mao under the banner of *da bianlun* 大辯論, or public debate. In 1966, the first year of the Cultural Revolution, public debate reached its ubiquitous climax. The whole country was politicized and filled with ideological zeal. Many eloquent speakers emerged at this time, and political persuasion became the symbolic expression of power struggle and ideological battles. You (1998) recalled a scenario he witnessed firsthand:

> It was an evening in September, 1966. A huge crowd filled the south side of Zhong Lou Avenue. A female college student from the University of Transportation was denouncing the provincial government of Shaanxi while standing on a fruit stand. A cadre-like male stepped up to the stand and refuted her denouncement. The debate was characterized by logical progression and the formal use of language. Many people were attracted to this debate. They divided themselves into small groups and started their own debate. . . . The debate lasted until next morning. The audiences showed no sign of waning enthusiasm. (11)

Public debate was usually staged by two different factions in the public arena. Both sides staked their claim to being truly revolutionary and accused the other side of being fraudulent, counterrevolutionary, and anti–Chairman Mao. Argument by authority and argument by example were the two most common techniques used in the debates. Topics varied from the definitions of revolutionary terms to the evaluation of certain political figures. Mostly the debates were centered around *chusheng lun* 出身論 (theories about class origin or family background). Some Red Guards from "revolutionary cadres" families coined the saying "Dragons bear dragons, phoenixes bear phoenixes, and mice sons know how to dig holes." Song lyrics expressed a similar message: "If the father is a revolutionary, the son is the successor of revolution. If the father is a reactionary, the son will be a bastard." These views on lineage, or blood line, as the determining factor for political attitudes and behaviors triggered great debates among different factions in schools and workplaces. Zhai (1992) cited an example of such debate:

> Yingqiu is from a good family [one of the five red categories] and she's the most revolutionary. "Do any of you know someone from a bad family [one of the five black categories] who has done so well in this revolution?" A person from the crowd argued, "What you said is right. Yingqiu is in the vanguard of the revolution in our school. I agree that family plays an important role in forming one's political views. But society, schools, and the media also have an influence. In fact, many famous revolutionaries came from exploitive families. Our beloved Premier Zhou for one. How do you explain this?" The first person was enraged, "How dare you use Premier Zhou to bolster your position! Don't smear Premier Zhou!" The opponent responded calmly, "All right, forget Premier Zhou. Let's talk about a person, a member of the Red Guards for example, whose father is a revolutionary cadre today. What if the father gets convicted as a member of the black gang tomorrow? What would this Red Guard member become? Would he be changed from a hero to an asshole overnight?" . . . The debate continued with each side quoting Mao's sayings and making personal attacks. Another supporter joined in, "We are born red! The red comes with us from our mothers' wombs, and I say right here you are born black! What can you do about us?" (80)[7]

The debate ended with each side calling the other names and using vulgar expressions. Not all public debates ended with personal attacks. In addition to the use of examples as in the case above, other rhetorical techniques were also employed to create the desired persuasive effect. One interviewee shared her experience in a debate between two factions of Red Guards: "Both sides claimed to be defenders of Chairman Mao and accused the other side of being 'infidels' of Mao Zedong's Thought. Everyone came to the debate with Mao's Little Red Book. The debate started with an assertion which was supported by reading a quotation from Mao. The opposition refuted the argument by citing another of Mao's sayings. The debate became a contest for how well one could remember and appropriately apply Mao's teachings. One was judged a good debater on the basis of how fluently one used Mao's words and how quickly one counter argued by using Mao's quotations." Many Red Guard leaders were charismatic and effective debaters. Liang (1998) described a female Red Guard leader, nicknamed "Pan Ersao" (Number Two Sister-in-law), who was well known for her eloquent debating style in the city of Harbin. In Liang's words, "She was calm, glib-tongued, well-articulated, and non-stop while talking. Her wording was sharp and spicy; her answers to questions were quick and clear; her logic was lucid. Her speech was filled with irony, satire, and humor. She was fluent in citing the doctrines of Marxism and Leninism. She was familiar with classical and contemporary works. The debate lasted more than three hours and no one could beat her" (377).

Rhetorical devices employed during public debates included slogans, Mao's poems, and revolutionary songs. Oftentimes such devices helped create a unified force and shared identity among opponents. Zheng (1998) describes his firsthand experience of a debate at Beijing Institute of Geology between the two Red Guards factions, the "East Red Commune" and the "Struggle-Criticism-Transformation Fighting Team":

> Each side selected three representatives who were positioned in front of the audience. The representatives from the East Red Commune accused the other team of making serious mistakes in directing the campaign of the Cultural Revolution on campus. The opponent disagreed. As the argument intensified and nearly led to violence, one side started shouting slogans and reading Mao's poems; the opposing group joined in. This act triggered a long round of applause and created a solemn atmosphere among the participants. Afterwards, the other side began to sing "The East Is Red" to show their loyalty and love for Mao. Then Red Guards from both sides (about 5000) stood up and sang the song together. (187–88).

In this way the two opposing groups were temporarily united, and a shared sense of revolutionary crusade was engendered through emotional appeals to the same authority.

Ancient strategies, drawn from "The Art of War" by Sunzi,[8] were also used in these debates. Liang (1998) recollected a debate between two groups of Red Guards at a train station where many Red Guards were waiting to go to Beijing to see Mao Zedong. A group of people calling themselves the "Persuasion Team" were trying to stop the Red Guards from going to Beijing, claiming that Beijing needed stability and that the influx of people to that city would cause trouble for Mao Zedong. This "reason" was met with furious refutations, for example: "Beijing is the heart of the battlefield for class struggle. If we do not go there, who will go? 'Stability in Beijing' is a slogan aimed at confusing the people's minds. You must have an ulterior motive!" (212). According to Liang's analysis of the debate, the second debate team used the technique of "gaining mastery by striking only after the enemy has struck." This technique involves letting one's opponent speak, waiting for the right moment to find fault, and then attacking back. This proved an effective technique, especially suited for situations in which the debater's argument was weak.

In sum, rhetorical devices from China's ancient past were employed during the Cultural Revolution. However, public debates during this time aimed at attacking one's opponents rather than taking the opportunity to reach a higher level of understanding on an issue. These public rituals were enacted as social dramas with elements such as actors, scenes, plots, agency, and action used to communicate political motives and accomplish political goals.

Impact of Political Rituals

Along with other types of discursive devices discussed in previous chapters, the political rituals observed and practiced during the Cultural Revolution exerted a strong influence on Chinese thought, culture, and communication behavior. Some rituals were rooted in Chinese tradition and were appropriated and extended to further the political aims of the powerful, while others were new inventions of the Communist Party and the communist masses with outcomes that deviated from traditional Chinese cultural values to varying degrees. At any rate, through mass participation in political rituals during the Cultural Revolution, the Chinese people who lived through that historic experiment created their own mythology, along with a fanatical and sometimes twisted social drama. The experience left many of China's citizens with psychological and communication problems in subsequent years.

Impact on Thought

The ritual of Fighting Selfishness and Denouncing Revisionism forced the individual to conform to political norms of criticism and self-criticism under intense public scrutiny and peer pressure. Under such conditions it became extremely difficult, if not impossible, to think critically and independently due to fear of social ostracism and political persecution. Further, conformity to this political ritual assured acceptance by one's peers and the possibility of becoming a role model. Fighting Selfishness and Denouncing Revisionism sessions also created a surveillance system among the participants in that everyone's behavior was closely watched and judged by a set standard of political criteria. Superficially the goal of such a ritual was to foster the moral goodness of the individual, which would in turn benefit society. At a deeper level participants were deprived of their critical thinking abilities and forced into a state of acquiescence. In this context one's ideas were formulated on the basis of what was expected, rather than according to one's conscience and reasoning. This ritualistic format was definitely an effective way of controlling behavior as it played on the needs and fears of the participants, gauging their psychological susceptibility and desire to conform and be accepted. In the words of one interviewee, "I tried so hard to reform myself and conform to political requirements, to the point that I had no thoughts of my own. I did not know who I was. I was doing everything in accordance with social norms and in reaction to political pressure. My own thought had been suppressed for too long and I didn't know how to think anymore." Edelman (1977) sums up this type of highly politicized climate well: "The denial of personal autonomy through politicization of virtually all facets of life is the key device through which authoritarian governments control their population" (121).

Rituals deifying Mao perpetuated the cult of Mao, involving millions of Chinese in the collective making of a living god. The iconography of Mao badges, portraits of Mao, and communist-inspired murals were designed to evoke absolute loyalty to Mao and dedication to the communist cause. The rituals of the three wishes, the Everyday Readings from the Little Red Book, and Mao's reviews of Red Guards in Tiananmen Square all served to communicate the purported majesty and absolute power of Mao. The extent of Mao's deification has no historical parallel, with the possible exception of Alexander the Great (356–23 B.C.E.), who allowed his portraits to be displayed everywhere in his empire and his image printed on coins, buildings, pottery, and other art forms (Taylor 1990). In the Chinese context, the traditional Chinese concept of filial piety for one's parents and ancestors was redirected toward piety for Mao. The Red Guards' ardent trips throughout the country and their crusading spirit in annihilating class enemies were inspired by this underlying sense of piety. Through a dramatic enactment of the mythology related to Mao and emotionally charged symbols, the Chinese people were conditioned into what Bennett (1980) calls "primary process thinking." In contrast to rational thought, Bennett describes primary process thinking as "characterized by projection, fantasy, the incorporation of nonverbal imagery, a high emotional content, the easy connection of disparate ideas, the failure to make underlying assumptions explicit, and the generation of multiple levels of meaning" (169).

When power and authority are centered on one political figure and differing views are considered heresy, independent and critical thinking is severely stifled. Blind faith combined with fear of being considered an infidel characterized the mind-set of many Chinese during the Cultural Revolution. In addition, the ritualistic deification of Mao promoted polarized and dogmatic thinking, as anyone who disagreed or refused to participate in such rituals was considered a class enemy and targeted for punishment by the Red Guards or zealous individuals. To this day many former Red Guards carry tremendous guilt for the sufferings they inflicted during the Cultural Revolution. Thurston (1987) recorded the testimony of one former Red Guard: "I feel I must apologize to my country and my people. . . . I must fall on the ground on my knees and beg for their forgiveness. Because if we fanatic young Red Guards had not done what we did, the country would not have been paralyzed" (249). In reflecting on the causes of such damage the Red Guard in question acknowledged his accountability: "On the one hand, it is true that we were used by the Gang of Four. But on the other hand, in terms of the entire history of what happened, we, I, my generation, still have a share of the responsibility. We doubted. We recognized they [the Gang of Four] were evil. We opposed them in our hearts. But we did not oppose them openly" (249).[9] This statement and countless others make it clear that much of the damage associated with the Cultural Revolution was caused by the loss of the ability to think critically and independently or the fear of being punished for speaking out. Even when members of the Red Guards did think and question, they did not have the courage to share their thoughts or challenge the authority. Those few who found the courage to speak out, such as Yu Luoke and Zhang Zhixin, were tortured and sentenced to death.[10]

Since the end of the Cultural Revolution the cult of Mao has continued unabated in some quarters or been resurrected after a period of decline in others. Some continue to worship Mao at their family altars, praying to him for peace and safety. According to Xiao Di (1993), peasants in a rural area in China still erected a temple to Chairman Mao, and thousands of people visit the temple each day burning incense and kowtowing to images of Mao, even years after the Cultural Revolution had ended (177). It is common today to see little pictures of Mao in automobiles; drivers believe that Mao will grant them safety and bring them good luck.[11] Books and songs about Mao Zedong are enjoying a popular resurgence, and Mao badges are again worn by some individuals. Many of today's college students have undertaken the serious study of Mao's five volumes of selected works. It is hard to say whether this resurrection of the cult of Mao stems from nostalgia or from a negative reaction to the current regime. One thing is certain, however: Mao has become an integral part of Chinese culture and psyche. Whether hated as a despotic leader or loved as a kind of god/saint, his ghost will continue to haunt Chinese people. Myths and legends about him will continue to loom large.

For many Chinese people today, one of the enduring legacies of the cult of Mao is a kind of cynicism toward religion in general and ritualistic practices in particular. Many people feel that they were manipulated into participating in rituals deifying Mao. Hence they have become disillusioned and even disgusted with any expression of religious sentiments. Having participated in fanatical rituals deifying Mao, they now refuse to take part in any religious ceremonies and are easily repulsed by religious preaching and attempts at conversion. Further, they are wary of affective communication aimed at arousing emotional commitment. Many interviewees shared that after believing in Mao they cannot bring themselves to believe in anybody, any ideology, or any religion. In the words of one interviewee, "There are a lot of similarities between the rituals of Christianity and the rituals of the Cultural Revolution, such as the practice of worshipping a sacred figure, and engaging in Bible study and group discussions. I was once invited to attend some church activities. I found the rituals very familiar. Having experienced the Cultural Revolution, I could not stand this any more. I was disgusted by the forms of the rituals even though I know there are some good things in the Bible and Christianity." This reaction is simply a lingering form of thoughtlessness as the person in question made a judgment about a religion on the basis of superficial associations with the Cultural Revolution.

Rituals associated with various kinds of political activities and public debates reinforced polarized thought patterns and black-and-white perceptions of reality. They also promoted Mao's teachings as infallible, absolute truth. The rituals of "Remembrance of the Bitter Past" and denunciation rallies elicited emotional responses, bred hatred for class enemies, and encouraged cruelty. Acts of violence were rationalized and justified through emotional pleas and a rhetoric of dehumanization. Moreover, public debates were not aimed at exchanging ideas and exploring different perspectives, but rather at enforcing strict adherence to one version of truth—Maoist ideology. The goal of these debates was to defeat their opponents and level charges against them. This dogmatic thinking and style of debating are still in evidence among those who grew up during the Cultural Revolution. In my own experience, when in the company of Chinese friends I frequently encounter the situation in which some issue becomes a topic of debate. Typically each side holds strongly to its own views and tries to beat the other side by assuming an attitude of moral superiority, laying out overgeneralizations as absolute truth and engaging in polarized thinking. One interviewee lamented, "Every time I get involved in an argument, I hear extreme views expressed. When I disagree with the person who is presenting different views, I am accused of something that attacks my moral character. This even happens with family members. Now I try to avoid getting into an argument for fear of being attacked or ruining relationships."

Rowland and Frank (2002) exemplified Kenneth Burke's concept of the entelechial principle in their scrutiny of the Israeli/Palestinian conflict. The entelechial principle is the tendency of defining the other as absolutely evil and take the symbols to the end of the line. Such a "symbolic extremism" as Rowland and Frank contend, is dangerous and deceiving as it is often presented in a perfectly logical fashion. Moreover, this "rhetorical violence often leads to societal violence" (299). The public debates and Red Guard factions during the Cultural Revolution were led by the entelechial principle and induced both rhetorical violence and societal violence.

Impact on Culture

Scholars have pointed out many striking parallels between the Confucian tradition and Communist political rituals (Chu 1977; Huang 1996; Pye 1968), parallels that strengthened the foundation of the communist experiment and eased the transition from the observance of tradition to the practice of revolution. For example, the rituals of "asking instructions in the morning" and "reporting in the evening" were observed piously and naturally by many during the Cultural Revolution. According to Huang (1996), this was because "for hundreds of years, people used to kneel before statues in Buddhist or Taoist temples confessing wrong doings, pouring out troubles and bitterness, or begging for help. The practice was basically the same, only the statue of the god had changed" (144). Indeed, Confucius emphasized moral idealism, believing that an individual could become a virtuous person and a society could become orderly through moral indoctrination and ritualistic practices. While the Confucian moral ideal is that of *ren* (benevolence), communist propaganda celebrated the virtue of *wusi* 無私 (selflessness). Confucius advocated rituals such as ancestor worship as means of maintaining the hierarchical ordering of society, while communism relied heavily on ritualistic practices deifying Mao. Confucius emphasized the self-cultivation of *junzi* (gentleman), while Mao used confession and self-criticism as means of remolding the new Communist person. In addition the communist approach seems to share important similarities with the legalist school of governing. For example, Han Feizi, the key legalistic philosopher, advocated a balance between a tight political control and the delegation of power by the ruler. The ruler should trust no one but instead design a system of surveillance so that his subjects could monitor each other's conduct (Han 1992). The political rituals of the Cultural Revolution served these functions. To be more accurate, the communist propaganda machine appropriated traditional Chinese cultural values, making ideological conversion more effective and ritualistic practices more familiar and acceptable. As Chu (1977) points out, "the possibility remains that because these [traditional] ideas and views have been part of the Chinese culture, not alien, their infusion into the Chinese Communist ideology may have made it less difficult for the Chinese people to accept the indoctrination and pressure tactics employed by the Party" (24).

In many ways, however, the political rituals employed during the Cultural Revolution show more differences than similarities with traditional Chinese cultural values. Confucian tradition used rituals to further the cause of social order and stability. Rituals were performed in order to insure that everyone knew his or her place and observed the appropriate rules and etiquette. In contrast, the political rituals of the Cultural Revolution were intended to promote uniformity of thought and action, strengthen the proletarian dictatorship, divide and isolate people according to their family origins and class backgrounds, and intensify sanctions against class enemies. On the one hand, the Confucian tradition of self-cultivation purported to maintain harmonious human relations through restraint and politeness. Communist self-criticism sessions, on the other hand, aimed at exposing people's weaknesses and pitting one against the other, thus causing human relations to be fraught with tension and mistrust. Chinese traditional values revolved around concepts of saving face and helping others do the same (Ting-Toomey 1993; Jia 2001). The possibility of losing face was an important feature of behavior control. In contrast, in Fighting Selfishness and Denouncing Revisionism sessions participants were not only made to feel shame about their own weakness but were also expected to shame and humiliate others. Such public spectacles amounted to a veritable orgy of face-losing rituals, which, in the words of Yue Daiyun, made "everyone increasingly jittery and self-protective, placing a great strain on human relationships. Many people would volunteer incriminating information about others to the Red Guards, their assertions of loyalty a desperate effort to protect themselves from harm" (cited in Wakeman 1985, 170). Furthermore, the Confucian motto "Do not do unto others what you do not want others to do unto you" was constantly violated under communism. Rituals deifying Mao were imposed on the masses, and many confessions or acts of self-criticism were involuntary. In addition, Chinese tradition promoted a love of humanity rooted in the Confucian concept of *ren* and the Mohist tenet of *jian ai* 兼愛 (mutual love),[12] while political rituals such as denunciation rallies engendered hatred and encouraged violence.

Impact on Communication

Chu (1977) points out that Chinese communication takes both vertical and horizontal forms. On the one hand, the vertical form is characterized by communication from top political leaders to the populace, through various sources of official media. The content of this type of communication is mostly informational and ideological. Horizontal communication, on the other hand, refers to communication between and among citizens in small group settings and informal networks. In this context face-to-face communication and small-group dynamics allowed for the mutual influence of behaviors related to confession and self-criticism, in the interest of showing reverence to Mao and exhibiting hatred of class enemies. Because they were under pressure, it was not uncommon for people to invent or fabricate their confessions in order to prove their loyalty to Mao. In these cases control was exerted through peer pressure and surveillance among the participants. The means of communication was psychological and emotional. Nevertheless, this horizontal style of political discourse was intertwined with vertical communication channels as the participants in face-to-face and small-group formats were heavily influenced by the rhetorical form and content disseminated from the upper echelons of the Communist Party.

Horizontal communication strategies forced people into group situations and often put them on public display, thus pressuring them to conform to ritualistic norms and rules. This type of communication took place under formal or semiformal conditions. Typically people were required to speak or made to speak whether or not they had anything to say. Ironically, during the Cultural Revolution communication at home and in informal settings between family members and friends was kept to a minimum. In Yue Daiyun's account, "When the children had gone to sleep we would sit together, unable to read or make small talk, absorbed in our separate thoughts. Lao Tang [Yue's husband] never spoke of his ordeal or shared with me his pain, though he would occasionally comment upon the inability of human beings to control their own fate" (cited in Wakeman 1985, 153). One interviewee told me that out of fear of being overheard by a neighbor who was a Rebel, she and her family members spoke to each other only when necessary to facilitate their daily routines. They never shared their inner thoughts with one another. If the children had doubts and questions, they had to write them down on a piece of paper, and their parents would write back telling them to have faith in Mao and the party. Another interviewee commented, "I never knew what other people thought about the rituals and bizarre things going on during the Cultural Revolution. I considered some of them problematic and foolish, but I never dared to say so. I couldn't speak my mind and I didn't trust what other people said, as I was afraid of being betrayed or persecuted." As in the story of "The Emperor's New Clothes," everyone knew, or at least suspected, during the Cultural Revolution that the emperor (Mao) could not live one thousand years, but no one dared to commit the heretical act of speaking such thoughts out loud.

The endless stress on thought reform and ubiquitous Fighting Selfishness and Denouncing Revisionism sessions left scars on many Chinese people's psychological well-being. One interviewee shared the following: "Because of my family background, I was labeled one of those 'rectifiable children.' Ever since, I have suffered from low self-esteem. I always think I am not good enough and that I have some serious moral defects. Even to this day, I do not have confidence in myself. This has severely affected my job performance and interpersonal relations." Further, because of the overemphasis on self-criticism, many Chinese people formed the habit of saying only negative things about themselves and others in the context of their interpersonal interactions. This has had detrimental effects on the quality of their lives. One interviewee commented, "I do not know how to give or respond to compliments. I seldom say positive things to my husband and children. I always ask them as well as myself, to look at our weaknesses, with the belief that this approach can help us improve ourselves."

Self-criticism sessions also encouraged the telling of lies since speaking the truth would be used against the individual in question. People often lied in order to prove their loyalty to Mao and protect themselves. As a result deception was commonplace in offering information and expressing one's thoughts. During the Cultural Revolution many innocent people were persecuted and tortured because of the fabricated testimonials provided by others. Once trust was breached, it was difficult to reestablish. One of the most tragic legacies of the Cultural Revolution is the extreme difficulty most survivors of that time still encounter when trying to trust people.

Political rituals are powerful tools of persuasion, mind and behavior control, and social change as they are rooted in indigenous cultural traditions and skillfully aimed at promoting ideological agendas. The symbolic and structural function of rituals during the Cultural Revolution fostered both alienation and false identification, escalated fanaticism, and dehumanized an entire group of people. The negative impacts of such rituals on thought, culture, and communication behavior linger even years after the Cultural Revolution.

A Rhetorical Analysis of Post–Cultural Revolution Political Discourse

It [the Cultural Revolution] is a huge tragedy created by the force of discourse. It has also become a laughing stock as in a comic presented by the force of language. Unfortunately, not everyone has learned a lesson from this part of the history. At present, one can still find those who are obsessed with the Cultural Revolution mentality trying to seek opportunities to scare others by the force of the Cultural Revolutionary language/discourse.

Meng Wang, *Wang Meng san wen ji* (Wang Meng's Selected Essays)

The scale on which the CCP mobilized the propaganda apparatus across the country to attack and slander Falun Gong was comparable to the "great struggle sessions" of the Cultural Revolution. And the threats, detentions, and criminal prosecutions directed toward Falun Gong members were also not much different from the persecution of the Cultural Revolution.

Binyan Liu, "Unprecedented Courage in the Face of Cultural Revolution–Style Persuasion," in *Falun Gong's Challenge to China*

The so-called "Proletarian Cultural Revolution" ended in 1976 following Mao's death on 9 September of the same year. The "ten years of chaos" had brought economic devastation and cultural destruction to China. In fact, the Sixth Plenum of the Eleventh Central Committee of the Chinese Communist Party issued a resolution on 27 June 1981 stating: "The 'cultural revolution,' which lasted from May, 1966 to October, 1976 was responsible for the most severe setbacks and the heaviest losses suffered by the Party, the state, and the people since the founding of the People's Republic" (Martin 1982, 198). It conceded that Mao was responsible for "the grave left error" as "he confused right with wrong and the people with the enemy" (199).[1] However, the document also credited Mao with having good intentions in launching the Cultural Revolution. In addition it asserted that Mao had made efforts to resist the Gang of Four's influence and to protect some leading party officials from harm. This conflicting assessment of Mao left his mythic status intact, primarily attributing the cause of the disaster to the Gang of Four, who were alleged to have taken advantage of Mao, abusing their power and committing politically motivated crimes behind his back. The statement did not include statistics on the loss of life and economic damages of the Cultural Revolution; it also did not call for analysis of the rhetorical strategies that led to polarized and radical thinking, which in turn inflamed hatred and violence against class enemies. This momentous social and political upheaval was summarized in one understated sentence: "History has shown that the 'cultural revolution,' initiated by a leader laboring under a misapprehension and capitalized upon by counter-revolutionary cliques, led to domestic turmoil and brought catastrophe to the Party, the state and the whole people" (Martin 1982, 200).

After a brief interim during which Hua Guofeng served as Mao's appointed successor to the chairmanship of the Communist Party,[2] Hu Yaobang took his place. The de facto leader of China, however, was Deng Xiaoping.[3] In December 1978, during the conference of the Third Plenum of the Eleventh Central Committee of the CCP, Deng officially charted a new route for China: "economic reform and an open door policy." Since that time China has been moving at an accelerated rate in the direction of economic development and greater openness to the outside world. Consequently the living standard of the average Chinese citizen has been vastly improved. Billboards once used to display Mao's portraits and quotations are now covered with advertisements and slogans promoting economic development. Ideological control has loosened up to some degree. According to Hsu's (1990) observation of this period, "The revolutionary rhetoric and cultural intolerance which had rendered China an intellectual desert of artistic insipidness gave way to some degree of relaxation and freedom of expression" (46). However, one must dig deeper in order to understand how and to what extent this ideological transformation has taken place. It is also important to ask whether the rhetoric of the Cultural Revolution still influences official Chinese discourse and if so, what effect such influence has on the lives of ordinary Chinese people.

Many Chinese believed that China has grown out of the shadow of the Cultural Revolution and can move forward toward economic development. I will argue that the rhetoric of this tragic movement still has a lingering effect on the thinking process and discursive behavior of Chinese people. In particular, little change has been made in the political discourse and official language with regard to forms of speaking. I maintain that although the content of propaganda has changed, linguistic and rhetorical styles, as well as the mind-set created by symbols and symbolic activities, still closely resemble those of the Cultural Revolution. Data for the analyses that follow were drawn mostly from the official media and CCP publications.

Post-Mao Rhetorical Exigencies and Responses

In his article "The Rhetorical Situation," Lloyd Bitzer (1968) identifies four components in a rhetorical situation: exigency; a rhetorical audience; constraints; and fitting responses. Exigency refers to a perceived or real problem in need of being addressed. A rhetorical audience is one that is capable of bringing about change to an undesirable situation. Constraints are defined as challenges faced by the speaker, such as audience perceptions and the speaker's use of ethical, emotional, and rational appeals. A fitting response is one that rhetorically remedies the exigency by providing visions or solutions or by satisfying the audience's needs and expectations. Multiple factors can have an impact on a rhetorical situation. Power, for example, is diffused throughout multiple social sites in the form of discourse. As a result, those who wield the most power can use discourse and other available means of persuasion to shape a given situation or a sense of reality. In the post-Mao era Chinese leaders faced rhetorical exigencies and constructs that needed to be addressed.

Similarly, Herbert Simons (1970) developed a theory of persuasion for social movements known as RPS. "R" stands for rhetorical requirements in promoting new ideology and execute rhetorical visions by the leaders. "P" is short for rhetorical problems or challenges and constraints generated by the changing political situation and demands from multiple audiences. "S" refers to rhetorical strategies chosen by political leaders to legitimize their positions/actions and to attract followers in efforts to transform the society. The post-Mao era in China faces rhetorical requirements to demystify Mao's legacy and move toward a market economy in order to improve the living standard of the Chinese people. Moreover, the Communist Party, functioning as a vanguard of Marxist/Maoist ideology, has evolved into what Simons and Mechling (1981) call a CIMO (Counter-Institutional Movement Organization) with its primary purpose being to provide social services rather than ideological guidance. However, in doing so, Chinese leaders also face the rhetorical challenge of reconciling Mao's utopian idealism with expedient pragmatism. What follows is a textual analysis of rhetorical strategies chosen by Chinese leaders from Deng Xiaoping to Jing Zemin in response to ideological transitions in China and an illustration of how the Cultural Revolution rhetoric still has its lingering effects in the forms of persuasion during the transitional period.

The Rhetoric of Deng Xiaoping's Regime
Demystification of Mao. Toward the end of the Cultural Revolution those who had been faithful to Mao's Marxist ideology began to question the validity and even the morality of much that they had previously embraced. Many felt betrayed and confused, having witnessed and experienced firsthand the chaos and tragedy of the Cultural Revolution. The image of an always-knowing, always-wise demigod was shattered. The fitting response to such disillusionment required the demystification of Mao. Unlike the de-Stalinization process in Soviet Russia, marked by Khrushchev's secret speech,[4] the mistakes made by Mao during the Cultural Revolution were openly acknowledged. In 1978 wall posters and articles began to undermine Mao's status as an almighty living god. One poster stated, "Mao was a human being, not a god. In order to truly uphold Marxism-Leninism and the teachings of Mao, we must ascribe to him the status he deserved. Without an accurate understanding of Mao, freedom of speech is empty talk. It is time for all Chinese to shake off the shackles on their thoughts and behavior" (cited in Hsu 1990, 49).

Similarly, Deng Xiaoping ([1979] 1987) advised party officials, "We have broken off from the Gang of Four's spiritual shackle. We must hold the position that a leader is a human being, not a god. . . . Only in this way are we truly faithful to

Mao Zedong's Thought" (11). Marshal Ye Jianying (1979) reiterated the same point in his speech on the thirtieth anniversary of the founding of the People's Republic of China. In his words, "Leaders are not gods. It is impossible for them to be free of mistakes or shortcomings. They should definitely not be deified" (Hsu 1990, 51). In a speech addressing the provincial leaders, Hu Yaobang (1980) criticized the practice of personal adoration and cultism without mentioning Mao's name: "The leader of the CCP deviated from his own correct thought and made mistakes. In all past years, especially when the Gang of Four were in power, an individual was deified and adulated and was thought to be one hundred percent correct" (520). Hu regarded such behavior as feudalistic, anti-Marxist, and mentally confining. In 1981 the resolution issued by the Sixth Plenum of the Eleventh Central Committee of the Chinese Communist Party offered the following explanation of Mao's conduct during the Cultural Revolution: "Comrade Mao Zedong's prestige reached a peak and he began to get arrogant at the very time when the Party was confronted with the new task of shifting the focus of its work to socialist construction, a task for which the utmost caution was required. He gradually divorced himself from practice and from the masses, acted more and more arbitrarily and subjectively, and increasingly put himself above the Central Committee of the Party" (Martin 1982, 207).

The above official discourse from new Chinese leaders served to demystify the image of Mao as a living god. At the same time, however, Mao's excesses and serious errors in judgment were excused to the extent that he was portrayed as an unwitting victim of the Gang of Four. Post-Mao Chinese leaders still wrestle with the ambiguity of Mao's legacy. Deng Xiaoping, in particular, distanced himself from Mao's revolutionary idealism but did not sever himself completely from Mao at the personal level. Nevertheless, the discourse of demystification has depoliticized public rhetoric and relaxed the political environment to some degree. As Martin (1982) observes, "Since Mao's death the leadership has refrained from holding up Maoism as the sole continuation of orthodox doctrine and from denouncing all other currents or tendencies outside of China as revisionism" (149).

Socialism with Chinese characteristics. In the wake of Mao's death and the downfall of the Gang of Four, there emerged a sense of ideological crisis among mainland Chinese. Sinologists note that during this time China was "at an ideological crossroad" (Tu 1994, xiii). This rhetorical exigency called for a fitting response from the government and a unified sense of purpose and confidence in China's future. Ideographs used in this post-Mao era took a diachronic turn toward pragmatism and ideological contradiction. Deng Xiaoping directed China's ideological transition to economic pragmatism and in some subtle and some not so subtle ways abandoned Mao's moral idealism with his proposal of "Socialism with Chinese Characters."

China has been tenaciously seeking its way toward modernization since the overthrow of the last dynasty and the miscarriage of Kang Youwei's "Hundred-Day

Reform" in 1898.[5] At first China attempted to embrace the democratic ideology and political structure of the West, under the leadership of Sun Yat-sen, but it failed to thrive due to the Sino-Japanese war and infighting among Chinese warlords. Eventually, Mao led China toward independence by adopting Marxist ideology and the Leninist model of a one-party dictatorship, but he also failed miserably, with the disastrous Cultural Revolution bringing China to the brink of total collapse. Having witnessed these tragic social experiments and having experienced the personal rise and fall as a high-ranking party official, Deng Xiaoping was keenly aware that the only way to save China and maintain the legitimacy of Communist Party rule after ten years of chaos was to abandon ideological orthodoxy and embrace a pragmatic orientation. His top priority after resuming power as premier of China was to develop China's economy and improve living standards for the common people.

By 1979, under the leadership of Deng Xiaoping, an urgent sense of economic pragmatism prevailed. For the first time in twenty years slogans in the *Red Flag* began to set goals for modernization in its headlines. These were known as the "Four Modernizations" (modernization of industry, agriculture, national defense, and science and technology (vol. 5, 1979). This slogan sent a signal to the Chinese people that priorities had shifted from political correctness and class consciousness to an objective of modernization and economic development. During that same year the *Red Flag* promoted the slogans "Seeking Truth from Facts" and "Liberation of the Mind" (vols. 2, 3, 1979), suggesting an ideological switch to a rational and empirical approach for dealing with economic problems and signaling an end of the dogmatic adherence to Marxist-Maoist ideology. Such slogans also called for contemplation and reflection on the ideological battle that had taken place over the previous thirty years for which the Chinese people had paid a heavy price.

Deng's pragmatic strategy was supported by liberal-minded party officials but opposed by conservative hard-liners who worried that China would become a capitalist society. To strike a balance between liberal-minded reformers and old-guard conservatives so as to maintain the harmony within the party, Deng proposed the concept of "socialism with Chinese characteristics." In explaining this concept Deng ([1984] 1987) asserted, "Capitalism did not work in China; China must remain a socialist society" (52). The ideological foundation of Chinese socialism, according to Deng, was "The Four Adherences" (adherence to the proletarian leadership; to the Party's leadership; to Marxism, Leninism, and Mao Zedong's Thought; and to the socialist path), and the main task of socialism was to improve the living standard of the Chinese people through economic development and an open-door policy" (52–53).[6] Thus, "Socialism with Chinese Characteristics" would mean little change to the political system. However, in a concerted effort to improve China's standard of living Western science, technology, and management techniques could be adapted to the Chinese situation.

The slogan "Socialism with Chinese Characteristics" was ambiguous and confusing to the Chinese and foreigners alike. In terms of overarching social structure, China identified itself as a socialist country; however, the economic development brought by reform and China's open-door policy resembled that of a capitalistic society, with its increase in private ownership of property and move toward a market economy. Such developments would appear to be inconsistent with the communist ideology. On the one hand, the spirit of the slogan "Socialism with Chinese Characteristics" could be understood as "China remains fundamentally a socialist country though with some capitalistic practices." On the other hand, it could be interpreted as "China combines strong government control (communist ideology) with a flexible trade policy and economic measures (market economy), as a unique feature of its political and economic situation." At any rate, "Socialism with Chinese Characteristics" was certainly a different socialism than the socialism practiced during the Mao era. While the CCP coined this slogan to address ideological inconsistencies and to assert its legitimacy, for ordinary Chinese people the slogan sent the message that it was acceptable to pursue capitalism. At the same time it was understood that the government would neither relinquish its political and ideological control nor change its one-party ruling system.

David Wen-Wei Chang (1988) argues that Deng's insistence on the Four Adherences Principles" was strategic and expedient in that they helped Deng gain support from the old guards, unite the nation, and pave the way for the acceptance of his central tenet: Practice is the only criterion for determining truth. As Chang explains,

> In short, the Four Cardinal Principles [the Four Adherences] are of political necessity. They are superficial policy guiding premises without ideological depth. The four principles are politically necessary for the leadership to disarm internal resistance. At the propaganda level, these principles help build unity and permit the government-controlled media to indoctrinate the public with the view that communism shall win out at last, that only socialism can guarantee a decent living for all citizens in relative equality, that socialist democracy and legality are superior to the Western rule of law and capitalist democracy, and that China can be strong only through the practice of socialism. (50)

Such a strategy legitimized what Kluver (1996) calls "the national myth," that is, the notion that economic modernization is "another stage in the inevitable history of China" (47).

Related slogans include "Stability and Unification" and "Spiritual and Material Civilization." Such slogans aimed to persuade the public not to challenge the legitimacy of the Communist government but instead to follow the guidance of the CCP in order to accomplish the modernization of China. However, these slogans did not produce the desired persuasive effect for everyone concerned. Indeed, the emphasis on economic development, along with the open-door policy with regard to Western influence, introduced fresh ideas and the desire for a truly democratic society into the post-Maoist era. These factors led directly to the student demonstration in Tiananmen Square in 1989.

The Rhetoric of Jiang Zemin's Regime

"Three Representatives." As promised, Deng left China with a booming economy and an improved standard of living when he stepped down from leadership of the CCP

and then passed away in 1997. However, the ideological crisis remained unsolved, and this had led to moral decline, corruption, and a widening gap between rich and poor. Leaders of Jiang Zemin's regime faced a rhetorical exigency in addressing these issues. Consequently a new set of ideographs was created. The most prominent of these was Jiang Zemin's "Three Representatives"—representing the developmental needs of advanced forces of production, the forward direction of advanced culture, and the fundamental interests of the majority of the Chinese people. According to the interpretation offered in a CCP article, the first category identified economic development as the number one priority of the party. The second category celebrated the advancement of socialist values, including patriotism and collectivism. Further, it advocated a socialist culture with Chinese characteristics that would bring together the most advanced cultural expressions from China and around the world under the guidance of Marxist ideology. The third category established the importance of serving the interests of the majority. The article went on to praise the "Three Representatives" as "scientifically conceptualized," asserting that "Comrade Jiang has creatively applied and developed Marxist doctrines in Party building" (*San Ge Daibiao Xuexi Du Ben* 三個代表學習讀本 2000, 2).

Jiang first introduced the concept of the Three Representatives in his speech of 25 February 2000 during his trip to Guangdong Province. Jiang regarded the Three Representatives as "fundamentals of Party building, principles of governing, and a source of energy" ("On the Publication of Jaing Zemin's Three Representatives," *People's Daily*, 9 August 2001).[7] This speech and others by Jiang were edited and put into a book titled *On the Three Representatives* (published in August 2001 by the CCP Archive Press). According to the *People's Daily*, the publication "promoted the study, propagandizing and practice of the three representatives and has united the thoughts of the whole Party" (Wu Huanqing, 16 August 2001). Jiang was lavishly praised for "having a panoramic view of the winds and clouds of the world and standing on the peak of history regarding the construction of the Party and socialism with Chinese characteristics" (Xia Changyong, *People's Daily*, 25 June 2001).

Jiang's tenet of the Three Representatives signals a bold step to legitimize the economic reform and it is rhetorically a fitting response to the changing function of the CCP. According to Herbert Simons (2003), the Chinese Communist Party has moved away from "its strident condemnation of the capitalist devils and feudal landlords with the utopian rhetoric of Marx's classless society" (10). He has observed that Post-Mao rhetoric in China has become more pragmatic and deradicalized, although often times exhibiting characteristics of ambiguity and paradox. To some degree, Jiang's rhetorical strategy in promoting the Three Representatives is even more pragmatic and expedient than Deng's "socialism with Chinese characteristics" as it has largely abandoned the adherence to any ideology and placed economic development as the top priority of the CCP.

However, even though the content of the CCP's propaganda has changed, the form of public communication remains largely the same.

Reporting on the success of the Three Representatives–inspired study sessions around the country, the same article stated, "The importance of the Three Representatives has been rapidly received and well supported by the whole Party. . . . The head of the Party Committee from Zhengtai Incorporated, in Wenzhou, gladly told reporters that the Three Representatives 'speaks to our hearts. We feel more secure and confident in doing our work'" (Xia Changyong, "The Three Representatives Always Guide Us Forward," *People's Daily,* 25 June 2001). In the same article a party secretary from a local village was quoted as saying, "Party members and cadres have implemented the essence of the Three Representatives. Villagers will become rich. When they are rich, they will support the Communist Party." Such testimonials bear close resemblance to the rhetorical practices known as *jiangyong hui* (Sharing Experience in Applying Mao's Teachings) and *xinde tihui* (reflections and experiences) of the Cultural Revolution. The use of Three Representative discourse has become a symbol of political correctness and means of consolidating Jiang's regime. At the present time nearly all the public speeches mention Jiang Zemin's Three Representatives as the cardinal principles and ideology of the Communist Party. Political jargon associated with the Three Representatives has been proliferated in the speeches of party officials and used frequently by the government-controlled media.

Eulogy of past achievements and goals for the future. The rhetorical theme of eulogizing Mao, the party, and the nation through revolutionary songs has continued to the present time in the speeches of high-ranking government officials, although the focus has shifted to praise for the party rather than for a particular figure. In almost every official speech of the last few years China has been praised for its movement from a problematic past to a prosperous present. This achievement is attributed to the leadership of the Communist Party. For example, Zhu Rongji (2001b), China's past premier, proudly reported to the audience at the Sixth Conference of the World Overseas Chinese Business Economics that the Chinese economy is still booming and that this achievement has been recognized by the entire world. He also reported that China is moving toward more openness and prosperity. Zhu attributed these achievements to the correct leadership of the party.

In addition to promoting ideological and moral principles, speeches by Chinese leaders currently put more emphasis on clarifying tasks/challenges and outlining the steps needed to ensure a prosperous future. In his lengthy speech on the eightieth anniversary celebration of the Chinese Communist Party, Jiang (2001b) outlined the current challenges facing the Communist Party in the areas of administration, serving the people, preventing corruption, liberating minds, and taking a leadership role in economic development. In his Chinese New Year address (23 January 2001a) the premier charted the tasks for the coming year, including reform of all state-owned industry, development of the western region of China, anticorruption activities, and strengthening of the legal system. Similar phraseology can be found in almost every speech by a high-ranking official and in almost every official newspaper. This type of repetition can be understood as *baguwen* 八股文 (fixed style of writing in classical Chinese) in its party-bureaucratic form.

References to history and historical figures. While American politicians like to tell personal stories (for example, former president Ronald Reagan was well known for his story-telling ability in conveying political messages) in their political speeches, Chinese leaders prefer national narratives. In nearly every speech by a Chinese leader the speaker pays tribute to past leaders, praising their contributions and inspiration in leading the country and envisioning the future. This rhetorical strategy lends a lofty air of legitimacy to the speaker.

Chinese political leaders appeal to their audiences by means of shared cultural knowledge and history of their nation. For example, Jiang (2001b) gave a brief review of the modern history of China, from the Opium War to Sun Yat-sen's 1911 Revolution, from the birth of the Communist Party to the founding of the People's Republic of China. These aspects of Chinese history are familiar to the average, educated Chinese citizen. On the occasion of the ninetieth anniversary celebration of Tsinghua University, Jiang (2001a) made reference to well-known scientists and their significant contributions to the country. A speech by Qian Qichen (23 January 2001), the vice premier, on the issue of China's unification with Taiwan painted the picture of a weak China split by imperialist powers and overrun by the Japanese. Finally, Li Ruihuan (2001), chairman of the Chinese Committee of Political Consultation, reminded the Chinese people, "We cannot forget the revolutionary martyrs who sacrificed their lives. Without their brave struggle, we would not have what we have today. We cannot forget the important advances several generations have fought hard and paid a high price for" (1).

Making reference to the past was one of the key rhetorical features of classical Chinese rhetoric (Jensen 1992). It was also a prominent characterization of the cultural-revolutionary rhetoric, especially in the rhetoric deifying Mao. Today the same pattern is repeated by the leaders of Jiang's regime. Nearly all official party speeches make reference to Deng Xiaoping for his vision of "Socialism with Chinese Characteristics" that has brought China economic prosperity and a better living standard. And while American leaders tend to end their speeches by saying "God Bless America," atheistic Chinese leaders predominantly close their speeches with the same formalized sequence of sentences such as "Let us closely unite under the core leadership of Comrade Jiang Zemin, raise high the great flag of Deng Xiaoping's theory, follow and practice the important ideas expressed in the 'Three Representatives' and strive for further victory in building the cause of socialism with Chinese characteristics." Although the content has been changed, the form of these set phrases and banal clichés is reminiscent of the Cultural Revolution.

Rhetorical features. Michael McGee (1980) contends that words and concepts that convey values and moral principles in political settings serve the functions of creating myth and fostering political consciousness. In his words, "ideology in practice is a political language, presented in rhetorical documents, with the capacity to dictate decision and control public belief and behavior" (427). Deng's "Socialism with Chinese Characteristics," Jiang's "Three Representatives," and other such formalized slogans were fitting responses to the exigencies of the post-Mao era. They served the function of calling for a collective commitment to national goals through appeals to cultural ideals. These slogans defined the causes and political realities of the time and justified proposals for future actions in light of prevailing cultural values/heroes and political ideology. In the Chinese context, both past and present, references to the glorious history of the party and past leaders have been the primary means of legitimization. As observed by Townsend and Womack (1986), "the tendency to cast political discourse in terms of historical events and personalities did not die with the end of the imperial system in 1911. Despite marked differences in vocabulary and interpretations required by a Marxist approach, the Chinese Communists remain highly sensitive to the political uses and implications of Chinese history and have continued to find legitimization in China's past for the domestic and external developments of her most recent present" (30).

Highly formalized, politically correct language was a common feature of communist discourse prior to, during, and after the Cultural Revolution. Such language tended to be ambiguous and abstract in meaning and, therefore, open to different interpretations, as in the case of "Socialism with Chinese Characteristics." In fact, as Kluver (1996) points out, "the power of these formulations lies largely in their ambiguity" (124). This is especially true when the terms are coined by authorities and defined in general terms in connection with cultural values and national sentiment. However, because of the ambiguous, abstract, and general nature of such slogans, it was difficult for ordinary people to challenge and question their validity. Out of a need for ideological correctness they would simply be repeated and recited without any real understanding of what was being communicated.

Chinese leaders like to use numbers in laying out policies and articulating future actions. Number sequences range from a total of three for a short speech to eight for a long one. Typically, after initial explanation of the numerated slogans, future reference only uses the numbers and omits the elaboration of the statement. The habit of enumerating slogans has the advantage of putting complex and intricate ideas into simple, easy-to-remember phrases. Designed not only for easy memorization but also for easy deployment in oral and written political discourse, this practice is especially effective for illiterate and less-educated party bureaucrats. The use of numbered phrases, or *chengyu* 成語 (four-character idioms), is common in Chinese spoken language. Not coincidentally, most political ideographs and symbols, vague and ambiguous as they seem to be, are associated with numerical references that give them a false air of specificity and precision. Pre–Cultural Revolution slogans such as "Three Antis" and "Four Clean-ups" were replaced during the Cultural Revolution with a new set of numerated slogans such as the "Five Red (or Black) Categories," the "Four Olds

(News)," the "Three Loyalties," and the "Four Boundless Loves." Numerated slogans after the Cultural Revolution have included the "Four Modernizations," "Five Unifications," "Four Adherences," and more recently, the "Three Representatives." Numerated slogans have been dominant features of the CCP's history and powerful means of political persuasion. In fact, Chinese political rhetoric in general is much characterized by its number-based propaganda.[8]

While American politicians generally use rhetoric to teach, to move, and to please their audiences, rooted in the Ciceronian tradition, Chinese leaders are primarily interested in the teaching function in relation to their audiences. Further, instead of employing a variety of stylistic devices, which are abundant in the Chinese language, Chinese political discourse is characterized by what Schoenhals (1992) calls "formalized language"—in effect, a restricted code deemed politically appropriate by party officials. Schoenhals argues that such formalization becomes a form of power for the already powerful since it is the language of the state. Worse, as this formalized language is used repeatedly in every political speech it becomes dry and cumbersome, leading to linguistic impoverishment and thought deprivation.

Rhetoric Condemning Falun Gong

Falun Gong (also known as Falun Dafa), a religious sect, was founded by Li Hongzhi in 1992. It is a branch of Qi Gong practice,[9] a type of movement meditation based on tenets of traditional Chinese Taoist philosophy and Buddhism, and it involves breathing exercises and hand movement around an imaginary wheel. According to Li Hongzhi (1994), the slow-motion meditation exercises are designed to improve health and facilitate a mental state of truthfulness, compassion, and tolerance that gives rise to moral living. Though the group has no apparent physical location and no articulated political agenda, it does have its own official publications, websites, E-mail networks, and leaflet distribution system. The group is organized secretly underground within China and often holds demonstrations throughout the United States and worldwide.

In the early stages of Falun Gong's development the government did not interfere. Instead it recognized the merits of the practice in improving public health, later honoring Li Hongzhi with the Award for Advancing Frontier Science and allowing the publication of his book *Zhuan Falun* by a government-run publisher.[10] However, with a drastic increase in Falun Gong's popularity, by the end of 1999 the number of practitioners reached two million according to the Chinese government and seventy million by the Falun Gong estimates.[11] Moreover, many members of the Communist Party were also Falun Gong practitioners. In May 1998 a scientist named He Zuoxiu criticized the group on television for promoting "pseudo science." A year later He Zuoxiu published an article in *Youth Reader* that cited the group as "disrupting the public order of the society" and its activities "similar to heretical cults in the West" (cited in Schecter 2001, 19).

Fearing that such a charge would cause Falun Gong to be banned, practitioners in Tianjin held a protest, which soon escalated into a riot. On 25 April 1999 ten thousand

Falun Gong practitioners, mostly women and retired workers, held a peaceful demonstration outside the Appeal Office (the location for filing complaints), which is next to Zhongnanhai Compound, the Communist Party's headquarters and residence of its top-ranking officials. Demonstrators demanded the release of forty-five Falun Gong members arrested by police during the Tianjin riot. These actions by the members of Falun Gong alarmed and stunned the government. Perceiving the sect as a threat to social stability and fearing that it might evolve into an antigovernment political organization,[12] the government launched a crackdown. On 22 July 1999 the Ministry of Civil Affairs of the People's Republic of China made a televised announcement labeling Falun Gong an "evil cult" and banning its practice along with the distribution of Falun Gong materials. Subsequently the government launched an intensive propaganda campaign through the government-controlled media to defame Falun Gong and its founder. A series of reports were issued in government media about how Falun Gong had killed people, ruined families, and driven people to insanity. Meanwhile, China's police force began investigating and arresting Falun Gong members. Some were imprisoned without trial. According to a Falun Gong data source, by 2002, 370 members were tortured to death; 100,000 were detained; and 20,000 were sent to labor camps (www.Falundafa.org).

Personally, I am not a believer of Falun Gong, nor do I feel attracted to its practice. My interest is in the rhetorical elements of the government's propaganda campaign against the group to the extent that such rhetorical elements are reminiscent of those employed during the Cultural Revolution. Rhetorical themes of the campaign against Falun Gong that resemble closely the rhetoric of the Cultural Revolution include: (1) moral and scientific appeals; (2) emotional and logical appeals; (3) conspiracy theory; and (4) rhetorical styles. The data used for the following analysis are government newspapers and publications condemning Falun Gong.

Moral and Scientific Appeals
Moral appeals against Falun Gong were communicated through two types of rhetoric. The first centered around discrediting Li Hongzhi, and the second focused on the alleged harm caused by the sect and the significance of the crackdown against them in the interest of ensuring China's future stability. Echoing Jiang Zemin's characterization of Falun Gong as "an evil cult threatening the Chinese people and society" (*The Guardian,* 30 October 1999), the *People's Daily* and other government-controlled media published a series of articles and commentaries denouncing the practice and, in particular, its founder Li Hongzhi, now residing in the United States. The sect leader was charged with having an ulterior motive of attempting to "replace the government and rule the world by deifying himself and by engaging in anti-government activities" (commentary, *People's Daily,* 28 July 1999). Li was portrayed as "a liar," "a charlatan," "a glib person," and "an evil person" who fleeced his followers, ruining their health and their lives and having a disastrous effect on society.[13] Further, Li was accused of fabricating his résumé, claiming to have supernatural abilities, changing his birthday to the birthday of Sakyamuni[14] (implying that he was the reincarnation of the Buddha), living

a luxurious life in America, and relying on foreign powers to subvert the Chinese government. His ideas were dismissed as "malicious fallacies," and his political ambition was labeled "wicked" and "viperous." China's official media coverage was filled with righteous and sometimes hyperbolic expressions denouncing Li Hongzhi, reminiscent of terms used to denounce "class enemies" during the Cultural Revolution.

Moral appeal also was exerted by delegitimizing Falun Gong as an evil cult. The CCP propaganda characterized the crackdown against Falun Gong as a serious political struggle. For example, Zhou Dai (1999) asserted in the opening statement of the booklet *Ten Denunciations of Falu Dafa* that this struggle "concerns the fundamental belief system of the Communists, concerns the fundamental ideology of the Chinese people, and concerns the future destiny of our Party and country" (1). A series of similar denunciation articles were published in a booklet under the authorship of the editorial board of *Seeking Truth,* formerly the *Red Flag.*[15] Falun Gong was described as "an evil cult that opposes science, humankind, society, and government" (Niu Aimin and Wang Leiming, "The Sky Is Clear When the Evil Is Eradicated," *People's Daily,* 22 July 2000).[16] The group was further condemned for allegedly "agitating the masses, provoking riots, ignoring the law and public interests, creating chaos, and plotting, inciting, and deceiving followers" (Dai 1999, 3). According to this view, Falun Gong was touted not as a spiritual practice, as claimed by Li Hongzhi, but instead as a serious threat to social stability and order. Such rhetoric appeals to the current mentality of many Chinese who passionately pursue both material well-being and a stable social environment, at all costs. It also serves to justify the government's repressive actions against the group as these actions are staged in the name of protecting the people.

To simply label the sect "evil" was not sufficient, for this characterization merely expressed the government's opposition to Falun Gong's practice. It did not explain why Falun Gong was evil, which was one of the rhetorical exigencies the government faced in persuading the public. To do so, the government propaganda machine used the appeal of science or scientific rationalism. China's intellectuals have placed a high value on science since the beginning of the twentieth century; it symbolizes modernization, progress, and truth-finding. Evaluations of Mao claim his most significant error to be his failure to use scientific thinking and a scientific approach to address the Chinese situation. And though China did not experience a clear transition from Judeo-Christianity to a scientific paradigm, as occurred in the West, many Chinese considered Mao's era of ideological confinement the Chinese equivalent of the Dark Ages and sought science as a source of enlightenment after the Cultural Revolution.

Guided, in denunciation articles, by the premise that science is the measure of truth and knowledge, authors cited Copernicus and other scientific visionaries to refute Li Hongzhi's spiritual explanation of the universe. In this way Falun Gong was dismissed as the "denial of all scientific truth and in complete opposition with modern science and civilization" (*Ten Denunciations of Falun Gong* 1999, 15). Falun Gong's real motive for allegedly denying the validity of science, according to anonymous commentaries, was to "deify Li Hongzhi and portray him as a savior" (55). Another motive was to "promote superstition and present a gloomy picture of the future of humankind" (76). According to government propaganda, Falun Gong's worldview was in complete opposition to science. The conflict between Falun Gong and communism, as asserted by a commentary in the *People's Daily* of 27 July 1999, "was a struggle between theism and atheism, superstition and science, idealism and materialism." This highly polarized depiction of science and religion created a dichotomous view of reality. Further, the scientific worldview was legitimized as moral and truthful, while the discourse of Falun Gong was branded as evil and deceptive. However, the privilege of scientific rationalism also can be harmful. As Kluver (1996) points out, "the absoluteness of this position [science as the only criterion for truth] is inherently as dangerous as an earlier authority, as it soon can turn to coercion of the 'scientific' perspective" (136).

Interestingly, the scientific perspective that the Chinese government seeks to uphold includes not only the scientific explanation of the workings of the universe (natural science) but also the theoretical framework of Marxism as articulated by Deng Xiaoping (social science). As expressed in an editorial in *Seeking Truth*, "No matter what hardships or difficulties we encounter, as long as the Chinese people rely on our own scientific theory—the theory of Deng Xiaoping— and stand behind our comrade Jiang Zemin, the core of the CCP Committee, we can solve all our problems with a spirit of historical perspectives" (*Ten Denunciations of Falun Gong* 1999, 89). This statement implies that Deng Xiaoping's theory of "Socialism with Chinese Characteristics" and Jiang Zemin's precept of "Three Representatives" are scientifically proven tenets that party members should follow. Such an assumption again reinforces the importance of ideological correctness and absolute obedience to authority, a prominent rhetorical feature of the Cultural Revolution. So-called scientific rationalism is reduced to a rhetorical strategy; the real motive of such propaganda is to consolidate the power base of the current regime.

Emotional and Logical Appeals

To convince the public that Falun Gong was an evil cult harmful to individuals and society, the government flooded the media with stories of broken families, suicides, and murder cases, all allegedly resulting from deep beliefs in Falun Gong. Consider the following story, one of many told in the *People's Daily:* Tian's family had practiced Falun Gong since 1997. The parents wanted their fifteen-year-old son to join them. The boy quit school and devoted himself totally to Falun Gong. School authorities and teachers came to their home many times trying to get the boy to return to school, but his parents insisted that practicing Falun Gong was more important than going to school. Later the father divorced his wife because he wanted to go to a higher level of consciousness in his practice of Falun Gong. The wife left home and never came back. The grandfather was so saddened and devastated by his broken family that he became seriously ill and eventually passed away (Xinhua reporters, "Destroy the Beloved Relations; Brutalize a Family," 6 April 2001). According to this story the family was torn apart, the child was deprived of his education, and the grandfather lost his life—all because of blind adherence to Falun Gong.

The *People's Daily* stories and televised accounts also reported a Tiananmen incident caused by a middle-aged man named Liu Yunfang. Since Liu began practicing Falun Gong he had become reticent and refused to talk to family members. It was reported that he stopped working and no longer helped his wife with housework. Liu was reportedly convinced by Li Hongzhi's preaching that the best way to reach a higher level of consciousness characterized by supernormal capabilities and special powers and to let go of all attachments was to go to Nirvana. He then decided to kill himself by soaking his body with gas and burning himself in Tiananmen Square (Xinhua reporters, "The Evil of Cult," 1 March 2001). Many more stories were told of sons killing their parents, mothers deserting their families and children, and people committing suicide. All such tragedies were attributed to the evil influence of Li Hongzhi and the unscientific notion that one must give up all his or her *zhizhuo* 執著 (adherence/attachments) in order to reach *yuanman* 圓滿 (freedom from the cycle of life and death). The *People's Daily* reported the findings of a study claiming that by January 2001, "1,600 followers had died of suicide or refusal to be treated for their sickness; 651 people had begun to hallucinate; fourteen were murdered, and 144 people were disabled; thousands of people lost their harmonious and happy family lives" (commentary, 11 January 2001).

These reports made strong emotional appeals because the Chinese value their families, education, and filial piety to parents above all else. According to government-sponsored reports, Falun Gong followers violated these values and caused personal/family tragedies that in turn destabilized society and brought disharmonious social relationships. The persuasive effects of such emotional appeals were further enhanced by the statistical evidence regarding loss of lives and broken families caused by blind adherence to Falun Gong.

Conspiracy Theory

Conspiracy theories were a common feature of the rhetoric of the Cultural Revolution in identifying and denouncing class enemies. The same rhetorical theme was used to denounce Falun Gong. According to Falun Gong's Web site (www.Falundafa.org), before Falun Gong was officially banned, Jiang Zemin gave a speech to the Politburo of the Central Committee claiming, "The issue of 'Falun Gong' has a very deep political and social background and even a complicated international background. . . . It is the most serious incident since the political turbulence of 1989" (No. 30 Highly Confidential Document, 1999). At the time of Falun Gong's peaceful demonstration on 25 April 1999, Jiang wrote a letter to the members of the Politburo charging that there were "masterminds behind the scenes" of the incident who were "planning and issuing commands" (No. 14 Highly Confidential Document, 1999). There was even a suspicion that there were "senior insiders in the Chinese government who might be manipulating and directing the whole thing" (Schechter 2001, 29). In the same rhetorical tone articles in the *Ten Denunciations of Falun Gong* accused Li Hongzhi of "aiming to enslave people and enlarge his own political power" (117). Li was accused of "conspiring to overthrow the government and gain power that is above the law and government" (3). He was even indicted for "conspiring to establish a separate nation under his control" (127). In responding to the Tiananmen self-immolation incident, the *People's Daily* called it "a vicious activity that is organized, well plotted, well planned, and following a well specified procedure" (Xinhua reporters, "The Evil of Cult," 1 March 2001).

While Li Hongzhi, in a U.S. interview, denied any political intention in promoting the practice of Falun Gong, the Chinese government insisted that he had strong political ambition and motive. In support of this claim, an editorial in the *People's Daily* argued that Li Hongzhi had disseminated the view that the government was useless and could not solve social and moral problems; furthermore, he had recruited party members to his sect, aiming to insinuate his preaching into the party and to sabotage the ideological foundation of the party. In addition Li was accused of instigating all Falun Gong demonstrations. He was described as "shamelessly relying upon anti-China foreign forces, stirring up anti-government sentiments and defying the Chinese people and the Chinese government." The article concluded with, "Falun Gong is an evil cult; it is a political tool manipulated by a Western enemy force to overthrow the Chinese government and China's socialist system" ("Expose Li Honzhi and Falungon's Vicious Motive," 8 January 2001).

To this day law enforcement authorities have found no evidence of a Western-backed political conspiracy with regard to Falun Gong. However, the rhetoric of conspiracy theory continues to permeate the government-controlled media, playing into the psychology of fear and insecurity. Li Hongzhi is portrayed as a traitor. The practice of denouncing political dissidents as traitors or tools of foreign interests has been an effective persuasive strategy as it stirs up nationalism and antiforeigner sentiments.[17] Conspiracy theories have been a regular feature of communist propaganda used as a rationale to launch and legitimize political movements. Schechter (2001) captured this strategy when he wrote, "Chinese leaders have been ideologically schooled and taught by history to suspect conspiracies and hostile internal political factions. The assumption is that people are incapable of organizing and mobilizing without someone in authority pulling the strings" (29). Similarly, conspiracy theories have been used to justify the incarceration of Japanese Americans during World War II, the extermination of Jews in Nazi Germany, and McCarthyism in the United States during the 1950s.

Rhetorical Styles
The denunciation papers and commentaries against Falun Gong in the government-controlled media closely resembled the organizational structure of Chinese wall posters, characterized by a syllogistic progression that began with an assumed major premise, usually expressed in a strong moralistic tone, and then proceeded with evidence in support of the accusations. The opening paragraphs typically consisted of a set of accusations against Li Hongzhi and Falun Gong. The evidence in support of

these accusations would then be presented in the form of testimonies by Falun Gong practitioners, accounts of Li Hongzhi's personal fraud and wanton lifestyle, and reports of Falun Gong's "antigovernment activities" (that is, demonstrations). The rhetorical flavor of such denunciation is reminiscent of the wall posters denouncing class enemies during the Cultural Revolution. The "evidence" provided points to the seriousness of the life-or-death struggle between the party and Li Hongzhi and confirms Li's evil intentions to subvert the government and ruin people's lives.

Further, the CCP propaganda campaign used the techniques of confession and alienation popular during the Cultural Revolution. Former Falun Gong practitioners were pressured to make confessions of their experiences. Such confessions usually had three parts: first, the person would give a detailed account of the harm Falun Gong had brought to his/her family; second, the person would express profound regret for having believed in Li Hongzhi and allowing him to harm the family and society; and third, the person would advise other Falun Gong practitioners to awaken from the evil spell of Falun Gong and to come back to truth and reality. In the early stage of the Falun Gong crackdown Li Qihua, a prominent People's Liberation Army lieutenant general, published his confession in a Cultural Revolution style conforming to the party line. Among other things, he stated: "The Party's decision is very wise, very correct, and very timely" (Schechter 2001, 200). Willingly and unwillingly, former Falun Gong practitioners signed letters disavowing the group. Thousands have been sent to reeducation camps and are required to make confessions and undergo self-criticism regarding their Falun Gong involvement in a manner reminiscent of the Cultural Revolution. A letter by Tsinghua University students and teachers to government officials protested the unfair treatment received by Falun Gong practitioners and described how some were forced to give up the practices. They wrote, "These people could not resume their education or work unless they took a stand against Falun Gong and promised not to practice any more. Under pressure from both the university and parents, some of us wrote the 'confession' unwillingly. Those who refused were put under house confinement to achieve 'mind changing'" (Schechter 2001, 80).

The strategy of the anti–Falun Gong campaign was to persuade the majority to abandon the practice. The *People's Daily* article by Niu Aimin and Wang Leiming ("chanchu xie-e qiankun lang" [The sky is clear when the evil is eradicated], 22 July 2000) stated: "In the very beginning of handling the Falun Gong problem, the Party and the government emphasized that we must educate, unite, and persuade the majority; we must isolate and attack the extreme minority." The article went on to report that "after sincere, patient, and careful thought work, 98% of practitioners have freed themselves from Li Hongzhi's mind control, distanced themselves from the cult, come back to their normal social activities, and regained their human dignity." Moreover, people were encouraged to identify and report Falun Gong practitioners among their neighbors and coworkers. Once identified, such people have been expelled from the Communist Party, and some have been fired from work. In serious cases when criminal charges were brought, practitioners have been imprisoned. Most have been sent to reeducation camps where they have had to make confessions and vow to sever their ties to the cult before being released. The whole process is reminiscent of the rituals of induced criticism and self-criticism, and of the study of the approved documents aimed for thought reform and ideological rectitude during the Cultural Revolution.

In further efforts to dismantle the organization the government deployed the legal system to level charges against some Falun Gong practitioners suggested of engaging in antigovernment activities (such as conducting public demonstrations without a permit and registration) and activities that have driven other members to murder or suicide. The legal card, like the science card, has been played a great deal during the reform era. It is the new rational/moral appeal used to persuade the public.

When asked if they see any evidence of the language of the Cultural Revolution in post-Mao China, many interviewees pointed to the language used by the government media to discredit Falun Gong. They noted many words and sentences that were familiar because those expressions were used frequently during the rhetorical drudgery of the Cultural Revolution in slogans, wall posters, and ritualistic practices. Examples of familiar words and phrases used to describe an enemy's behavior include *chiluoluo* 赤裸裸 (blatantly), *gudong* 鼓動 (agitate), and *shandong* 煽動 (stir up). Others such as *da baolu* 大暴露 (big exposé), *Tiaoliang xiaochou* 跳梁小丑 (contemptible scoundrel), *ban qi shitou za ziji de jiao* 搬起石頭砸自己的腳 (lift a rock only to drop it on one's own feet), *chuisi zhengzha* 垂死掙扎 (a last-ditch struggle), and *qiongtu molu* 窮途末路 (dead end) are often used to indicate the enemy's inevitable failure. Phrases including, for example, *ba . . . jinxing daodi* 把 . . . 進行到底 (carry . . . till the end) and *Jiechuan . . . xian'e zhengzhi yongxin* 揭穿 . . . 險惡政治用心 (expose . . . vicious political motive) are clichés expressing the will and determination to carry on the revolutionary cause. During the four-year campaign against Falun Gong all denunciation papers and articles have used similar language, employed similar structure, and drawn similar conclusions.

Rhetoric condemning Falun Gong has had different effects on different groups of people. It can be effective in relation to those who are familiar with the expressions but have never given any critical thought to the effects. On the one hand, these people may find the denunciation articles persuasive as the use of language recalls a familiar, though largely unconscious, rhetorical experience during the Cultural Revolution. On the other hand, for those who have been conscious of the use of such language and have given some critical thought to it, the repeated use of the same clichés may have an adverse effect. In the words of a Beijing academic, "It's a stupid policy. It is creating enemies where there are no enemies" (McCarthy 1999, 50). Clearly, for this portion of the audience at least, such propaganda is perceived as "totalitarian paranoia."

Through a massive Mao-style propaganda campaign and some degree of coercion, Falun Gong as a spiritual movement has been crushed, and the government has proclaimed itself victorious. Currently, however, Falun Gong is the largest dissident group in China and overseas, with its worldwide "virtual" organization and network. Further, the handling of the Falun Gong crisis has raised many concerns in China that the government has failed to address. The rise and popularity of the sect indicate a need for spiritual comfort that rapid economic development and the pursuit of materialism cannot fulfill. The formalized language and tedious rhetoric of party bureaucrats have lost their appeal; Maoism has lost its ideological attraction. Millions in China feel a spiritual void as the country transitions from a Marxist socialist economy to a Western market economy. As noted by Schechter (2001), "Falun Gong offers an individual-centered self-improvement philosophy, rather than a top-down collective approach" (17). Moreover, in facing the moral crisis and spiritual void, people often turn to indigenous cultures for insights and enlightenment. Falun Gong's eclectic mix of traditional Taoism and Buddhism plus its practical application of traditional healing techniques had widespread appeal. The government's predictable response to Falun Gong continued the rhetorical themes and styles of the Cultural Revolution while adding scientific and legal appeals to the mix. Ultimately, government propaganda still operates under a nondemocratic system in which only one version of truth is allowed and legitimated. Falun Gong's preaching is not given its due as an alternative worldview and valid means of personal empowerment in the face of economic and spiritual woes; it is instead branded as heresy in contrast to scientific rationalism and Marxist ideology. Unfortunately, the Chinese government has once again lost an opportunity to engage in dialogue with the common people and delayed the process of democratization.[18]

Rhetoric of Anti-American Sentiments

In the 3 September 2000 airing of the U.S. television program *60 Minutes,* CBS senior correspondent Mike Wallace interviewed Jiang Zemin, China's president. During the interview Jiang used a nature metaphor to describe U.S.-China relations: "Our relations have experienced wind, rain, and sometimes clouds or even dark clouds. However, sometimes it clears up. We all sincerely hope to build a constructive partnership between China and the United States." Indeed, the history of Sino-U.S. relations has had its ups and downs, its clear skies and dark clouds. John Starr (1981) describes it as like "a pendulum swing[ing] between euphoria and disenchantment—illusions giving way to disillusionment" (257).

The historic handshake between Mao Zedong and Richard Nixon in 1972 marked the beginning of normalized relations between China and the United States. The most dramatic change in relations between the two countries has occurred in the last twenty years since China launched its open-door policy and economic reforms in 1982, paving the way for a significant increase in trade.[19] Strained relations over controversial issues have often overshadowed the economic partnership between the two countries, however.[20] Since the 1989 Tiananmen Square incident the United States has imposed certain sanctions against China for alleged human rights violations as well as infringement of "intellectual property" rights. Moreover, after the collapse of the Berlin Wall and the former Soviet Union in 1989, which brought an end to the cold war, certain elements within the U.S. government and media began to perceive China as an increased threat and to argue for the necessity of sanctions against China (Krauthammer 1995; Lilley 1997). At the same time the Chinese government was indignant at the U.S. government's issuance of a visa to Taiwan's president Li Denghui as well as America's unfavorable votes against China becoming a member of the World Trade Organization and China's bid to host the Olympic games in the year 2000 in Beijing. China retaliated with harsh rhetoric, accusing the United States of interference in China's internal affairs and intentionally blocking China from the realization of its quest for modernizations. China claimed that America's ultimate motive was to maintain hegemony and world domination by thwarting China's economic development and deliberately targeting China as an enemy. More recent events such as the U.S. bombing of the Chinese embassy in Yugoslavia and the collision of a U.S. spy plane with a Chinese fighter jet further inflamed the rhetoric of anti-America and pro-nationalistic sentiment.

The Rhetoric of Anti-Americanism in China Can Say No

China Can Say No (Song, Zhang, and Qiao 1996a) was authored by young intellectuals professionally engaged as reporters, poets, and free-lance journalists.[21] When the book was first published in May 1996 the first run of fifty thousand copies sold out instantly. The book was written in response to mounting tensions in Sino-American relations that had been on the increase since the 1989 Tiananmen Square massacre.

In content and style *China Can Say No* resembles the Chinese government's anti-American rhetoric, while claiming to represent public opinion and the common people. It was written in a format of refutation and argumentation and filled with anecdotes, sarcastic remarks, catchy phrases, Maoist pronouncements, threats of retaliation, and profane language. Most Chinese commentaries on the book regarded it as having revealed the true feelings of contemporary Chinese youth and having reflected the Chinese people's dissatisfaction with American policy toward China (Song, Zhang, and Qiao 1996b, 418–18). However, non-Chinese commentaries described the book as attacking America's cultural invasion, a work of extreme nationalism, and anti-American. Several sources characterized the book as emotionally charged and filled with bias and stereotypes (Cheng Li 1996; Jianhong Lin 1996).

Rhetorical argument in the book: American hegemony and an anti-China policy. According to the authors of *China Can Say No,* the United States has two clear purposes in relation to the world and in particular to China: to maintain and exercise American hegemony in the world; and to thwart China's economic development through sabotage and a policy of containment.

The U.S. quest for world domination has intensified, according to the authors, since the end of the cold war with the former Soviet Union. They warn, "The ghost of hegemony lingers in the world" (Song et al. 1996a, 305), and that ghost is the United States of America. Evidence of the U.S. hegemonic campaign includes the fact that the United States "plays the role of the world's police force" (65), "wants to dominate the world" (227), and "always strives for the status of world leadership" (310). A prime example of the American hegemonic impulse is U.S. interference in the Middle East and Asia (210, 241), the authors contend. What is frightening, the authors assert, is that the U.S. desire for world domination hides behind the pretense of concerns for "humanitarianism and justice" while in fact "its appetite [to eat the world] is bigger than a Heavenly dog" (241). The American lust for hegemony, according to the authors, is most evident in the U.S. policy of containing China. They believe that the United States "has placed obstacles everywhere to block China from its economic development" (195). Two explanations for U.S. hostility toward China are given: first, it would be boring for the United States not to have an enemy after the cold war; and second, the United States has always been hostile to China and has never wanted China to be economically strong. In the judgment of the authors, "The strategy of the U.S. is to contain China and ultimately to reduce China to chaos" (325). Further, they state, "The U.S. tried its best and took every opportunity to achieve the goal of containing China" (328). To insure that China remains the enemy the United States has proposed the theory of the "China threat," describing China as "evil, menacing, and in violation of international rules" (82).

The authors imply that such evil intentions and this hostile attitude toward China would naturally be followed by numerous evil acts against China. The authors identify U.S. actions taken to achieve its hegemonic ends and plot against China. For example, the United States organized an anti-Chinese club with a large membership, the CIA plotted the instance involving Harry Wu[22] and supported the publication of the book *The Private Life of Chairman Mao* (144), and the United States prevented China from joining the World Trade Organization and voted against China's hosting of the Olympic games in the year 2000. Further examples cited by the authors are that the United States exports Coca-Cola with a much higher sugar content to China than that sold in the United States and that the cigarettes exported to China have a higher nicotine content than those sold in the United States.

Examining the logic of the authors' arguments makes it clear that all alleged anti-China acts are presented not as data for inducing and rendering a conclusion but as confirmation of the U.S. hegemonic designs against China. In other words, the U.S. hegemonic impulse, combined with America's evil intentions toward the Chinese, determined and explained American policy-making and communication with regard to China. Such an argument is a powerful means of persuasion as the end is justified by the means and the action is explained by the motives. For Chinese readers with doubts about American motives for sanctioning China, the authors provide a deductive explanation. That is, the U.S. role in the world combined with an anti-Chinese bias predetermines that the United States will act against China in every way possible.

Form of rhetoric: Syllogism, repetitiveness, anecdotes, and emotional language. The syllogistic form is evident in the pentadic analysis of purpose-act ratio (Burke 1969a)[23] in that the purpose is proposed as a well-accepted principle that the United States is hegemonic and hostile toward China. The U.S. actions against China fit the description of their purpose, and accordingly the United States is motivated by the evil intention of making China into an enemy. This deductive reasoning process was characteristic of Cultural Revolution rhetoric by which an individual in question was accused of being a "capitalistic running dog," "counterrevolutionary," or "traitor" based purely on allegation. Next the Red Guards or masses would contrive a list of "evildoings" as "evidence" that would prove the accusations. Many Chinese who lived through the Cultural Revolution are accustomed to this form of argumentation. The book *China Can Say No* in some way recalled their symbolic experiences with this type of rhetorical strategy and satisfied their desire to understand and interpret the motives and actions of the United States vis-á-vis China.

The repetitive form used in *China Can Say No* is exemplified by repeated references to the decline and degradation of American culture and by demonstrating how American cultural influence has disgraced China's national character and pride. American culture is described as "naive," "degenerate," and "lacking a sense of history and depth of thought" and as "having no value for tradition" (Song et al. 1996a, 25, 219). American people are portrayed as "obnoxious," "arrogant," and "ignorant" (33); as "lazy" (128); and as having "lost interest in independent thinking" (25). Americans also are described as "lacking self control, being cold in human relationships, lacking a sense of responsibility for each other, lacking love and care, and showing numbness toward public and political life" (127). American politics are depicted as corrupt. Hollywood films are "trash" and are "filled with sex and violence and should be burned" (122–25). Moreover, in the authors' eyes the United States poses a serious threat to the world as it is "the biggest terrorist country. No matter where you live, everyday you can feel the effects of the reign of U.S. terror, which has power all over the world" (247). The authors assert, "A world without America would be better because it would have no threat of a nuclear war, no cultural imperialism and economic looting. People of the world would have more peace and would enjoy a shared human civilization" (305).

In describing the United States as a nation Song et al. (1996a) claim that the "American personality is biased and arrogant" and has "lost its soul" (304); "it is shallow, short-sighted, and rude" (305). The authors conclude that given the current state of affairs in the United States, "the U.S. will decline, and this will come sooner than we thought" (28). Further, they disqualify the United States as a world leader, stating that "Americans do not have empathy and sympathy for other nations. From educated to ordinary people, they cannot understand the inner world of people of other cultures. They are, therefore, not qualified to lead the world" (34). "They lack the [moral] character for an advanced nation"(25).

The corrupting influence of the American culture is conveyed through anecdotal evidence such as the following: American soldiers' rape of Japanese girls; American police brutality with regard to illegal Mexican immigrants; the former CBS anchorwoman Connie Chung's accusation that Chinese students are spies; and the plight of a Chinese man who was repeatedly refused a U.S. visa and eventually died of disease on a boat going to the United States. These stories, not backed up by any sources or specific contexts, are what Kenneth Burke (1969b) calls "representative anecdotes."

According to Burke, a representative anecdote is "a form in conformity with which the vocabulary is constructed" (59). Such a form appeals to the reader's conventional symbolic experience and defines reality in a highly selective fashion. Rueckert (1969) interprets Burke's notion of a representative anecdote as "the paradigmatic embodiment of the 'pure' or 'ideal' . . . the archetypal myth, the perfect imitation of the pure essence" (381). In other words, representative anecdote has a rhetorical power to shape reality, to frame certain circumstances, and to draw out cultural meanings. According to Madsen (1993), the selection of a representative anecdote is a conscious choice on the part of the rhetor in order to depict a reality and respond to a rhetorical situation in a particular way; in his words, "Rhetors may employ the representative anecdote as they try to produce a representative text to round out a situation" (209). The anecdotes used in *China Can Say No* were deliberately selected for their negative portrayal of American culture and the American people, in response to U.S. hostility against China and as a means to promote Chinese nationalism. This rhetorical strategy created and reinforced stereotypes related to American culture, perpetuating the image of the "ugly Americans." More important, it sent a message to the Chinese people that they should maintain their cultural esteem and dignity, and establish a new national identity rooted in Chinese civilization and tradition.

In addition to the use of anecdotes, value statements, and labels, the authors seem fond of catchy phrases, metaphors, Maoist pronouncements, and sometimes even profanity. Phrases such as "stumbling blocks," "a group of crows," and "upstart" were used to describe the United States and its politicians. The phrase "pushed into the trial of history" was used to suggest what will happen to the United States in the future, and the phrase "burn the Hollywood" was used to inspire resistance to American cultural imperialism. The Maoist slogan "A just cause enjoys abundant support while an unjust cause finds little support" was also employed by the authors of *China Can Say No* in reference to the inevitable demise of the United States. All these terms were popular during the Cultural Revolution when they were leveled against class enemies and the international superpowers—namely the United States and the former Soviet Union. These terms are emotionally charged, giving vent to frustrations and hatred, and holding out hope that good will triumph over evil in the end. However, they do not allow the reader to engage in rational and critical thinking but instead invite surrender to the rhetor's version of reality as well as to the immediate gratification of verbal attack.

The rhetorical form used in *China Can Say No* can be a powerful means of persuasion when the reader is able to identify with the author's use of language, the manner of presenting a syllogistic argument with a strong element of moral condemnation (that is, the United States is evil) and emotional involvement (Chinese national dignity), and the desire to understand U.S. motives and culture. However, the book would not be persuasive for those with the ability to detect the logical fallacies in the presentation of its arguments nor to those who engage in critical thinking and arrive at conclusions based on factual evidence rather than on preferential judgments and personal feelings. The book would also not be persuasive for these readers who have benefited from firsthand exposure to American culture and become genuinely acquainted with American people. These more discriminating readers would consider the argumentative form and the use of language biased, overly emotional, and invalid. The authors would quickly lose their credibility with such readers.

In his analysis of Hitler's rhetoric Burke (1957) identifies four persuasive devices used by Hitler as means of unifying German people: (1) inborn dignity; (2) a projection device; (3) symbolic rebirth; and (4) commercial use (173–74). By means of these rhetorical devices Hitler provided a successful recipe for addressing the rhetorical exigency in Germany during the 1930s and 1940s. The rhetoric of *China Can Say No* is characterized by these same strategies. The authors portray the Chinese people as a morally superior race, project enemy status on the United States, establish the need for the Chinese to redefine their mission and identity in the world, and promote anti-American sentiments. In so doing they attempt, through symbolic discourse, to satisfy the Chinese yearning for national dignity and a new sense of national identity rooted in the conviction of moral superiority. According to Burke (1961), such a shift in identity or perspective is experienced as a kind of redemption. The end result of redemptive process is an infusion of new purpose and meaning into further actions. Through anti-American, pro-Chinese rhetoric the authors of *China Can Say No* completed the process of redemption and achieved some sense of new national identity or rebirth for the Chinese people.

Anti-American Sentiments from the Official Discourse
Just as Sino-American relations began to move in a positive direction with the state visits of the two leaders in 1997 and 1998, anti-American rhetoric resumed and intensified with the U.S. bombing of the Chinese embassy in Belgrade, the issuance of the "Cox Report," and U.S. policy toward Taiwan. The following identifies political antagonism toward the United States through an examination of media reports in the government-controlled *People's Daily* and various speeches of government leaders.[24]

U.S. hegemony. On 8 May 1999 the NATO air force, operated by the United States, bombed the Chinese embassy in Belgrade, causing three deaths, over twenty injuries, and severe property damage. While the U.S. government claimed that the bombing was a mistake and apologized on various occasions, the Chinese government refused to believe the U.S. explanation. As Jiang declared during the *60 Minutes* interview aired on 3 September 2000, "All the explanations that they [U.S.] have given us for what they call a mistaken bombing are absolutely unconvincing."

China was infuriated by the bombing, and the *People's Daily* subsequently issued a series of articles and commentaries condemning the United States. An editorial dated 11 May 1999 in the *People's Daily* stated: "This [the bombing] is a brutal crime against humanity. It demonstrates the hypocrisy of American humanism and thoroughly exposes America's real motive of trampling on other countries' sovereignty and human rights." The commentary characterized the United States as "invaders" and "a chief criminal of the human disaster," asserting that "the bombing was a crime against the Chinese people plotted by the U.S. and that the Americans were lying when they claimed the bombing was a mistake." The article concluded by arguing that the United States wants to provoke wars and create human disasters in order to impose its own values on other societies ("The Evil Criminal of the Human Disaster," *People's Daily*, 11 May 1999). In subsequent editorials the U.S. bombing was labeled "an invasion," "an international crime," and "an exercise in hegemony" (15 May 1999). An anonymous article titled "On the New Development of American Hegemony" asserted that "American hegemony has been inflated since the end of the Cold War" and that "American hegemony and power politics are the source of threats to world peace and stability" (27 May 1999). This rhetoric of condemnation, along with the images of the bombing of the Chinese embassy, provoked Chinese nationalism and brought long-held anti-American sentiments to the fore. In an article authored by Huang Hong and Ji Ming, Chinese readers were reminded that "it [the bombing] made us see the U.S.'s intent of containing China and its ambition of becoming a world superpower" ("Condemning U.S.-Led NATO's Atrocity," *People's Daily*, 1 June 1999). An article issued by China's Human Rights Committee charged that the United States violated China's rights of sovereignty in the name of protecting U.S. human rights and that the American theory of human rights above sovereignty right was by definition an excuse for hegemony.[25]

Sabotaging U.S.-China relations. On 25 May 1999 the United States issued the "Cox Report" on Chinese espionage in the United States. The report detailed allegations of the systematic theft of U.S. nuclear secrets by Chinese spies. The Chinese government categorically denied all charges. In retaliation, China's News Office of the State issued a lengthy article dismissing the charges against China and calling such accusations a blatant act of discrimination against Chinese Americans and a devastating humiliation of the Chinese people.[26] The article indicted the "Cox Report" as "returning to the McCarthyism of the 1950s in America and an indication of hatred toward China and the Chinese economic development among some American politicians" ("The Cox Report: An Anti-Chinese Policy," *People's Daily*, 16 July 1999). Further, it was considered a means of spreading the theory of the "China threat" and a justification for containing China. An editorial of 26 May 1999 in the *People's Daily* cited a statement issued by China's Xinhua News Agency calling the report "absurd" and "a fabrication by those who have hatred and prejudice against China." Zhu Bangzao, a spokesperson for the Ministry of Foreign Affairs, was quoted as saying, "They [the United States] adhere to a Cold War mentality and act against the tide of history. They spread the 'China Threat' theory and sabotage friendly relations between China and the U.S." At the same time Zhao Qizhen, a spokesperson for the News Office of the State Council, hosted a press conference protesting the report. In his speech, published in the *People's Daily*

("The Cox Report Harmed U.S.-China Relations," 1 June 1999), Zhao argued that "the Cox Report had the ulterior motive of acting against China. The purpose of the report was to provoke anti-Chinese sentiment, degrade China's image, hinder the development of Sino-American relations, and contain China to the detriment of its economic development."

U.S. hegemony and the violations of international law. On 1 April 2001, according to reports by the U.S. media, a U.S. surveillance plane collided with a Chinese fighter jet near the Chinese seashore of the South China Sea, causing the death of one Chinese pilot and the emergency landing in China of the U.S. plane. Twenty-four American crew members were detained by the Chinese government. China demanded an apology, while the United States seemed primarily concerned with the safe return of its crew members. Anti-America rhetoric in China intensified once again.

In reporting the incident China first claimed that the U.S. spy plane was flying near Chinese air space close to the Chinese province of Hainan. Wang Wei, the pilot of the Chinese fighter jet, was on routine duty following and monitoring the U.S. plane. Suddenly the U.S. plane made an unexpected turn and collided with Wang Wei's jet. Wang Wei lost control, and his jet plunged into the sea. China protested that this was an act of aggression against China's sovereignty and that the United States must take full responsibility for the accident (Xinhua reporters, *People's Daily,* 3 April 2001).

A series of articles condemning American hegemony and the U.S. arrogance of refusing to apologize followed the initial report. "Hegemonic Action and Hegemonic Logic," the *People's Daily* editorial, described the U.S. jet's collision with the Chinese jet and consequent landing without permission as "a blatant act of hegemony"; the American explanation regarding the territory issue was dismissed as "an excuse that can only make sense according to hegemonic logic" (5 April 2001). The *People's Daily* also reported the public reaction to this incident. For example, one local official was quoted as saying, "We are all extremely indignant at America's hegemonic attitude concerning our air space. We consider the U.S. action a typical form of hegemony. It was an invasion of our country's sovereignty and air space" (Xinhua reporters, "China's Protest Against the United States," *People's Daily,* 3 April 2001, 1.). A CEO of a shoe manufacturing company was quoted as saying, "I was very angry to hear that the U.S. invaded our air space and collided with our fighter jet. The U.S. always regards itself as the world's police, so they think they can come into another country's air space without permission. This is a typical act of aggression and it is intolerable to the Chinese" (Xinhua reporters, "People in Beijing, Shanghai, and Hainan Condemn with Indignation American Hegemonic Behavior," *People's Daily,* 4 April 2001). Many such statements were quoted, each repeating exactly the same wording and formalized language set by the government-controlled media.

In addition to moralist appeals, the government also employed legal appeals in condemning the United States for the incident. In an article titled "Examining the Incident of the China-U.S. Plane Collision through the Lens of International Law" the author, Qin Li, cited Articles 56 and 58 of the United Nations Sea Agreement. According to the agreement, the air space where the collision took place belonged to China's economic zone. Although foreign planes were allowed to fly in that zone, there was to be consideration for the sovereignty of the affected country. Li charged that the United States violated international law as well as the basic principle of respecting the rights of sovereignty of other nations (16 April 2001). The *People's Daily* also reported the findings of China's legal experts, who expressed the view that the U.S. "excuses" for not taking full responsibility and refusing to apologize "found no basis in international law" and that, further, their "arrogance is a manifestation of American hegemony, power politics, and the Cold War mentality" (Xinhua reporters, "The Attitude of Hegemony Will Not Help Resolve the Conflict between China and the United States," *People's Daily,* 20 April 2001).

In addition the government-controlled media used this opportunity to promote nationalism and heroism. Wang Wei was immediately granted martyrdom and was mourned as such by the entire nation. His picture was printed on the front pages of major newspapers throughout the country, and his collision with the U.S. plane was portrayed as a heroic attempt to protect the motherland. The *People's Daily* published an article written by a middle-school student in memory of "Uncle Wang Wei"; the article was titled "Give Me Back My Beloved Uncle Wang Wei" (Xinhua reporters, 20 April 2001). In addition to praising Wang Wei as a conscientious pilot and real-life hero, the author, Jingjing Ge, asked the United States: "Why didn't you fly in your own sky? Why did you come to our air space to spy on us? If you had not invaded our air space and collided with our jet, my beloved Uncle Wang would not have lost his life." Jingjing Ge then demanded that the United States take full responsibility for the incident and not send any more spy planes to China in the future.

A few days after the incident the *People's Daily* (7 April 2001) published a letter written by Wang Wei's wife and addressed to President George W. Bush. In the letter Wang's wife expressed her deep sorrow and grief over losing her husband and described how the tragedy had affected the whole family. She expressed grave dismay at how the United States reacted to the incident. She described the U.S. refusal to apologize as a degradation of conscience and humanity. She demanded that justice be done and that President Bush give back her husband. Obviously both the article and the letter were drafted by the government and expressed views in accordance with the government's denouncement and demands of the United States. Such emotional appeals also were used after the U.S. bombing of the Chinese embassy to evoke anti-American sentiments and inspire nationalism. Because of the one-sided reporting of the issue and appeals to national pride, many ordinary Chinese blindly embraced the government's view and used the same type of language in denouncing the United States, even in private conversations.

Impact of Post–Cultural Revolution Rhetoric on Thought, Culture, and Communication

Three areas of post–Cultural Revolution rhetoric have been described: that of Deng and Jiang's regimes, that condemning Falun Gong, and that of anti-America sentiments. Clearly, rhetorical themes and features of the official discourse of the post–Cultural Revolution period remain fundamentally the same even though the Cultural Revolution ended over twenty-eight years ago. Since then China has been transformed economically from a state-controlled economy to a semimarket economy and is Westernized in many aspects of life.

Similarities and Problems

Rhetorical features such as formalized language, numerical associations, deductive reasoning, and the use of emotional appeals permeated the period of the Cultural Revolution in the interest of promoting revolutionary zeal and dehumanizing class enemies. Such features can still be discerned in assertions of the new ideological agendas, the denouncements of Falun Gong, and the anti-America rhetoric. Ritualistic practices such as confession, criticism and self-criticism, and group studies have been performed to convert or alienate individuals and have been employed in the "reeducation" of Falun Gong practitioners. Moreover, although China's leaders are no longer deified, as was the case with Mao Zedong, adulation of Deng Xiaoping and Jiang Zemin is still in evidence to a different degree. Deng has been praised as the architect of China's economic reform. His theories have been published and made widely available, and his deeds have been the subject of many documentaries and movies. Like Mao, he is a legendary figure in modern Chinese history. Jiang, Deng's successor, is regarded as the core leader in today's China, and his portrait has been placed alongside Deng Xiaoping's and Mao Zedong's in public places. Like Mao, his pronouncements are considered the model of ideological correctness and are frequently quoted in political speeches and government media. Furthermore, post–Cultural Revolution slogans share features of ambiguity and abstractness with those of the Cultural Revolution and serve the same ideological functions of unification and justification of means. The official language of today's China is characterized by politically correct clichés to the detriment of artistic merit. The sentence structure of political discourse is rife with formalized phrases designed to achieve various political goals. Critical thinking is stifled to the extent that official discourse is presented as the only version of truth and reality; alternative views and perspectives are either condemned as heresy or totally negated. The radical views of the authors of *China Can Say No* closely resemble those of the Red Guards during the Cultural Revolution.

The unchanging form of official Chinese discourse and the lack of a varied linguistic repertoire are directly responsible for thought deprivation on a massive scale. For example, the one-voice interpretation of the Falun Gong movement prevented many individuals from critically considering alternative views and challenging the dominant version disseminated by the government-controlled media. When the media began labeling Li Hongzhi a "liar" and the sect an "evil cult," many Chinese people at home and overseas followed suit, using the same terms in reference to the group. They readily took the side of the government without informing themselves and examining all sides of the issue. In the case of anti-American rhetoric the language of moral righteousness in *China Can Say No* and official discourse on Sino-American conflicts provoked hatred of the "international enemy" while fanning the flames of ethnocentrism and a virulent nationalism.

The emotional language and argumentative style used by the Chinese to provoke anti-America sentiments seem to suggest that confrontation is the only means of communication in Sino-American relations. In fact, in the second book published by the authors of *China Can Say No,* titled *China Can Still Say No* (Song, Zhang, and Qiao 1996b), the authors assert on the book's cover, "Confrontation is an important form of human communication." Such confrontation would be commendable if it were based on an honest exchange of opinions, mutual respect, a spirit of cooperation, and a sincere effort to resolve misunderstandings and problems rather than on hostility, verbal attack, threats, and attempts at retaliation. One cannot overlook the irony of attacking American hegemony while promoting Chinese superiority, of criticizing American stereotypes of China and the Chinese people while spreading stereotypes of American culture and the American people. Likewise, for the United States to overlook Chinese apology protocol stands at odds with a denial of hegemony. Indictment of Chinese notations of human rights may exude an arrogance that denies various interpretations of human rights not upheld within U.S. borders. Surely the world would be a better place if we all engage in honest exchange and take more responsibility for the manner in which we communicate.

Differences and Hopes

In some important respects the rhetoric of the post–Cultural Revolution era has deviated from the rhetoric of the Cultural Revolution. Generally the progress has been made toward depoliticization and the establishment of a more relaxed atmosphere, even by the government-controlled media. For example, the use of profane, vulgar, and inflammatory speech in the condemnation of internal and external enemies has been greatly reduced. Indeed, rhetorical evidence suggests that the language of the post–Cultural Revolution period emphasizes content over style, aiming to inculcate rather than to move or please. In fact, unlike classical Chinese rhetoric, characterized by its lack of interest in logic (Oliver 1971), contemporary Chinese speech appears to be too rational and "scientific." Metaphors, analogies, and stylistic devices are rare in the speeches made by today's Chinese leaders. This may account for the lack of persuasive effect in public discourse. In fact, the readership of the *People's Daily* has dwindled, and not all members of the general public are interested in listening to official speeches or watching news on Chinese Central Television (CCTV), the official channel for news reports.

The China of the twenty-first century is filled with contradictions. Rhetorical paradox is simply one of these contradictions. On the one hand, the Chinese government still holds the reins of ideological control tightly; on the other hand, its promotion of a market economy has allowed a great deal more freedom than the Chinese people enjoyed during the Communist era. In the past the Chinese people heard one official party line from one channel and read only one newspaper. Nowadays they can get information from a variety of sources with the help of internet and satellite television. In the post–Cultural Revolution period the gap between public and private rhetoric has increased dramatically. Citizens can now criticize government officials in private settings as long as they do not organize themselves or speak publicly against the regime. From his study comparing China's popular social language and its offical political language, Yu Zhang (2003) concludes that many Chinese poeple have created their own version of social reality through popular language and folk themes, and such a phenomenon indicates a crisis of the official language. The pragmatic orientation of Deng Xiaoping's era had a significant effect on the Chinese mentality, moving the masses from moral absolutism to materialistic utilitarianism and from a collectivistic orientation to a somewhat individualistic approach (Lu 1998a). The pursuit of material well-being is the number one priority in the minds of the majority of Chinese, and in this limited context there is more freedom of choice in the China of today.

Changes also have occurred with regard to authority. Though political leaders are still regarded as having absolute power mandated by heaven, they are no longer afforded the status of deities. Instead, nowadays eulogy songs or other forms of entertainment characteristic of the Cultural Revolution are mostly restricted to the subjects of the nation and people. Along with this shift away from deification of one great political leader, "China's leaders during the last two decades have abandoned pretensions to totalitarianism in favor of a more accommodating form of undemocratic rule" (Jacques deLisle, www.realization.org/page/topics/falun_gong.htm). As China is now a member of the World Trade Organization (WTO) and will be hosting the 2008 Olympic games in Beijing, its status on the world stage depends largely on the success of its democratization process. While economic reform has been proven successful, political reform has been slow. A logical place to begin such reform, as the ruling party has recognized in the past, may be in the realm of rhetoric and discourse. In other words, official Chinese discourse needs to move out of the shadow of the Cultural Revolution in order to be more effective and congruent with the market economy and globalization.

Conclusion and Implications

Reflecting upon my years during the Cultural Revolution, I realized that I blindly followed others. I never engaged in independent thinking. I hurt other people and was hurt and tortured by others. All my actions were influenced by the language we were exposed to and used at the time. I made some terrible mistakes and the entire nation made a terrible mistake.

Account from an interview

This ten-year political movement was a catastrophe for the Chinese people. It opened the Chinese people's eyes and greatly raised their self-awareness, to such a degree that they realized China needed a profound reform. The Chinese Communist Party and Chinese government must make a fundamental change.

Guangyuan Yu, *Wo xie wenhua da geming*
(I Wrote the Cultural Revolution)

The China that was once characterized by blue or gray Mao jackets, militant Red Guards, and wall posters with slogans has disappeared. The Chinese citizens of today are much more colorfully attired; people are busy making money rather than participating in political activities; and billboards are filled with commercial advertisements instead of political slogans. The stories people exchange are centered around ways to get rich quickly; the Cultural Revolution is hardly mentioned in official media or in private conversations. Since the arrest of Song Yongyi 宋永毅, a United States–based scholar doing research on the Cultural Revolution,[1] the government has censored information related to the Cultural Revolution. Further, the Chinese people, young and old, were reluctant to talk about the Cultural Revolution. It was as if this tragic event had never happened.

The Jewish people who survived the Holocaust and Japanese Americans who were sent to internment camps during World War II face a similar problem: they are reluctant to talk about the past (Wendy Ng 1991), not because they have forgotten but because it is simply too painful to recall the experience. The same can be said for many Chinese who survived the Cultural Revolution. For example, when I was interviewing my parents about their experiences during the Cultural Revolution, I had to stop several times because it was too painful for them to continue. They are both now in their midseventies; reliving the trauma of those times was torturous for them. However, the slate of history can never be wiped clean. Collective memory does not die, and in any case, there are always those who live to tell the story. Once the collective memory of the Cultural Revolution is unleashed, shared, and reflected on, the impact on the world and future generations in China will be enormous. Museums will be built, documentaries and films will be made, books will be published, memorials will be undertaken, and textbooks will integrate the experience for future generations. Unfortunately, China has not generated such a body of public discourse yet. The silencing of the experience is directly related to the abuse of political power and authority.[2] Ba Jin's request to establish a Cultural Revolution museum in China has not yet been granted.[3]

The Chinese government has never offered any compensation for those who lost their lives or suffered serious harm during the Cultural Revolution. Furthermore, the perpetrators have not been given the opportunity to repent, nor have they received any punishment for their crimes. Still, my parents and many others like them consider themselves lucky to have survived the Cultural Revolution. The experience has given them a greater appreciation of life. My father extended his hands and heart to those who beat and tortured him. Some Rebels apologized to him and asked for forgiveness. Some never did. Like many other victims during the Cultural Revolution, my parents have found inner peace. For those who inflicted much pain and suffering during that terrible time such inner peace has been elusive. In the words of one former member of the Red Guards, "Many of us feel guilty about the Cultural Revolution. I don't mean to suggest that we *should* feel guilty, that we really did something wrong. But still, I feel that this guilt is a good thing, not a bad thing. It shows that we still have a conscience, that our consciences are intact. And so long as we have our conscience, so long as they work, there is hope" (Thurston 1987, 247). Clearly, many Red Guards were themselves victims of the political chaos of the Cultural Revolution. Having lost their formative years to the revolutionary cause, they had to settle for second-rate jobs. Many of them are now putting pressure on their children to do well in school to make up for the education and opportunities they have lost.

The reasons so many people were caught up in what appears to have been crude propaganda were many. As one who lived through the turbulence of the Cultural Revolution and was affected by the political discourse at the time, I believe that in addition to the blind faith most Chinese people placed in Mao and the Communist Party, the idiomatic and metaphorical features employed in political discourse, frequent exposure to extreme and violent language, the endless repetition of the same expressions and rituals, and constant fear of punishment, ostracism, and even death all contributed to the acceptance of the mass hypnotic propagation. In short, language is powerful and those who control the means of communication control the minds of the people.

Thus far in this book the rhetoric of the Cultural Revolution and post–Cultural Revolution rhetoric have been described and analyzed. The impact of such rhetoric on Chinese thought, culture, and communication as a result of the use of particular symbols and symbolic practices has been discussed. In addition an examination has been done of certain aspects of traditional Chinese cultural values and rhetorical practices that provided soil for the practice of the Cultural Revolution rhetoric. This final chapter will summarize major rhetorical themes of the Cultural Revolution; review and discuss the impact of the revolution on thought, culture, and communication (largely from the interviewees' perspectives); and discuss the challenges China faces today in the areas of critical education, culture rebuilding, and public communication. Lowell Dittmer (1991) once said, "National cultures that undergo a particularly devastating formative experience often seek to draw some redeeming 'lesson' from it" (19). The main purpose of this concluding chapter is to explore the lessons that can be drawn from the Cultural Revolution so that recurrence of such a tragedy can perhaps be prevented. In other words, as Dittmer suggests, perhaps some redemption from the madness of the Cultural Revolution can be found so that those who suffered and died will not have done so in vain.

Major Rhetorical Themes of the Cultural Revolution

To conclude, five themes dominated the rhetoric of the Cultural Revolution: (1) the rhetoric of moral appeals; (2) the rhetoric of mythmaking; (3) the rhetoric of conspiracy theory; (4) the rhetoric of dehumanization; and (5) the rhetoric of radicalization. Some of these themes can be traced to classical Chinese rhetoric, and some bear close resemblance to the rhetoric of Stalin's Russia and Nazi Germany.

The Rhetoric of Moral Appeals

Appeals to morality constitute a dominant rhetorical theme in classical Chinese rhetoric. This appeal was primarily based in Confucian humanism and manifested in benevolent governing, compassion for other human beings, righteousness, and virtuous conduct toward family and friends. While governing in the West is exercised primarily through the observation of laws, governing in traditional China is shaped by the cultural notion of the "Mandate of Heaven," or *Tian Ming*, with its powerful persuasive appeal in overthrowing a corrupt regime and legitimizing the new order. According to this notion, a ruler is mandated by heaven if he or she exercises benevolence and is a moral exemplar. A ruthless ruler will lose heaven's mandate and will be overthrown. Ultimately in ancient China the moral appeal of the Mandate of Heaven was made by the emperor's ministers and advisers to the emperors who made up their audience.

During the Cultural Revolution the moral appeal of the Mandate of Heaven was appropriated into the communist concept of historical progression, and the audience for the appeal became the Chinese masses as opposed to the ruler. According to the Maoist interpretation of the Marxist view on history, human history proceeds in five stages: from slavery to feudalism, to capitalism, to socialism, and finally to communism. Each society is more advanced than the previous one, with communist society as the ultimate goal, guaranteeing equality and the best possible life. This historical progression cannot be changed; any attempts to reverse the flow of history will only return people to the poor living conditions of the past. The Chinese people were persuaded by this communist theory of moral progression. The progression from slavery to communist society is believed to be the only path of social evolution. With all the negative propaganda about capitalism, the Chinese masses believed that capitalism was doomed and that communism would ultimately prevail.

One reason the Cultural Revolution was so attractive to so many people in China was that the masses embraced Mao's argument that a handful of people within the CCP were attempting to subvert the Communist revolution and turn China into a capitalistic society. Accordingly, all the slogans and accusations displayed in the form of wall posters attacked traditional Chinese cultural values (symbols of the old society), as well as people who were labeled "capitalist roaders" and anybody who had connections with the past or with the Western world. Mao's view of history established the moral authority of the CCP and provided the necessary justification for launching the Cultural Revolution. Thus, it is not surprising that symbols and symbolic practices during the Cultural Revolution were highly moralistic, targeting the "evil motives" of capitalistic roaders and defending China's socialistic society headed by Mao Zedong. While the ancient Chinese used parables and analogies in moral persuasion, contemporary Chinese favored more abstract and formalized language. As long as the rhetoric contained a moral message, it was deemed to have persuasive effects.

Moralistic language has universal application. It has been used to justify religious wars, terrorism, and counterterrorism.[4] Moralistic language is evident in the official discourse of the post–Cultural Revolution period. Some interviewees observed that China's political dissidents living overseas typically use highly moralistic language as well. A typical slogan is "Comrades, sacrifice for the great cause and strive with great effort for Chinese democracy." Here the sentence structure and moralistic overtones are reminiscent of the sloganeering of the Red Guards during the Cultural Revolution.

Throughout China's history moralistic language and political language have never been separated. Political messages from the ruler were tantamount to moral sermons. If Mao said that only the Cultural Revolution could turn back the tide of capitalism in China, it must be so. If the government declared that Falun Gong was an evil cult, then such must be the case. If the government asserted that the United States was attempting to exercise hegemony over China, America must be China's enemy. During the Cultural Revolution the use of politically correct language (formalized clichés, Mao's quotations) along with the expression of hostility toward class enemies demonstrated a person's high moral character. An ethical and effective speaker would indicate his or her unswerving loyalty to Mao, intimate familiarity with Mao's poems and quotations, and resolute condemnation of class enemies. Perry Link (1999) pointed out the danger of such moralistic language. In his opinion, when language becomes moralistic, the user tends to simplify the complex situation under consideration; this sets a limit on alternative ways of solving the problem. Further, when language becomes moralistic, the speaker gains a false sense of confidence and superiority, which can easily lead to justification of the action by any and all means (28). A case in point is the mind-set of the Red Guards under the influence of moralistic language: "We thought it was our turn, our moment, our chance to move away from the established order and contribute to a new China, our chance to march, fists in the air, shouting political slogans and making our loyalty to the Party visible. We were good; they—anyone who dared disagree with us—were evil" (Chihua Wen 1995, 6).

Moral appeals also were used at the individual level during Mao's era. Mao had consciously or unconsciously adopted Mencius's idea that human nature was inherently good and that therefore people were naturally attracted to moral preaching. Accordingly, human beings were malleable and perfectible if provided with the right examples and opportunities to engage in self-criticism. As Lifton (1989) notes, "it is this lingering Confucian spirit which has caused the Chinese Communists to make an ideological fetish of moralistic personal re-education" (391). The model emulation of Lei Feng, the promotion of heroes in revolutionary model operas, and the never-ending political study sessions were examples of moral reeducation aiming to modify individual behavior in the direction of selflessness and conformity to Maoist teachings. Rituals of criticism and self-criticism were means through which one could engage in thought reform and align with the party and Mao Zedong.

The paramount importance of ideology and thought reform during the Cultural Revolution can be traced to the traditional ideal of benevolent government and the righteousness of the individual, except that in the contemporary Chinese context morality was cast in terms of Marxist-Maoist ideology. Furthermore, the Chinese government was more adamant about influencing individual behavior with state ideology and communist appeals. In this sense Mao adopted traditional rhetorical strategies to maximize his political control and persuasive appeal. Ironically, as Link (1994) lamented, China's primary problem throughout its history has been the inculcation of moralistic language. Indeed, Jiang Zemin's current insistence on *yi de zhi guo* 以德治国 (governance by morality and virtue) signals China's continued attempt to combine morality with political persuasion and governing.

The Rhetoric of Mythmaking

Mythmaking exists in all cultures. In Western rhetoric mythology has played an important role in shaping a collective sense of reality. Greek mythology existed long before the codification of rhetoric. Mythology was a dominant rhetorical feature in the medieval period with regard to Christian conversion. Mythmaking has moral implications; it defines cultural values and provides a rhetorical vision for the future. Mythmaking is characterized by the worship of a mythical figure, participation in religious ceremonies, and the use of mythic terms in public discourse. The rhetoric of the Cultural Revolution demonstrates all these characteristics of mythmaking. Mao was mythologized as a living god, a savior of China. Mao Zedong's Thought was revered as the guiding principle of every aspect of life. Millions of Chinese participated in the use of symbols and symbolic practices characterized by a strong religious flavor. This myth-making phenomenon took various rhetorical forms: from slogans of boundless love and loyalty to songs or eulogies, ritualistic practices of worship, public and private discourses, and literature and films.[5] The Cultural Revolution is perhaps the best example of the power of mythmaking that history has yet given us.

Mythmaking is often accomplished through stories and fables. In the United States, President George Washington's confession of cutting down his father's cherry tree is a national myth that has been incorporated into elementary-school textbooks. As Washington is known as the "founding father of the country," the myth of the cherry tree sets a moral example of honest and upstanding character. Similarly, in the Chinese context the deeds and utterances of Mao Zedong, the founding father of the People's Republic of China, have become national narratives. His very human story has been transformed through various forms of mythmaking into a spiritual and religious cult. Willingly or otherwise, nearly every person in China has participated in the process of deifying Mao. Needless to say, Lin Biao and other faithful followers of Mao have exerted enormous pressure in promoting the myth-making process. The phenomenon also has revealed a national need for an absolute authority figure and a mentality that has been deeply rooted in the Chinese psyche and Chinese culture. Even Walter Fisher's (1987) rhetorical model of "narrative coherence" and "narrative fidelity" proved inadequate in the face of the Cultural Revolution as fanaticism swept away common sense and the ability to think and question.[6]

Traces of the tendency to deify Mao can still be discerned in today's China. His presence still looms large in the nation's psyche. For example, in the same way that an American might say "Swear to God," a Chinese person would say "Swear to Chairman Mao." The idealization surrounding Mao is still so thick that the worst he has been accused of in launching the Cultural Revolution is having made an innocent mistake. No subsequent leader has dared to criticize or denounce him for the damage he brought to China and the Chinese people.

The myth-making process continued in the post-Mao era with Deng Xiaoping's scheme of "Socialism with Chinese Characteristics," which has become a euphemism for making money and getting rich. It functions as an "archetypal metaphor" (Osborn 1967) in that it is popular, is used frequently, and was coined on the basis of cultural experience and conditions. It also has became a shared ideograph in that it has bonded the Chinese masses together in the interest of material pursuit. Last, it has created a new sense of political and social pragmatism in the aftermath of the Cultural Revolution. The Chinese people are once again engaged in the mystification of Deng Xiaoping as a charismatic leader and the guiding light of post-Mao reform.

The rhetorical process of mythmaking is powerful and persuasive because it attends to the audience's desires and moral ideals and is rooted in cultural traditions. Mythic pronouncements tend to be couched in emotional, moral, and high-sounding terms and expressions that serve to incite passion for a particular cause or reinforce blind faith in an identified authoritative figure. Skillful mythmaking can easily deprive its audience of the ability to think and question. This occurred in Nazi Germany when Hitler used the myth of German ascendancy and the superiority of the Aryan race to justify the extermination of Jews. Clearly mythmaking is a powerful tool for good or for evil in the world. It is therefore important to be vigilant with regard to mythic formulations worldwide, especially at the national level when mythmaking elevates cult figures and engenders a kind of mass hypnosis.

The Rhetoric of Conspiracy Theory

The CCP's political movements since the Yan'an period have operated largely in the framework of conspiracy theories. The most noticeable example in modern history is the anti-rightist movement of 1958, brought about because Mao ,suspected that the intellectuals, who had been encouraged to criticize the party in the first place, were plotting to overthrow communist rule. The conspiracy-theory framework also served as a justification for launching the Cultural Revolution as Mao accused Liu Shaoqi of secretly setting up a capitalist headquarters within the Communist Party and aiming to turn China into a capitalistic society. Further, the primary function of *dazibao* (wall posters) was to level charges of conspiracy against party officials, intellectuals, and other types of class enemies. Evidence for these charges was based on family backgrounds, fabricated facts, or enforced confessions. Once someone was labeled a class enemy, the assumption was that he or she must have been conspiring to sabotage the proletarian cause or pose a threat to Chairman Mao in some form of disguise.

Some scholars tend to link the Chinese conspiracy-theory mentality with that of Soviet Russia. For example, Andrew Walder (1991) asserts that "the theme of hidden conspiracy, as expressed during the CR [Cultural Revolution], is borrowed directly, with only minor emendations, from the Stalinist political culture of the era of mass liquidations and show trials" (43). Indeed, Mao and Stalin used almost identical language with regard to conspiratorial musings: the exploitive class that had been overthrown was still plotting its eventual return to power. The bourgeoisie would fight back in more insidious ways to regain their power. Bourgeois ideas still lingered in the minds of party officials who would inevitably betray the communist cause. The only difference between Mao and Stalin, according to Walder, was that "Mao resurrected this old class-based conspiracy theory, on an equally grand but more dramatic scale" (44).

In fact, Mao's mentality of conspiracy theory may have been fostered more by the classical Chinese statecraft of *shu* than by the influence of Stalin. *Shu* 術 can be translated as "tact" or "strategy." This concept was advocated by Han Feizi as a means of imperial control over the ministers of state. Han assumed that ministers were motivated by self-interest and that some were motivated by a desire to undermine the ruler. Thus the ruler would do well by looking closely for the motivation behind the ministers' behavior and by using pretense and cunning strategies to expose their real intent. Once the underlying motives were exposed, the offending minister would be duly punished (Liao 1939, 16.38.188, 9.30.281). As an art of statecraft *shu* has been practiced for over two thousand years in China's political arena as a means of suppressing opposition to the ruler and removing any threat posed to his power. Given this historical backdrop, Mao's accusation against Liu Shaoqi can be understood as an exercise of *shu*. Though Liu had made a concerted effort to please Mao by proposing Mao Zedong's Thought and helping to establish the cult of Mao through his writings and speeches (Dittmer 1998), Mao never trusted Liu; instead Liu was perceived as a threat and an enemy in disguise. In the early stages of the Cultural Revolution, Mao deliberately left Beijing and allowed Liu to be in charge of the movement. When Liu tried to control the chaotic situation by sending work teams to universities,[7] Mao returned to Beijing and posted his "Big-Character Poster: Bombarding the Capitalist Headquarters," indirectly targeting Liu and accusing him of suppressing the masses and attempting to subvert the revolutionary movement.

The same mentality of conspiracy also was in operation in the denunciation of Falun Gong for allegedly plotting to subvert the government and manipulate the masses. Li Hongzhi was considered the front man of the conspiracy. Behind him were the anti-China overseas forces that had long desired the collapse of the Chinese Communist government. The United States was suspected of being the mastermind behind the scenes as it had created obstacles to China's modernization and was well known for its hegemonic role in the world. The sanctions and containment methods imposed after the 1989 Tiananmen Square incident along with a series of conflicts over Sino-American relations were the primary evidence of an American conspiracy against China.

Conspiracy-theory rhetoric plays into the psychology of fear as it rests on the assumption that hidden enemies are always more dangerous than those who are out in the open. It also serves as a major premise for the formulation of an argument against the target enemy. In that sense it has moral overtones as well. More important, conspiracy theory rhetoric serves to justify atrocities or violent actions against the enemy. History has recorded several such atrocities: the purge and persecution of Soviet party officials by Stalin; the extermination of Jewish people by the Nazis; and Pol Pot's killing rampage in Cambodia, to name a few. In most cases conspiracy charges were based on assumptions with no hard evidence whatsoever. In the case of the Chinese Cultural Revolution, no conspiracy against Mao or the socialist system has ever been proven (except the case of Lin Biao). And yet there has been no apology and no compensation from the government or from the zealous individuals who committed countless crimes against humanity and inflicted untold suffering during the course of the Cultural Revolution.

Americans remember the witch-hunt experiences of the McCarthy period, and they should not forget the lockup of Japanese Americans during World War II, both based on charges of conspiracy.[8] The rhetoric of conspiracy theory is dangerous. First, assumptions of conspiracy may be based on bias, prejudice, political ideology, racism, or outright paranoia. Second, conspiracy-theory rhetoric alienates people, creates enemies, leads to conflict, and causes a vicious cycle of violence. In a world where peace and allies are in short supply, conspiracy-theory rhetoric can be nothing but detrimental to cooperation and mutual understandings. Third, conspiracy-theory rhetoric causes paranoia to spread like wildfire. The notion that "someone is plotting to get you" creates excessive mistrust and a climate of fear. For example, Parry-Giles's (1994) study illustrates that American anticommunist propaganda and cold-war rhetoric, with its basis in conspiracy theory, engendered much paranoia and hysteria during the cold-war era. The legacy of that era lingers to this day.

History has shown that conspiracy-theory rhetoric can manifest in both domestic and international contexts. It can be employed by both democratic societies and totalitarian societies and is inextricably linked to power politics and attempts at political persuasion. For all these reasons it is vitally important to be alert to the effect of such rhetoric and to combat ungrounded assumptions, prejudicial remarks, and racist tendencies as well as to examine all sides of an issue, engage in critical thinking, and build trust whenever possible.

The Rhetoric of Dehumanization

In comparing the language of totalitarian societies Young (1991) summarizes six major components of what he calls the "Orwellian Model": "(1) the intent of the rulers to control thought and behavior through language; (2) exaltation of the state over the individual; (3) violence; (4) vilification; (5) euphemism; and (6) special political terminology" (215). The rhetoric of dehumanization during the Cultural Revolution exhibited several features of the Orwellian Model. It also had several stark elements in common with the rhetoric of dehumanization characteristic of other totalitarian societies.

During the Cultural Revolution the rhetoric of dehumanization was often presented in the form of animal metaphors. Class enemies were likened to undesirable animals in the Chinese cultural context. For example, the official media referred to class enemies as "cow ghosts and snake spirits," "monsters and demons," "parasites," and "vermin." The Red Guards called them "pigs," "dogs," and "vampires." These dehumanizing metaphors permeated Chinese spoken and written discourse. They were used in slogans and wall posters as well as at denunciation rallies and political study sessions. Detention centers were called "cowsheds"; the song class enemies were forced to sing was called the "ghost song"; and children of class enemies were called "sons of bitches." In the swirl and storm of revolution such terms were symbols of tearing down social structure, expressing hatred for the enemy, and showing loyalty to Mao Zedong.

The rhetoric of dehumanization was also presented in the form of negation (Wander 1983). The voice of class enemies was literally and symbolically silenced. For example, during his one-year imprisonment my father was not allowed to speak. His confession was presented in written form only. For a period of time after he was released Father could not speak properly; when he did try to speak he would only slobber. We thought he had lost the physical ability to vocalize and speak coherently. It took him a long time to recover the ability to speak normally. In this and many other ways class enemies were deprived of their human dignity as well as their most basic human rights.

Another feature of the rhetoric of dehumanization was the use of euphemism to conceal the truth. For example, the pillaging and violence of the Red Guards were termed *geming xing dong* 革命行動 (revolutionary action). Being incarcerated and tortured was referred to as *xuexi gaizao* 學習改造 (study and reform). This use of euphemism was reminiscent of Nazi practices in relation to the Jews: deportation was termed "installation," and extermination was "the final solution." One went for a "shower" and instead was gassed to death. Such terms camouflaged and sanitized the horror of reality.

The rhetoric of dehumanization creates a climate that divides people into categories of good and evil, morally superior and subhuman—a climate in which political enemies must be eliminated. Further, such rhetoric functions as justification for torture and violence, neutralizing and minimizing the severity of the atrocities. It alienates and persecutes entire groups of people on the basis of, for example, family background, political affiliation, nationality, race, and gender. Such rhetoric is especially effective when the speaker appeals to the audience's bias and prejudice against a group. It is a language of totalitarian as well as democratic societies when the political situation involves identification and alienation and calls for a justification of action for a political agenda.

Accordingly, we must be on guard against rhetorical practices that reduce human beings to objects and animals. Humanity has paid too high a price for objectifying our fellow human beings in these ways. The mindful person can choose to reject the conceptual linkages in the use of metaphors in transferring one version of reality to another. It is important to be aware of social and political consequences in the use of dehumanizing metaphors. The practice is inhumane and threatens the continued existence of the human race, indeed of the entire planet.

The Rhetoric of Radicalization

Ying-shih Yu (1994) points out that "twentieth-century China has been so inundated with radicalisms from the West that thorough and rapid radicalization was hardly avoidable" (133). China's process of radicalization began with the May Fourth movement in 1919, when Confucianism was repudiated and blamed for keeping China a backward country. Subsequently, Mao adopted Marxism as the new state ideology, believing that a radical change in the political and economic structure would bring China closer to modernization. He advocated a total deconstruction of Chinese tradition as a precondition to the building of a new society.

Mao had been a radical thinker in his early years. The young Mao Zedong (1927) organized the peasants in his home province of Hunan to join a radical uprising against local landlords and gentry. He professed admiration for Lu Xun, who was in the vanguard of antitraditionalism, having been instrumental in the establishment of a new mass culture completely cut off from tradition. Yu (1994) characterizes Mao as "Chinese Marxist radicalism incarnate" (135) capable of only one thing: the destruction of Chinese tradition. At the inception of the Cultural Revolution, Mao issued his famous directive "To Rebel Is Justified," calling for the destruction of the "Four Olds." He mobilized and encouraged the Red Guards to engage in the radical acts of purging and denouncing party officials and intellectuals, tearing down the party apparatus, and destroying anything related to traditional culture.

The rhetoric of radicalization was expressed through slogans, wall posters, and revolutionary songs. Extreme political views were the order of the day, and as such, they were lavishly and extravagantly articulated. Phrases such as *zalan* 砸爛 (tear down), *fensui* 粉碎 (smash to pieces), and *xiaomie* 消滅 (annihilate) were ubiquitous in public and even private discourse during the Cultural Revolution. Likewise, military metaphors were commonly used against class enemies, engendering a belligerent view of the world.[9]

As the Sapir-Whorf Hypothesis asserts, language shapes thought, perceptions of reality, and action. The rhetoric of radicalization employed during the Cultural Revolution promoted hatred, excited fanaticism, polarized thinking, and justified brutal action. As such rhetoric escalated, the hatred of class enemies intensified and members of the Red Guards became increasingly fanatical and irrational. In their world there were no longer shades of gray, only blacks and whites. Consequently their actions became increasingly violent. In this sense the rhetoric of radicalization gave the Red Guards the incentive to be brutal and relentless; it unleashed rabid emotions and transformed some of them into monsters and killers. Ironically, all such criminal acts were justified in the name of defending Mao Zedong and promoting the revolutionary cause. The damage caused by the rhetoric of radicalization can never be adequately measured. It was immense.

The rhetoric of radicalization began to lose its appeal toward the end of the Cultural Revolution. In the post–Cultural Revolution era the official media has refrained from radical rhetoric. However, the mentality of radicalism can still be discerned among some Chinese. This spirit has been exemplified in the anti-American rhetoric of the best-seller *China Can Say No.*

Impact of the Cultural Revolution

By the end of the Cultural Revolution many who grew up with the revolutionary slogans, songs, model operas, wall posters, and loyalty dances of the ten years of chaos became disillusioned with politics and began to pursue material well-being. The horror of revolution was over, but its impact on Chinese thought, culture, and communication lingers to this day. As Yung Wei (1972) predicts, "we can be quite sure that this event [the Cultural Revolution], unprecedented in the history of Chinese polity, or anywhere in the world, is going to have long-lasting effects both on the Communist regime and on the social and political life of the Chinese people as a whole" (6). Indeed, the rhetorical themes and features described and analyzed in this book have fundamentally altered the way the Chinese think and communicate. They have also changed the face of Chinese culture. For those interviewed for this project some changes were positive, but most were not.

Impact on Thought

Scholars are in general agreement that traditional Chinese thinking is characterized by a pattern of synthesis, holism, and the integration of opposites (Kincaid 1987; Lin Yu-tang 1936; Nakamura 1964). However, repeated exposure to the polarized views expressed in slogans, wall posters, revolutionary songs, and operas has engendered polarized thinking among the Chinese. To this day many Chinese people tend to categorize their world into black versus white and good versus evil. This type of either/or thinking has affected every aspect of Chinese life, from judgment made about international crisis to personal interactions and intrapsychic life. Because of the intense exposure to dogmatic and radical language, Chinese thinking has become increasingly dogmatic and radicalized. Such dogmatic and radical thinking in turn gives rise to more dogmatic and radicalized language in a vicious cycle of escalating rhetorical aggression and violence.

The rhetorical landscape of the Cultural Revolution lends support to the Sapir-Whorf Hypothesis that language influences or determines thought and affects human perceptions of reality. The deification of Mao as a savior of the Chinese people and a living god through speeches, songs, and rituals promoted blind faith in Mao's teachings that was applied to every aspect of Chinese life. His image was worshiped as that of an emperor, except with an even greater fervor and fanaticism. His Little Red Book became the bible of the entire nation. Ji Li Jiang (1997) says it well: "To us Chairman Mao was God. He controlled everything we read, everything we heard, and everything we learned in school. We believed everything he said. Naturally, we know only good things about Chairman Mao and the Cultural Revolution. Anything bad had to be the fault of others. Mao was blameless" (265). With the whole nation engaged in Mao-speech during the Cultural Revolution, thinking became stifled, mechanical, and confined. Language influences thought, and exposure to only one linguistic system created a cog mentality that severely curtailed critical thinking.

The climate of thoughtlessness is still evident in today's China. One interviewee, for example, told me that when he raised doubts about the government's version of the Chinese-U.S. plane collision that blamed the United States for causing the accident, his entire family verbally attacked him and called him a traitor. The interviewee was reportedly surprised and disappointed at this behavior: "They are all highly educated, but they do not seem to think and question beyond what the government tells them. They refuse to listen to alternative views. Whenever they hear any criticism of China, they get angry and become defensive." To this day many Chinese people are not well equipped to engage in an argument when evidence is presented and logical inferences are drawn. Instead they typically make assertions and claims and regard them as truth.

While most firsthand accounts of the Cultural Revolution are overwhelmingly negative in the assessment of its lingering influence, some interviewees reported feeling that they had actually benefited from their Cultural Revolution experiences in that they had been inspired to become more critical in their thinking processes. They no longer blindly follow what the official media says but instead question and criticize. One interviewee said, "Traditional Chinese education never taught us how to be independent and critical thinkers. Like many others, I followed Mao and believed him. I learned a big lesson from the Cultural Revolution. I am not easily persuaded by political rhetoric anymore. I have learned to question the major premise of an argument, examine all sides of an issue, and analyze the weaknesses in the argument. I am more immune to the rhetoric of agitation and my critical thinking ability has increased." Another interviewee shared a similar view: "The education we received before and during the Cultural Revolution simplified our thinking processes. We could not think in a critical and complex manner. After the experience of the Cultural Revolution, I began to question the validity of claims and the use of biased and emotional language in the official media. Without the experience of the Cultural Revolution, I may not be as critical as I am now."

Some interviewees went to the other extreme, explaining that after the Cultural Revolution they felt so betrayed and disillusioned that they no longer trust anything the Chinese government propagates and have totally lost interest in political arguments and activities. Material pursuit has become the defining feature of their lives. However, without reflecting on their thought processes and consciously cultivating critical-thinking skills, they risk falling into the same rhetorical traps when facing the bombardment of persuasive messages from commercial sources. They have simply switched from Mao as the god of political correctness to capitalist propaganda as the new god of material consumption.

Impact on Culture

Radical change at the political and ideological level will bring radical cultural change. The rich and long history of traditional Chinese culture was transformed beyond recognition during the Cultural Revolution. Cultural artifacts were smashed, temples were burned, traditional arts and rituals were eradicated, and classical books were banned. But what is even more devastating and takes longer to heal is the destruction of traditional Chinese values and practices. Traditional Chinese culture valued harmony; the Cultural Revolution stirred up enormous conflict between factions and in interpersonal relations. Traditional Chinese culture emphasized balance; the Cultural Revolution was radically out of balance in both form and content, to an extent unprecedented in Chinese history. Traditional Chinese culture emphasized family unity; during the Cultural Revolution family members were encouraged to disown one another for "counterrevolutionary crimes." Traditional Chinese culture stressed loyalty to superiors and friends; during the Cultural Revolution the practice of betraying superiors and friends was applauded as a "true revolutionary act." Traditional Chinese culture valued the saving of face and upholding of human dignity; the humiliation, torture, and violence many individuals experienced during the Cultural Revolution brutally stripped them of their dignity and sometimes even their basic right to live. Traditional respect for authority and order, the notion of trust in human relations, and the indirect style of communication were all very much changed during the Cultural Revolution. Challenging authority at home, at school, and in the workplace was the new fashion, and Mao was the only authority to be obeyed and worshiped. Humiliating others in the public was not only acceptable but required in the name of revolutionary zeal. People no longer confided in each other for fear of being betrayed or accused of counterrevolutionary acts. During the Cultural Revolution a generally peace-loving nation became militant and belligerent toward perceived domestic and international enemies. A colorful tapestry of cultural richness was bleached white by the bright red sun of communist ideology and tattered beyond recognition. During the ten years of the Cultural Revolution, under the leadership of Mao Zedong, the Chinese people managed to destroy a tradition and culture that had taken over five thousand years to create.

Interviewees shared two observations on the impact of the Cultural Revolution on culture. One was that the Cultural Revolution resulted in the disappearance of civilized behavior, and the other impact was the disappearance of humane and well-rounded individuals. The Cultural Revolution encouraged the use of vulgar language and boorish, rude behavior toward class enemies. One interviewee remarked, "I was ten years old when the Cultural Revolution started. I spent most of my time in the streets watching parades and denunciation rallies. I learned and saw how people treated each other rudely and brutally. It took me a long time to get rid of these bad influences in my personal upbringing. I see many people going through the same process. Some people may carry these traces for the rest of their lives."

The traditional Confucian education system aimed at the cultivation of a *junzi,* or gentleman, who possessed the qualities of *ren* (benevolence), *yi* (righteousness), *li* (knowledge of rites), *zhi* (wisdom), and *xin* (trustworthiness). Traditional China was concerned not only about the knowledge a person possessed but also about the moral, humane character of the individual. One can still identify these qualities in the older generation of Chinese intellectuals. However, those who grew up during the Cultural Revolution did not receive this type of instruction. All they learned in schools were Mao's directives and revolutionary songs, as well as how to write wall posters and participate in political rituals. Influenced by the rhetoric of the Cultural Revolution, the Cultural Revolution generation, often referred to as the "lost generation," was not given the proper environment and instruction in developing humanistically. Instead some people of that generation have inherited the terrible legacy of post-traumatic stress disorder characterized by psychological problems and twisted personalities. One interviewee commented, "The traditional qualities of a person, such as gentleness, and even-tempered disposition, kindness, courteousness, restraint and magnanimity are not evident in the younger generation. The Cultural Revolution has wiped out these teachings and values. It was an extermination of the best part of the Chinese culture."

Unlike the older generation, who received a Confucian education that taught people to love others, the generation that came of age during the Cultural Revolution was taught to hate class enemies and love only Mao Zedong and the Communist Party. Confucian education taught people to respect teachers and obey authority; the Red Guards were taught by Mao that "Rebellion Is Justified" and that violence against class enemies was acceptable and praiseworthy. Confucian education taught people to be respectful to each other and follow the rules of etiquette; the Red Guards were taught to be uncivil and to reject the rules and norms governing traditional culture.

Indeed, many of the best aspects of Chinese culture, such as moderation, balance, and harmony, were eradicated from mainland China as a result of the Cultural Revolution. Some aspects of traditional culture were preserved in Hong Kong, Taiwan, and overseas. However, since the end of the Cultural Revolution some traditional cultural practices have resurfaced. The Chinese people have begun to enjoy their rich traditions in the performing arts and physical and mental healing. They have also begun again to appreciate the sacredness of ancient sites and cultural relics. They have begun to identify themselves more with Chinese culture than with Chinese politics. However, realistically, the damage done by the Cultural Revolution will take several generations of conscious effort to heal fully.

Impact on Communication

The Cultural Revolution had a profound influence on the manner in which the Chinese people communicate at both official and interpersonal levels. As was previously discussed, several repercussions of exposure to various symbolic, myth-making, and political rituals include lack of tolerance for different views, polarized and dogmatic thinking, political conformity, and a general decline of self-esteem. From interviewees' perspectives there are three additional rhetorical patterns characteristic of the Cultural Revolution in relation to communication styles: aggressive speech, formalized speech, and humorous speech.

Aggressive speech. Unfortunately, aggressive verbal attacks against one's perceived enemies are still quite common in the China of today. One noticeable example was the official denunciation of Falun Gong. According to one interviewee, "The language used to attack Falun Gong is exactly the same language as that used to attack 'cow ghosts and snake spirits' during the Cultural Revolution. On hearing such language, I felt like the Cultural Revolution had returned." Another interviewee pointed out, "There is definitely a trace of the cultural-revolutionary style even in the writings of political dissidents. I am a regular reader of their publications *Chinese Spring* and *Zheng Ming* (Contention). The language they use to attack the CCP is very similar to the Red Guard style. They use Mao's style of verbal aggression to condemn Mao. They have not advanced very far from Mao's dictatorship style." This observation was shared by another interviewee, who said, "The overseas political dissidents have continued using the language of the Cultural Revolution. Instead of engaging in meaningful exchange and contention, they attack each other's character and politicize everything; this is very reminiscent of the Cultural Revolution." A few interviewees also mentioned the use of verbal attacks and vulgar language on the internet. One interviewee shared, "The forums on the internet are filled with verbal fights. Every one is expected to share the same view, especially on international issues such as Sino-American relations. If one person disagrees with the majority's view, this person will be attacked, cursed, and humiliated. It is very much like the debates I witnessed during the Cultural Revolution." This type of confrontational communication is also evident in some Chinese language schools in the United States. One interviewee witnessed such a conflict in a school in the Chicago area: "Several Chinese parents shouted at the principal, pressing her to make clear how she had allocated the tuition. They wrote articles verbally attacking the principal in the school newsletter. The format was similar to that of *dazibao*. The principal was finally forced to resign. After the principal left, the parents divided themselves into different factions and each faction attempted to gain control of the school. The verbal attack finally escalated into a physical fight."[10] This type of scenario was quite common during the Cultural Revolution. The language and techniques used to humiliate, attack, and discredit someone are reminiscent of those employed by the Red Guards at that time.

Formalized speech. Though today's private language is much freer and more creative and colorful, public language still shows traces of the formalized, abstract, high-sounding, and dry communication style popularized during the Cultural Revolution. Some interviewees admitted that they still feel the need to use formalized, ideologically correct language in public settings. Otherwise they feel they run the risk of being ostracized one way or another. They report feeling pressured to conform to this type of discursive behavior.

The confessional format of the Cultural Revolution is still in evidence today, as one interviewee observed: "At meetings, I often hear people say 'from now on, I will study hard President Jiang's Three Representatives, raise my awareness, continue to make progress in thought reform, and establish a correct worldview." Political leaders, in particular, are thoroughly immersed in language rules, clichés, and jargons of public speech. As noted by one interviewee, their speeches are rife with such pat phrases as "Raise high Deng Xiaoping's great flag of reform" and "Unite under the Party's Central Committee with Comrade Jiang Zemin as the core." Such language remains mostly at the official level and is generally spoken by party bureaucrats.

During the Cultural Revolution such formalized public language made its way into the private domain in the form of family conversations and diaries. Although nowadays it is rare to hear family members using official language, there are still some representative cases. For example, one interviewee confided that her ex-husband, a party official, had been haranguing her son with formalized and ideologically correct speech. He advised his son to be loyal to the party and serve the party wherever he goes. Before his son left for the United States to study, the father warned him to be careful not to be influenced by bourgeois ideas and not to be manipulated by capitalism. The interviewee said that her ex-husband has always used the language that appears in official newspapers and that there is little variation between his speech at work and that at home. He apparently does not have a vocabulary and thoughts of his own.

Humorous speech. In describing the Chinese sense of humor, Lin Yu-tang (1936) commented that for Chinese, "Humor often takes a tolerant view of vice and evil and instead of condemning them, laughs at them, and the Chinese have always been characterized by the capacity to tolerate evil" (63). Some of the radical expressions of the

Cultural Revolution have been appropriated to make humorous sense of the current situation. Interviewees offered the following examples. A boss's opinion of a company is referred to as "the highest directive" (a phrase used to describe Mao's words); this expression is also frequently used by husbands to refer to their wives' opinions. The expression "reactionary academic authority" was used derogatorily in reference to intellectuals during the Cultural Revolution; now it is used to refer to well-known and well-established experts in certain fields. "Petty bourgeois sentiments" were denounced during the Cultural Revolution; now the phrase is used to refer to caring behaviors between lovers. The slogan "Revolution is not a dinner party" was a Maoist pronouncement used by the Red Guards as justification for violent action; nowadays it is used by employers when making demands of employees to work extra hard. The slogan "If father is a revolutionary, the son is a hero" was used during the Cultural Revolution to classify people by their political backgrounds; it is now used in reference to children who do well in school and make their parents proud. "A single spark can start a prairie fire" was a Mao saying used by the Red Guards during the Cultural Revolution to symbolize the infectious nature of the revolutionary spirit; it is now used as a metaphor for investment in the stock market. Normally these expressions would have negative meanings as they are associated with the Cultural Revolution. However, instead of crying over memories of the past triggered by these expressions, the Chinese people choose to laugh at the link these expressions make between the miserable past and the current situations. One interviewee stated, "My wife and I both grew up during the Cultural Revolution. We are very familiar with the expressions of that era. I often use these expressions in our daily life to create humor and release tension. I even used these expressions in our annual letter of New Year Greetings to our friends. Only those who experienced the Cultural Revolution can appreciate the humor and share the laughter." In fact, Culture Revolution humor can be found in comedy shows, informal exchanges, tabloid articles, and films depicting dogmatic personalities and mass hysteria, as a reminder of the crazy and painful past as well as a means of healing.

Challenges Facing China

China has gone through rapid change in its economic development in the last two decades. The standard of living of the average Chinese person has drastically improved. The Chinese enjoy much more freedom than they did twenty years ago; they have the freedom to make money, to choose a career, and even to criticize the government in private settings. At the same time, however, China faces a serious moral dilemma. To prevent chaos and maintain social stability and political conformity, the government still has to employ many of the techniques characteristic of authoritarian control. If China wants to avoid another Cultural Revolution it must address the challenges of critical education, culture rebuilding, constructive communication, and civic discourse. Changes have to be made at both political and economic levels. Attention must be paid to the use of language as well as to channels of communication.

Critical Education

During the Cultural Revolution passion and mythmaking prevailed at the sacrifice of rational and critical thinking. The Red Guards, under the banner of Maoism, spoke and acted in the name of protecting the interests of the proletarian class while committing crimes against humanity. According to Hannah Arendt (1963), the use of language is directly linked to thought; restricted use of language leads to thought deprivation, which is the cause of evil. There are two types of evil. The first is intentional evil, such as committing a crime with the knowledge that one's act will do harm to others. Such evil is easy to identify and clearly deserves punishment. The second type of evil is not motivated by evil intent but is caused by blind adherence to certain linguistic rules and by not engaging in independent thinking. In examining the speech of Adolf Eichmann during his trial for war crimes, for example, Arendt noticed that Eichmann was incapable of thinking beyond the bounds of Nazi rhetoric, and she concluded that therefore it was his sheer thoughtlessness that had led to his criminal acts against humanity. The linguistic rules Eichmann followed had predisposed him to act in the ways that he did, with no conscious intent to do harm. In fact, Eichmann considered himself "the victim of a fallacy" (248). Consequently, Arendt reminds the reader, "what had happened to him might happen in the future to anyone, the whole civilized world faces this problem" (247). Arendt argues that ordinary people are susceptible to "banality of evil" (252) to the extent that they view morality as obedience to authority and fail to think critically and independently. This would be no less true of the Chinese experience during the Cultural Revolution than it was of the Germans during World War II. Through immersion in the rhetoric of the Cultural Revolution the Chinese masses were deprived of their critical-thinking abilities. Thought patterns became simplistic, dogmatic, and polarized, and they came to see the world in black and white terms. Edelman (1977) says it well: "Banal language evocative of fears, hopes, or personal interests engenders firm, single-minded cognitions that change with altered social situations. That political spectators are rarely in a position to express anything but a dichotomous choice doubtless encourages this outcome" (19). Collectively, Chinese people had committed "banality of evil" and were guilty of entelechialization: taking symbols to the end of the line (Burke 1969b).

To prevent banal expressions of evil from dominating China's political and cultural climate in the future, China needs to abandon moral absolutism and give more attention to critical education. In this regard Hammond and Gao (2002) point out that the educational system in today's China still emphasizes one-sided lecturing and rote memorization. Students are not given opportunities to interact with one another, and teachers are more interested in test scores than in allowing students to engage in the critical examination of questions and claims. Hammond and Gao contend that China should take the approach of dialogical learning, which is rooted in Chinese tradition as well as promoted by Western scholars. This approach encourages the active participation of students and helps develop critical thinking skills, such as the ability to examine an issue from multiple perspectives and avoid dichotomized thinking. Moreover,

Hammond and Gao believe that this kind of approach "will enable Chinese students to succeed in the global economy" (239).

Another way to avoid committing banal acts of evil is to engage in self-dialogue, turning to one's own conscience and being vigilant in one's use of language. In Arendt's (1963) words, it is important "to make judgments in terms of individual moral responsibilities" (297). It is equally important to question claims of moral superiority and emotional appeals devoid of sound reasoning and well-considered judgment. One must think independently and critically in rhetorical situations. Blind faith in authority and the mindless following of orders can impede a person's dialogue with his or her own conscience. In this aspect the Western conception of "the authentic self," rooted in the philosophy of existentialism, may be instructive. According to Kierkegaard and Sartre, the leading thinkers of existentialism, one's authentic self is achieved through the processes of choice-making and self-examination, which are guided by one's deeply committed values. This authentic self cannot be confined to rigid categories or misled by illusions and deception (Smith 1998, 274–83).

This "authentic self" can be achieved through a rational engagement with self and/ or an enhancement of one's rhetorical repertoire. In an effort to find a rational approach to moral discourse Perelman and Olbrechts-Tyteca (1969) propose a new rhetoric that, among other things, includes considering self as an audience in that one engages in a dialogue with oneself to reach a reasonable decision about moral issues that require adherence and beliefs. In this process one raises questions, asks for clarifications, and develops a counterargument to the publicly accepted truth/beliefs. Through this rational process one chooses to speak and act based on the universal concerns and well-being of humanity rather than favoring certain people, certain situations, or local prejudices.

Another way to cultivate the authentic self is to engage in rhetorical enrichment, that is, exposure to a variety of language arts. Repeated exposure of this type will lead to what Heidegger called "poetizing thought," which will free the self from the herd mentality and inspire transcendent truth. Heidegger's "poetizing," as interpreted by Smith (1985), meant "thinking and speaking in inventive ways that uncover and reveal the transcendent truth . . . authentic discourse allows the emergence of logos, the voice of being" (285). This process entails engagement in authentic intrapersonal dialogue in which a person relates to his or her own inner voice or the voice of conscience. In other words, to combat the herd mentality and the tendency toward conformity one needs to construct and reconstruct oneself through a creative use of language, engagement of a rational self-dialogue, and acceptance of responsibility for one's choice. Nietzsche's skepticism on language and the Taoist view of freeing oneself from the bondage of language also help one become a critical thinker and mindful consumer of language. Many people during the Cultural Revolution lost their individuality and rationality; willingly or unwillingly they allowed themselves to be confined to Mao's speech only. In this way they submitted to the construction of the politically correct, public self and failed to take personal responsibility for their actions.

Culture Rebuilding

China has been searching since the beginning of the twentieth century for a cultural formula for the achievement of modernization. For example, the May Fourth movement was based on the rationale that Confucianism, the foundation of traditional Chinese culture, was largely to blame for China's backwardness. Left-wing and Western-educated intellectuals launched a relentless attack on traditional Chinese culture, aiming to replace it with Western democratic ideals. This radical approach found continuity in Mao's launch of the Cultural Revolution as Mao believed strongly that a new proletarian culture, serving the interests of the masses rather than elites, would not be established without a complete eradication of the old culture. In the post–Cultural Revolution discussion of the role of culture, Chinese intellectuals once again attributed China's lag in modernization to the mind-set and practices characteristic of traditional culture.[11] Thus the modern history of China has been characterized by a radical perception of traditional Chinese culture. Changfu Chang (2002) points out that such radicalism treats culture "as a totality rather than a web of complex relationships" and, further, that the source of this totalistic attitude was "dichotomous thinking" (72). Though an attempt was made by the culture discussion movement in the early 1990s within China to restore Confucian tradition, the movement's total rejection of Western culture and hegemonic tendencies regarding the "Neo-Pacific Rim" made the notion less appealing for many.[12] Like other developing countries, China has been wrestling with the dilemma of modernity versus traditionality and Westernization versus national identity. Given that China now embodies a seemingly contradictory combination of authoritarian government and market economy, the path to culture reconstruction seems even more uncertain and unsettling.

China is currently enjoying a cultural revival in the performing arts and religious practices, even though it would seem that many aspects of traditional Chinese culture were damaged beyond repair during the Cultural Revolution. This is especially true regarding the destruction of cultural sites and artifacts and the near eradication of well-rounded, even-tempered, psychologically balanced, and humane individuals. In their highly acclaimed works the contemporary Chinese literary critics Yu Qiuyu 余秋雨 and Nobel laureate Gao Xingjian 高行健 have both lamented the loss of traditional Chinese culture as a result of the Cultural Revolution.[13]

On the other hand, as a result of the economic reforms of the 1980s China has adopted Western economic structures and management styles, and this has caused a dramatic cultural shift. The open-door policy and media/internet access have exposed China to Western cultural influences as well, and whether we like to admit it or not, Western cultural influence is a strong presence in contemporary China. Culture rebuilding and the search for new identity in a globalized world are formidable challenges facing China today.

In response to these new challenges, Jiang Zemin proposed his "Three Representatives" tenet, claiming that the CCP represents the forward direction of an advanced culture. According to Yunshan Liu's (2000) analysis, this "advanced culture" is a "socialist culture with Chinese characteristics" that "must be guided by Marxism-Leninism, Mao Zedong's Thought and Deng Xiaoping's theory; must emphasize the core values of patriotism, collectivism, and socialism; must combine the best elements of traditional Chinese culture and foreign culture; must be based on future modernization and globalization, and finally, must be rooted in national and mass culture" (10). In general, Chinese intellectual discussions on the rebuilding of culture seem to unequivocally agree on the importance of combining indigenous culture with imported culture. However, the intellectuals believe that this process must be guided by Marxism-Leninism, Mao Zedong's Thought, and Deng Xiaoping's theory. This formula is broad and self-contradictory. On one hand, it recognizes that both internal and external factors are needed to bring about a culture revitalization. On the other hand, it maintains that the changes must be determined by Marxism, Leninism, Maoism, and Deng's ideology. Moreover, it remains vague on the subject of what aspects of indigenous culture should be continued and what aspects of foreign culture should be borrowed and adopted. The rhetoric used to make these claims provides a contemporary example of formalized language and ideological adherence.

Another approach to culture rebuilding by Chinese intellectuals entails the wholesale rejection of tradition, deemed backward and not applicable to current challenges and conditions. This approach remains purely theoretical. The path of Westernization is also considered problematic as what has worked in other countries may not work in China. For example, Li, Sun, and Sun (2001) propose that China be "forward looking" and "creative" in culture rebuilding. They assert that China must be placed at the center and that the creation of a new culture must be based on empirical knowledge (129). This view is problematic as it is not only ethnocentric but also rejects what has been constructed by other civilization, both Eastern and Western, and lacks concrete methods and substance and clear direction.

Instead of adopting a dichotomized or ambiguous view on this subject, it is my opinion that China's cultural rebuilding must be based on an integration of indigenous and imported cultures. A multicultural approach would enrich China's cultural terrain and linguistic repertoire. The Tang dynasty (618–907 C.E.), the most prosperous period in China's history, was marked by the adoption of Western cultural elements combined with traditional Chinese culture. Japan is well known for its ability to borrow the Western political system and economic structure while maintaining the practice of its own indigenous culture and religion. Early in the twentieth century Liang Qichao 梁啓超, a well-known reformer, initially followed his teacher's suit in condemning Confucianism. His view changed after he made a trip to Europe in 1920. He returned to China convinced that instead of eliminating Chinese culture, Western and Chinese culture should complement each other. A combination of the two cultures could create a new world civilization (Ouyang 2002).

Liang Shuming 梁漱溟 (1989), a well-known Chinese scholar, divided world cultures into three categories—Western, Chinese, and Indian—arguing that each takes a different path and has a different emphasis. He predicted that Chinese culture would be revitalized in the future and realize its potential. This view was in direct opposition to the popular notion that Western culture was superior and Chinese culture inferior. In fact, researchers have attributed eastern Asia's economic management success to the Confucian values of mutual dependency and humanistic interpersonal relations. The Confucian ethocracy, characterized by a strong sense of duty and a paternalistic, authoritarian management style, has inspired high productivity and skillful rhetorical strategies in Taiwan's modernization process (Gold 1996; King 1996). Rita Mei-Ching Ng (2002) contends that the Confucian practices of respecting authority and ordering society along hierarchical lines have been appropriated by the Chinese government as means of encouraging the quest for material success. Furthermore, Zhaohui Hong and Yi Sun (1999) assert that the Chinese cultural values of balance, moderation, and compromise should be maintained and revitalized to benefit political democratization and economic growth; in their words, "this ancient philosophy [Confucianism] has demonstrated remarkable resilience, for it is ingrained in the Chinese mentality. As the guiding philosophy and code of ethical behavior for centuries, Confucianism still has much to offer" (37).

A cultural renaissance is needed in China to allow for the revival of traditional teachings and the creative flowering of cultural expressions. At the same time continued efforts should be made to promote cultural diversity and literacy, rather than dogmatic adherence to moral absolutism, nationalism, and ideological confinement. Reflection is also needed on the practical application of Marxism-Leninism and Mao Zedong's Thought to the contemporary Chinese situation. In the West there has been an increasing appreciation of Eastern wisdom and practices. Chinese culture can be enriched by learning and borrowing from the West as well. However, China will have to carefully consider its own needs in borrowing from other cultures and consciously resist postcolonial and hegemonic influences. At the same time China can learn from the West's greater familiarity with the processes of modernization. Liang Shuming (1987) has identified four aspects of Western culture that are lacking in the Chinese tradition: "sense of community, habits of following the rules, organizational ability, and the spirit of law-governing" (64). Echoing Liang, Zhaohui Hong and Yi Sun (1999) suggest the cultivation of a "modern" citizen who is "law-abiding, hardworking, fair-minded, trustworthy, civilized, and willing to help others" (39). As China becomes a member of the international community, these Western cultural values will help China grow into a more rational and rule-governed society. A multicultural perspective will help China with its economic pursuit as well as with political stability. In this regard Kluver and Powers (1999) have predicted, "The future [of China] is likely to bring an even more diverse set of ideas into a culture and a society that is rapidly constructing a new identity, a new perspective, and a new Chinese view" (22).

Communication and Civic Discourse
Culture and communication mutually influence one another. While culture provides scripts for communication, the forms and dynamics of communication also become the impetus for cultural transformation. In the course of human history the phonetic

alphabets and the prints medium transformed the ancient world from an oral to a logo-centric tradition; electronic communication has transformed the world into an information age and a global village. In the Chinese context the new culture movement of the 1920s, the first attempt to modernize China, was facilitated by the *Baihua* movement, a system of language reform that transformed the classical Chinese written language into a vernacular form. The radical rhetoric of the Cultural Revolution changed the face of Chinese culture from an orderly and harmonious society to one of madness and chaos. Deng's ideograph of "Socialism with Chinese Characters" transformed China into a semicapitalistic society and brought the country in alignment with the global economy.

Needless to say, communication is crucial to China's future development. China faces two areas of challenge in communication. One is communication effectiveness at the official level. Formalized, politically correct, and sloganlike official language and clichés, to the detriment of artistic expression, have lost their persuasive appeal and become a new type of *bagu,* or fixed writing/speaking style. Likewise, the current emphasis on scientific determinism limits the scope and variety of linguistic expressions. In fact, as Schoenhals (1992) points out, "The use of a 'scientific' criterion is somewhat misleading in the sense that what is being judged is not the scientific verifiability or truthfulness of a formulation but its political utility" (9). In other words, people use these formulations merely for the sake of political expediency rather than out of genuine commitment to a scientific perspective.

During the Cultural Revolution public language infiltrated the private domain and the entire country spoke one revolutionary language. After the Cultural Revolution the political power of the CCP was diminished and the nation's leaders no longer enjoyed the level of cult status that Mao had achieved. In fact, increasing numbers of ordinary people became more critical and cynical of the government and began to deviate from their style of speech. They created their own set phrases and formulas for ridicule as ways of expressing their dissatisfaction. These set phrases and formulas spread rapidly with the help of electronic communications. At the same time readership numbers dropped dramatically with regard to the official channels of news reporting and official newspapers and magazines. This caused an even larger gap between official language and the unofficial language spoken by the common people. As a result avenues of public persuasion would be severely curtailed and the authority of government would be considerably weakened.[14]

Political leaders in particular need to learn public communication skills, especially skills for engaging in dialogue with their constituents. Jia (1999) cites the example of Li Peng's confrontation with student representatives of the Tiananmen Square demonstration in 1998. On the one hand, during the confrontation Li (China's premier at the time) appeared to be condescending and arrogant. On the other hand, the student representatives publicly rebuked Li and directly challenged his authority instead of showing respect for an elderly, authoritative figure, as might have been expected if Confucian values had influenced the interaction. Jia argues that such rhetorical confrontation caused television viewers "to more firmly identify themselves with the prodemocracy force, thus legitimizing the prodemocracy sentiment" (69).

To bridge the gap between public discourse and private discourse and increase the likelihood of political persuasion, a society must provide its citizens with opportunities and forums to voice their attitudes and views. This is the rhetorical foundation of a civil society. Powers and Kluver (1999) define a civil society as one that is "created through the discursive practices of the people who identify with the society" (2). According to Habermas (1987), who formulated his argument in reaction to the Nazis's irrational appeals during World War II, a society must provide its citizens with optimum speaking opportunities during which they are allowed to question claims and scrutinize received knowledge through public debates. For Habermas, this interactive process of critical argumentation in the public sphere is a key to overcoming the problem of ideological domination and blind adherence to beliefs in a society. To avoid the type of chaos that ensued during the Cultural Revolution these channels of communication must be organized and structured. Current television programs in China, such as *Shihua Shishuo* 實話實說 (Speaking with Honesty), are examples of the attempt to integrate the private voice into the public domain. More forums of this sort should be made available at all levels and on a variety of topics. The time is long overdue for China to deemphasize the language of "correct formulations" and bring out more voices of the people. China must become more flexible and sophisticated in its discursive practices. Democracy is not simply a form of government; it is a way of life and a way of speaking.

Broadly speaking, China faces the daunting challenge of attempting to legitimize one-party rule against a global trend of democratization. It also faces the challenge of moving toward globalization while maintaining national identity. A good place to start in dealing with these challenges is the reform of political rhetoric and public discourse. Despite these challenges, China is optimistic about its future. Signs have already indicated China's progress in international settings in communicating its goals as well as in negotiating its bargains (Heisey 1999; Heping Zhao 1999). In joining the WTO and becoming a member of the global village, and with more avenues of information opening up, China will have to break down its ideological constraints and move toward a more pragmatic orientation, as charted by Deng Xiaoping. At the same time China must learn to appreciate its own cultural traditions while selectively absorbing Western influences. China's future remains difficult to predict. However, one thing is certain: the age of ideological totalitarianism is over. The Chinese people now have the potential to learn a huge lesson from the trials and tribulations of the Cultural Revolution. The nightmare of the Cultural Revolution may still haunt those who survived the experience, but the nightmare will have done its work if it serves to inspire their waking lives with efforts to ensure that such a catastrophic event never again happens in human history. This book is one such effort.

Notes

Introduction

1. The Rebels were also known as Radicals. They consisted of workers and low-ranking party officials. While the Red Guards seized the power at schools, the Rebels took control of the factories and administration apparatus throughout the urban areas of the country. They tended to hold radical views and take violent actions against class enemies. See Parris Chang (1973) for a more detailed description of the Rebels.

2. The "Gang of Four" were the high-ranking officials, namely Zhang Chunqiao, Yao Wenyuan, Wang Hongwen, and Jiang Qing, Mao's wife. They were trusted by Mao and given the power to control the country throughout the Cultural Revolution. After Mao's death in 1976 they were arrested, charged, and found quilty of various crimes against humanity.

3. Based on a Marxist theory of class struggle, Mao divided the Chinese people into either proletarian or bourgeois class. The latter group, composed of people from rich family backgrounds, rightists, counterrevolutionaries, and criminals, were regarded as class enemies. During the Cultural Revolution most class enemies fell under the first three categories.

4. Lin Biao was the claimed successor to Mao during the Cultural Revolution. He gave speeches on different occasions, and these speeches set the tone for the movement as well as the style for the use of political language.

5. Studies of the same topic by Chinese scholars, although limited because of the government's ongoing censorship, remain largely an abbreviated history of movement events.

6. The site has been censored and is therefore not accessible in China.

Chapter 1—My Family Caught in the Cultural Revolution

1. A woman with bound feet was considered physically attractive by elite men in ancient China. According to many sources on the history of foot-binding, the practice began during the Five Dynasties period (907–60 C.E.), first among female courtesans and dancers in the imperial court, and later among wealthy women to enforce a moral-sexual code of conduct during the Southern Song dynasty (1127–1279). The practice was abolished first by Empress Dowager Ci Xi of the Qing dynasty in 1902 but continued in northern China among Han women until the 1940s. See Wen Shu Lee (1998) for a detailed review on the foot-binding process and nineteenth-century discourse against foot-binding.

2. Starting in November 1965, under Mao's directive, government-controlled newspapers and journals were bombarded with criticism of Wu Han's play *Hai Rui Dismissal of Office*. The play was thought to speak for Peng Dehuai, a general and top government official, who had been dismissed from office because of his open disagreement with Mao

Zedong. Since May 1966 newspaper articles had also targeted Deng Tuo, Wu Han, and Liao Mosha, known as *San Jai Cun* (Three-Family Village). The three were high-ranking officials and top-level intellectuals who coauthored a column in a journal titled *Three Family Village*. They were accused of spreading counterrevolutionary ideas and using the column against the party. See Yan and Gao (1996) for a more complete account of the early development of the Cultural Revolution.

3. "The Announcement of the Central Committee of the Chinese Communist Party," *People's Daily*, 17 May 1966.

4. "Big-character poster" is a literal translation of *dazibao*, or "wall posters." The first version of Mao's poster appeared in the *Beijing Daily* on 2 June 1966. Mao posted his big-character poster on 5 August 1966 in Zhong Nan Hai, the residential compound for high-ranking officials. The final version was disseminated at the Eleventh Session of the Eighth Chinese Communist Party Central Committee on 7 August 1966 and then further disseminated to all levels of government on 17 August 1966. Many Red Guards copied the poster and posted those copies throughout the country. See Xi and Jin (1996).

5. While the Red Guards were mostly young students, the Rebels were mostly workers and lower-level public officials.

6. In October 1966 a united worker's organization was formed in Shanghai. With the support of Zhang Shunqiao, one of the "Gang of Four" members, the organization seized control of the Shanghai municipal government in January 1967. This seizure was known as "January Storm." Rebels in other provinces soon followed suit. This marked the beginning of overthrows throughout the country at every level of government and administration. See Xiao Di (1993).

7. The term "roader" was accusatory. A roader was a person taking the road to capitalism.

8. The cap is referred to as *gao mao* 高帽, literally translated as "tall cap." In his "Report on an Investigation of the Peasant Movement in Hunan," Mao ([1927] 1975) described the use of such caps in the parade of the evil gentry by peasants and praised such practices as the "vanguard of revolution" (30). The tall paper cap was used by the Communist Party during the 1930s in Yan'an, the Communist base in Shaanxi Province, and in the 1950s in the land reform movement as a way to publicly humiliate class enemies and political dissidents.

9. People who committed suicide because of the political charges leveled against them were considered criminals who used suicide to cover up their crimes. Their family members would be negatively affected as the result of this label.

10. The land reform was launched earlier in the northeast regions of China.

11. A file was kept on every person beginning at a young age and throughout the person's life. Only certain people (usually in leadership positions or party officials) had access to these files. The screening process for joining any organization and for promotion depended on what was in the person's file. The file was a powerful means of surveillance and control. A part of Mother's job was to keep the files of the employees in her workplace.

12. Along with a dozen other "class enemies" in Father's factory, we were forced to move out of our self-contained apartment a year after the Cultural Revolution began. The new apartment we were assigned to had only one bedroom. We shared a tiny kitchen and bathroom with another family.

13. During the Yan'an period (1936–47) Mao and his comrades lived in caves, wore identical uniforms, and grew crops to feed themselves. This revolutionary tradition of the Chinese Communist Party was expected to be recaptured in the cadre school to reform party officials and intellectuals.

14. For an English translation on the life of the May Seventh Cadre School, see Yang Chiang (1986).

15. "A pair of ragged shoes" is the literal translation of the Chinese term *poxie* 破鞋, used for women who have extramarital affairs. The term was very demeaning and humiliating.

Chapter 2—Language, Thought, and Culture in the Chinese Political Context

1. Hoijer argues that if linguistic categories related to color are different, then thought pattern related to color are also different. Henle concludes that vocabulary is related to perception and conception. Bloom's study reveals that the lack of counterfactual markers in the Chinese language does not lead to a lack of abstract thinking among Chinese speakers. Heider and Oliver's study on color provides counterevidence to Hoijer's, concluding that individuals in a speech community can identify color differences even if there is no vocabulary in their language to distinguish the difference. Rodda and Grove's study indicates that children with hearing disabilities have the same cognitive skills as hearing children. See Steinfatt (1989) for a more complete review of these studies.

2. I do not mean to suggest that all those who have traveled are liberal and open-minded while all those who have not are conservative. There are many other factors contributing to one's perspectives of the world. However, I do believe that traveling and being exposed to diverse cultures helps cultivate open-mindedness and reduce ethnocentrism. Most great thinkers in both Eastern and Western cultures are/were also great travelers.

3. For a chronology of Communist political movements, see Chu (1977, 170–71). The major movements were for land reform (1950–52), thought reform (1952), the anti-rightist campaign (1957), and the "four cleans" (1962).

4. Instead of relying on the urban proletarian, as suggested by Marx and accomplished by Lenin in the Russian Revolution, however, Mao situated his powerbase in rural China through the support of the peasants. This strategy eventually enabled him to take over the urban centers and the entire country.

5. The spelling "Mao Tse-tung" is in accordance with the Wade-Giles system of romanization of Chinese characters. It is a system used by early sinologists. Contemporary scholars and library systems all use the pinyin system to replace the Wade-Giles system. The spelling "Mao Zedong" is in accordance with the pinyin system.

6. There is a top-down organizational structure in the Chinese propaganda system. At the top is the Ministry of Propaganda under the direct leadership of the Political Bureau. A branch of the Ministry of Propaganda is operated at every provincial, municipal, and country level. A member in charge of propaganda is assigned to every workplace, village, army unit, and business sector. This organizational structure expedites the dissemination of information and directives issued from the central government to ordinary citizens.

7. Eight-legged writing was a form of scholarly writing in the imperial times. It has a fixed structure and norms and is the standard form in imperial exams. It is used as a metaphor to refer to the party's bureaucratic writing characterized by a fixed style in wording and structure.

8. Peasants were not the only segment of the population to participate in land reform. Students, professors, and cadres were dispatched to rural areas to lead the mass accusation meetings. Chen (1960) recorded his personal observation of the participation of students and professors: "On their return each person had to write his [*sic*] 'thought conclusions' or his 'impressions.' Conclusions acceptable to the Party were published in the press for propaganda purposes. At one time when the land-reform movement was in full swing, the Communist newspapers and magazines were practically flooded with articles written by professors, scholars, and men of note reporting their experience of class struggle" (23).

9. In mid-1956 the Communist Party launched a campaign of "Letting a hundred flowers bloom, letting a hundred schools of thought contend." For the first time the party directly solicited criticism from citizens. The dissatisfaction and bitterness unleashed in the name of criticism shocked Mao, who subsequently launched the anti-rightist movement in 1957. Those who spoke openly against party policies were charged with being rightists or counterrevolutionaries during the campaign. Those labeled "rightists" and other outspoken intellectuals had to write confession reports and engage in self-criticism of "wrong thought" and antiparty tendencies. See Chen (1960, Appendix B) for a list of published confessions by prominent intellectuals.

Chapter 3—A Rhetorical Analysis of Political Slogans

1. Starting in 1933 Stalin ordered a purge of party leaders and members considered the "enemies of people" in the Soviet Union. For example, between 1936 and 1938 an estimated 850,000 members, or 36 percent of the total membership, were purged from the party. According to more recent data, almost 700,000 were executed and a similar number were sent to concentration camps and prisons between 1937 and 1938. In addition around 20,000 were sentenced to exile. Sources also show that 1.4 million were arrested for "counter-revolutionary crimes" and almost 300,000 were arrested for "anti-Soviet agitation" in those years. See Sheila Fitzpatrick (1999, 264–65).

2. The movement took place on 4 May 1919 in reaction to a decision at the Versailles Peace Conference in Paris. The decision rejected demands by the Chinese delegation to rescind the privileges of imperialist forces residing in China along with twenty-one unfair treaties imposed on the Chinese. The decision also rejected the Chinese delegate's demand to take back Qingdao (German-leased territory) in Shangdong Province from Japan. On hearing the news students in Beijing staged a large-scale protest through demonstrations and by boycotting classes. The fervor of patriotism soon spread to the whole country. The movement is also known as the new culture movement, with its promotion of Western science and democracy, the introduction of Marxism to China, and the denunciation of the Confucian tradition by Chinese intellectuals.

3. Political slogans are often disseminated by the government-controlled media. For example, recently the government issued fifty slogans at the fiftieth anniversary celebration of the founding of the People's Republic of China. The slogans were published in newspapers throughout the country.

4. The term "ideograph" also has a specific meaning in the linguistic field; it is used to describe the pictographic feature of Chinese characters in that certain words resemble the actual objects to which they refer. In this study the use of the term "ideograph" differs from

this linguistic designation and reference to Chinese language. In fact, modern Chinese characters have gone through much modification, simplification, and standardization over time, and many words no longer bear close resemblance to actual objects. Moreover, the social and rhetorical meaning of ideographs/slogans as a type of political discourse created through Communist propaganda was far more influential in shaping the political reality of Chinese people.

5. As the designated successor to Mao during the Cultural Revolution, Lin Biao made appearances at many mass rallies and gave speeches on different occasions. Often the main points made during these speeches were adopted as slogans. See *Quotations of Vice Chairman Lin* (Beijing: Chinese People's University Editorial Group, 1969).

6. See Xu (1999) for a list of official and unofficial slogans used during the Cultural Revolution.

7. In the 1950s there were three major political movements in China. The first was the "Three Antis and Five Antis" campaign launched in 1952 against corruption among government officials. The second was the "Anti-Rightist Campaign" initiated by Mao in 1957, which aimed at suppressing critics (mostly intellectuals) of the party. This movement was followed by the "Great Leap Forward" in the next year, which sought to accelerate the pace of Chinese economic development but proved an economic disaster. By the early 1960s support for Mao's economic strategies had weakened. Liu Shaoqi, the second in command, began to take charge of economic planning.

8. In June 1956 a widespread strike took place in Poland, during which the workers demanded a salary increase. The police violently quelled the uprising. Fifty-three died and 270 were injured in the crackdown. Polish communists learned an important lesson from this event. They resisted pressure from Russia and elected Gomulka as the chairman of the party. In October 1956 Hungary revolted against its Communist government. The Soviets sent tanks to Budapest and put down the uprising within two days. Many executions followed, and the movement was suppressed.

9. In the campaign to let "one hundred flowers bloom and one hundred schools contend" Mao allowed intellectuals and party members to voice their dissent and make suggestions to the party. However, when many openly criticized the party and the government, Mao considered them dangerous and launched the anti-rightist movement in 1957.

10. The *Red Flag* was the official publication of the CCP from the early 1960s to the late 1980s. Written by top party officials and high-ranking radical intellectuals of the CCP, the *Red Flag* was, for almost three decades, the most authoritative voice with regard to China's ideological direction and policy-making. The publication's name was changed to *Qiu Shi* (Seeking Truth) in 1988. Since that time the journal has lost its political influence and its readership has declined.

11. Da Qing is the first oil field discovered in northeastern China. It was the model for industry and enterprises during the Cultural Revolution. *Da Qing ren* represents the spirit that promotes total devotion and personal sacrifice to the country.

12. It is known that a student named Zhang Chengzhi 張承志 came up with the idea of establishing the Red Guards organization..

13. Mao's new directive was announced through official newspapers and radio programs. Every time Mao's new directive was issued, people took to the streets singing and dancing to celebrate.

14. The Chinese term *yiqie* 一切 (all) was inclusive as well as ambiguous. It did not specify the parameter for the label to be used. Instead, it was loosely applied to all class enemies.

15. The Gang of Four included Mao's wife and three other men who took control of Chinese politics and propaganda when Mao became seriously ill.

16. Lin Biao, Mao's chosen successor, betrayed Mao in a failed coup d'état and died in a plane crash on 13 September 1971. The anti-Confucius campaign was associated with the condemnation of Lin Biao for his "counterrevolutionary acts."

17. The practice of Confucianism has serious limitations, such as absolute obedience to authority and the suppression of women. Confucianism had been the ruling class philosophy in ancient China and was used to control and subjugate the Chinese people.

18. *Wan shou wu jiang* appears in "xiaoya: xin nan shang" and "xiaoya: pu tian." *Wan nian* has the same meaning as *wan sui*, which appears in "xiaoya: zhan po luo yi."

19. The "Little Red Book" is a metaphor for the *Quotations of Chairman Mao*, the only book studied all over China during the Cultural Revolution. It is a pocket-sized book with a red cover.

20. Confucian classics were learned by memorization and recitation at an early age. This is especially so with Confucius's *Lun Yu*, or *The Analects*, in which Confucius used proverbs, parallelism, and analogies.

Chapter 4—A Rhetorical Analysis of Wall Posters

1. Sun Yat-sen (1866–1925) was the first Westernized Chinese leader. He led the 1911 revolution that overthrew the last Chinese dynasty and was also the founder and temporary president of the Republic of China. He reformed the Nationalist Party and coined the doctrines of nationalism, democracy, and livelihood as the means and goals of a new Chinese order.

2. See Anne Thurston (1987) for a collection of testimonies from the victims (most of them were children at the time) of the Cultural Revolution.

3. In fact, Lu Xun was the only writer whom Mao admired and promoted. Mao's own writing was similar to that of Lu Xun in style and in its sharp criticism of the Chinese tradition.

Chapter 5—A Rhetorical Analysis of Revolutionary Songs and Model Operas

1. The term "model opera" was an invention of the Cultural Revolution. Such opera was characterized by a clear ideology of class struggle and politicized messages and images. There were only eight such operas sanctioned and performed during the Cultural Revolution. All were performed under the direct supervision of Jiang Qing, Mao's wife.

2. The other five components are rituals, archery, horseback riding, writing, and arithmetic.

3. See Kraus (1989) and DeWoskin (1985) for more detailed descriptions of Chinese ceremonial music and its functions.

4. A news release from Xinhua News Agency on 25 December 1967 reported that within the first year of the Cultural Revolution 80 million copies of *The Selected Works of Mao Zedong,*350 million copies of *Quotations from Chairman Mao* (Little Red Book), and 57 million copies of Mao's books of poetry were published and sold (Xiao Di 1993).

5. Most quotation songs indicated that Li was the composer, even though it was not a common practice to give credit to individuals. However, Li's name was removed from all such songs after he was accused of being involved in Lin Biao's conspiracy against Mao and the party.

6. Jinggangshan, situated in Shaanxi Province, is where Mao established his first armed force fighting against the Nationalists. It became a symbol of the establishment of the first Communist base.

7. The vanguard of the language reform movement known as *bai hua wen yundong* 白話文運動 was Hu Shi, an American-educated scholar and student of John Dewey. The classical style of the Chinese language known as *wenyan wen* 文言文 was the language of the literati and had been the dominant form of scholarly discourse for over two thousand years. Hu Shi and other reform-minded Chinese intellectuals, such as Chen Duxiu, advocated the abolishment of classical Chinese writing and its replacement with a vernacular form of Chinese. It was their belief that reform in language would lead to reform in thought and culture.

8. According to Wong (1984), the song was written by Eugene Pottier and set to music by Pierre Degeyter in 1871. The song was associated with the European labor movement and was sung at strikes and demonstrations. It was the official song of the French Communist Party and a battle hymn of the Bolshevik Revolution (119).

9. *Duilian* is a traditional form of writing, with a poemlike verse that must have an exact number of words and antithetical meanings. On the top of a door a short phrase is posted summarizing the key message of the *duilian*. People compose them during New Year's celebrations as well as for celebratory occasions in general.

10. Sources show that before 1958 Mao was against personal idolatry and against attempts by his colleagues to elevate Mao Zedong's Thought. However, in 1958 he delineated two kinds of personal idolatry, a correct one and an incorrect one. Afterward colleagues such as Liu Shaoqi, Kang Sheng, and Lin Biao began to promote Mao idolatry and Mao Zedong's Thought as the absolute truth. See Xiao Di (1993, 150–52).

11. In some cases the musical components of popular songs have been kept while the lyrics have changed.

Chapter 6—A Rhetorical Analysis of Political Rituals

1. Falun Gong is a religious sect borrowed from a combination of traditional Chinese Taoist philosophy and Buddhist meditation. It was established in 1992 and banned in 1999 by the Chinese government with the charge of being an "evil cult." Practitioners have been protesting the government's action against the sect. A more detailed discussion of the sect and the rhetoric surrounding it will be offered in chapter 7.

2. *Kowtow*, with a physical position of kneeling down and nodding one's head on the ground, is a traditional way of showing deference to the emperor and the elderly members of a family in ancient China.

3. Religion was banned when the Communists took over China in 1949. Religious practices and references to God were considered bourgeois and counterrevolutionary. The Communists prided themselves on being stark materialists and atheists.

4. The quote was given at a meeting of the Chinese Communist Party standing committee on 10 June 1966.

5. The "Three Old Essays," or *Lao San Pian* 老三篇 in Chinese, were strongly promoted by Lin Biao as required readings. They were widely studied and recited. Some paragraphs have been made into songs, and the main character in each essay was regarded as a hero.

6. The color red symbolizes happiness and good luck in Chinese culture. It is the color of weddings and celebrations. The Communist Party has co-opted the color to symbolize revolution and the communist cause. Some examples are Red Army, Red Guards, Red Scarf (a symbol worn by young pioneers), and *Red Flag* (the CCP's mouthpiece).

7. See Li Zhensheng (2003) for a collection of photographs on denunciation allies from Heilongjiang Province.

8. The Chinese title is *Sunzi Bing Fa* 孫子兵法. The book was supposedly written by Sun Wu or Sunzi at the end of the Spring-Autumn and Warring State period (772–221 B.C.E.). It is a well-known Chinese classic on war strategies. The key to winning the war, according to Sunzi, was not physical strength but persuasion through moral appeals as well as employment of various strategies. See Steven Combs (2000) for a good discussion of these persuasive strategies.

9. At the end of the Cultural Revolution the government gave an official evaluation of the movement and attributed much of the damage to the Gang of Four, charging them with manipulating power and acting against Mao's will.

10. Zhang Zhixin wrote to the party leaders in 1969 criticizing adulation of Mao and Lin Biao and citing human rights violation. She was charged as a "counterrevolutionary" and imprisoned in 1969. There she was tortured and finally sentenced to death in 1975. Her reputation was rehabilitated in 1979. See Jing Wen (1994).

11. An anecdote was spreading throughout China. It said that a group of trucks fell off a cliff and all the drivers died except the one who had Mao's portrait hanging on his front mirror. It was believed that Mao's spirit protected the driver.

12. The concep of *jian ai* was coined by Mozi (475–390 B.C.E.), who is the founder of the School of Mohism. However, the Confucian concept of *ren* is selective love/benevolence based on one's relationship with others, while the Mohist notion of *jian ai* advocates universal love based on equality and mutual benefits (see Lu 1998b).

Chapter 7—A Rhetorical Analysis of Post–Cultural Revolution Political Discourse

1. "The grave left error" refers to Mao's severe mistakes as committed by a radical or far left approach to revolution.

2. Hua's legitimacy was granted by Mao's handwritten will, in which he stated: "With you [Hua] in charge, I am at ease." The will was published in the official press. Because it was written during the time when Mao was seriously ill and might have been manipulated by the Gang of Four, there have been doubts about its authenticity.

3. Deng Xiaoping was made an outcast during the Cultural Revolution when Mao identified him as the number two capitalist roader in China after Liu Shaoqi. However, in the last year of his life, 1975, Mao invited Deng to return as vice premier of China in charge of economic development. After being in power for a year Deng was severely criticized by the Gang of Four as the mastermind of the "April 5th" incident, when Beijing residents held gatherings in memory of the late premier Chou En-lai. Deng was once again removed from office, but he returned to power after the downfall of the Gang of

Four. By the time Hu Yaobang became chairman of the CCP, Deng had resigned from positions of power except one: the chairmanship of the Central Military Committee. Before his death in 1997 Deng had been the real power behind China's political scene.

4. De-Stalinization in the Soviet Union began after Stalin's death in March 1953. Khrushchev delivered a secret speech titled "The Personality Cult and Its Effects" at the twentieth party congress on 25 February 1956. The speech was said to have triggered the Polish and Hungarian uprisings. At the same time in China, Mao was still in defense of Stalin. The Chinese media was critical of Soviet abandonment of Stalin's canon, calling the Soviets "revisionists."

5. Influenced by Western-educated and liberal-minded intellectuals, Emperor Guang Xu launched a reform (also known as "Wuxu Reform") of political and economic structures, in addition to the military and education, on 11 June 1898. The reform was the first attempt at Westernization and the first move toward modernization. However, Empress Dowager Cixi staged a coup d'état on 21 September 1898 and put the emperor under house arrest. Consequently the reform movement lasted only 103 days.

6. The "Four Adherences" were endorsed by Deng Xiaoping and later included in the Chinese constitution as the guiding cardinal principles and dominant ideology of the Chinese people.

7. All the sources cited from the *People's Daily* are from its overseas version. The major news, especially political messages between the overseas and inland versions, are the same.

8. Richard Smith (1983) notes that Confucius's sayings, especially the four-characer idioms and numerated aphorisms, helped bridge the gap between the intellectual elites and common people. Many of Mao's quotations and the party propaganda slogans served the same purpose.

9. A traditional Chinese way of healing and maintaining good health through the flow and manipulation of *qi* (energy) in the body, the exercise is in the form of slow body movement and meditation.

10. The award was given by the Beijing Oriental Health Expo. The publisher was China Broadcasting and Television Publishing House. The book became a best-seller in 1995.

11. The CCP has sixty million members. The fact that the number of Falun Gong members exceeded the number of CCP members threatened the government.

12. China's Taiping Rebellion in the nineteenth century started off as a religious organization and turned into a cult that triggered a civil war and the loss of a million lives. Falun Gong is reminiscent of such a movement.

13. According to government reports, some practitioners died of illness because they refused to receive any medical treatment. They were told by Li Hongzhi that medicine would not be good for their health.

14. Sakyamuni (560–480 B.C.E.) is the name of Buddah, the founder of Buddhism.

15. The *Red Flag* was the party's most prominent journal with articles and rhetoric that represented the central policy and political ideology of the party. These articles were required readings for party members. The journal changed its name to *Seeking Truth* in the 1980s.

16. The citations from the *People's Daily* in this section are all from its overseas version.

17. The same denunication strategy was used to describe political dissidents of the Democracy Wall in 1979 as well as the Tiananmen student demonstration in 1989.

18. The Tiananmen student demonstration in 1989 provided an opportunity for dialogue between the government and students. Li Peng's authoritarian style during the televised dialogue and the students' open defiance over authority contributed to the failure of the dialogue, which led to the massacre of hundreds of students.

19. Since the 1980s China has become the world's fastest-growing economy with its average GDP of 8–9 percent a year. Statistics show that in the last decade of the twentieth century economic interdependence between the United States and China has increased substantially. Currently, China is the biggest buyer of U.S. aircraft; the United States has become the second-largest investor in China. According to Richard Haass (2002), the director of Policy Planning Staff on U.S.-China Relations, China's GDP stands at more than $1.1 trillion. China's foreign trade grew at about 13 percent a year.

20. The United States was concerned with the trade deficit, national security, human rights conditions in China, and China's influence on the U.S. presidential campaign. China, at the same time, was vexed by U.S. trade policies with China (its bid to join the World Trade Organization and the termination of the annual review of most-favored-nation [MFN] status), American pressure on human rights issues, and the U.S. policy on Taiwan. In the last three years anti-American rhetoric has intensified with NATO's bombing of the Chinese embassy in Belgrade, while suspicion that China may be spying on U.S. intelligence has accelerated with the case of Wen-Ho Lee.

21. None of the authors had been to the United States before the publication of the book, and their account and charges against the United States are mostly derived from secondary materials and the Chinese government news media. The authors identified themselves as nationalists who were once devout believers in Western values. All confessed to once admiring the American culture and loving American movies. They smoke Marlboros and wear jeans, and one of them speaks English.

22. Harry Wu, who grew up in China and was persecuted during the Cultural Revolution, shot a film describing life in the Chinese prison. He was arrested by the Chinese government and accused of spying for the United States. The U.S. negotiation with China led to the release of Wu, who is now an American citizen. The book *The Private Life of Chairman Mao,* authored by Li Zhisui, Mao Zedong's private doctor, revealed Mao's private life and the political backgrounds of many unknown Chinese. The Chinese version of the book was published in 1994 by China Times Publishing Company in Taiwan, and the English version was published by Random House in 1994. The book was banned in China but gained popularity in the United States.

23. Burke's framework of pentadic criticism consists of the identification of act, agent, agency, scene, and purpose typically present in a drama. The critic's job then is to pair two of the elements in the pentad and to discover how the first term affects the second. The analysis will allow the critic to name the motive of the rhetor. See Sonja Foss (1996) for a more detailed description of the rhetorical method.

24. All the citations of the *People's Daily* are from its overseas version.

25. On 28 February 2000 the *People's Daily* cited a document issued by the News Office of the State Council titled "American Records of Human Rights in 1999." The document cited examples and instances of violations of human rights, such as discrimination and racism in the United States. The sources of the information were the American and

Western media. This document was in response to the "1999 Country Reports on Human Rights Practices," which identified China's record of violations of human rights (released by the Bureau of Democracy, Human Rights, and Labor, U.S. Department of State, 25 February 2000).

26. This accusation refers to the case of Wen-Ho Lee, who was a Taiwan-born nuclear scientist. Lee spent nine months in solitary confinement after the government accused him of downloading computer files. The prosecution asserted that the files contained top secrets of the U.S. nuclear program. Prosecutors dropped fifty-eight out of fifty-nine charges against Lee and set him free on 13 September 2000. U.S. district judge James Parker issued an apology to Lee and called the whole handling of the case a national embarrassment. See Lee and Zia (2001).

Chapter 8—Conclusion and Implications

1. Song was conducting archival research on the Chinese Cultural Revolution in Beijing and was arrested in 2001 on the charge of smuggling government secrets and spying for anti-Chinese foreign forces. He was later released, but books on the Cultural Revolution have been banned since then and doing research on the Cultural Revolution has become politically risky. Overseas Chinese scholars and researchers in the areas of sociology and communication studies have become the primary targets.

2. The underlying assumption is that public reflection on the Cultural Revolution would threaten Mao's legitimacy, which in turn would threaten the legitimacy of the CCP. The prevailing slogan since Deng's era is to "maintain stability." There is a fear among members of the central government that activities reflecting on the Cultural Revolution would lead to chaos.

3. In his "Collection of Reflections" (1987) Ba Jin proposed to establish a Cultural Revolution museum so that this ten-year tragic experience can be remembered and those who persecuted others can learn to take responsibility for what they did. Due to the government's censorship on this topic, this proposal still remains merely an idea.

4. For example, American president George W. Bush declared to the international community, "you are either with us or against us" in combating terrorism after the terrorist attack of the World Trade Center in New York on September 11, 2001. He also branded Iran, Iraq, and North Korea the "axis of evil."

5. Many novels, plays, and poems were written and films made eulogizing Mao and Mao's works. They are not included in this book due to space limitation. See Lan Yang (1998) for information on the literature of the Cultural Revolution

6. Fisher (1987) asserts that a narrative is persuasive to the audience if it has internal coherence and is believable. Fisher's theory is based on the assumption that audience members will have a general sense of life experience and basic rational thinking ability. During the Cultural Revolution the fidelity of narratives of Mao's deeds was taken for granted and never questioned. Coherence of these narratives was not important as Mao was perceived as a mythical and almighty figure.

7. Work teams were dispatched by Liu Shaoqi to defuse students' attacks against university administrators in twenty-four universities throughout Beijing. Some student representatives, such as Kuai Dafu 蒯大富, were denounced. Mao was dismayed at this situation and

openly supported the students. This turned the situation against Liu Shaoqi and his work teams. Many work teams were driven out of universities by students. Mao criticized Liu Shaoqi, and subsequently Mao's followers accused Liu of having ulterior motives and suppressing the Cultural Revolution.

8. Under Executive Order No. 9066 by President Roosevelt, in the spring of 1942, 110,000 Japanese Americans were relocated to ten internment camps throughout the country following the Pearl Harbor attack on 7 December 1941. Two-thirds of the Japanese Americans interned were native-born Americans. The incarceration was deemed a "military necessity" as the U.S. government was operating under the assumption that persons of Japanese ancestry would forge an alliance with Japan against America. Japanese Americans were forced to leave their homes and property and lived in harsh conditions in internment camps for over three years until the end of the war. Not one act of espionage was found.

9. Similarly, in the vocabulary of the Nazis militant language such as "extinguished," "mercilessly annihilated," and "exterminated" were used in reference to the killing of Jewish people.

10. These parents are new immigrants to the United States and experienced the Cultural Revolution in their teenage years.

11. This was exemplified by the documentary *He Shang* (River Elegy), made by a few intellectuals in 1988 and televised throughout China. China was characterized as "earth culture," while Western countries were labeled "sea cultures." The film portrayed the Chinese people as lacking adventurous spirits and as psychologically inferior

12. According to Zhang, Zhang, and Wang (1994), the "Neo-Pacific Rim" has four layers, with mainland Chinese culture as its core, or the first layer; Taiwan, Hong Kong, and Macao constituting the second layer; all overseas Chinese as the third layer; and Asian countries with Chinese cultural influence as the fourth layer (Chang 2002, 71).

13. Yu's *A Bitter Journey of Culture* and *Diaries in the Mountains* and Gao's *Soul Mountain* all center on the theme of how much traditional Chinese culture, its sites, and its practices have been destroyed. The authors call for reflection on this loss.

14. Tony Saich (1994) notes that there has been a widening gap between official party rhetoric and social practices since the 1980s and that the party is no longer perceived as having a monopoly on higher truth. The criteria for determining the party's legitimacy has switched to the ability to raise the standard of living and deliver on promises of economic prosperity.

Bibliography

Ahn, Byung-Joon. 1972. *Chinese Politics and the Cultural Revolution: Dynamics of Policy Processes.* Seattle: University of Washington Press.

An, Tai Sung. 1972. *Mao Tse-Tung's Cultural Revolution.* Indianapolis: Pegasus.

An, Wenjiang 安文江. 1998. "Wo bu chanhui" 我不忏悔 (I Will Not Confess). In *1966: Women na yidai de huiyi* 我们那一代的回忆 (1966: The Memories of Our Generation), edited by Youyu Xu 徐友渔, 93–122. Beijing: China Literature Association Press.

Ana, O. S. 1999. "Like an Animal I Was Treated: Anti-Immigrant Metaphor in US Public Discourse." *Discourse & Society* 10 (April): 191–224.

Announcement of Scientific Revolution. 科学革命宣言 1967. "Wei ziran kexue jinru Mao Zedong sixiang xin shidai er zhandou" 为自然科学进入毛泽东思想新时代而战斗 (Fighting for the Natural Science in the New Mao Zedong Era). *Ke da hong weibing* 科大红卫兵 (Red Guards of the University of Science) 15:1–7.

Arendt, Hannah. 1951. *Totalitarianism.* New York: Harcourt Brace Jovanovich.

———. 1958. *The Human Condition.* Chicago: University of Chicago Press.

———. 1963. *Eichmann in Jerusalem: A Report on the Banality of Evil.* New York: Penguin Books.

Asante, Molefi K. 1998. "Identifying Racist Language Linguistic Acts and Signs." In *Communicating Prejudice,* edited by Michael L. Hecht, 87–98. Thousand Oaks, Calif.: Sage.

Augustine. 1990. "On Christian Doctrine, Book IV." In *The Rhetorical Tradition: Readings from Classical Times to the Present,* edited by Patricia Bizzell and Bruce Herzberg, 386–422. Boston: Bedford Books of St. Martin's Press.

Aune, James Arnt. 1994. *Rhetoric and Marxism.* Boulder, Colo.: Westview Press.

Ba, Jin 巴金. 1987. *Sui xiang lu* 隨想錄 (A Collection of Reflections). Beijing: Life, Reading & New Knowledge.

Bacon, Francis. 1952. "Novum Organum." In *Great Books of the Western World,* edited by Hutchins et al. Chicago: Encyclopedia Britannica.

Bakhtin, Mikhail. 1973. *Marxism and the Philosophy of Language.* Cambridge: Harvard University Press.

Ball, Terence. 1988. *Transforming Political Discourse: Political Theory and Critical Conceptual History.* Oxford, U.K.: Blackwell.

Barcata, Louis. 1967. *China in the Throes of the Cultural Revolution.* New York: Hart Publishing Company.

Barnouin, Barbara, and Changgen Yu. 1993. *Ten Years of Turbulence: The Chinese Cultural Revolution.* London and New York: Kegan Paul International.

Bennett, W. Lance. 1980. "Myth, Ritual, and Political Control." *Journal of Communication* 30 (winter): 166–79.

Berlin, Isaiah. 1956. *The Age of Enlightenment: The Eighteenth Century Philosophers*. Boston: Houghton Mifflin Company.

Bitzer, Lloyd. 1968. "The Rhetorical Situation." *Philosophy and Rhetoric* 1 (winter): 1–14.

Bloom, A. 1981. *The Linguistic Shaping of Thought: A Study in the Impact of Language in Thinking in China and the West*. Hillsdale, N.J.: Lawrence Erbaum.

Boas, Franz. 1942. "Language and Culture." In *Studies in the History of Culture: The Disciplines of the Humanities*, 178–84. Menasha, Wis.: Banta (published for the Conference of Secretaries of the American Council of Learned Societies).

———. 1974. "Introduction to the Handbook of American Indian Languages." In *Language, Culture and Society*, edited by Ben G. Blount, 12–31. Cambridge, Mass.: Winthrop Publishers.

Bormann, Ernest G. 1972. "Fantasy and Rhetorical Vision: The Rhetorical Criticism of Social Reality." *Quarterly Journal of Speech* 58 (December): 396–407.

Branham, J. Robert. 1999. "'God Save the _____!': American National Songs and National Identities, 1760–1798." *Quarterly Journal of Speech* 85 (February): 17–37.

Bredeck, Elizabeth. 1992. *Metaphors of Knowledge: Language and Thought in Mauthner's Critique*. Detroit: Wayne State University Press.

Broman, Barry M. 1969. "Tatzepao: Medium of Conflict in China's Cultural Revolution." *Journalism Quarterly* 46, no. 1 (spring): 100–104.

Burke, Kenneth. 1941. *The Philosophy of Literary Form: Studies in Symbolic Action*. New York: Vintage Books.

———. 1957. *The Philosophy of Literary Form by Kenneth Burke*. New York: Vintage Books.

———. 1961. *The Rhetoric of Religion: Studies in Logology*. Berkeley: University of California Press.

———. 1966. *Language as Symbolic Action: Essays on Life, Literature, and Method*. Berkeley: University of California Press.

———. 1968. *Counter-Statement*. Berkeley: University of California Press.

———. 1969a. *A Grammar of Motives*. Berkeley: University of California Press.

———. 1969b. *A Rhetoric of Motives*. Berkeley: University of California Press.

Carter, David. 1980. "The Industrial Workers of the World and the Rhetoric of Song." *Quarterly Journal of Speech* 66 (December): 365–74.

Cassirer, Ernst. 1964. *Language and Myth*. New York: Harper & Brothers Publishers.

Chan, Anita. 1985. *Children of Mao: Personality Development and Political Activism in the Red Guard Generation*. Seattle: University of Washington Press.

Chang, Changfu. 2002. "Chinese Culture and Its (Post) Modern Fate: Three Debates and One Critique." In *Chinese Communication Studies: Contexts and Comparisons*, edited by Xing Lu, Wenshan Jia, and Ray D. Heisey, 65–83. Westport, Conn.: Ablex Publishing Corporation.

Chang, David Wen-Wei. 1988. *China under Deng Xiaoping: Political and Economic Reform*. New York: St. Martin's Press.

Chang, Jung. 1991. *Wild Swan: Three Daughters of China*. New York: Simon & Schuster.

Chang, Parris. 1973. *Radicals and Radical Ideology in China's Cultural Revolution*. New York: Columbia University Press.

Chen, Theodore H. E. 1960. *Thought Reform of the Chinese Intellectuals*. Oxford: Oxford University Press.

Chu, Godwin C. 1977. *Radical Change through Communication in Mao's China*. Honolulu: University Press of Hawaii.

Chu, Godwin C., and Philip H. Cheng. 1978. "Revolutionary Opera: An Instrument for Cultural Change." In *Popular Media in China: Shaping New Cultural Patterns,* edited by Godwin C. Chu, 73–103. Honolulu: University Press of Hawaii.

Chu, Godwin C., and Francis L. K. Hsu. 1979. "Communication and Cultural Change in China: A Conceptual Framework." In *Moving a Mountain: Cultural Change in China*, edited by Godwin C. Chu and Francis L. K. Hsu, 2–24. Honolulu: University Press of Hawaii.

Chu, Godwin, Philip Cheng, and Leonard Chu. 1972. *The Roles of Tatzepao in the Cultural Revolution*. Carbondale: Southern Illinois University Press.

Chu, Leonard L. 1978. "Sabers and Swords for the Chinese Children: Revolutionary Children's Folk Songs." In *Popular Media in China: Shaping New Cultural Patterns,* edited by Godwin C. Chu, 17–50. Honolulu: University Press of Hawaii.

Combs, C. Steven. 2000. "Sun-zi and the Art of War: The Rhetoric of Parsimony." *Quarterly Journal of Speech* 86 (August): 276–94.

Condit, Celeste, and John Lucaites. 1993. *Crafting Equality: America's Anglo-African Word*. Chicago: University of Chicago Press.

Confucius. 1992. *Lun Yu baihua jinyi* 論語白話今譯 (Translation of Analects). Edited by Chengyi Gou 勾承益 and Yadong 李亚东 Li. Beijing: China Books.

Dai, Zhou. 戴舟. 1999. "Yi chang yansu de zhengzhi douzheng" 一場嚴肅的政治門爭 (A Serious Political Struggle). In *Shi Pi "Falun Da Fa"* 十批法輪大法 (*Ten Denunciations of Falun Gong*), 1–13. Beijing: Red Flag.

Deng, Xiaoping 鄧小平. [1979] 1987a. "Jianchi sixiang jiben yuanze" 堅持四項基本原則 (Adherence to the Four Basic Principles). In *Jianchi sixiang jiben yuanze, fandui zichanjieji ziyou hua* 堅持四項基本原則, 反對資產階級自由化 (Adherence to the Four Basic Principles, Opposition to Bourgeoisie Freedom), 9–23. Beijing: People's Press.

————. [1984] 1987b. "Jianshe you zhongguo tese de shehui zhuyi" 建設有中國特色的社會主義 (Building Socialism with Chinese Characteristics). In *Jianshe you zhongguo tese de shehui zhuyi* 建設有中國特色的社會主義 (Building Socialism with Chinese Characteristics). In *Building Socialism with Chinese Characteristics: A Collection of Deng Xiaoping's Speeches,* 51–56. Beijing: People's Press.

Denisoff, Serge R. 1983. *Sing a Song of Social Significance*. 2d ed. Bowling Green, Ohio: Bowling Green State University Popular Press.

Denton, Robert. 1980. "The Rhetorical Functions of Slogans: Classifications and Characteristics." *Communication Quarterly* 28 (spring): 10–18.

DeWoskin, Kenneth J. 1985. "Philosophers on Music in Early China." *World of Music* 27:33–45.

Dittmer, Lowell. 1979. "Cultural Revolution and Cultural Change." In *Moving a Mountain: Cultural Change in China,* edited by Godwin C. Chu and Francis L. K. Hsu, 207–36. Honolulu: University Press of Hawaii.

———. 1991. "Learning from Trauma: The Cultural Revolution in Post-Mao Politics." In *New Perspectives on the Cultural Revolution,* edited by William Joseph, Christine Wong, and David Zweig, 19–40. Cambridge: Harvard University Press.

———. 1998. *Liu Shaoqi and the Chinese Cultural Revolution.* Rev. ed. Armonk, N.Y.: M. E. Sharpe.

Dong, Leshan 董乐山. 1999. "Zhongguo de yijiu basi: Lun zhongguo zhishi fenzi de ruanruo xing" 中国的一九八四：论中国知识分子的软弱性 (China's 1984: On the Weakness of Chinese Intellectuals). In *Gongchan zhongguo wushi nian* 共产中国五十年 (Fifty Years of Communist China), edited by Jin Zhong 金钟, 49–62. Hong Kong: Kaifang Magazine.

Edelman, Murray. 1977. *Political Language: Words That Succeed and Politics That Fail.* New York: Academic Press.

Esmein, Jean. 1973. *The Chinese Cultural Revolution.* Garden City, N.Y.: Anchor Books.

Eulogy of Mao Zedong: Collection of Songs 毛澤東頌：歌曲集. 1978. Shanghai: Art Press.

Fairbank, John. 1976. "The Chinese Pattern." In *Comparative Communism: The Soviet, Chinese, and Yugoslav Models,* edited by Gary Bertsch and Thomas W. Ganschow, 51–64. San Francisco: W. H. Freeman and Company.

Fisher, Walter R. 1987. *Human Communication as Narratives: Toward a Philosophy of Reason, Value, and Action.* Columbia: University of South Carolina Press.

FitzGerald, Charles P. 1976. *Mao Tsetung and China.* London: Hodder & Stoughton.

Fitzpatrick, Sheila. 1999. *Everyday Stalinism: Ordinary Life in Extraordinary Times: Soviet Russia in the 1930s.* New York: Oxford University Press.

Foss, Sonja. 1996. *Rhetorical Criticism: Exploration & Practice.* 2d ed. Prospect Heights, Ill.: Waveland Press.

Foucault, Michel. 1972. *The Archaeology of Knowledge.* Translated by A. M. Sheridan Smith. New York: Pantheon.

———. 1980. *Power/Knowledge.* New York: C. Golden, 1980.

———. 1981. "The Order of Discourse." In *Untying the Text: A Post-Structuralist Reader,* edited by Robert Young, 48–78. Boston: Routledge & Kegan Paul.

Gao, Xingjian 高行健. 1990. *Ling Shan* 靈山 (Soul Mountain). Taiwan: Lian Jing Inc.

Gold, T. B. 1996. "Civil Society in Taiwan: The Confucian Dimension." In *Confucian Traditions in East Asian Modernity: Moral Education and Economic Culture in Japan and the Four Mini-dragons,* edited by Wei-ming Tu, 244–58. Cambridge: Harvard University Press.

Gong-Sun, Long 公孫龍. 1986. *Gong-Sun Long jin zhu jin yi* 公孫龍今注今譯 (Interpretation of Gong-Sun Long). Edited by Guimiao Cheng 陳癸淼 Taipei: Shang Wu Printing House.

Gonzalez, Alberto, and John Makay. 1983. "Rhetoric Ascription and the Gospel According to Dylan." *Quarterly Journal of Speech* 69 (February): 1–14.

Green, David. 1987. *The Language of Politics in America: Shaping Political Consciousness from McKinley to Reagan.* Ithaca and London: Cornell University Press.

Haass, Richard (2002). "China and the Future of U.S.-China Relations." Speech given to the National Committee on U.S.-China Relations, New York. December 5. http://www.whitehouse.gov/

Habermas, Jurgen. 1987. *The Philosophical Discourse of Modernity: Twelve Lectures*, translated by Frederick Lawrence and edited by Thomas McCarthy, x. Cambridge: MIT Press.

Hammond, Scott, and Hongmei Gao. 2002. "Pan Gu's Paradigm: Chinese Education's Return to Holistic Communication in Learning." In *Chinese Communication Studies: Contexts and Comparisons*, edited by Xing Lu, Wenshan Jia, and Ray D. Heisey, 227–43. Westport, Conn.: Ablex Publishing Corporation.

Han, Feizi. 韓非子. 1992. *Han Feizi quanyi* 韓非子全譯 (The Collected Works of Han Feizi). Edited by Zhang Jue. Guiyang: Guizhou People's Press.

Havel, Vaclav. 1985. "The Power of the Powerless." In *The Power of the Powerless*, edited by John Keane, 23–96. London: Hutchinson.

He, Shu 何蜀. 2000. "Wenhua dageming zhong de gequ" 文化大革命中的歌曲 (Songs of the Cultural Revolution). Virtue Museum of the Cultural Revolution, *China News Digest* 235, 18 October. http://www.cnd.org/cr.

Heider, E. R., and D. C. Oliver. 1972. "The Structure of the Color Space in Naming and Memory for Two Languages." *Cognitive Psychology* 8 (April): 337–54.

Heisey, D. Ray. 1999. "China's Rhetoric of Socialization in Its International Civic Discourse." In *Civic Discourse, Civil Society, and Chinese Communities*, edited by Randy Kluver and John Powers, 210–20. Stamford, Conn.: Ablex Publishing Corporation.

Heng, Liang, and Judith Shapiro. 1983. *Son of the Revolution*. New York: Vintage Books.

Henle, P. 1958. "Language, Thought, and Culture." In *Language and Culture*, edited by P. Henle, 1–24. Ann Arbor: University of Michigan Press.

Hoijer, Harry. 1974. "The Sapir-Whorf Hypothesis." In *Language, Culture and Society*, edited by Ben G. Blount, 120–31. Cambridge, Mass.: Winthrop Publishers.

———, ed. 1965. *Language in Culture*. Chicago: University of Chicago Press.

Hong, Zhaohui, and Yi Sun. 1999. "In Search of Re-ideologization and Social Order." In *Dilemmas of Reform in Jiang Zemin's China*, edited by Andrew J. Nathan, Zhaohui Hong, and Steven R. Smith, 33–50. Boulder, Colo.: Lynne Rienner Publishers.

Hsia, Adrin. 1972. *The Chinese Cultural Revolution*. London: Orbach and Chambers.

Hsu, Immanuel C. Y. 1990. *China without Mao: The Search for a New Order*. 2d ed. New York: Oxford University Press.

Hu, C. T. 1972. "Communist Education: Theory and Practice." In *Communist China: A System-Functional Reader*, edited by Yung Wei, 141–55. Columbus, Ohio: Charles E. Merrill.

Hu, Yaobang 胡燿邦. 1980. "zuo yige chedi de weiwu zhuyi zhe" 做一個徹底的唯物主義者 (Be a complete materialist). In *sanzhong quanhui yi lai zhongyao wenxian* 三中全會以來重要文獻 (Important documents since the Third Assembly). Beijing: People's Press, 518–31.

Huang, Shaorong. 1996. *To Rebel Is Justified: A Rhetorical Study of China's Cultural Revolution Movement 1966–1969*. Lanham, Md.: University Press of America, 1996.

———. 2000. "Power to Move the Masses in a Mass Movement: An Analysis of Mao's Rhetorical Strategies during China's Cultural Revolutionary Movement." In *Chinese Perspectives in Rhetoric and Communication*, edited by D. Ray Heisey, 207–22. Stamford, Conn.: Ablex Publishing Corporation.

Huberman, Leo. 1967. *Cultural Revolution in China: A Socialist Analysis*. Boston: New England Free Press.

Hyland, Drew A. 1973. *The Origins of Philosophy: Its Rise in Myth and the Pre-Socratics.* New York: Capricorn Books.

Irvine, R. James, and Walter G. Kirkpatrick. 1972."The Musical Form in Rhetorical Exchange: Theoretical Considerations." *Quarterly Journal of Speech* 58 (October): 272–84.

Jackson, Ronald L. II, and Thurmon Garmer. 1998. "Tracing the Evolution of 'Race,' 'Ethnicity,' and 'Culture' in Communication Studies." *Howard Journal of Communications* 9 (January–March): 41–55.

Jensen, Vernon. 1992. "Values and Practices in Asian Argumentation." *Argumentation and Advocacy* 28 (spring): 155–66.

Ji, Xianlin 季羨林. 1998. *Niupeng zayi* 牛棚杂忆 (Memory of Cowshed). Beijing School of Chinese Communist Party Press.

Jia, Wenshan. 1999. "From Kaihui to Duihua: The Transformation of Chinese Civic Discourse." In *Civic Discourse, Civil Society, and Chinese Communities,* edited by Randy Kluver and John Powers, 52–66. Stamford, Conn.: Ablex Publishing Corporation.

Jia, Wenshan. 2001. *The Remaking of the Chinese Character and Identity in the 21st Century: The Chinese Face Practices.* Westport, Conn.: Ablex Publishing.

Jiang, Ji Li. 1997. *Red Scarf Girl: A Memoir of the Cultural Revolution.* New York: HarperCollins.

Jiang, Zemin 江澤民. 2001a. "Zai qingzhu qinghua daxue jianxiao jiushi zhounian dahui shang de jianghua" 在慶祝清華大學建校九十周年大會上的講話 (speech given at the ninetieth anniversary celebration of the founding of Tsinghua University [29 April 2001]). *People's Daily,* 30 April.

———. 2001b."Zai qingzhu zhongguo guochandong chengli bashi zhounian dahui shang de jianghua" 在慶祝中國共産黨成立八十周年大會上的講話 (speech given at the eightieth anniversary celebration of the founding of the Chinese Communist Party [1 July 2001]). *People's Daily,* 2 July, p. 1.

Jin, Fu 晋夫. 1998. *Wenge qian shinian de zhongguo* 文革前十年的中國 (Ten Years Prior to the Cultural Revolution in China). Beijing: Chinese Communist Party History Press.

Joseph, William A., Christine P. W. Wong, and David Zweig. 1991. "Introduction: New Perspectives on the Cultural Revolution." *In New Perspectives on the Cultural Revolution,* edited by William A. Joseph, Christine P. W. Wong, and David Zweig, 1–16. Cambridge and London: Harvard University Press.

Jowett, S. Garth, and Victoria O'Donnell. 1999. *Propaganda and Persuasion.* 3d ed. Thousand Oaks, Calif.: Sage.

Kincaid, Lawrence D. 1987. "Communication East and West: Points of Departure." In *Communication Theory: Eastern and Western Perspectives,* edited by D. Lawrence Kincaid, 331–40. San Diego: Academic Press.

King, A. Y. 1996. "The Transformation of Confucianism in the Post-Confucian Era: The Emergence of Rationalistic Traditionalism in Hong Kong." In *Confucian Traditions in East Asian Modernity: Moral Education and Economic Culture in Japan and the Four Mini-dragons,* edited by Wei-ming Tu, 265–76. Cambridge: Harvard University Press.

Kirk, G. S., and J. E. Raven. 1957. *The Presocratic Philosophers: A Critical History with a Selection of Texts.* New York: Cambridge University Press.

Kluver, Alan R. 1996. *Legitimating the Chinese Economic Reforms: A Rhetoric of Myth and Orthodoxy.* Albany: State University of New York Press.

Kluver, Randy, and John Powers, eds. 1999. *Civic Discourse, Civil Society, and Chinese Communities.* Stamford, Conn.: Ablex Publishing Corporation.

Koenigsberg, Richard. 1975. *Hitler Ideology: A Study in Psychoanalytic Sociology.* New York: Library of the Social Sciences.

Kosokoff, Stephen, and Carl W. Carmichael. 1970. "The Rhetoric of Protest: Song, Speech, and Attitude Change." *Southern Speech Journal* 35 (summer): 295–302.

Kraus, Richard C. 1989. *Pianos and Politics in China: Middle-Class Ambitions and the Struggle over Western Music.* New York: Oxford University Press.

Krauthammer, Charles. 1995. "Why We Must Contain China." *Time,* 31 July, 72.

Kroll, J. L. 1985–87. "Disputation in Ancient Chinese Culture." *Early China* 11–12:118–45.

Lakoff, George, and Mark Johnson. 1980. *Metaphors We Live By.* Chicago: University of Chicago Press.

Lee, Wen-Ho, with Helen Zia. 2001. *My Country Versus Me.* New York: Hyperion.

Lee, Wen Shu. 1998. "Patriotic Breeders or Colonized Converts: A Postcolonial Feminist Approach to Antifootbinding Discourse in China." In *Communication and Identity Across Cultures,* edited by D. V. Tanno and A. Gonzalez, 11–33. International and Intercultural Communication Annual 21. Thousand Oaks, Calif.: Sage.

Legge, J. Li Chi. 1967. *Book of Rites.* New Hyde Park, N.Y.: University Books.

Leys, Simon. 1997. *The Analects of Confucius.* New York and London: W. W. Norton & Company.

Li, Cheng. 1996. "Fallacies of Extreme Nationalism in China Can Say No." *Sino U.S. Weekly,* 27 December, 4.

Li, Deshun, Meitang Sun, and Weiping Sun 李德順，孫美堂，孫偉平. 2001. "Wenhua jianshe zhong de san zhong daoxiang" 文化建設中的三種導向 (Three Views on Culture Construction). *Xinhua wenzhai* 新華文摘 (New China Magazine) 12:126–29.

Li, Dun. 1978. *The Ageless Chinese.* 3d ed. New York: Charles Scribner's Sons.

Li, Gucheng 李古城. 1992. *Zhongguo dalu zhengzhi shuyu* 中国大陆政治术语 (Political Language of Mainland China). Hong Kong: Chinese University Press.

Li, Hongzhi. 李洪志 1994. *Zhuan Falun* 轉法輪 (Wheeling of Falun). Beijing: China Broadcasting and Television Publishing.

Li, Ruihuan 李瑞環. 2001. "Zia quanguo zhenxie jiujie sici huiyi bimuhui shang de jianghua" 在全國政協九屆四次會議閉幕會上的講話 (speech given at the closing ceremony of the fourth session of the nineth Chinese People's Assembly [12 March 2001]). *People's Daily,* 13 March.

Li, Zhensheng. 2003. *Red-Color News Soldier.* London: Phaidon Press.

Liang, Mingyue. 1985. *Music of the Billion: An Introduction to Chinese Musical Culture.* New York: Heinrichshofen Edition.

Liang, Shuming 梁漱溟. 1987. *Zhongguo wenhua yaoyi* 中國文化要義 (Essence of Chinese Culture). Hong Kong: San Lian Books.

———. 1989. *Dongxi wenhua ji zhexue* 東西文化及哲學 (Eastern and Western Cultures and Philosophy). Jinan: Shandong People's Publisher.

Liang, Xiaosheng 梁晓声. 1998. *Yige hongweibing de zibai* 一个红卫兵的自白 (Confession of a Red Guard). Xi'an: Shaaxi Tourism Publishing House.

Liao, W. K. 1939. *The Complete Works of Han Fei Tzu*. London: Arthur Probsthan.

Lifton, Robert Jay. 1972. "Thought Reform: The Cultural Perspectives." In *Communist China: A System-Functional Reader,* edited by Yung Wei, 163–73. Columbus, Ohio: Charles E. Merrill.

———. 1989. *Thought Reform and the Psychology of Totalism: A Study of "Brainwashing" in China*. Chapel Hill: University of North Carolina Press.

Lilley, R. James. 1997. "The 'Fu Manchu' Problem." *Newsweek,* 24 February, 36.

Lin, Biao. [1966] 1968. "Zaiban qianyan" 再版前言 (Preface). In *Mao zhuxi yulu* 毛主席語錄 (Quotations from Chairman Mao), 1–3. Beijing: Political Bureau of the People's Liberation Army.

Lin, Jianhong. 1996. "What Kind of Nationalism Do the Chinese Need?" *U.S. China Tribune,* 20 September, 2.

Lin, Jing. 1991. *The Red Guards' Path to Violence: Political, Educational, and Psychological Factors*. New York: Praeger.

Lin, Yutang. 1936. *My Country and My People*. London: Heinemann.

Link, Perry. 1994. "China's 'Core' Problem." In *China in Transformation,* edited by Tu Wei-ming, 189–205. Cambridge: Harvard University Press.

———. 1999. *Ban Yang Sui Bi* (Notes across the Ocean) 半洋随笔. Taibei: Sanmin Shuju.

Liu, Binyan. 2001. "Unprecedented Courage in the Face of Cultural Revolution–Style Persuasion." In Danny Schechter, ed., *Falun Gong's Challenge to China: Spiritual Practice or "Evil Cult"?,* 204–20. New York: Akashic Books.

Liu, Pingping, Liu Yuan, and Liu Tingting 刘平平，刘源，刘亭亭. 1987. "Shengli de xianhua xiangei nin" 胜利的鲜花献给您 (Presenting You with the Victory Flowers). In Lishi zai zheli shensi 历史在这里沉思 (Reflection of History), 1–48. Beijing: Huaxia Publications.

Liu, Yunshan 劉云山. 2000. "Shizhong jianchi xianjin wenhua de qianjin fangxiang: fanrong fazhan you zhongguo dese de shehui zhuyi wenhua" 始終堅持先進文化的前進方向：繁榮發展有中國特色的社會主義文化 (Always Adhere to the Forward Direction of Advanced Culture: Developing Socialist Culture with Chinese Characteristics). *People's Daily,* 1 June, p. 1.

Locke, John. 1959. *An Essay Concerning Human Understanding*. Vols. 1–2. Edited by Alexander Campbell Fraser. New York: Dover Publications.

Lu, Guang, and Xiaoyu Xiao. 2000. "Beijing Opera during the Cultural Revolution: The Rhetoric of Ideological Conflict." In *Chinese Perspectives in Rhetoric and Communication,* edited by D. Ray Heisey, 223–48. Stamford, Conn.: Ablex Publishing Corporation.

Lu, Xing. 1998a. "An Interface between Individualistic and Collectivistic Orientations in Chinese Cultural Values and Social Relations." *Howard Journal of Communication* 9 (April–June): 91–107.

———. 1998b. *Rhetoric in Ancient China, Fifth to Third Century B.C.E: A Comparison with Classical Greek Rhetoric*. Columbia: University of South Carolina Press.

Lu, Xun 鲁迅. 1970. *Lu Xun lun wenyi* 魯迅論文藝 (Lu Xun on Literary Art). Hong Kong: Art and Education Press.

Luo, Zi-Ping. 1990. *A Generation Lost: China under the Cultural Revolution.* New York: Henry Holt and Company.

Lucy, John. 1992. *Language Diversity and Thought.* Cambridge: Cambridge University Press.

MacIntyre, Alasdair. 1981. *After Virtue.* Notre Dame, Ind.: University of Notre Dame Press.

Madsen, Arnie. 1993. "Burke's Representative Anecdote as a Critical Method." In *Extensions of the Burkeian System,* edited by James W. Chesebro, 208–29. Tuscaloosa: University of Alabama Press.

Mao, Zedong 毛澤東. [1927] 1945. "Report on an Investigation of the Peasant Movement in Hunan." In *Selected Works of Mao Tse-tung [Zedong].* Vol. 1. Peking: Foreign Languages Press.

———. 1958. "Introduction of a Co-operative." In *Selected Works of Mao Zedong.* Vol. B. Beijing: China Youth Press.

———. [1940] 1965. "On New Democracy." In *Selected Works of Mao Tse-tung.* Vol. 2. Peking: Foreign Language Press.

———. [1942] 1965b. "Talks at the Yan'an Forum on Literature and Art." In *Selected Works of Mao Tse-tung.* Vol. 3. Peking: Foreign Language Press.

———. 1967. *Quotations from Chairman Mao Tse-Tung.* Edited by Stuart R. Schram. New York: Bantam Books.

———. 1968. *Mao zhuxi yulu* (Quotations from Chairman Mao). Beijing: General Ministry of Politics of the People's Liberation Army.

———. [1962] 1974. "Speech at the Tenth Plenum." In *Mao Tse-tung Unrehearsed,* edited by Stuart Schram, 188–89. Harmondsworth, U.K.: Penguin.

———. [1943] 1975. "Get Organized." In *Selected Works of Mao Tse-tung.* Vol. 3. Peking: Foreign Language Press.

———. [1945] 1975. "On Coalition Government." In *Selected Works of Mao Tse-tung.* Vol. 3. Peking: Foreign Language Press.

———. [1937] 1975. "On Practice." In *Selected Works of Mao Tse-tung [Zedong].* Vol. 1. Peking: Foreign Languages Press.

———. 1976. *Mao Tsetung Poems.* Beijing: Shangwu Publishing.

———. [1945] 1977. "The Situation and Our Policy after the Victory in the War of Resistance against Japan." In *Selected Works of Mao Tse-tung.* Vol. 4. Peking: Foreign Language Press.

———. [1957a] 1977. "Speech at the Chinese Communist Party National Conference on Propaganda Work." In *Selected Works of Mao Tse-tung.* Vol. 5. Peking: Foreign Language Press.

———. [1957b] 1977. "Wenhuibao de zichan jieji fangxing yingdang pipan" 文匯報的資產階級方向應當批判 (Denounce the Bourgeois Ideas in Wenhui Daily). In *Mao Zedong xuanji: di wu juan* 毛澤東選集：第五卷 (Selected Works of Mao Zedong). Vol. 5. Beijing: People's Press.

———. [1962] 1978. *Zai kuoda de zhongyang gongzuo huiyi shang de jianghua* 在擴大的中央工作會議上的講話 (speech at the session of the extended Central Committee). Beijing: People's Press.

Markham, James W. 1967. *Voices of the Red Giants: Communications in Russia and China.* Ames: Iowa State University Press.

Martin, Helmut. 1982. *Cult & Canon: The Origins and Development of State Maoism.* Armonk, N.Y.: M. E. Sharpe.

Marx, Karl. 1859–72. "Zhengzhi jingji xue pipan xuyan" 政治經濟學批判序言 (Introduction of the Criticism of Political Economy). In *Makesi Engesi xuanji* 馬克思恩格斯選集 (Selected Works of Marx and Engels). Vol. 2. Beijing: People's Press.

Marx, Karl, and Frederick Engels. [1848] 1965. *The Communist Manifesto.* Translated by Samuel Moore. New York: Washington Square Press.

McCarthy, Terry. 1999. "Inside the Falun Gong." *Time,* 9 August, 48–50.

McGee, Michael. 1980. "The 'Ideograph': A Link between Rhetoric and Ideology." *Quarterly Journal of Speech* 66 (February): 1–16.

Meisner, Maurice. 1999. *Mao China and After: A History of the People Republic.* 3d ed. New York: Free Press.

Mencius. 1992. *Mengzi baihua jin yi* 孟子白話今譯 (The Translation of Mencius). Edited by Li Shuang. 李雙 Beijing: China Books.

Michael, Franz. 1971. "The Struggle for Power." In *China in Ferment: Perspectives on the Cultural Revolution,* edited by Richard Baum, 52–59. Englewood Cliffs, N.J.: Prentice-Hall.

Milgram, Stanley. 1969. *Obedience to Authority.* New York: Harper and Row.

Munro, D. J. 1977. *The Concept of Man in Contemporary China.* Ann Arbor: University of Michigan Press.

Nakamura, H. 1964. *Ways of Thinking of Eastern Peoples: India, China, Tibet, and Japan.* Honolulu: University Press of Hawaii.

Ng, Rita Mei-Ching. 2002. "Culture and Modernization: The Case of the People's Republic of China." In *Chinese Communication Studies: Contexts and Comparisons,* edited by Xing Lu, Wenshan Jia, and Ray D. Heisey, 33–45. Westport, Conn.: Ablex Publishing Corporation.

Ng, Wendy. 1991. "The Collective Memories of Communities." In *Asian Americans: Comparative and Global Perspectives,* edited by Shirley Hune, Hyung-chan Kim, Stephen S. Fugita, and Amy Ling, 103–12. Pullman: Washington State University Press.

Nietzsche, Friedrich. 1979. "On Truth and Lies in a Nonmoral Sense." In *Philosophy and Truth: Selections from Nietzsche Notebooks of the Early 1870's,* translated and edited by Daniel Breazeale, 79–100. Atlantic Highlands, N.J.: Humanities Press.

Niu-Niu. 1995. *No Tears for Mao: Growing Up in the Cultural Revolution.* Chicago: Academy Chicago.

Oliver, Robert. 1971. *Communication and Culture in Ancient India and China.* Syracuse, N.Y: Syracuse University Press.

Orwell, George. 1949. *1984.* San Diego: Harcourt Brace Jovanovich.

———. 1956. "Politics and the English Language." In *The Orwell Reader,* 355–66. New York: Harcourt Brace Jovanovich.

Osborn, Michael. 1967. "Archetypal Metaphor in Rhetoric: The Light-Dark Family." *Quarterly Journal of Speech* 53 (April): 115–26.

Ouyang, Junxi 歐陽軍喜. 2002. *Wusi xinwenhua yundong yu ruxue* 五四新文化運動与儒學 (The May Fourth New Cultural Movement and Confucianism). Xi'an: Shanxi People's Publisher.

Parry-Giles, Shawn J. 1994. "Rhetorical Experimentation and the Cold War, 1947–1953: The Development of an Internationalist Approach to Propaganda." *Quarterly Journal of Speech* 80 (December): 448–67.

Perelman, Chaim, and L. Olbrechts-Tyteca. 1969. *The New Rhetoric: A Treatise on Argumentation*. Translated by John Wilkinson and Purcell Weaver. Notre Dame, Ind.: University of Notre Dame Press.

Perris, Arnold. 1985. *Music as Propaganda: Art to Persuade, Art to Control*. Westport, Conn.: Greenwood Press.

Perry, Steven. 1983. "Rhetorical Functions of the Infestation Metaphor in Hitler Rhetoric." *Central States Speech Journal* 34 (winter): 229–35.

Philipsen, Gerry. 1987. "The Prospect for Cultural Communication." In *Communication Theory: Eastern and Western Perspectives*, edited by D. Lawrence Kincaid, 245–54. San Diego: Academic Press.

Plato. 1960. *Gorgias*. Translated by Walter Hamilton. New York: Penguin Books.

———. 1961. *Cratylus*. Translated by Benjamin Jowett. In *The Collected Dialogues of Plato*, edited by Edith Hamilton and Huntington Cairns. New York: Bollingen Foundation.

———. 1973. *Phaedrus*. Translated by Walter Hamilton. New York: Penguin Books.

Poon, David Jim-tat. 1978. "Tatzepao: Its History and Significance as a Communication Medium." In *Popular Media in China: Shaping New Cultural Patterns*, edited by Godwin Chu, 184–221. Honolulu: University Press of Hawaii.

Powers, John, and Randy Kluver. 1999. "Introduction: Civic Discourse and Civil Society in Chinese Communities." In *Civic Discourse, Civil Society, and Chinese Communities*, edited by Randy Kluver and John Powers, 1–7. Stamford, Conn.: Ablex Publishing Corporation.

Pye, Lucian. 1968. *The Spirit of Chinese Politics: A Psychocultural Study of the Authority Crisis in Political Development*. Cambridge: MIT Press.

———. 1979. "Communication and Political Culture in China." In *Moving a Mountain: Cultural Change in China*, edited by Godwin C. Chu and Francis L. K. Hsu, 153–78. Honolulu: University Press of Hawaii.

———. 1985. *Asian Power and Politics*. Cambridge: Harvard University Press.

———. 1992. *The Spirit of Chinese Politics*. Cambridge: Harvard University Press.

Qian, Qichen 錢其琛. 2001. "Zai jian zeming zhuxi wei shujin zuguo tongyi dayie de wancheng er jixu fengduo zhongyao jianhua fabiao liu zhounian zuotanghui shang de jianghua" 在江澤民主席［為促進祖國統一大業的完成而繼續奮鬥］重要講話發表六周年座談會上的講話 (speech given at the sixth anniversary of Chairman Jiang Zemin's speech on the continued efforts of completing the cause of uniting the motherland [22 January 2001]). *People's Daily*, 23 January.

Relie zanyang geming yangbanxi zhiquweihushan 熱烈讚揚革命樣板戲智取威虎山 (Enthusiastic Praise of Model Opera Taking Tiger Mountain by Strategy). 1969. Hong Kong: Hong Kong Sanlian Books.

Rodda, M., and C. Grove. 1987. *Language, Cognition, and Deafness*. Hillsdale, N.J.: Lawrence Erlbaum.

Ross, R. James. 1994. *Caught in a Tornado: A Chinese American Woman Survives the Cultural Revolution*. Boston, Mass.: Northeastern University Press.

Rowland, C. Robert, and David Frank. 2002. *Shared Land/Conflicting Identity: Trajectories of Israeli & Palestinian Symbol Use.* East Landsing, MI: Michigan State University Press.

Rueckert, William H. 1969. "Tragedy as a Representative Anecdote." In *Critical Responses to Kenneth Burke, 1924–1966,* edited by William H. Rueckert, 380–95. Minneapolis: University of Minnesota Press.

Rybacki, Karyn, and Donald Rybacki. 1991. *Communication Criticism.* Belmont, Calif.: Wadsworth.

Saich, Tony. 1994. "Discos and Dictatorship: Party-State and Society Relations in the People's Republic of China." In *Popular Protest and Political Culture in Modern China,* 2d ed., edited by Jeffrey N. Wasserstrom and Elizabeth J. Perry, 246–67. Boulder, Colo.: Westview Press.

San Ge Daibiao Xuexi Du Ben 三個代表學習讀本 (On the Study of Three Representatives). 2000. Beijing: CCP Central Committee Party School Publisher, 2000.

Sapir, Edward. [1929] 1949. "The Status of Linguistics as a Science." In *The Selected Writings of Edward Sapir in Language, Culture, and Personality,* edited by D. G. Mandebaum, 160–66. Berkeley: University of California Press.

———. 1974."The Unconscious Patterning of Behavior in Society" and "Language." In *Language, Culture and Society,* edited by Ben G. Blount, 32–45 and 46–66, respectively. Cambridge, Mass.: Winthrop Publishers.

Schechter, Danny. 2001. *Falun Gong's Challenge to China: Spiritual Practice or "Evil Cult"?* New York: Akashic Books.

Schoenhals, Michael. 1992. *Doing Things with Words in Chinese Politics.* Berkeley: Institute of East Asian Studies, University of California.

———, ed. 1996. *China's Cultural Revolution, 1966–1969: Not a Dinner Party.* Armonk, N.Y.: M. E. Sharpe.

Schwartz, I. Benjamin. 1994. "Culture, Modernity, and Nationalism—Further Reflections." In *China in Transformation,* edited by Tu Wei-Ming, 233–53. Cambridge: Harvard University Press.

Shalom, Stephen R. 1984. *Deaths in China Due to Communism Propaganda Versus Reality.* Tempe, Ariz.: Center for Asian Studies.

Shankel, George. 1941. *American Mottoes and Slogans.* New York: H. W. Wilson Co.

Sharp, Horald. 1984. *Advertising Slogans of America.* Metuchen, N.J.: Scarecrow Press.

Shuo Yuan (The Garden of Talks). 1992. Edited by Liu Xiang. Guiyang: Guizhou People's Press.

Simons, Herbert. 1970. "Requirements, Problems and Strategies: A Theory of Persuasion for Social Movements." *Quarterly Journal of Speech* 56 (February): 1–11.

———. 2003. "China in Transition: An RPS Approach." Paper presented at the 89th National Communication Association Convention, Miami Beach, Fla. November 20–23.

———, and Elizabeth Mechling 1981. "The Rhetoric of Political Movements." In *Handbook of Political Communication,* edited by Dan Nimmo and Keith Sanders, 417–44. Beverly Hills, Calif.: Sage Publications.

Slobin, D. T. 1979. *Psycholinguistics.* Glenview, Ill.: Scott Foresman.

Smith, Craig. 1985. "Martin-Heidegger and the Dialogue with Being." *Central States Speech Journal* 35:269.

———. 1998. *Rhetoric and Human Consciousness: A History*. Prospect Heights, Ill.: Waveland Press.

Smith, Richard J. 1983. *China's Cultural Heritage: The Ching Dynasty 1644–1912* Boulder, Colo.: Westview Press.

Solomon, Richard. 1998. *Mao's Revolution and the Chinese Political Culture*. Ann Arbor: Center for Chinese Studies, University of Michigan.

Song, Qiang, Zhang Zangzang, and Qiao Bian. 1996a. *China Can Say No*. Beijing: Chinese Industry Trade United Press.

———. 1996b. *China Can Still Say No*. Beijing: Chinese Cultural Federation Press.

Starr, John. 1981. *The Future of US-China Relations*. New York: New York University Press.

Steinfatt, Thomas M. 1989. "Linguistic Relativity: Toward a Broader View." In *Language, Communication, and Culture: Current Directions*, edited by Stella Ting-Toomey and Felipe Korzenny, 35–75. Newbury Park, Calif.: Sage.

Stewart, Charles, C. A. Smith, and R. Denton Jr. 1995. "The Persuasive Functions of Slogans." In *Propaganda*, edited by Robert Jackall, 400–422. New York: New York University Press.

Tan, Fang, and Wumian Zhao. 1996. *Highlights of Da-zi-bao during the Cultural Revolution*. Hong Kong: Mirror Books.

Taylor, P. M. 1990. *Munitions of the Mind: War Propaganda from the Ancient World to the Nuclear Age*. Wellingborough, U.K.: Patrick Stephens.

Ten Denunciations of Falun Gong. 1999. Beijing: Red Flag.

Thurston, Anne. 1987. *Enemies of the People*. New York: Alfred A. Knopf.

Ting-Toomey, S. 1993. "Communicative Resourcefulness: An Identity Negotiation Perspective." In *Intercultural Communication Competence*, edited by R. Wiseman and J. Koester, 72–111. Thousand Oaks, Calif.: Sage.

Townsend, James. 1972. "Political Participation." In *Communist China: A System-Functional Reader*, edited by Yung Wei, 261–74. Columbus, Ohio: Charles E. Merrill.

———, and B. Womack. 1986. *Politics in China*. 3d ed. Boston, Mass.: Little, Brown and Company.

Tu, Wei-Ming. 1994. "Introduction: Cultural Perspective." In *China in Transformation*, edited by Wei-Ming Tu, xi–xxvii. Cambridge: Harvard University Press.

Urdang, L., and C. Robbins, eds. 1984. *Slogans*. Detroit: Gale Research Company.

Van Dijk, Teun A. 1995. "Discourse Semantics and Ideology." *Discourse & Society* 6 (April): 243–89.

Wagner, Vivian. 1999. "Songs of the Red Guards: Keywords Set to Music." Indiana East Asian Working Paper Series on Language and Politics in Modern China. http://www.easc.indiana.edu/Papers/Easc/working-papers/

Wakeman, Carolyn. 1985. *To the Storm: The Odyssey of a Revolutionary Chinese Woman*. Berkeley: University of California Press.

Walder, Andrew. 1991. "Cultural Revolution Radicalism: Variations on a Stalinist Theme." In *New Perspectives on the Cultural Revolution*, edited by William Joseph, Christine Wong, and David Zweig, 41–62. Cambridge: Harvard University Press.

Wander, Philip. 1983. "The Ideological Turn in Modern Criticism." *Central States Speech Journal* 34 (spring): 1–18.

———. 1984. "The Third Persona: An Ideological Turn in Rhetorical Theory." *Central States Speech Journal* 35 (winter): 197–216.

Wang, Huo 王火. 1998. *Zhai zhong zi qi xia tiaowu* 在忠字旗下跳舞 (Dancing under the Loyalty Banner). Beijing: Chinese Literature Association Press.

Wang, Meng 王蒙. 2001. *Wang Meng san wen ji* 王蒙散文集 (Wang Meng's Selected Essays). Zhe Jiang: Zhe Jiang Art Press.

Wang, Minmin. 2000. "Mao Zedong's Talks at the Yenan Forum on Literature and Art." In *Chinese Perspectives in Rhetoric and Communication*, edited by D. Ray Heisey, 179–96. Stamford, Conn.: Ablex Publishing Corporation.

Wang, Shaoguang 王紹光. 1996. "Tuozhan wenge yanjiu de shiye" 拓展文革研究的視野 (Extending the Vision of the Cultural Revolution Studies). In *Wenhua da geming: shishi yu yanjiu* 文化大革命: 史實与研究 (The Cultural Revolution: History and Studies), edited by Qingfeng Liu 劉青峰, 515–30. Hong Kong: Chinese University Press.

Wang, Xiaobing, ed. 2001. *Hongqi piaopiao: hongse jingdian gequji* 紅旗飄飄: 紅色經典歌曲集 (Red Flag Waving: Songs of Red Classics). Beijing: Heichao.

Wang, Xizhe 王希哲. 1996. *Wang Xizhe zizhuan: Zou xiang heian* 王希哲自傳: 走向黑暗 (Walking toward Darkness). Hong Kong: University of Democracy Press.

Wang, Youqin 王友琴. 1996. "1966: xuesheng da laoshi de geming" 學生打老師的革命 (1966: The Revolution of Students Beating Teachers). In *Wenhua da geming: shishi yu yanjiu* 文化大革命: 史實与研究 (The Cultural Revolution: History and Studies), edited by Qingfeng 劉青峰 Liu, 17–35. Hong Kong: Chinese University Press.

———. 2000. "Bian Zhongyun: Beijing diyi ge bei dasi de jiaoyu gongzuo zhe" 卞僆耘: 北京第一个被打死的教育工作者 (Bian Zhongyun: The First Educator Who Was Beaten to Death). www.chinese-memorial.org/bianzhongyun, 16 October.

Wasserstrom, Jeffrey N. 1991. *Student Protests in Twentieth-Century China: The View from Shanghai*. Stanford, Calif.: Stanford University Press.

Watson, Burton. 1968. *The Complete Works of Chuang Tzu*. New York: Columbia University Press.

Wei, Yung. 1972. "Introduction." In *Communist China*, edited by Yung Wei, 1–13. Columbus, Ohio: Charles E. Merrill.

Wen, Chihua. 1995. *The Red Mirror: Children of China's Cultural Revolution*. Boulder, Colo.: Westview Press.

Wen, Yu 文聿. 1994. *Zhongguo zuo huo* 中國左禍 (Disasters of Leftism in China). Hong Kong: Tian Di Books Limited.

Wenhua da geming yu xinren 文化大革命育新人 (New Persons Cultivated during the Cultural Revolution). 1976. Beijing: China Youth Publisher.

Wenyi pinglun ji 文藝評論集 (Collection of Articles on Literary Criticism). 1974. Beijing: People's Literature Press.

Whillock, R. 1995. "The Use of Hate as a Stratagem for Achieving Political and Social Goals." In *Hate Speech*, edited by Rita Whillock and David Slayden, 28–54. Thousand Oaks, Calif.: Sage.

Whorf, Benjamin L. 1952. *Collected Papers on Metalinguistics*. Washington, D.C.: Department of State, Foreign Service Institute.

———. 1974. "The Relation of Habitual Thought and Behavior to Language." In *Language, Culture and Society,* edited by Ben G. Blount, 67–87. Cambridge, Mass.: Winthrop Publishers.

Whyte, Martin K. 1979. "Small Groups and Communication in China: Ideal Forms and Imperfect Realities." In *Moving a Mountain: Cultural Change in China,* edited by Godwin C. Chu and Francis L. K. Hsu, 207–36. Honolulu: University Press of Hawaii.

Wiesel, Elie. 2002. "How Can We Understand Their Hatred?" *Chicago Tribune Parade Magazine,* 7 April.

Winance, Eleutherius O. S. B. 1959. *The Communist Persuasion: A Personal Experience of Brainwashing.* New York: P. J. Kenedy & Sons.

Wong, Isabel K. F. 1984. "Geming Gequ: Songs for the Education of the Masses." In *Popular Chinese Literature and Performing Arts in the People's Republic of China 1949–1979,* edited by Bonnie S. McDougall, 112–43. Berkeley: University of California Press.

Woodward, G. C., and R. E. Denton Jr. 2000. *Persuasion & Influence in American Life.* 4th ed. Prospect Heights, Ill.: Waveland Press.

Xi, Xuan 席宣, and Chunming Jin 金春明. 1996. *Wenhua da geming jianshi* 文化大革命简史 (A Brief History of the Cultural Revolution). Beijing: CCP History Press.

Xiao, Di 晓地. 1993. *Wenge zhi mi* 文革之谜 (The Myth of the Cultural Revolution). Beijing: Chaohua Press.

Xie, Quan 解全. 1998. "Wo zai wenhua da geming zhong de jingli" 我在文化大革命中的經歷 (My Experience during the Cultural Revolution). In 1966: *Women na yidai de huiyi* 我们那一代的回忆 (1966: The Memories of Our Generation), edited by Youyu Xu 徐友渔, 145–70. Beijing: China Literary Association Press.

Xu, Yongyu 徐友渔. 1999. *Xingxing sese de zaofan: hongweibing jingshen suzhi de xingcheng ji yanbian* 形形色色的造反：紅衛兵精神素質的形成及演變 (Various Kinds of Rebellion: The Formation and Change of Red Guards Spirit). Hong Kong: Chinese University Press.

Yan, Jiaqi 嚴家其, and Gao Gao 高皋. 1986. *Wenhua da geming shi nian shi* 文化大革命十年史 (Ten Years of the Cultural Revolution). Hong Kong: Chao Liu Press.

———. 1996. *Turbulent Decade: A History of the Cultural Revolution.* Translated by D. W. Y. Kwok. Honolulu: University Press of Hawaii.

Yang, Chiang. 1986. *Six Chapters of Life in a Cadre School: Memoirs from China's Cultural Revolution.* Translated by Djang Chu. Boulder, Colo.: Westview Press.

Yang, Lan. 1998. *Chinese Fiction of the Cultural Revolution.* Hong Kong: Hong Kong University Press.

Yang, Rae. 1997. *Spider Eaters: A Memoir.* Berkeley: University of California Press.

You, Xilin 尤西林. 1998. "Wenge jingkuang pianduan" 文革境況片斷 (Episodes of the Cultural Revolution). In 1966: *Women na yidai de huiyi* 我们那一代的回忆 (1966: The Memories of Our Generation), edited by Youyu Xu 徐友渔, 1–16. Beijing: China Literary Association Press.

Young, W. John. 1991. *Totalitarian Language: Its Nazi and Communist Antecedents.* Charlottesville: University Press of Virginia.

Yu, Daizong 余岱宗. 2001. "Lun yangbanxi de jiaose dengji yu chouhen shijiao" 論樣板戲的角色等級与仇恨視角 (On the Discussion of Characters and Hatred in Model

Operas). Virtue Museum of the Cultural Revolution, *China News Digest* 272, 4 November. http://www.cnd.org/cr

Yu, Frederick T. C. 1964. *Mass Persuasion in Communist China.* New York and London: Praeger.

———. 1968. *Mass Persuasion in Communist China.* New York: Praeger.

———. 1972. "Communication and Politics." In *Communist China: A System-Functional Reader,* edited by Yung Wei, 275–82. Columbus, Ohio: Charles E. Merrill.

Yu, Guangyuan 于光遠. 1997. *Wo xie wenhua da geming* 我寫文化大革命 (I Wrote the Cultural Revolution). Hong Kong: Jing Bao Cultural Corperate.

Yu, Luowen 遇罗文. 2000. *Wo jia* 我家 (My Family). Beijing: China Social Science Press.

Yu, Qiuyu 余秋雨. 1992. *Wenhua kulu* 文化苦旅 (A Bitter Journey of Culture). Shanghai: Oriental Publishing Center.

———. 1995. *Shan ju biji* 山居筆記 (Diaries in the Mountain). Taiwan: Erya Publication Inc.

Yu, Ying-shih. 1994. "The Radicalization of China in the Twentieth Century." In *China in Transformation,* edited by Tu Wei-Ming, 125–50. Cambridge: Harvard University Press.

Yuan, Gao. 1987. *Born Red: A Chronicle of the Cultural Revolution.* Stanford, Calif.: Stanford University Press.

Zhai, Zhenhua. 1992. *Red Flower of China.* New York: Soho Press.

Zhandi xinge 戰地新歌 (News Songs in the Fighting Front). 1972. Beijing: Cultural Section of the State Department.

Zhang, Bingnan 張秉楠. 1991. *Jixia gou-chen* 稷下鈎沉 (The Study of Jixia). Shanghai: Shanghai Classics.

Zhang, F., Y. Zhang, and Y. Wang. 1994. "Cong xiandaixing dao zhonghua xing:xin zhishixing de tanxun" 從現代性到中華性：新知識型的探尋 (From modernity to Chineseness: Inquiry into a new model of knowledge). In *wenyi zhengming* 文藝爭鳴 (Debates of Literature and Arts), 2:10–20.

Zhang, Mei. 1999. "From Lei Feng to Zhang Haidi: Changing Media Images of Model Youth in the Post-Mao Reform Era." In *Civic Discourse, Civil Society, and Chinese Communities,* edited by Randy Kluver and John H. Powers, 111–24. Stamford, Conn.: Ablex Publishing Corporation.

Zhang, Wenhe 张文和, and Yan Li 李艳. 1998. *Kouhao yu Zhongguo* 口号与中国 (Slogan and China). Beijing: History of the Chinese Communist Party Press.

Zhang, Yu. 2003. "China's Popular Social Language vs. Official Political Language." Paper presented at the 89th National Communication Association Convention, Miami Beach, Fla. Nov. 20–23.

Zhao, Feng 赵丰. 1999. *Hongse niupeng* 红色牛棚 (The Red Cowshed). Xining: Qinghai People's Press.

Zhao, Heping. 1999. "Rhetorical Adaptability in China's Argument for Most Favored Nation Status." In *Civic Discourse, Civil Society, and Chinese Communities,* edited by Randy Kluver and John Powers, 236–50. Stamford, Conn.: Ablex Publishing Corporation.

Zhao, Wumian 趙無眠. 1996. "Chong Du Dazibao" 重讀大字報 (Reading Wall Posters Again). In *Highlights of Da-zi-bao during the Cultural Revolution,* edited by Tan Fang and Zhao Wumian, 11–21. Hong Kong: Mirror Books.

Zheng, Ben 正本. 1998. "Ba huiyi de cailiao liu gei lishi 把回憶的材料留給歷史 ." In
  1966: Women na yidai de huiyi 我们那一代的回忆 (1966: The Memories of Our Generation), edited by Youyu Xu 徐友渔, 183–90. Beijing: China Literary Association
  Press.
Zhu, Meng 朱夢. 2001. *Da fengbao* 大风暴 (Big Storm). Wulumuqi: Xijiang People's Press.
Zhu, Rongji 朱鎔基. 2001a. "Zai shunjie tuanbai hui shang de jianghua" 在春節團拜會
  上的講話 (speech given at the Chinese New Year celebration [23 January 2001]).
  People's Daily, 24 January.
———. 2001b. "Zai di liu jie shijie huashang dahui zhongguo jingji luntan shang de yan-
  jiang" 在第六屆世界華商大會中國經濟論壇上的演講 (speech given at the sixth
  conference of the World Overseas Chinese Business Economic Forum [19 September
  2001]). *People's Daily*, 20 September.
Zuguo renmin huoxue huoyong Mao Zedong sixiang de zhanxin mianmao 祖國人民活學活用
  毛澤東思想的嶄新面貌 (The New Face of Studying Mao Zedong Thought by
  People in the Motherland). 1969. Hong Kong: Ministry of Propaganda in Kowloon.

Chinese Names and Terms Index

Ba Jin	巴金	10
Ba . . . jinxing daodi	把 . . . 進行到底	169
Baguwen	八股文	160
Baihua wen yundong	白話文運動	213
Ban qi shitou za jizi de jiao	搬起石頭砸自己的腳	169
Changan	長安	62
Chen Boda	陳伯達	64
Chengyu	成語	161
Chiluoluo	赤裸裸	169
Chuisi zhengzha	垂死掙扎	169
Chushen lun	出身論	143
Da	大	88, 116
Da baolu	大暴露	169
Da bianlun	大辯論	74, 142
Da chuanlian	大串聯	135
Da fang	大放	74
Da gou dui	打狗隊	92
Da ming	大鳴	74
Daqing ren	大慶人	56
Dazibao	大字報	73
De	德	126
Deng Xi	鄧析	74
Dongfang Hong Dajie	東方紅大街	62
Dou	鬥	72
Dou gui tai	鬥鬼台	60
Dou si pi xi	鬥私批修	127
Douzheng	鬥爭	48
Du she	毒蛇	92
Duilian	對聯	113
Fandi	反帝	62
Fapei	發配	21
Fensui	粉碎	192

Fu Lei	傅雷	19
Gao	高	116
Gao Mao	高帽	208
Gao Xingjian	高行健	201
Geming qunzhong	革命群眾	82
Geming shengdi	革命聖地	136
Geming xingdong	革命行動	191
Gou	狗	92
Gou zaizi	狗崽子	23, 92
Gudong	鼓動	169
Gui Jian Chou	鬼見愁	113
Gui tou	鬼頭	23, 60
Guojia	國家	121
Hao ge	嚎歌	114
He	和	72
Hong Xiuquan	洪秀全	98
Hui shi	惠施	90
Hundan	混蛋	89
Ji Ge	繼革	62
Ji Hong	繼紅	62
Jian ai	兼愛	150
Jian Baozan	翦伯讚	20
Jian yanwang	見閻王	89
Jiangui	見鬼	89
Jiangyong hui	講用會	138
Jiechuan . . . de xian'e zhengzhi yongxin	揭穿 . . . 的險惡政治用心	169
Jieji douzheng	階級鬥爭	48
Jinggangshan	井岡山	109
Jixia	稷下	142
Junzi	君子	47, 94
Kui Dafu	蒯大富	217
Lantian	藍天	62
Lao She	老舍	19
Lao San Pian	老三篇	214
Li	禮	97, 126
Liang Qichao	梁啓超	202
Liang Shuming	梁漱溟	202
Lu Xun	魯迅	94
Luo Ruiqing	罗瑞卿	12

Luxian douzheng	路线鬥爭	48
Min'ge	民歌	102
Min'yao	民謠	112
Niu gui she shen	牛鬼蛇神	59
Peng Dehuai	彭德懷	65
Pi	譬	90
Pidou hui	批鬥會	26
Poxie	破鞋	209
Qiongtu molu	窮途末路	169
Quan	全	116
Qujing	取經	136
Ren	仁	63
Renai	仁愛	122
San Ge Daibiao Xuexi Du Ben	三個代表學習讀本	158
San jing san zhu	三敬三祝	132
Shandong	煽動	169
Shanfeng dianhuo	煽風點火	136
Shi Jing	詩經	65
Shihua Shishuo	實話實說	205
Shu	術	188
Sixiang douzheng	思想鬥爭	48
Sixiang wenti	思想問題	138
Song yongyi	宋永毅	182
Su Buqing	蘇步青	23
Sunzi Bingfa	孫子兵法	214
Ta ma de	他媽的	89
Tian Ming	天命	79
Tiantian du	天天讀	138
Tiaoliang xiaochou	跳樑小醜	169
Wan huibao	晚彙報	133
Wan nian	萬年	65
Wan shou wu jiang	萬壽無疆	65
Wei Dong	衛東	62
Wengongtuan	文工團	98
Wenyan wen	文言文	213
Wusi	無私	148

Xiang Dong	向東	62
Xiao	孝	120
Xiao Bing	小兵	62
Xiaomie	消滅	192
Xiaoren	小人	94
Xiehe	協和	62
Xinde tihui	心得體會	138
Xuexi ban	學習班	20
Xuexi gaizao	學習改造	191
Yangbanxi	樣板戲	115
Yi de zhi guo	以德治國	186
Yi he wei gui	以和爲貴	72
Yiku fan	憶苦飯	140
Yiku sitian	憶苦思甜	139
Yinyang tou	陰陽頭	141
Yiqie	一切	212
Yongyuan	永遠	86
Yu Qiuyu	余秋雨	201
Yuanman	圓滿	166
Yue	樂	97
Zalan	砸爛	192
Zao qingshi	早請示	133
Zhan Guoce	戰國策	90
Zhang Chengzhi	張承志	211
Zheng ming	正名	31
Zhengfeng	整風	42
Zhizhuo	執著	166
Zhong	忠	120, 134
Zhong Dong	忠東	62
Zhong Hong	忠紅	62
Zhong zi wu	忠字舞	133
Zhongyong	中庸	71
Zhu	豬	92
Zhuangzi	莊子	34
Zui	最	88
Zui da	最大	88
Zui gao zhishi	最高指示	66, 88
Zui hong	最紅	88

General Index

"Aesopian language," 49

alienation, 24; and conspiracy theory, 189; and dehumanization, 60–61; and political slogans, 68; and thought reform, 46, 47

ancient Chinese rhetoric. *See* classical Chinese rhetoric

ancient Greece, philosophy of, 31, 97

anti-Americanism, 8, 123, 173, 185, 189; rhetorical analysis of, 177–78. *See also* post-Mao China, and anti-Americanism; *China Can Say No*

anti-rightist campaign, 43–44, 48, 54, 59, 75, 188

Arendt, Hannah, 1, 3, 28, 36–37, 52, 72, 199

Azalea Mountain (model opera), 115

Ba Jin, 1, 10, 183

Bacon, Francis, 32, 34

Bakhtin, Mikhail, 35–36

Ball, Terrence, 39

"banality of evil." *See* Arendt, Hannah

Battle in the Plains (model opera), 115

Bay of Panshi (model opera), 115

Beijing opera, 115, 116

"Beloved Chairman Mao" (song), 133

betrayal. *See* false testimony; family betrayal

"big character posters." *See* wall posters

Bitzer, Lloyd, 153

blood line. *See* family background; five black and five red categories

Boas, Franz, 29

Book of Odes (*Shi Jing*), 65, 98, 120–21

Bormann, Ernest, 70

bourgeoisie. *See* class enemies; class struggle; denunciation; family background; five black and five red categories

Broman, Barry, 73

Burke, Kenneth, 37–38, 70, 79, 84, 126, 148, 172, 173–74, 175

cadre schools. *See* May Seventh Cadre Schools

capitalism. *See* post-Mao China, and economic development

capitalist roaders, denunciation of, 13, 14, 81–82, 85, 123, 185

Cassirer, Ernst, 70

chengyu (four-character idioms), 161

Chiang Kai-shek, 13

China Can Say No, 179, 180; and condemnation of American hegemony, 171–72; rhetorical analysis of, 172–75

Chinese Communist Party (CCP), 6, 12; and anti–Falun Gong propaganda, 164, 168; goals of, 40, 54; and ideological transformation, 4, 40–46; moral authority of, 185; in post-Mao China, 154, 158, 160; praised in revolutionary songs, 104–5; pre–Cultural Revolution rhetoric of, 46–50,

class consciousness, development of, 40, 43, 52, 55

class enemies: and confession and self-criticism, 128–30; denunciation of, 4, 5, 15, 79, 153, 185, 190; political rituals denouncing, 140, 149; revolutionary

class enemies (*continued*)
    music denouncing, 117–18, 123; wall
    posters denouncing, 77–78, 79, 81–84
class struggle: and communist ideology, 24,
    35, 41, 47, 48, 79; and dehumanization,
    59, 69; and polarized thinking, 71, 93;
    and political slogans, 53–57, 68; and
    wall posters, 85. *See also* Marxism-
    Leninism
classical Chinese rhetoric, 4, 31, 40, 48, 65,
    86, 180; and appeals to morality, 184;
    appropriation of, 7, 186; and historical
    references, 160; and metaphors, 90–91;
    and mythology, 59; and political slo-
    gans, 52; and public debates, 144–45
Communist Manifesto, 53
confession, 11, 20, 22, 28, 38, 197; Lu
    Rong and, 17; and political rituals, 42,
    43–44, 149; in post-Mao China, 179;
    and revolutionary songs, 114; and wall
    posters, 77
Confucianism: appropriation of, 44–45,
    128, 132, 139; as classical Chinese ide-
    ology, 40, 92–93, 94, 106; denuncia-
    tion of, 4, 7, 40, 63–64, 78–79, 122–23,
    191; and language, 31–32; and music,
    97–98; and political rituals, 69, 126–27,
    142, 148–49,; similarities to Maoism,
    47, 71; values of, 47, 48, 71, 91–93, 94,
    184. *See also* traditional Chinese culture
conspiracy theory, 4, 81–84, 188–90. *See
    also* capitalist roaders, denunciation of;
    class enemies, denunciation of; family
    betrayal; party officials, denunciation of
"Core of Leadership for Our Cause Is the
    Chinese Party" (song), 107
counterrevolutionaries, 12, 26, 41–42, 80;
    denunciation of, 58, 88, 135, 141; and
    family background, 55, 86
cow ghosts and snake spirits, 15, 20, 59–
    61, 69, 92, 190
"Cox Report," 175, 176–77
criticism. *See* self-criticism and criticism
cult of Mao. *See* Mao Zedong, deification of

Cultural Revolution: goals and effects of,
    2, 4–5, 6, 152–53, 188; government
    not held accountable, 6, 152–53, 183,
    189; historical context of, 10–11, 12,
    76; ideology of, 4, 6, 7, 29, 32, 35, 37,
    79, 186; impact on communication,
    196–98; impact on culture, 194–96;
    impact on thought, 192–94; remem-
    bering, 182–83; rhetoric of, 5–7, 29,
    32, 35, 36, 141–42, 153–54, 184–92
Cultural Revolution Virtual Museum, 8

da (big), 88
da bianlun (holding great debates), 74, 76,
    142
Da Chuanlian (the great exchange) and
    Red Guards, 135–36
da fang (voicing one's views freely), 74, 76
da gou dui (dog beating team), 92
da ming (speaking out loudly), 74, 76
dazibao (wall posters). *See* wall posters
de (virtue), 126
deductive and inductive reasoning, and
    wall posters, 86–87, 95
dehumanization, 4, 7, 23, 60, 69, 190–91;
    and language of wall posters, 89–92, 95;
    and political rituals, 151; political slo-
    gans, 53, 59–61. *See also* metaphor; cow
    ghosts and snake spirits
Deng Xiaoping, 8, 9, 32, 105, 121, 165;
    denunciation of, 18, 74, 77, 80, 86, 88–
    89; rhetoric of regime, 79, 153, 154–
    57, 202; "Socialism with Chinese
    Characteristics," 155–57, 158, 187
denunciation: of class enemies, 15–15, 20,
    26, 77–78, 80, 87, 140–42; language of,
    89–90, 92, 141–42; of Lu Rong, 2, 89; of
    teachers, 23, 78, 83, 110, 135, 141; and
    wall posters, 77–78, 80, 81–82, 83, 87
denunciation rallies, 2, 11, 20, 28, 82, 110,
    125, 135, 140–42, 148, 190; and dehu-
    manization, 60; and Lu Rong, 15
"Destroy the four olds and establish the
    four news" (political slogan), 61–64, 67

diaries, and confession and self-criticism, 48, 131–32

dou (fight), 72

dou gui tai (stage of the ghost), 60

dou si pi xiu (Fighting Selfishness and Denouncing Revisionism), 127

douzheng (to struggle), 48

drama, social. *See* political rituals

"dramatism." *See* Burke, Kenneth

dress and appearance, as revolutionary traits, 62–63, 78, 110, 117

du she (poisonous snake), 92

dualistic thinking. *See* polarized thinking

"East Is Red" (song), 23, 101–3, 112, 138, 144

education, 5, 199–200; and class struggle, 55, 56; and deification of Mao, 65; and political indoctrination, 23–24, 26, 36; and rebellion, 57, 59

Eulogy of Mao Zedong, 101, 102, 103, 104

"Everyday Reading" (ritual), 138

factionalism, 11, 25, 34, 109, 143–45

false testimony, 18, 19–20; and Lu Rong, 24; and political rituals, 46, 131, 135, 150, 151; and wall posters, 13, 77, 82–83, 85, 86, 92

Falun Dafa. *See* Falun Gong

Falun Gong, 8, 126, 162, 170; conspiracy theory and rhetoric condemning, 166–67; denunciation of, 185, 189, 196; and emotional and logical appeals of and rhetoric condemning, 165–66; and moral and scientific appeals of and rhetoric condemning, 163–65; styles of rhetoric condemning, 167–70

family background, 16, 19, 22, 27, 83, 93, 198; and class struggle, 46, 55–56, 82, 86; and dehumanization, 59; and political rituals, 129–30, 143, 149; and revolutionary songs, 113–14. *See also* five black and five red categories

family betrayal, 25–26, 27, 55, 60, 83; and

Lu Rong, 17; and political rituals, 141; as rebellion, 58–59; and revolutionary songs, 106; and wall posters, 81–82

fapei (exile), 21

femininity, as counterrevolutionary trait, 19, 63, 90, 109–10, 123

fensui (smash to pieces), 192

Fighting Selfishness and Denouncing Revisionism sessions, 127–28, 130, 145, 149

five black and five red categories, 23, 32, 55–56, 59, 129, 123, 143, 161–62. *See also* family background

five red categories. *See* five black and five red categories

folk songs, and revolutionary songs, 106, 101, 102, 112–13

"Foolish Old Man Who Moved a Mountain" (song/essay), 24, 107, 138

formalized language, 48–49, 52, 96, 162, 177. *See also* political slogans, language of; post-Mao China, rhetoric of; wall posters, language of

Foucault, Michel, 3, 36

"Four Adherences," 156, 157

four olds and four news, 4, 61–64, 67, 78–79, 161–62, 191

Gang of Four, 2, 5, 63, 146–47, 152, 154–55

Gao Xingjian, 201

geming qunzhong (revolutionary masses), 82

geming shengdi (sacred revolutionary lands), 136

geming xing dong (revolutionary action), 191

Gong-Sun Long, 31

gou (dog), 92

gou zaizi (sons of bitches), 23, 92

"Great Purge," 1, 42, 52, 84

"Gui Jian Chou" (song), 113

gui tou (ghost hair), 23, 60

guo (state), 121

Guomin Dang. *See* Nationalist Party (Guomin Dang)

Han Feizi, 142, 188
Harbin, 12, 13, 14, 18, 184
he (harmony), 72
"He Will Not Fall If You Do Not Beat
    Him" (song), 107
He Zuoxiu, 162
Heraclitus, 31
Hitler, Adolf. *See* Nazi Germany
Hoijer, Harry, 29, 30
Hong Xiuquan, 98
How to Be a Good Communist (Liu Shaoqi),
    45
Hsueh-Hsi (political study sessions), 45
Hua Guofeng, 153
human rights, violation of. *See* dehuman-
    ization; torture and violence
Hume, David, 33, 34
hundan (bastard), 89–90

ideographs, 39, 52–53, 57, 155, 187
ideological indoctrination, theories of, 32–
    39, 52
ideology: communicated through music,
    98–124; of Cultural Revolution, 4, 6, 7,
    29, 32, 35, 37, 79, 81, 186; indoctrina-
    tion into, 1–2, 71, 32–39; lack of alter-
    nate, 68–69, 122, 146; as limiting
    thinking and language, 93–94; Marxist-
    Leninist, 35, 127–28, 144; of post-Mao
    China, 152–55, 158–60, 180, 205; pre–
    Cultural Revolution, 46–47; transfor-
    mation of, 40–41, 51–53, 61–64
"In Memory of Norman Bethune" (song),
    24, 107, 138
inductive reasoning. *See* deductive and
    inductive reasoning, and wall posters
intellectuals, 75, 134, 198; as anti-rightists,
    75; and class struggle, 40; and confes-
    sion and self-criticism, 43–44, 128–30;
    dehumanized, 59; denunciation of, 10,
    12, 26, 56, 75
international law, American violation of,
    177–78
"Internationale" (song), 112

Ji Xianlin, 60–61
jia (family), 121
jian ai (mutual love), 150
jian yanwang (meet your death), term on
    wall posters, 89–90
Jiang Qing, 115, 116, 120
Jiang Zemin, 8, 157–62, 186, 197; and
    post-Mao China, 154, 166, 179; rheto-
    ric of, 160–62; *60 Minutes* interview,
    170, 175; and "Three Representatives,"
    157–59, 161, 165, 201
jiangui (go to hell), 89–90
jiangyong hui (sharing experience in apply-
    ing Mao's teachings), 138–39, 159
jieji douzheng (class struggle), 48
jinggangshan (Jinggang Mountain), 109
Judeo-Christian tradition, 3, 34, 44, 49, 99
junzi (gentleman), 94, 122, 149, 195

labor camps. *See* May Seventh Cadre
    Schools
land reform movement, 43, 48
language: aggressive, 94–95; ambiguity of,
    33, 62, 161–62; anthropological theo-
    ries of, 29–31; of anti–Falun Gong rhet-
    oric, 169; as constructive of reality, 28,
    29–34, 84, 93–94, 183; critical theories
    of, 35–37; impoverishment of, 3, 7, 26,
    37, 48–49, 52, 72, 96, 162, 179–80,
    193–94, 197; inadequacy of, 32, 34, 37;
    as legitimizing violence, 89–90; philo-
    sophical theories of, 31–35; and politi-
    cal rituals, 139; rhetorical theories of,
    37–39
Lei Feng, 48, 131–32, 138, 186
Lenin, Vladimir, 40, 41, 52
li (rituals), 97, 126, 195
Li Hongzhi, 162, 163, 179, 189; denuncia-
    tion of, 163–64, 165–67
Li Jiefu, 107–108
Li Peng, 204
Liang Shuming, 202–3
Lin Biao, 5, 53, 93, 91, 131, 133, 187;
    denunciation of, 63; and Fighting

Selfishness and Denouncing Revision-ism sessions, 127–28; and four olds and four news, 61; and Mao Zedong's Thought, 65–66, 107

"linguistic relativity." *See* Sapir-Whorf Hypothesis

Little Red Book (*Quotations from Chairman Mao*), 24, 26, 107, 193; and political rit-uals, 132–33, 135, 141, 145; and politi-cal slogans, 65, 66

Liu Shaoqi, 56; denunciation of, 16–17, 77, 80, 81–82, 89; and Mao Zedong, 6, 188–89; and self-criticism, 45

Locke, John, 33, 34, 88

loyalty dance, 102, 133–34, 138, 142

Lu Xun Academy of Arts and Literature, 98

Lu Xun, 94–95, 191

Lucy, John, 29

Luo Ruiqing, 12, 88

luxian douzheng (line struggle), 48

"Make Up Your Minds" (song), 108

"Marching Song of the Courageous Army" (song), 111

Mandate of Heaven, 79, 120–21, 184

Mao badges, 134–35, 141

Mao Zedong, 6, 79, 91, 95, 99, 170; death of, 2, 152; demystification of, 154–55; and establishment of People's Republic of China, 39; and political rituals, 136–37; and self-criticism, 45, 128; and wall posters, 12, 74, 76, 90; **deification of,** 32, 104, 121, 131, 132–38, 145, 186–87; and political rituals, 137, 147; and political slogans, 53, 64–65, 70; and revolutionary music, 101–6, 112, 121, 122; and wall posters, 80–81, 87; **loy-alty to,** 19, 22, 26, 47, 64–65, 106, 183, 185; and family betrayal, 58–59; and Lu Rong, 12, 13–14; and political rituals, 44, 133–35, 140; Red Guards and, 57, 136–37; and revolutionary music, 113; and wall posters, 79, 80–81; **quotations**

and poems, 15, 24, 185; and political rituals, 24–25, 138–39, 144; and politi-cal slogans, 53, 58, 65–67; and revolu-tionary music, 103, 106–111; and wall posters, 80, 85, 87

"Mao Zedong's Thought," 32, 55, 61–62, 186; demystification of, 154–55; estab-lishing legitimacy of, 42–43; and model operas, 115, 119; in post-Mao China, 155, 156, 202; and rebellion, 57–58; and revolutionary songs, 103, 104, 108; and wall posters, 75, 81, 87, 92

Maoism: and Marxism-Leninism, 4, 24–25, 41–42, 65–66, 120, 191; similarities to Confucianism, 47, 71; as single and absolute truth, 26, 34, 42, 65, 69, 81, 87, 93, 94, 108, 142, 148, 186

"Marching Song of the Courageous Army" (song), 111

Marxism-Leninism, 34, 35, 53, 40, 43, 127, 144, 184–85; in post-Mao China, 154, 156, 202. *See also* Maoism, and Marxism-Leninism

mass singing, 98–114

May Fourth movement, 52, 69, 94, 111, 191, 201

May Seventh Cadre Schools, 21–22, 60, 129

McGee, Michael, 38–39, 160–61

Mein Kampf, 105

Mencius, 63, 128, 142, 186

metaphor: in *China Can Say No,* 174; and dehumanization, 4, 33, 59–61, 69, 92, 190; and political slogans, 59–61, 68, 69; and revolutionary songs, 103–4, 113, 114; and wall posters, 90–92

min'ge (layman's songs), 102

minyao (folk verse), 112–13

model operas: and expression of hatred, 117–18; impact on communication, 122–24; impact on culture, 120–21; impact on thought, 121–22; language of, 118–20; and persuasion, 97, 115–16; and polarized thinking, 118, 123; and

model operas (*continued*)
revolutionary heroes, 116–17; rhetorical analysis of, 114–20
modern Chinese culture, and conflict, 7, 27, 48, 68, 72, 180, 195–97
monsters and demons, 190
moralistic language. *See* class enemies, denunciation of; polarized thinking; Mao Zedong, loyalty to; Mao Zedong, quotations and poems
Mozi, 142
music, rhetorical functions of, 97–100. *See also* model operas; revolutionary songs
myth, as rhetorical tool. *See* Mao Zedong, deification of

names, changing of, 62, 110
Nationalist Party (Guomin Dang), 16, 22, 40, 42, 80, 86
Nazi Germany: and dehumanization, 69–70; and political rituals, 58; and propaganda, 52, 84, 100; similarity to Cultural Revolution, 1, 6, 7, 36–37, 38, 65, 91, 167, 175, 187–88, 189
"Never forget the class struggle" (slogan), 53–57, 118
new Communist person, 40, 44, 47, 128, 139, 149
Nie Er, 111
Nie Yuanzi, 75, 76
Nietzsche, Friedrich, 33, 34, 200
nui gui she shen (cow ghosts and snake spirits), 59
numbered concepts, as rhetorical tool, 71, 76, 156, 157, 161–62

Ode to the Dragon River (model opera), 115
Olympic games, 171, 172, 181
On the Docks (model opera), 115, 116, 117, 119
Orwell, George, 96, 118, 122, 190

Parmenides, 31
party officials, 4, 54, 55, 74, 129, 188;

denunciation of, 12, 26, 74, 77, 83, 87, 141
Peng Dehuai, 65
Peng Zhen, 80, 88
People's Daily, 8, 25, 45, 180; and anti-American rhetoric, 175–77, 178; and condemnation of Falun Gong, 163–64, 165–66, 167, 168–69; and political slogans, 53, 54, 55, 57, 59, 61; and political rituals, 128, 136; and revolutionary music, 107; and "Three Representatives," 158, 159; and wall posters, 75, 76
personal reeducation. *See* confession; self-criticism and criticism; political study sessions
persuasion, 4, 24, 29, 38, 42, 79, 105, 154, 179; in *China Can Say No,* 172, 174–75; and classical Chinese rhetoric, 86; and political rituals, 44, 125–27, 140; and political slogans, 51–53; and public debates, 142–45; and revolutionary music, 97, 99–100, 102, 105, 108, 112, 118–20; and wall posters, 74
pi (metaphor), 90
pidou hui (denunciation rallies), 140–42
pipan gao (denunciation papers), 26
Plato, 31, 97
polarized thinking, 31, 32, 34, 37, 38, 71–72, 93, 153, 191, 194, 196, 199; in *China Can Say No,* 173; and political rituals, 146–47, 148; and political slogans, 52, 57, 67, 68; in post-Mao China, 165, 180; and revolutionary music, 118, 122–23; and wall posters, 76, 78, 88, 96
"Policy and Tactics Are the Life Force of the Party" (song), 107
political and social reality, construction of 3, 7,; and language, 28, 29–34, 35–37, 38–39, 84; and political slogans, 53, 67–68; in post-Mao China, 174, 181; and wall posters, 92
political consciousness, cultivation of, 35–36, 76, 118–20, 139, 160–61. *See also*

model operas; political rituals; political slogans; revolutionary music; wall posters

political rituals, 26, 28, 32, 139, 151; and deification of Mao Zedong, 132–38, 145–46; denunciation rallies, 2, 11, 20, 28, 82, 110, 125, 140–42, 148; emotional appeal of, 142, 136–37; loyalty dance, 102, 133–34, 138, 142; impact on communication, 150–51; impact on culture, 148–50; impact on thought, 145–48; functions of, 125–25, 145, 149; and justification of violence, 148; and persuasion, 125–27, 140; and political slogans, 58, 137, 139, 140, 141; political study sessions, 11, 45–46, 159, 186, 190; public debates, 12, 124, 128, 142–45; and self-criticism, 45, 127

political slogans, 11, 28, 35, 36, 71, 81, 142, 186; attacking traditional Chinese values, 185; and deification of Mao Zedong, 64–65, 134; denouncing Lu Rong, 13, 20; emotional appeals of, 67; functions of, 51–53; impact on thought and action, 71–72; justifying violence, 15, 53, 57, 59, 62, 71; language of, 49, 53, 59–61, 68, 69, 192; and metaphor, 59–61, 68, 69; and political rituals, 128, 139, 140, 141, 144; in post-Mao China, 156, 157, 161, 179; and revolutionary music, 110, 118–20; rhetorical analysis of, 67–71

political study sessions, 11, 45–46, 159, 186, 190

politically correct language. *See* class enemies, denunciation of; Mao Zedong, loyalty to; Mao Zedong, quotations and poems; polarized thinking

politicization, of symbolic practices, 97–100, 116, 123, 126–27, 135–36

post-Mao China: and anti-Americanism, 170–178; challenges facing, 198–205; and Deng Xiaoping, 154–57; and communication and civic discourse, 203–5; and culture rebuilding, 201–3; and eco-nomic development, 153, 156, 170–72, 181, 198, 201; and education, 199–201; and "Four Adherences," 156, 157; ideological crisis of, 155, 158; and Jiang Zemin, 157–62; and pragmatism, 155–57; rhetoric of, 154, 155, 159–60, 161, 163–65, 170, 179–3; and "Socialism with Chinese Characteristics," 160, 161, 165, 187

profanity, as rhetorical tool, 23, 89–90, 95, 110, 113, 141, 143, 171, 195

proletarian. *See* class struggle; family background; five black and five red categories

propaganda. *See* model operas; political rituals; political slogans; revolutionary songs; wall posters

public debates, 11, 24, 28, 142; and argument by authority and example, 143–44; and polarized thinking, 148; and political slogans, 144; and Red Guards, 143–45

Quintilian, 99

qujing (getting the script), 136

Quotations from Chairman Mao. See Little Red Book (*Quotations from Chairman Mao*)

radio broadcasts, of revolutionary music, 101, 112, 115

Raid on the White Tiger Regiment (model opera), 115, 116, 117

rebellion, 57–59, 108, 112

"Rebellion Is Justified" (song), 108

Rebels, 5; and persecution of Lu Rong, 13–16, 20; and public debates, 24; torture and violence, 2, 15–16, 25; and wall posters, 12–13

Red Army, 42, 100

Red Detachment of Women (model opera), 115, 117, 118

Red Flag, 8, 45, 90, 156; and political slogans, 53, 54, 55, 60, 61, 63, 65

Red Guards, 3, 5, 8, 57, 109, 191; and
    confession, 131; and deification of Mao
    Zedong, 64–65; and four olds and four
    news, 61–62, 63; language of, 90–91,
    95, 186,; and political rituals, 135–36,
    145, 146–47; and public debates, 24,
    143–45, 148; and rebellion, 57–59;
    reflecting on Cultural Revolution, 183;
    and revolutionary songs, 101, 107, 108;
    and torture and violence, 15–17, 25,
    26, 63, 199
Red Guards' Fighting Songs, 113
Red Lantern (model opera), 115, 117, 118
"Remembering the Bitterness of the Past
    and Appreciating the Sweetness of the
    Present" (ritual), 139–40, 148
ren (benevolence), 63, 19, 122, 128, 148–
    49, 150, 195
"Revolution is not a dinner party" (slogan/
    song), 15, 107, 108, 141, 198
revolutionary songs, 2, 11, 22, 142, 187;
    and appropriation of folk songs, 101,
    102, 106, 112–13; and deification of
    Mao Zedong, 101–6; emotional appeals
    of, 100, 122; functions of, 99–100,
    106–111, 120; impact on communica-
    tion, 122–24; impact on culture, 120–
    21; impact on thought, 121–22; and
    justification of violence, 108, 109, 113,
    121; and loyalty dance, 133–34; and
    Mao Zedong's quotations and poems,
    106–111; and metaphor, 100, 103–4,
    113, 114; and persuasion, 97, 105, 108;
    radicalization, 111–14; rhetorical analy-
    sis of, 100–114
rhetoric, 37, 79, 97–99, 153–54, 162
rhetoric of Cultural Revolution. See Cul-
    tural Revolution, rhetoric of; political
    rituals; political slogans; wall posters
rhetorical analysis: of anti–Falun Gong dis-
    course, 167–70; of Deng Xiaoping's
    regime, 154–57; of Jiang Zemin's
    regime, 159–62; of model operas, 114–
    20; of political rituals, 127–45; of

pre–Cultural Revolution discourse, 46–
    50; of revolutionary songs, 100–114; of
    wall posters, 77–84
rituals. See political rituals
rumors. See false testimony
Russian Revolution, 40

"Sailing the Sea Depends on the Helms-
    man" (song), 23, 103
san jing san zhu (three respects and three
    wishes ritual), 132–33
Sapir, Edward, 28, 29, 30
Sapir-Whorf Hypothesis, 3, 30–31, 193
Seeking Truth (formerly Red Flag), and con-
    demnation of Falun Gong, 164, 165
Selected Works of Mao Zedong, 66
self-criticism and criticism, 20, 38, 125,
    130, 186; and Confucianism, 44–45;
    and denunciation of Falun Gong, 168–
    69; and Lu Rong, 17; and political ritu-
    als, 46, 149, 150; post-Mao China, 179;
    and thought reform, 42–43, 44–45; and
    wall posters, 77, 90
"Serve the People" (essay/song), 24, 107,
    138
"Seven Absolute: Militia Women" (song),
    109–10
Sha Jia Village (model opera), 115, 116
Sha-jia-bang Symphony (model opera), 115
shanfeng dianhuo (inflaming and agitating),
    136
Shaorong Huang, 73
"Sharing Experience in Applying Mao's
    Teaching" (ritual), 138–39, 159
Shi Jing. See Book of Odes (Shi Jing)
shu (strategy), 188–89
Simons, Herbert, 154
"Singing for the Motherland" (song), 105–6
Sino-American relations, 170–71, 175,
    176–77, 189
sixiang douzheng (thought struggle), 48
sixiang wenti (thought problem), 138
"Sixteen Directives," 76
slogans. See political slogans

social drama. *See* political rituals

"Socialism with Chinese Characteristics," 160, 161, 165, 187

"Song of Cow Devils and Snake Spirits" (song), 114

Song Yongyi, 182

"Sons of Heaven" concept, 101

Sophists, 3, 31

Soviet propaganda, and wall posters, 74

Soviet Russia, and similarity to Cultural Revolution, 1, 7, 9, 40, 84, 154, 188, 189; and political slogans, 52; and thought reform, 42, 43, 44; and wall posters, 74, 76

"spitting bitter water," 43, 48

Stalin, Joseph. *See* Soviet Russia

stereotypes. *See* polarized thinking

suicide, 12, 16, 19–20, 60, 465, 466

swearing. *See* profanity, as rhetorical tool

"Sweeping away all the monsters and demons" (political slogan), 59–61, 67

symbols and symbolic practices. *See* political slogans; wall posters; revolutionary songs; model operas

ta ma de (damn you), 89–90

Taking Tiger Mountain by Strategies (model opera), 115, 116–17, 118

"Talks at the Yan'an Forum on Literature and Art" (lecture), 99, 100, 115, 127

Tao Zhu, denounced as counterrevolutionary, 82, 87

teachers. *See* denunciation, of teachers; education

Ten Denunciations of Falun Gong, 164, 165, 166

"There Will Be No New China without the Communist Party" (song), 104

thought processes, 29–32, 35, 92–94, 122; and loss of critical thinking, 7, 11, 26, 33, 34, 37, 49, 69, 71–72, 187, 193–94, 199; and music, 99, 120; and political rituals, 126–27, 145; in post-Mao China, 179

thought reform, 42–46, 47, 186; and political rituals, 127–32; and political slogans, 52–53. *See also* self-criticism and criticism; confession; political rituals

"Three Main Rules of Discipline and the Eight Points for Attention" (song), 100

Tian Han, 111

Tian Ming (Mandate of Heaven), 79

Tiananmen Square, 64, 101, 105, 107, 112, 126, 136, 157, 170, 189

Tianjin riot, 162–63

tiantian du (Everyday Reading ritual), 138

"To rebel is justified" (political slogan), 57–59, 67, 191

torture and violence, 5, 15–16, 23, 25, 89, 93, 113; and dehumanization, 60; justification of, 26, 59, 90, 92, 95, 113, 148, 189, 191; of Lu Rong, 2, 13–16; and political rituals, 140, 147, 148

traditional Chinese culture: and authority, 58, 65, 70–71, 187; denunciation of, 4, 5, 7, 27, 41, 71–72, 93, 185, 191, 194; and confession, 44; and literature, 109; and music, 98, 100, 120–21; and political rituals, 137; and political slogans, 61–64, 67; and public debate, 142; and self-criticism, 44–45; values of, 46–47, 78–79, 92–93, 95, 101, 121, 122, 174, 194–95

Tsinghua High School, 57

vandalism. *See* torture and violence

violence. *See* torture and violence

wall posters, 3, 11, 19, 28, 188; and anti–Falun Gong rhetoric, 167, 168; and conspiracy theory, 81–84; as constitutional right, 76, 96; and cultural and linguistic behavior, 94–95; and deification of Mao Zedong, 80–81; and demystification of Mao Zedong, 154; denouncing Lu Rong, 13; and denunciation, 12, 13, 74–77, 81–84; and family betrayal, 81–82; functions of, 77; history of, 74, 75; language of, 84–86, 87–92, 95, 192;

wall posters (*continued*)
  and metaphors, 90–92; moral/ethical
  appeals of, 77–80; and revolutionary
  songs, 110
wan huibao (reporting in the evening ritual),
  133
wan nian (long life), 65
wan shou wu jiang (a thousand years of life),
  65
Wang Guangmei, 92
Wang Wei, 177, 178
"We Must Have Faith in the Masses and
  We Must Have Faith in the Party"
  (song), 107
Wei Jungsheng, and wall posters, 93
weidong (Protecting Mao Zedong), 84
Wengongtuan (performing teams), 98
Western music, influence in Chinese revolutionary music, 98, 108, 116, 120
White-Haired Girl (model opera), 115, 112,
  118
Whorf, Benjamin, 30
Wiesel, Elie, 10
World Trade Organization, 171, 172, 181
wusi (selflessness), 148

"Xi Jiang Yue: Jinggangshan" (song), 109
Xian Xinghai, 111
xiao (filial piety), 120
xiaomie (annihilate), 192
xiaoren (base persons), 94
Xiaosheng Liang, 54
xin (trustworthiness), 195
xinde tihui (reflections and experiences),
  138–39, 159
Xinghai Revolution, 40
xuexi ban (study groups), 20
xuexi gaizao (study and reform), 191
Xunzi, 142

yangban xi (model operas). *See* model operas

"Yellow Banner Rebellion," 52
yi (righteousness), 195
yi de zhi guo (governance by morality and
  virtue), 186
yi he wei gui (valuing harmony), 72
yiku fan (recalling bitterness meal), 140
yiku sitian (Remembering the Bitterness of
  the Past and Appreciating the Sweetness
  of the Present Ritual), 139–40
yinyang tou (ghost hair), 141
yongyuan (always), term used on wall
  posters, 86
Young Pioneers, 22–23
Yu, Frederick T. C., 28, 42, 120
Yu Luojin, 132
Yu Luoke, 55–56, 93, 132, 147
Yu Quiyu, 201
yuanman (freedom from cycle of life and
  death), 166
yue (music), 97

zalan (tear down), 192
zao qingshi (asking instructions in the
  morning ritual), 133
Zhan Guoce (Intrigues), 90
Zhang Zhixin, 93, 147
Zhao Ziyang, 80–81
zheng ming (rectification of names), 31
zhengfeng (reform of work style), 42, 43
zhi (wisdom), 195
zhizhuo (adherence/attachments), 166
zhong (loyalty), 120, 134
zhong yong (the middle way), 71
zhong zi wu (loyalty dance), 133–34
Zhou En-lai, 103
zhu (pig), term on wall posters, 92
Zhu De, 85–86
Zhu Rongji, 159
Zhuangzi, 34
zui (absolute, most), 88
zui gao zhishi (highest directives), 66